THE SOCIAL WEB: BRIEF

An Introduction to Sociology Second Edition

John and Erna Perry
Cuyahoga Community College

Canfield Press, San Francisco
A Department of Harper & Row, Publishers, Inc.
New York, Hagerstown, London

Cover Design: John Sullivan

Photo Credits

Chapter 2: 26—Ken Heyman. 33—Gerhard Gscheidle, Jeroboam. 38—Gunther Reits/Leo de Wys, Inc. 43—John Bacchus, DPI.

Chapter 3: 60—Ken Heyman. 64—Jerry Frank, DPI. 84—Sovfoto. 88—Alon Reininger, DPI.

Chapter 4: 95—Jim Jowers, Nancy Palmer Photo Agency, Inc. 101—Lynn McLaren, Rapho/Photo Researchers. 103—Optic Nerve, Jeroboam.

Chapter 5: 137—Ken Heyman. 151—Hank Lebo, Jeroboam.

Chapter 6: 166—United Press International. 186—Jim Jowers, Nancy Palmer Photo Agency, Inc. 189—Chie Nishio, Nancy Palmer Photo Agency, Inc. 196—Henri Cartier-Bresson, Magnum.

Chapter 7: 206—Ken Heyman. 208—Chris Reeberg, DPI. 213—Jerry Frank, DPI. 228—© Larry Keenan, 1975, Nest, S.F.

Chapter 8: 248—Robert Mark Altman. 254—Magnum. 257—Ken Heyman. 262—Leo de Wys, Inc. 276—Kenneth Murray, Nancy Palmer Photo Agency, Inc.

Chapter 9: 315—Charles Harbutt, Magnum.

Chapter 10: 327—Ken Heyman. 337—Robert Mark Altman. 353—Alex Webb, Magnum.

The Social Web: Brief
An Introduction to Sociology, *Second Edition*

Library of Congress Cataloging in Publication Data
Perry, John Ambrose, 1931–
The social web.
Includes bibliographies and index.
1. Sociology. I. Perry, Erna, joint author.
II. Title.
HM51.P44 1977 301 77-22690
ISBN 0-06-386766-4

78 79 80 10 9 8 7 6 5 4 3 2 1

Contents

vi Preface
viii A Word to the Student

1

1 THE SOCIAL WEB

What Is Sociology?
A New Road to Knowledge
The Scientific Method in Sociology
Summary
24 Terms to Remember
25 Further Readings

2

26 GROUPS: FROM TWO TO MILLIONS

A Life Lived in Groups
The Nature of Groups
Social Interaction and Social Processes
Social Organization
Summary
56 Terms to Remember
57 Further Readings

3

59 SOCIETY AND CULTURE

Society
Society and Culture
Cultural Content
Culture as Structure: An Organized System of Behavior
Cultural Differences and Uniformities
Ideal Versus Real Culture
Subcultures and Countercultures
Summary
91 Terms to Remember
92 Further Readings

4

94 THE INDIVIDUAL IN SOCIETY: SOCIALIZATION AND DEVIANCE

What Is Personality?
Cultural Determinism
Normal Versus Abnormal Personality?
Summary
124 Terms to Remember
125 Further Readings

5

126 RANKING AND STRATIFICATION

Stratification
Class, Status, and Power
How Sociologists Determine Social Class
Social Mobility
Summary
156 Terms to Remember
157 Further Readings

6

158 WE AND THEY: MAJORITY AND MINORITIES

Minorities
Ethnicity
Prejudice
Discrimination
The Struggle to Belong
Black Americans
Jews
Spanish-Speaking Minorities
American Indians
Asian Minorities
Women
Summary
199 Terms to Remember
200 Further Readings

7

201 SOCIAL AND CULTURAL CHANGE IN THE MODERN ERA

Social and Cultural Change
Processes of Social and Cultural Change
Sociocultural Changes
Population
Urbanization
Formal Organizations and Bureaucracy
Formal Organizations
Bureaucracy
Summary
244 Terms to Remember
245 Further Readings

8

246 COLLECTIVE BEHAVIOR

Determinants, Mechanisms, and Theories of Collective Behavior
Crowds
Other Forms of Collective Behavior
Publics and Public Opinion
Social Movements
Summary
279 Terms to Remember
281 Further Readings

9

282 PIVOTAL INSTITUTIONS: THE FAMILY, EDUCATION, RELIGION

Pivotal Institutions
The Family
Basic Patterns of Family Organization
Religion
Contemporary Trends
Education
Summary
321 Terms to Remember
322 Further Readings

10

324 PIVOTAL INSTITUTIONS: ECONOMY AND GOVERNMENT

The Sociology of Economics
Economic Decision Making
Economic Systems of Industrial Societies
Three Economic Systems
Social Problems and the Economy
Is the Work Ethic Dying?
Purpose and Function of Government
Political Power: Legitimacy and Authority
Political Ideology
Political Behavior in the Mass Society

Interest Groups: Purpose and Functions 358
Political Parties: Purpose and Functions 360
Citizen Participation in the Political Process
Summary 362
Terms to Remember
Further Readings

Index

Preface to the Second Edition

In the first edition of *The Brief Web* we addressed ourselves to a special problem. We were concerned that many students, initially enthusiastic about taking an introductory sociology course, soon lost interest in the discipline because of what they perceived as its lack of relevance. Student disinterest, however, is often justified. Students want to find out what makes them the types of individuals they are. They are curious about their society, or about what makes the society different from others, about which expectations for the future are probable or feasible, and about how much faith they should put in a science of society. If these students are confronted with long lists of terms that must be memorized, boredom or disinterest often can be the result.

We wanted to ensure that students would not undergo the sad metamorphosis from enthusiasm to disinterest when reading our textbook. To this end, we tried to minimize the number of concepts—which certainly must be presented and defined, else what does the discipline rest on?—and to define them in such a context that students could readily identify with them from their own experience. We tried to engage the student personally, to tell him or her, "Look, stratification is not just an abstract term whose meaning you must memorize in order to pass a test. Stratification characterizes the society in which you live. What you are, what you become, where you go to school, how well educated you will become, whom you marry, for whom you vote, where you live now and where you will live eventually—all these factors and many others are determined in large part by stratification. So you would be wise to familiarize yourself with the functioning of this system and decide, since presumably you are a free individual, whether to work for its maintenance or its change."

In this second edition, we remain committed to these original goals, and also have made many innovations. We cut down on some superfluous concepts and definitions. We begin with a more complete chapter on the nature of sociology and the scientific method which it employs. We now have a separate chapter on collective behavior and a greatly expanded chapter on sociocultural change. The chapters on institutions, and especially the one on the economic institution, are linked more firmly to basic sociological principles. In general, all chapters have been lengthened and made more comprehensive in answer to those critics who wanted elaboration.

In relation to pedagogy, we have also tried to improve the text. In addition to the summary, glossary, suggested readings, and annotated bibliography, we have added boxes in each chapter that highlight and capsulize pertinent sociological research, or describe sociological methodology, or simply explore points of human interest. In addition, provocative questions are placed in the margins relating sociological concepts to the student's own life experiences. Finally, we have retained and improved the clarity, readability, and general intelligibility of the material.

That there was a need for the type of text we offered in the first edition was confirmed for us by the favorable reception *Brief Web* enjoyed. We thank the many instructors and students who took the time to write to us, commending us—or sometimes chastising us—on some particular or other. We have tried to keep both commendations and criticisms in mind, and hope they are reflected in this new edition.

John and Erna Perry, 1977

A Word to the Student

MOST OF YOU know why you are here, taking this introductory course in sociology. The course may fulfill a requirement in the social sciences for those of you who are primarily oriented toward the physical sciences. Or you may be intending to major in the social sciences; an introduction to sociology will help you narrow down an area of specialization. Or you may be already familiar with sociology and plan to use this course as a steppingstone to becoming a sociologist. Or you may just be interested in finding out as much as possible about the society you live in.

But you may still have questions about what sociology really is. Perhaps you recognize the prefix *socio-*, which sounds like the word *social*. You may know that the suffix, *-logy*, means 'a study of.' But 'a study of social' still makes very little sense. Let's go back to the word *social*. It is used in many different contexts: social work, a church social, a social butterfly, social responsibility, social security. None of these contexts suggests a clear definition of sociology. If you look up these terms in a dictionary, you will begin to see that all of them refer to two or more people interacting. Thus, social work means trying to help certain groups of disadvantaged people. A church social is a friendly gathering of people associated with a church. A social butterfly is someone who likes being with other people most of the time. Social responsibility means a sense of commitment to other people; and your social security number is part of a system that, by keeping you safe from economic disaster, helps you maintain equal relationships with other people in society. Therefore, you can guess that sociology is the study of interrelationships among people. Sociology is a social science that attempts to discover how you interrelate with other people and how people relate to each other.

A Word to the Student

Since sociology is a social *science,* it follows that it has content, methodology, theories, and research of its own. In addition, it deals in concepts that are peculiar to itself. It is with these concepts that the first part of this book is concerned. You may wonder why well over one-half of the text is taken up with definitions, explanations, and discussions of concepts. These concepts in sociology are rather special. First, they present some difficulty because they are identical to the layperson's everyday vocabulary, yet often they have specific meanings that differ from the layperson's. For instance, when you say "a group of students," you mean any haphazardly gathered number of students standing or sitting together in the same place, at the same time. As you will see in chapter 2, the sociologist means something quite distinct and different when he* refers to "a group of students."

Second, concepts are the real tools of sociology. Theories are often the hypothetical, educated guesses about the how and why of human behavior in society. Research either bolsters or invalidates theories. But concepts are the tools of analysis with which sociologists dissect a situation, examine its component parts, and draw pertinent conclusions.

The first chapter defines the discipline of sociology, delineating its aims and scope, its methods and tools. You will note that although sociology calls itself a science, it is a rather special science, promising no certain results, no sure answers.

Subsequent chapters deal with the most important concepts of sociology: the facts that humans live in different kinds of groups, that patterns of behavior emerge through life in groups, that as individuals we hold certain statuses and play the attendant roles. Additional concepts include the facts that most people live in large groups called societies, that societies spawn cultures with both universal and particular characteristics, and that there exists a tendency for a member of each society to consider his or her culture the "best." Finally, we look at how socialization influences personality development; how collective behavior explains such unusual patterns of behavior as mobs, riots, panics, and hysteria; how social change affects societies and their individual members; how people are ranked by social classes and divided according to racial, ethnic, or religious groupings; and how bureaucracy and formal kinds of organization in industrial societies replace the informality of interaction found in simpler, more traditional societies.

The remaining portion of the text employs the concepts introduced in part I to probe beneath the surface of American institutions, or at least, of our most important ones: the family, education, religion, the economy, and government. All of these institutions are marked by the fact that all nations seem to have achieved or are attempting to achieve a

---

*The traditional use of the pronoun *he* has not yet been superseded by a convenient, generally accepted pronoun that means either *he* or *she.* Therefore, the authors will continue to use *he,* and take this opportunity to acknowledge the inherent inequity of the traditional preference for the masculine pronoun.

high level of industrialization. The resulting mass societies are more and more linked together in what may some day be an international society. These changes have taken place with extraordinary rapidity, encompassing only the last two centuries. Consequently, many problems have arisen at the same time that many dreams have been realized. The concepts, tools, and research of sociology are helping to analyze the impact of change on our social institutions.

[The Relevance of Sociology]

Max Weber, one of the great sociological thinkers, perceived a threefold function in the social sciences: the ability to control the forces of society, the training of future social scientists, and the attainment of intellectual clarity. It appears that the first two functions have been generally accepted by academicians, the second function having, in addition, been actively pursued. But the last function, which Weber considered the most important, has been neglected. Yet intellectual clarity would enable the individual citizens of a society to judge alternative courses of action because they would be aware of their present basis and future consequences.

It is to this last function, intellectual clarity, that this text addresses itself. It is only by attaining intellectual clarity that the first of Weber's functions—the ability to control the forces of society—can be considered a reasonable goal. For much of human history, people have been buffeted by forces beyond their control. Today, through technology, people can control many of these forces. But their control has been most successful in the physical world. In the social realm, people have remained slaves to tradition and provincialism, which limit their ability to perceive things as they are.

Sociology has no specific answers that will cure the ills of humanity or that will help to bring about utopia. But by relentlessly asking Why? and How? and by continually probing into causes, sociology can tear off some of the veils that have covered social reality for so long. It matters little how these veils were imposed—whether through ignorance, greed, or the thirst for power. What matters is that they be seen for what they are, not for what they appear to be. In bringing this about, sociology and its adherents are, and no doubt will be, faced with much antagonism. No one likes to see his idols shattered. No one likes to be told that the group he belongs to is not actually superior—that only his ethnocentrism, or belief in the superiority of his group, makes it seem so. No one likes to be told that the family he is trying to prevent from moving into his neighborhood is not inferior—that only his prejudice makes it seem so. No one likes to be told that his hate of communism is not patriotism but only a compensatory mechanism he has developed because he feels frustrated by changes beyond his control.

People must understand social reality if they are to become the true masters of their destiny and if they are to make rational, constructive choices and to experience complete lives. Unfortunately, even though we live in society and society is our immediate reality, we understand very little about it. (After all, we are living organisms, but this does not mean that we automatically understand biology!)

Sociology does not claim to be the only discipline that helps people understand and know society and its functioning. Sociology only claims to provide one means of achieving such understanding, but the means are uniquely appropriate to the exploration of a changed and changing world. Novelist James Joyce expressed his horror at some of the morbid aspects of human experience by saying that history was a nightmare from which he was trying to awake. Sociology may help us all to awake from the nightmares not only of history but of the present.

What do you think Joyce meant by saying that history was a nightmare from which he was trying to awake? Do you agree with this appraisal of history?

The social web

CAN PEOPLE LIVE without other people? Human beings have always wondered what it would be like to be truly solitary. Many people have become voluntary hermits; others have been thrust into solitary confinement or exile, as the worst punishment imaginable. We have always played with myths about people who were brought up away from human beings—Pecos Bill, raised by coyotes in the American West; Romulus and Remus, raised by a wolf and later to become founders of Rome; Sir Percival of King Arthur's Round Table. These myths express our curiosity about our own social nature, our wondering what we would be like if we were not shaped and molded by other human beings.

The title of this text, *The Social Web,* suggests ways in which we relate to the society around us. Each of us is part of the social web. We each have many connections to other people; and many common bonds. Human beings, like other animals, have never been able to exist solely as individuals. We are born from the union of two persons. We can survive our infancy only if other people take care of us. And we can become human only if others teach us what it is to be human. We are social animals who live in families, tribes, and communities. We build cities and nations. We form groups based on friendship, special interests, hobbies, or political ideas. Sure, we can become hermits, and some of us do want to live totally isolated. But we could not choose to live as hermits if we had not lived with others first, because we would have no basis on which to choose.

What other social sciences that you have studied are related to sociology? How do you think these sciences will help you with your study of sociology?

Being social animals means we have relationships with many other people. Some of these relationships are intimate (with families and some friends), and some are formal (with bosses and colleagues at work). Some are close in certain situations only (with teachers and fellow students), while others are much more impersonal (with local and national governmental agencies, economic agencies, and other bureaucracies). All these relationships form a web around us. Sometimes the web may feel like a trap, and at other times like a huge, supportive net, or telephone system that links us all together. But it is always there. Most of our behavior, most of our actions, affect in some way one or more of these relationships, and in turn evoke reactions in others that reflect back on us. The more we participate in relationships, the closer we weave ourselves into the web.

Sociology helps us untangle the social web, helps show us how and why we are part of it. Sociologists try to dig below the surface of the social structures we have made—parts of the social web—and build up a body of knowledge that will help us recognize and improve our relationships to others in the same web. Sociologists ask questions about how we behave toward one another and why. And finally sociologists use the methods of science to answer these questions.

[What Is Sociology?]

Sociology, then, can be variously defined as *the scientific study of human social behavior,* or as *the science of human interaction,* or as *the study of society.* The goals of sociology resemble the goals of most other sciences: the discovery of facts, the explanation of facts and causes of human behavior, and, ultimately, the prediction of behavior. The more we know about how we *do* behave, the more we can predict how we *will* behave in the future.

Sociology is a social science—*social,* because it is concerned with the relationships of people in society; *science,* because it uses the scientific method (the characteristics of which we will analyze later in the chapter). Still, definitions merely set the boundaries of a discipline. Sociologist Peter Berger suggests that one way of obtaining a clear image of what sociology is, is to list all the things that it is *not.* This can be done best, he says, by showing that the image the sociologist has acquired in the popular imagination is inaccurate.[1]

Not a boy scout. The first such inaccurate popular image is of the sociologist as someone who likes to work with and help people—the sociologist as Boy Scout. Although such an attitude can serve to motivate a beginning sociologist, there is nothing to prevent a person who dislikes and does *not* want to help people from being a successful sociologist. The insights of sociology may be used both for humanitarian and nonhumanitarian purposes.

Not a social worker. The sociologist is not a social worker, nor does he provide theories for social work. It is true that the early sociologists were

---

[1]Peter L. Berger, *Invitation to Sociology* (Garden City, N.Y.: Doubleday, 1963), pp. 1–16.

full of reformist zeal. But today sociology tries to understand *why* specific social conditions exist. In contrast, social work is the *practice* of a certain method for the improvement of social conditions. The facts uncovered by sociology can be used in the practice of social work, but the two are not synonymous.

For the same reasons, the sociologist is not usually considered a social reformer, although some sociologists might disagree. Again, sociological insights have been responsible for improving the living conditions of particular groups of people.

If a sociologists is not a social reformer, what should be his or her attitude toward social problems?

The same sociological insights, however, could be used by those who try to make conditions worse. The sociologist, then, is neither a social worker, nor a social reformer.

Not a statistician. The sociologist is not simply a gatherer of statistics about human behavior. The gathering of statistics, as a whole activity, is much more characteristic of agencies concerned with public opinion and market trends. Statistical analysis is one technique of the sociological methodology that is popular with a number of sociologists who prefer to do empirical research rather than to develop broad theories. Statistics can be a valuable tool to sociologists, but the data must be interpreted from a sociological perspective and frame of reference, or they are meaningless. The statistical information in the Kinsey reports on sex behavior is not in itself sociological. The information only becomes sociological when it is used to make statements about the institutions of marriage and the family, and about the values of our society in the area of sex.

Not totally detached. Finally, the sociologist is neither a totally detached observer and a cold manipulator of people nor a describer of human activities who does not participate in the activities. Such an image may have been suggested by the insistence of sociologists that they are scientists and that consequently they view their subject matter with as much objectivity as any scientist. However, it is one thing to place a cross section of animal tissue under the microscope, and another to place a cross section of the human species under sociological examination. The sociologist cannot ever be totally objective. Before being a scientist, he is a human being. The issue of objectivity versus subjectivity is a burning one in sociology. It involves the moral questions of how the sociologist uses the findings of his research, for what purpose and to whose benefit.

What, Then, Is Sociology?

The general characteristics of sociology may be listed for the sake of clarity and understanding. For example, in addition to being a social science, *sociology is categorical rather than normative.* This formulation means it is concerned with what *is* and not with what *ought to be.* Science in general does not attempt to probe into matters that are not perceived by the human senses. It is more concerned with empirical phenomena. Sociology, as a science, is likewise limited to the description of events as they are, were, or probably will be.

Furthermore, *sociology is a pure, and not an applied science.* Its goal is the acquisition of knowledge about the behavior of human beings in society, not the use of that knowledge. Knowledge acquired by sociologists is applied by workers in fields such as social work, diplomacy, admininstration, teaching, and so on.

Would you find it easy to describe the behavior of people in wartime without making judgments? Why or why not?

Sociology is *an abstract science, rather than a concrete one.* This distinction means that sociology is more concerned with the forms and patterns of human behavior than with the specific consequences of behavior. Sociologists are not interested in, for instance, the U.S. Steel Corporation as such, but in the human tendency to organize into various associations, such as corporations, to get things done. Sociologists are not interested in nations per se, but in the universality of human societies, which share structural similarities or patterns.

Related to the abstract nature of sociology is its involvement with general, rather than particular, principles governing human interaction. Sociologists are not interested in any *particular* society that waged war on another society and was strengthened as a result. They study that event only because it provides further evidence of the principle that external aggression tends to solidify the internal unity of a group.

Finally, *sociology is a general, and not a special, social science.* Sociologists seek out the principles that govern all interaction and social relationships, regardless of the area of human life in which they occur. Therefore, sociology differs from the rest of the social sciences, which make this distinction and treat only specific areas of human life. Economists, for example, analyze how people organize and interact in the production, distribution, and consumption of goods and services necessary to survival. Sociologists study the economy as one of the pivotal institutions of society, but economics is only one subfield of sociology, not its entire content. In addition, the sociologist looks at the economy with a special perspective.

How does sociology, as a study of human behavior, differ from psychology? From psychiatry?

Sociology and the Social Sciences

Although sociology's place is among the social sciences, its distinction from them may not seem clear. Someone may justly say, for instance, that history also deals with humans as they interact with others. Without interaction, there would be no history. History, however, focuses on the narration and explanation of a chain of past events to form a complete record of a society or a number of societies—American history, or the history of Western civilization, for example. Sociology, on the other hand, uncovers in the same events certain processes that occur when people relate with one another under certain circumstances. Sociologists want to know whether historical events show a definite pattern that repeats itself every time people find themselves in the same circumstances. They look for generalities in the events, not for specifics; they look for regularities, not for the exceptional; they look for the universal, not for the particular.

For example, whereas the historian would be concerned with the differences between the French and the American revolutions, the sociologist would be interested in the phenomenon of revolution in itself. The historian would be acquainted with the biographies of the great personalities of history, but the sociologist would wonder what made *these* persons, rather than others, leaders. History focuses on descriptions of particulars, of specifics, of the unique. Sociologists generalize, analyze, and find recurring variables. As sociologist Robert Bierstedt comments, "If the past is to be thought of as a continually unrolling cloth, then the historian would be interested in picking out the individual threads; the sociologist, in the overall pattern."[2]

The Sociological Perspective

A frequent criticism of sociology is that it merely takes a commonplace subject and couches it in scientific terminology; or that sociologists see the same reality and come to the same conclusions as other mortals, but they do it in a more roundabout way. (There is an often-repeated joke that a sociologist is a fellow who spends thousands of dollars in research to find the corner brothel.) Human interaction is the subject matter of sociology, and both the sociologist and the layperson look at the same reality. But they look at it in different ways.

How does a sociologist avoid the criticisms of saying nothing, but saying nothing in scientific jargon?

The sociological perspective looks beyond commonly accepted or officially defined goals of human behavior. It recognizes that human behavior can be interpreted at different levels, and that some motives of human behavior are hidden, rather than conscious. It implies a certain skepticism about the official interpretation of things, whether these concern religion, politics, or justice. Such a perspective results from the sociologist's objective recognition of the subjective nature of such official interpretations. This skepticism is only natural when the federal government issues a finding that states rich people tend to be happier than poor people. And this skepticism is not peculiar to sociology alone; thinkers throughout the ages and in all civilizations have looked behind and seen through official explanations. The rise of modern sociology is especially marked by certain circumstances of Western civilization that brought about a situation in which the accepted, official, and authoritative interpretations of societal and cultural goals were severely shaken. These jolts began with the breakup of European Christianity by the Reformation and came to a pitch when the French Revolution abolished the absolutist state. Sociology arose as a way of analyzing these tremendous reversals of the status quo.

---

[2]Robert Bierstedt, "Toynbee and Sociology," *The British Journal of Sociology* (June, 1959), pp. 95–104. Also, see Pitirim A. Sorokin, "On Sociology Among the Social Sciences," in Marcello Truzzi, ed., *Sociology: The Classic Statements* (New York: Random House, 1971), pp. 3–13.

Seeing Ourselves from the Outside

What would our own culture look like to a true stranger? Here is an imaginative and humorous example of how you can take an ordinary daily practice with which we are all familiar and see it in a new way:

> *The Nacirema have an almost pathological horror of, and fascination with, the mouth, the condition of which is believed to have a supernatural influence on all social relationships. Were it not for the rituals of the mouth, they believe that their teeth would fall out, their gums bleed, their jaws shrink, their friends desert them, and their lovers reject them. They also believe that a strong relationship exists between oral and moral characteristics. For example, there is a ritual ablution of the mouth for children that is supposed to improve their moral fiber.*
>
> *The daily body ritual performed by everyone includes a mouth-rite. Despite the fact that these people are so punctilious about care of the mouth, this rite involves a practice that strikes the unitiated stranger as revolting. It was reported to me that the ritual consists of inserting a small bundle of hog hairs into the mouth, along with certain magical powders, and then moving the bundle in a highly formalized series of gestures.*

Horace Miner, "Body Ritual Among the Nacirema," *American Anthropologist* 58 (1956): 503–507. (The Nacirema are, of course, Americans—spelled backwards.)

The word *cosmopolitan* is derived from roots that roughly mean *citizen of the world.* Why might being a citizen of the world, as opposed to a citizen of a country, make one more open to ideas?

History shows that the sociological perspective develops best in a cosmopolitan atmosphere. New ideas have always seemed to catch on first in the large cities where people were exposed to others who came from faraway places and who represented strange cultural customs. As our socieites become more and more urban, we begin to appreciate other ways of thinking and acting, and we shed some of the provincial idea that "our way is the best way." The open-mindedness that comes from maintaining a world view of human life—in contrast to a national or regional view—is essential to sociology.

Finally, sociology could not exist in a society that claims the absolute "rightness" or "truth" of its values. Traditional societies *have* made this claim, and thus their citizens have had a static idea of who they are and to what they can aspire. For example, in feudal times, if you were born a peasant, you died a peasant. Not too long ago, a villager from a Middle Eastern country could not conceive of ever, under any circumstances, leaving his native village or leading a different life. In traditional societies, people have definite and permanent identities.

Behind the Restroom Door

One of the more enterprising and controversial sociological investigations done in recent years was Laud Humphreys' study of the tearoom trade. "Tearoom" is the name given by homosexuals to those public restrooms where they engage in sex. Humphreys observed and made extensive notes on fifty such encounters, later interviewing many of the participants. What characterized these sexual encounters, Humphreys said, was the lack of involvement between the men—"kicks without commitment" is Humphreys' phrase—and their impersonality: in only fifteen of the cases did he hear as much as a single word spoken. Humphreys was able to observe men of all races, from all occupational and income levels, married and unmarried, those with both heterosexual and homosexual self-identifications, engaging in fellatio. Men came for a variety of reasons but they chose tearooms because they wanted their activities to remain secret and their personal involvement fleeting.

Humphreys' study raises some important ethical questions about sociological research. He was able to conduct his investigations by acting as the lookout, or "watchqueen," for the men. To only a few, and then only after establishing some rapport, did he reveal his real purpose for being there. To obtain interviews with many of the men, Humphreys resorted to noting the license numbers of their cars as they drove away. He traced the men down, noting their neighborhoods and gathering any public information he could about them. About a year later he changed his appearance and his automobile and went to their homes to interview them as part of a "social-health survey." To what limits do you think it is ethical for the researcher to go in inquiring into the lives and feelings of others?

Laud Humphreys, *Tearoom Trade: Impersonal Sex in Public Places* (Chicago: Aldine-Atherton, 1969).

But we live in a modern society, in which conflicting values are held and in which values change rapidly. Today we may aspire to a house in the suburbs and three cars in the garage. Tomorrow we may have exchanged these aspirations for life in a rural commune, growing our own food and making our own clothes. We can, and frequently do, change jobs, social positions, life-styles, friends. So we can look at the world from many points of view, and this multiple perspective forces us to say: "This is true; but that is also true." Truth becomes relative to time, place, and circumstance. We no longer see things in terms of black

What differing values on, say, lying, are held among your classmates? Can you agree on a definition of lying? How can you learn to tolerate different value positions?

and white, good and evil, truth and lie. Now when values are relative, as in our society, people tend to be confused and to hold contradictory beliefs; identity becomes tenuous, and anxiety mounts. Only when values are relative can we appreciate the sociological perspective. This perspective can perhaps help alleviate the anxiety, this "culture shock." We need to feel more at ease with relative values to be able to fully relate to others.

Theoretical Frameworks of Sociology

Sociologists believe that objectivity and a lack of bias are the most important prerequisites for scientific investigation. But none of us are born in a vacuum. We assimilate the attitudes we find in our immediate environment and even if we later reject them—because they go against more raional explanations—they still continue to affect us. No wonder different sociologists have approached the study of society from various points of view and have come to somewhat different conclusions. Perhaps because sociology is still a young discipline, it has not produced a sweeping theory that alone can be the basis for the science of society. We have to be satisfied, for the moment, with a number of general perspectives on the functioning of society and the interaction of people. These perspectives, when presented in a systematic and clear fashion, are called *theoretical models.* A discussion of the nature and content of theory may be found later in this chapter.

The evolutionary model. The evolutionary model patterns itself on the example of biology. In this model, society is believed to develop through a number of fixed stages. Like living organisms, society proceeds from a simple to a more complex form (in an evolutionary fashion). Since evolution has been equated with progress, the final stage of society should represent its most perfect form.

Do you feel that our society has reached a more perfect stage than the stage we were in at the time of the American Revolution? Why or why not?

This theory was the earliest sociological model, subscribed to by Auguste Comte and many other sociologists of the nineteenth and early twentieth centuries.

Today much evidence suggests that not all societies have passed through a fixed set of stages. The chaos of societies in the twentieth century does not necessarily indicate that we have reached a "higher" stage of development. The evolutionary model has lost some of its credibility, but has not been totally abandoned. Some sociologists believe that since societies are often different to begin with, they go through different stages of development (change). Even if they went through the same stages, the results might differ. This model is called *multilinear evolution.* General patterns, the multilinear evolutionists say, are visible nonetheless. All societies tend to grow away from large, conjugal families to small, nuclear ones. Industrialization and urbanization result in liberalized attitudes and reduce discrimination in most societies.

The Promise

The great transformations of the modern world, in constantly throwing up new challenges to cherished values, often leave people with a sense of being trapped and a feeling of being unable to cope in daily life, C. Wright Mills once said. What people needed, he believed, was a capacity of mind that would allow them to connect their personal feelings with public issues and larger historical processes. This capacity Mills called the "sociological imagination": the ability "to shift from one perspective to another, . . . to range from the most impersonal and remote transformations to the most intimate features of the human self—and to see the relations between the two." With the aid of this capacity, he believed, we could see the connection, for example, between personal marital troubles and larger social forces that result in a rising divorce rate, or relate our feelings about being unemployed to the workings of the business cycle. In this way, Mills believed, we would come to see that many problems, though personally experienced, are incapable of personal solution; instead, they require a knowledge of and involvement in larger social issues.

The sociological imagination would aid its possessor in clarifying the sources of contemporary feeling and in grasping the "interplay of man and society, of biography and history, of self and the world." This, he said, was the task and the promise of the sociological imagination. That he wrote a book highly critical of the dominant trends in sociology is indicative of how well he felt sociology was fulfilling that promise.

C. Wright Mills, *The Sociological Imagination* (New York: Oxford University Press, 1959), pp. 3–24.

The conflict model. Some sociologists feel that conflict is the most important and universal characteristic of social change. The most famous conflict theorist of the nineteenth century was Karl Marx (1818–1883). A number of other theorists contributed to the development of the conflict model. German sociologist Georg Simmel (1858–1918) maintained that social order was the result of competing forces of harmony and disharmony in society. There are conflicts between individuals, groups and the individual, and between various groups. Because of conflicts, you know who your friends and enemies are. Common enemies tie a group together. Conflict is a social relationship, and other social relationships follow from the resolution of conflict.

Can you think of ways in which conflict has helped you and other members of your family develop personally and as a group?

Marx's model is, of course, much more complicated. Although it has been criticized on several points, a number of sociologists have seen value in it. They have expanded the model and kept it alive through several decades when other models, based on consensus rather than conflict, were more popular. Now that conflict—racial, class, and sexual—is resulting in rapid social change, this model is once more popular with many sociologists. American sociologist C. Wright Mills was a conflict theorist, as is contemporary German sociologist Ralf Dahrendorf. The recent crop of sociologists, who variously refer to themselves as "radical," "activist," or "humanist," also like to be associated with this theoretical model.

The functional model. This model, like the Marxist conflict model, incorporates aspects of evolutionary theory. It too makes the analogy between society and a living organism. A living organism is made up of parts that contribute to the maintenance and survival of the whole organism. In the same way, the functionalists claim, a society consists of a number of systems that contribute to the maintenance and survival of the whole society. This contribution is their function (hence the name *functional model*), just as the function of the circulatory system in a living organism is to provide oxygen and nourishment ot the tissues, and to carry off waste material.

The functional model views society as existing in a delicate balance, like the aquatic life of a lake. If something happens to one of the parts of the system, all other parts are affected. The system then no longer functions well, and social problems arise. In the same way, water pollution may encourage algae, which may choke other forms of life. Although change occurs as a result of occasional malfunctioning of the system, stability tends to be restored. Stability and change are dual characteristics of the social system.

The various institutions of society will be discussed later in the book. Can you anticipate what a structural-functionalist might say about the function of the economic institution in society?

Functionalists stress the importance of structure as well as function. This model is also called *structural-functionalism.* By structures, structural-functionalists mean the various parts of the system. In society, the chief structures are societal institutions: the family, education, the economy, the government, religion, and so on. Each structure is thought to have a part in helping the society survive and persist. Structural-functionalist analysis tends to focus on the interrelationship among the various structures.

The social-scientific model. Underlying all other theoretical models is the social-scientific model. This model derives from the original idea that sociology should be totally guided by the scientific method of investigation. It assumes that the science of society is very much the same as the physical and biological sciences. During the period between World Wars I and II, a physical science model was very popular. Many sociologists attempted to quantify their data and sought to discover the operation of social laws by using the experimental research methods of the physical sciences. However, many other sociologists have insisted that sociology is not just a science. They claim it has artistic, even spiritual, overtones. In short, sometimes insight into human relationships is just as important as scientific data.

Today most sociologists accept the necessity of using the scientific method to accumulate empirical data. Yet they are aware that this method cannot be used exclusively. When people investigate matters pertaining to other people, strict objectivity can never be totally attained. So most admit that sociology is only part science. However, the social-scientific model is the hub of a controversy between action-oriented sociologists who are less interested in discovering laws of social behavior than they are in changing society for the better, and sociologists who believe that their job is to discover and present facts, not judge them.

Statistical and mathematical models are also used by some sociologists. These models cover specialized fields, and are beyond the scope of an introductory text. Finally, let us reemphasize that sociologists may use any of the theoretical models we just reviewed. No one model is more "right" than another. In sociology there are no invariable "laws" like the laws in the physical sciences. We cannot say that a person will always behave in a certain way under specific circumstances. We can only suggest that on the basis of having counted and sampled and interviewed innumerable persons under the same circumstances, we *think* that they *probably* may behave in a specific manner. We cannot guarantee it.

A New Road to Knowledge

Can strict objectivity ever be attained in any study of any subject? If not, why do people continue to strive for objectivity?

[A New Road to Knowledge]

Many of sociology's insights into the nature of people and society are identical with those of poets, playwrights, essayists, novelists, and philosophers. Throughout the centuries philosophers and artists have developed knowledge by using four main tools. One tool is *intuition*, a sudden insight, the source of which cannot be explained. A second is *authority*, or acceptance of statements by people who are specialists in a subject or who are thought to be divinely inspired. A third tool used is *tradition*, which is based on the belief that what has been considered right and true in the past should be considered so in the present. The last tool is *common sense*. The use of common sense is based on superficial observation, on incomplete data, and on the human senses, which are often inaccurate.

What kinds of subjective reasoning may affect conclusions reached by common sense?

These tools of inquiry are very useful. Many people continue to rely on them for most of their everyday knowledge. Knowledge gained through the use of such tools persists, if only because people tend to cling to accepted ideas and traditions. That is why people refused for so long to acknowledge the evidence that the earth was not flat and that it was not the center of the universe. That is why many superstitious beliefs and old wives' tales are still accepted today.

The search for truth and knowledge can be carried much further through the use of a new tool of inquiry: the scientific method. It is the scientific method, and not any particular body of content, that gives science a unique way of looking at things. The objective of the scientific method is to obtain verifiable evidence to the basic question, How does it work? Its basis is to make no judgment about even the most obvious facts until original suppositions are overwhelmingly supported by proof.

The Scientific Spirit

Underlying the scientific method is an attitude called the *scientific spirit.* The first principle of this spirit is that the scientist approaches everything with great *doubt* and *skepticism,* taking nothing for granted. This attitude is displayed even in regard to his own findings, which are always subject to change after further analysis. The second principle is *objectivity.* The scientist tries to rid himself completely of personal attitudes, desires, beliefs, values, and tendencies when confronting data. He must try to be completely dispassionate, not permitting his individual biases to affect his judgment. Naturally, objectivity is an ideal to which the scientist can only aspire. No one is totally objective all the time. Some scientists no longer believe that total objectivity is desirable. An increasing number maintain that the scientist as a human being has a moral obligation toward his fellow human beings. Therefore, he should not permit the products of his research to be used in immoral ways. We shall see later how this issue affects sociology.

Closely related to objectivity is the third principle of *ethical neutrality.* According to this principle, the scientist must not make value judgments about his findings. In his function as a scientific researcher, he cannot maintain that his conclusions are good or bad, right or wrong. He must be concerned only with whether they are true or false. Finally, the scientist's conclusions must never be considered final, absolute, or universal truths. His conclusions are always relative to the time and place in which they are made and always subject to change.

How is skepticism related to ethical neutrality? What kind of attitude should the scientist take toward his or her own opinions or conclusions?

The Scientific Method

The basic technique of the scientifc method is a special kind of observation. Above all, it must be accurate and precise. In collecting data, the scientist must subject it to careful checking, rechecking, and cross-checking. He must also subject it to careful measurement. For instance, he cannot permit himself to say, "The big universities are full of radicals." He would have to make, instead, this hypothetical statement: "In universities with enrollments of 15,000 and over, 60.5 percent of the students were found to be members of political action groups."

Scientific observation should take place under controlled conditons. The researcher should be able to make particular features of the environment remain constant. Then, when other features change, he can be sure which specific cause is determining which effect. This requirement is difficult to achieve in the social sciences because research on people cannot always be performed in a laboratory. Finally, scientific observation must be made by a trained observer. Only such a person knows which data are relevant and which are unimportant.

Scientific observation is not the same as looking at things. Those of us who have the use of our vision look at things all the time, but seldom arrive at scientific observations. Sometimes the evidence of our senses can be confirmed through the method of science. And sometimes that same method does not confirm the evidence. Scientific observation must also proceed systematically. The scientist must select and define a problem and then make an organized plan for collecting data. A haphazard collection of facts, taken from memory or from a small sample, obviously proves nothing.

Hypothesis. In defining his problem, the scientist forms a hypothesis. This is a statement, in general terms, of the problem and its probable solution. A hypothesis may be a hunch or guess by the researcher. Research may prove the hypothesis valid, may reform it, or may contradict it altogether. Its basis may be simply common sense or curiosity, or perhaps a "truth" rooted in tradition. The hypothesis may also derive from existing theoretical models and sociological research. Frequently it emerges from a review of the literature pertaining to a problem that interests the researcher. This review of the literature is a very important step in the scientific method. It connects new research with old, allows science to accumulate ideas, and helps tell the scientist what variables to control when he conducts his own research.

If you were beginning a sociological study of your classmates, what kinds of questions might you ask? Construct a hypothesis for such a study.

Data collection. The research plan following the statement of a hypothesis specifies from what group(s) and in what manner data are to be collected. The researcher must decide from whom and how best to obtain his data: by direct observation, by questionnaires, by interviews, and so on.

Data classification. After data have been systematically collected, the scientist must classify, organize, and record the data. Because human memory is imperfect and subject to personal prejudices, research that has not been recorded is considered invalid. The data must also be made public, so others may have access to both the findings and the procedures through which they were obtained. The scientist is obligated to make public his findings even if they displease him or endanger him.

If you were trying to test a sociological hypothesis about your classmates, how would you go about deciding what data to collect? How would you classify the data?

Data analysis. In this step, the researcher places the data according to a classificatory scheme. Then, various statistical methods are used to see whether the differences are substantial or so small that they are caused by chance.

Generalization. After analyzing the data, the researcher must decide whether the data warrant a firm conclusion of the hypothesis or only a broad generalization. The researcher must make this decision after taking into account the size of his sample and the thoroughness of his data analysis. Cautious researchers tend to make undergeneralizations, which keep their research from being useful to other researchers. Overconfident researchers tend to make overgeneralizations, which may lead to false hypotheses and wrong conclusions.

Methodology: Direct Observation

Direct observation, the basis of many sociological investigations, means simply that you observe people's behavior at first-hand rather than relying on their own reports or the reports of others about them. The idea is to observe systematically and report accurately what you see. One sociologist who uses this method (among others) is Erving Goffman. Though Goffman generalizes far beyond his own evidence, his work illustrates some possible fruits of direct observation.

How do people avoid bumping into each other on city sidewalks? Without official rules and without police to keep them in line, pedestrians nevertheless sort themselves into definite patterns and ordinarily obey a set of unspoken rules of conduct. Like vehicular traffic, Goffman observes, American pedestrian traffic tends to follow a two-way pattern separated by an imaginary line, with traffic going in your direction tending to be on the right of the line. Sometimes, however, pedestrians going either way move to the curb edge to achieve a faster pace. Pedestrians also follow a set of lane and passing rules. These are made possible, Goffman believes, by a method of "scanning," whereby pedestrians, like drivers, orient themselves to people around them, and by a body language people use to signal their course intentions to one another. At the edge of their awareness, pedestrians make themselves "into something that others can read and predict from." When collison with an oncomer seems probable, Goffman observes, a pedestrian will often first seek some recognition from the oncomer that he or she is aware of the imminent danger and then make some gesture as to an intended course. Once each has done so and seen that the other acknowledges this signal, they can turn their attention elsewhere. As oncomers come abreast of us, we will tend to forget about them, Goffman says, trusting that they will continue in their paths rather than abruptly change their course to force a collision. This is all evidence, Goffman argues, of the existence of some degree of mutual trust and order among strangers on city streets.

You could test this out in your community by making your own observations. What happens, for example, on a narrow path when oncomers meet? What techniques do people use to give way without appearing to lose face? Try to be as systematic and concrete as possible, recording your observations as you go along.

Erving Goffman, *Relations in Public: Microstudies of the Public Order* (New York: Basic Books, 1971), pp. *ix*–18.

If you conducted a study of your classmates, and then someone else collected the same types of information, with different results, how could you clear up the discrepancies in your research?

Verification. Since most research is subject to error—of which the researcher may or may not be aware—some prefer to add another step to the scientific method, that of verification. This consists of repeating the research project (called *replication*) and can be done either by the same researcher who did the original research, or by another researcher. In order for research to be considered successful, it must be capable of being repeated by another scientist with the same results.

[The Scientific Method in Sociology]

Sociology is considered a science because it uses the scientific method as its system of inquiry. Because it is a *social* science, it cannot use exactly the same methodology as the physical sciences do. The investigative method of sociology does, however, share with other sciences the use of concepts, theory, and research.

Concepts

People think in terms of *concepts* about things that they observe and experience. They express these concepts through language. Concepts are generalized ideas about people, objects, and processes that are related to one another. Concepts are abstractions, ways of classifying things that are similar. For instance, the concept of chair includes all those objects that people sit in. Although this concept embraces all variations of the object, each of us interprets it in his own way. Those who have been brought up in mansions may think of a gilded Louis XIV chair. Others are likely to think of plain chrome kitchen chairs. However, we all know and understand the generalized idea of chair.

Concepts are learned and are continually altered in our minds as we obtain additional information. The child who believes that all chairs are made of wood adds another dimension to his concept of chair when he discovers that some chairs are upholstered and covered with fabric.

Sociological concepts are generalizations made about human interaction. Conflict is a concept that we all understand; in sociology, *conflict* refers to a particular kind of behavior among a number of people. It may refer to a fistfight between two men who both want to dance with the same woman; it may refer to an argument between marriage partners when a large portion of the paycheck has been misspent; or it may refer to war. We know about conflict because we have experienced it ourselves. We have observed it among others. We have thought about it; and are therefore able to generalize about it.

Sociologists use concepts as their technical vocabulary. Statements of sociological concepts often have precise meanings that differ considerably from the layman's meaning. It is essential for a student of sociology to become acquainted with sociological concepts. Such concepts as *group, culture, society,* and *association,* to mention but a few, mean one thing to the man and woman in the street and another to sociologists.

The Disciplined Imagination

"Inventing a scientific hypothesis is as imaginative an act, as inexplicable an act, as inventing the theme and the personae of, let us say, John Keats' 'Ode on a Grecian Urn,' " the noted mathematician, biologist, and author of *The Ascent of Man,* J. Bronowski, has said. "The misconception is that science or any intellectual activity is done—or understood—by rational thought without imagination." People forget the role of imagination in science, Bronowski thinks, because they see only the final product—the orderly and dispassionate exposition of ideas—when in fact the process of discovery occurs in just the opposite way. The great discoveries of science have often been the result of intuition, chance happenings, or the joining together of apparently disparate ideas, sometimes by people who have only a vague sense of what they are seeking.

Rationality enters into the scientific process, says Bronowski, only at a later stage, as "the verification of the intuition by steps which can be communicated to others. That is what distinguishes science from nonsense, philosophy from mysticism, and the inspired work of Watson and Crick on the double helix from Hitler raving at Nuremburg."

George Derfer, "Science, Poetry and 'Human Specificity': An Interview with J. Bronowski," *American Scholar* 43 (Summer 1974): 386–404.

The concept of *group* is very important in sociology. What kinds of specific groups do you already associate with this concept? How did you develop these associations?

When dealing with sociological concepts, the student should be aware that they are generalized and abstract, rather than concrete and real. When they define the concept of group, sociologists do not mean to imply that each and every group has characteristics identical to those in their definition. They have no particular group in mind, but a generalized abstraction of a group. Concepts are guidelines that direct sociologists as they try to interpret and analyze reality.

Theories

Concepts form the basis of *theories.* Theories are sets of concepts and generalizations so arranged that they explain and predict possible and probable relationships among phenomena. They are also formulations of principles of behavior through which we try to increase our knowledge of human interaction. Theories are founded on observation and analysis. Their intent is to explain the connection between and among occurrences in human interaction. Without theories, the accumulation of sociological knowledge would be impossible, just as the formulation of theories would be impossible without concepts.

In sociology, theories not only help explain current situations but also help predict future ones. Suppose we use available data to theorize that, under conditions of large-scale unemployment, minority groups will vote the Democratic ticket. If analysis of election results proved our theory right, it would be reasonable to expect that these groups will vote similarly whenever they are faced with unemployment. This prediction does not mean that every member of a minority group will always vote Democratic. It simply suggests that, under the same circumstance, most will vote Democratic most of the time.

A theory does not have the force of a law. A law is an explanation of unchanging relationships among events. According to the law of gravity, an object always falls in the same direction under given conditions. Sociology has no laws because it deals with people, who are unpredictable. It has many theories, some of which, because data are unavailable, are really little more than hypotheses. Working with concepts as tools and using the techniques of the scientific method, the sociologist arrives at a theory. A theory, however, is never considered the final word on a subject. It is always open to change and even to total rejection if new evidence is presented to challenge it.

Research

Research tests and bolsters theories. The two aspects of the sociological method complement each other. Theory without the proper research remains in the realm of speculation, and research without theory is meaningless. However, most sociologists specialize in either one or the other. Either they refine the concepts from which theories are constructed, fitting concepts into a theoretical framework, or they engage in empirical research. Empirical research has already been described in general terms when we discussed the techniques of the scientific method. Sociological research makes heavy use of four fundamental formats: the sample survey, the case study, the experiment, and participant observation. In all of these formats, mathematical statistics have become a frequently used and valued research tool. But, before exploring these basic formats of sociological research we must concern ourselves with the question of variables.

Variables

Research may be defined as scientific inquiry conducted under controlled conditions in which data are carefully observed for the purpose of determining the relationship between one factor (for example, income) and one or more other factors (for example, child-raising techniques). The factors whose relationship sociologists try to uncover are called *variables.* Variables are characteristics that vary or differ in each individual case—from person to person, from group to group, from time to time, from place to place. The opposite of a variable is a *constant*—a characteristic that does not vary. Age, education, income,

Given a hypothesis that children raised by wolves will develop wolflike characteristics, how would you go about controlling the variables in research designed to test the hypothesis? What problems do you expect to encounter in testing the hypothesis?

religion, and political affiliation are the most frequent variables in sociological research.

When the sociologist tries to uncover the relationship between two variables, one variable is called *dependent,* and the other one is called *independent.* The independent variable always exerts some influence on the dependent variable. For example, income (independent variable) may influence child-raising techniques (dependent variable). More than one independent variable may influence the dependent variable. In addition to income, education and temperament may also influence child-raising methods. Every experiment consists of (1) keeping all variables constant except one; (2) changing that one variable; and (3) discovering what happens.

Sample Survey

The *sample survey* is a research design that consists of two separate features, the sample and the survey. The researcher decides to study a specific group, which he calls the *population.* The population can be anything from middle-aged bankers, to newly-registered voters, to college students enrolled in four-year schools. Since it is impossible to study every single middle-aged banker, or every individual new voter, or every college student across the land, the researcher selects a statistically valid sample of his population. There are procedures that allow the researcher to select such a sample of his population. The researcher must make sure that his sample is truly representative of the larger population.

Develop a questionnaire to test the political attitudes of your classmates as related to their families' income level. Be sure that the questions elicit the information you want.

Following the selection of his sample, the researcher proceeds to survey it. Surveying involves collecting data—members of the sample fill out questionnaires, personal interviews are conducted, data on specific questions are amassed, the attitudes of the members toward the subject matter are questioned, and, if the project demands it, the relationship among a number of variables is analyzed.

The sample survey is an accurate research design for some investigative questions, but not for others. It is comparatively easy to establish factual information with the sample survey technique. But in surveying attitudes and opinions, there is a greater margin for error. Consequently, the sample survey technique should be entrusted to a trained researcher who is aware of its shortcomings and pitfalls and who can try to compensate for them.

The Case Study

The *case study* research design is especially helpful when it is necessary to study a particular unit in depth, or several units for purposes of comparison. The unit may be a person, a family, a group of residents of an apartment complex or a neighborhood, employees of a particular plant, a clique, or a religious movement. The important thing is that in following the case study design, the researchers attempt to obtain a complete, detailed account of the behavior of the unit or event under consideration. Where the sample survey selects only a few characteristics for investigation—how middle-aged bankers feel about a woman having a career—the case study selects the total behavior of the unit for study.

Case studies are most valuable not because of their own accuracy, but because they often suggest hypotheses that can then be tested by other methods. A case study, particularly if it involves only one individual, cannot be used as a basis for generalizations. It is expensive and difficult to compute data from a large number of case studies, and they do not lend themselves to computation of a quantitative nature. But the researcher may see, in certain patterns of a subject's life, relationships that he then tests by another, perhaps more experimental, method. If the researcher's hypothesis is proven, the case study provides an excellent illustration of it.

Choose a partner from among your classmates and write case studies of each other, concentrating on political attitudes. Can you make generalizations about the whole class from such case studies? Why or why not?

Participant Observation

Somewhere between the case study technique and the sample survey technique we find a technique called *participant observation.* In this technique, the researcher tries to take part in the lives of the members of the group he is studying. He associates with members of the group as closely as possible, trying to gain their confidence, and attempting to share in their experiences and life-styles. A researcher who wants to study a labor union will join it, attend meetings, work in a shop, become active in union work, and perhaps become a union official or organizer. Some researchers in order to fit in better among those under scrutiny, do not reveal their identity. Rather they pretend to be one of the group. One example of such a study (although one test was not undertaken for the sake of sociological research) is that of a white novelist, John Griffin, who wrote *Black Like Me.* Griffin, disguised as a black with the aid of a skin-darkening drug, traveled around the South in the late fifties and was treated by the white Southerners as a black.[3] Many sociologists and anthropologists have used the participation technique to study ethnic and black street-corner culture.

The participant observation technique has its shortcomings. Much depends on the personality of the researcher, who has to develop trust in and friendship with the subjects. For another, there is the danger of the researcher becoming too involved with the subjects and thereby losing objectivity. The researcher might tend to overgeneralize, believing that what was found in the group studied is true of other such groups, when it may not be true. At the same time, the method of participant observation has given researchers many useful insights that can be tested and verified by more quantifiable techniques.

Do you think there might be any difficulties with accepting the observations of a participant such as Griffin in a group that he does not belong to? Would there be problems with the data collected by a member of the group itself?

[3]John H. Griffin, *Black Like Me* (Boston: Houghton Mifflin, 1961).

The Experiment

The experimental method is used in all sciences. In sociology, the experiment may take place either in a laboratory or in the field. In the laboratory experiment, people are recruited to serve as subjects (they can be volunteers or paid by the researcher). The researcher subjects them to a number of tests and records their responses. In an experiment on authority, social psychologist Stanley Milgram wanted to know if, and how many, subjects would press a button that they thought was inflicting pain (by electroshock) on other persons if told to do so by an authoritative figure—a scientist. The experiment showed that people obey the commands of authoritative persons even if they conflict with their moral convictions. Only a few people refused to push buttons in the name of science.[4] In the field experiment, the researcher goes out among the people, instead of the people being brought to him. In both the field and the laboratory, a variable is controlled, or held constant, and systematic observation or measurement of the result is made. In an experiment, a "control" group represents one variable and is compared to another chosen variable, or the "experimental" group.

If Milgram had been announced to the subjects of the study as a priest rather than as a scientist, do you think the results would have been different? As a policeman? As a convict?

Experimental and control groups are usually set up in either of two ways. In the *matched-pair* technique, for every person in the experimental group, another person is placed in the control group, as alike in every important variable as possible. In the *random-assignment* technique, persons are assigned to either the control of the experimental groups according to statistically random methods—every second, or third, or tenth person is assigned to the experimental group while the rest are assigned to the control group. This last method seems to be just as accurate and is much easier to set up than the matched-pair technique.

Experiments as a method of sociological research are also subject to shortcomings and pitfalls. Wide-ranging experiments in which thousands of people are involved are very expensive. The physical safety as well as the dignity of people as human beings must be safeguarded. Consequently, we cannot *force* people to act as subjects in an experiment, and the ethics of tricking them into acting as experimental subjects are questionable. Finally, when people are aware that they are the subjects of an experiment, their behavior tends to differ from their usual behavior. This tendency can ruin the experiment and make it invalid. Experiments on people are most reliable when the subjects are not aware of the true goals of the experiment but do know that some type of experiment is being conducted. Nevertheless, even harmless deception sometimes leads to intellectual dishonesty in interpreting results, and so the technique is not widely used by sociologists.

If you were told you were to participate in an experiment, and were then locked in a room, how would you behave? Would you behave differently if you were simply locked in a room? What are your assumptions in both cases?

None of the methods of sociology is 100 percent effective and errorproof. On the contrary, all methods have some shortcomings. The sample survey is perhaps the most popular with sociologists because it lends

[4] Stanley Milgram, *Obedience to Authority* (New York: Harper & Row, 1973).

itself to computer analysis and seems to be the most scientific. The case study, especially if used in a comparative framework, has also produced some milestone research, in spite of the danger of overgeneralization. Many sociologists use a combination of techniques, whichever seem to best fit the needs of their particular research designs. Some still use the historical, or impressionistic, study, which consists of describing and analyzing observations according to informal, but still coherent and purposeful guidelines.

Finally, the demographic method is also used by sociologists with good results. In this method, publicly available statistics are used for the compilation of data and comparisons. The classic study using this technique is Emile Durkheim's *Suicide,* in which Durkheim compared the suicide rates of several European countries and linked suicide with three

The Values of Detachment

Central to the debate over the goals of sociology is Alvin Gouldner, who, in his influential book *The Coming Crisis of Western Sociology,* argues that value neutrality is neither possible nor desirable. True objectivity is impossible, he believes, because people cannot leave themselves behind when, donning the costume of objective sociologists, they conduct research or concoct theories. People, sociologists included, are influenced by their pasts, their society, and their culture. Sociologists in addition are often influenced by their career ambitions within the university world and by their dependence on research funds from the world they vow to study objectively. Like everyone else, sociologists make assumptions about society and people, and these assumptions, whether conscious or not, shape the direction their ideas take. We cannot think about any aspect of social life without attaching some meaning to it, Gouldner asserts, and these meanings are inescapably laden with moral judgments and beliefs about their significance. Not only is every theory value-laden in its assumptions, but in its implications as well, tending to either justify or undermine the contemporary social structure.

The tasks of sociologists, Gouldner argues, are to become aware of their own assumptions and the political implications of their research. Most importantly, "sociologists must surrender the human but elitist assumption that *others* believe out of need whereas *they* believe because of the dictates of logic and reason."

Alvin W. Gouldner, *The Coming Crisis of Western Sociology* (New York: Avon Books, 1971), pp. 3–60, 481–512.

variables: religion, family, and political situation. He theorized that a lack of social integration resulted in the largest number of suicides.[5]

What are some of the major problems with trying to verify or replicate data concerning human beings? What kinds of qualifications must always be added to statements or theories about human behavior?

We must stress again that, in spite of the use of the scientific method, social scientists have more difficulty obtaining verifiable data than do physical scientists. Examining a piece of moon rock in the laboratory is very different from examining a human being as he relates to others. Not only does the human being not lend himself to many of the experiments that the inert moon rock does, but the human being also evokes a reaction from the researcher. The researcher can remain objective and perfectly impassive as he uncovers all the elements of the moon rock. But the researcher cannot help reacting positively or negatively to the human being he is analyzing. Thus, in sociology, there are no absolute conclusions and no absolutely objective interpretations.

[Summary]

Sociology is the scientific study of how humans interact in society—how they are all connected in a social web. It is a fairly new discipline, although its subject matter has for thousands of years occupied philosophers and thinkers. What is really new about the discipline is that it uses scientific methods to formulate generalizations and theories about human behavior in society. Previously, the social philosophers who were concerned with the same subject depended on their common sense and intuition, and on traditional and authoritative sources for the theories they set forth. Sociology, as one of the social sciences, is interested in studying man-made, rather than natural, phenomena.

While sociologists attempt to uncover the processes involved when humans interact with one another under specific circumstances, they are neither do-gooders, nor social workers, nor reformers, although some claim that they should be all these things. Neither are they totally dedicated to science, interested in statistics and numbers alone, and detached from human activity. Sociology is concerned with what is and not with what ought to be; it is a pure, rather than an applied, science; it is abstract, rather than concrete; it deals with generalities rather than with particulars; and it is a general and not a special social science. Sociologists approach their subject matter with a special perspective whose goal it is to "look behind" the common-sense and official explanations of why things are as they are. This perspective requires an attitude of skepticism and produces a multidimensional view of human relationships.

Added to this special perspective is the fact that sociologists, because they are thinking adults, necessarily bring preconceived ideas—a certain world view—to their study of society. Consequently, they approach society—about which they hope to formulate valid theories—within a

[5]Emile Durkheim, *Suicide* (Glencoe, Ill.: Free Press, 1951).

theoretical framework of their own. This framework, when presented in a systematic and clear fashion, is considered in terms of theoretical models. Most sociologists fall within three such theoretical models: (1) the evolutionary model, which maintains that society goes through a fixed and progressive number of stages; (2) the conflict model, which envisions society as the product of constant conflict and stress; and (3) the functional model, which views society as existing in a delicate balance between stability and change. The social scientific model underlies all others, stressing the importance of the scientific investigation of society as if society were no different than a natural or biological phenomenon.

Sociology uses the scientific method as a tool for its theory building. The scientific method implies that the researcher does his work with a set of attitudes that includes doubt, objectivity, and ethical neutrality. It also involves a specific technique, based on precise and systematic observation. This technique includes the selection and definition of problems and a plan for the collection of data; statement of hypothesis; collection of data; classification of data; analysis of data; generalization; verification; controlled conditions; and trained observers.

As applied to sociology, the scientific method consists of concepts, theories, and research. *Concepts* are abstract ways of classifying things that are similar. Sociological concepts are generalizations made about human interaction—for example, conflict, cooperation, group, class. Concepts are the technical vocabulary of sociologists and hence they have precise meanings that differ considerably from their everday meaning. Sets of concepts (and generalizations) arranged so as to explain and predict possible and probable relationships between and among phenomena are called *theories.* Theories explain current situations and try to predict future ones. Working with concepts as tools and using the scientific method in research, the sociologist arrives at a theory. A theory is never considered final, however, but is open to change and even to total rejection in the light of new evidence.

The third component of the scientific method is *research.* Research tests and bolsters theories, and the two complement one another: without the proper research, theories are merely speculations, and research without a theory behind it is meaningless. In sociology, research is conducted with the help of three fundamental techniques: the sample survey, the case study and participant observation, and the experiment. None of these techniques is completely foolproof and they all have shortcomings and pitfalls. Most sociologists use a combination of these techniques, or whichever technique lends itself best to their research project.

Sociology has no magic answers to the ills of humanity nor does it have formulas for bringing about utopia. All it can offer is a way to reach intellectual clarity, which is a first step in the understanding of our social reality. For this we need not wait for the sociologists themselves to become unanimous in the goals and methods of the discipline. Sociology shows us a way and we are all free to pursue it.

Terms to Remember

Sociology. The study of the human being as he relates with other human beings, or the study of humans in groups.

Intuition. A method of gaining knowledge through a sudden insight, the source of which cannot be explained.

Authority. A method of gaining knowledge through acceptance of statements by people who are experts.

Tradition. A method of gaining knowledge based on the belief that what has been considered right and true in the past should be considered so in the present.

Common sense. A method of gaining knowledge based on superficial observation, incomplete data, and the imperfect perception of the human senses.

Scientific spirit. A principle of the scientific method, requiring the scientist to approach everything with doubt and skepticism.

Objectivity. A principle of the scientific method, requiring the scientist to divest himself of personal attitudes, desires, beliefs, values, and tendencies when confronting data.

Ethical neutrality. A principle of the scientific method, requiring that the scientist not pass moral judgment on his findings.

Concept. A generalized idea about people, objects, or processes that are related to one another; abstractions; ways of classifying things that are similar.

Theory. A set of concepts arranged so as to explain and/or predict possible and probable relationships among phenomena.

Sample survey. A method of research consisting of an attempt to determine the occurrence of a given act or opinion within a given sample of people.

Case study. A method of research consisting of a detailed investigation of a single social unit.

Experiment. A method of research in which the researcher controls one variable and observes and records the results.

Research. A facet of sociological methodology that bolsters and complements theories. It uses three fundamental formats: the sample survey, the case study, and the experiment.

Evolutionary model. A theoretical model in sociology whose adherents maintain that society (as does the biological organism) progresses through a series of fixed stages of development. The *multilineal* evolutionists assert that not all societies go through the same stages.

Conflict model. A theoretical model in sociology whose adherents maintain that society is the product of conflicts and stresses in the relationships among individuals and groups.

Functional model. A theoretical model in sociology whose adherents maintain that society exists in a delicate balance between stability and change and that societal structures function to maintain stability.

Social scientific model. The basic theoretical model in sociology that states that the discipline must exclusively use the scientific method of investigation because the discipline is no different than the physical and biological sciences.

Variables. Factors whose relationship sociologists try to uncover; characteristics that differ (vary) in each individual case.

Suggestions for Further Reading

Aron, Raymond. *Main Currents in Sociological Thought.* Vols. 1 and 2. New York: Doubleday, 1970. The classical theories reinterpreted.

Bates, Alan P. *The Sociological Enterprise.* Boston: Houghton Mifflin, 1967. An analysis of sociology as both an academic and occupational field, and a discussion of the meaning and functions of sociology for society.

Berger, Peter. *Invitation to Sociology.* New York: Doubleday, 1967. A humanistic sociological perspective on the discipline and profession of sociology. Eminently readable and incisive.

Greer, Scott A. *The Logic of Social Inquiry.* Chicago: Aldine, 1969. The fundamental assumptions and methods of sociological research, as well as discussions of objectivity, the place of sociology in society, and the discipline as a symbol system.

Hammond, Philip E., ed. *Sociologists at Work: Essays on the Craft of Social Research.* New York: Basic Books, 1964. An aging, but readable and anecdotal account of how sociologists actually conducted their research products.

Labovitz, Stanford and Robert Hagedorn. *Introduction to Social Research.* New York: McGraw-Hill, 1971. Research methodology presented in a concise package.

Mills, C. Wright. *The Sociological Imagination.* New York: Oxford University Press, 1959. A classic by the well-known conflict theorist, who defines sociology from a new perspective.

Nisbet, Robert A. *The Sociological Tradition.* New York: Basic Books, 1967. The historical development of the concepts of community, authority, status, the sacred, and alienation and the classical social theorists who dealt with them.

Wallace, Walter L., ed. *Sociological Theory: An Introduction.* Chicago: Aldine, 1969. A collection of readings analyzing various conceptual models of sociology, in particular the structural-functionalist model as compared to the conflict model.

Groups: from two to millions

Make a list of all the groups that you are now or have ever been a member of, formal or informal, large or small.

Although we Americans often pride ourselves on our individuality, evidence that we are really group animals is all around us. Most people are members of a family, whether of their own making or one they were born or adopted into. Students may belong to one or more student groups: a social club; a political group; the student government; and so on. Instructors may belong to the American Association of University Professors or to the American Federation of Teachers; or to one or more professional associations and so on.

In the news media we hear ourselves being referred to in terms of aggregates and groups, as consumers, the public, the young, the old, the middle-aged, the affluent, the poor. The newspaper reports that the farmers are complaining about the high cost of feed, and the automobile workers are demanding another raise. The local public school teachers are threatening to strike. In the United Nations, hearings are being held about yet another nation that has lashed out against its neighbor.

Organizations and associations of every hue—families, communities, and nations—are referred to far more often in everyday life than are the individuals who make up these groups. Very few of us live in isolation of our own free will. Once in a while, of course, we do hear about people who have lost their sense of community or their membership in a group. These people may be old, living out the rest of their days in sterile convalescent homes where their physical needs may be taken care of, but where they seldom feel as if they belonged. Or they may be old people who live alone in their own homes, perhaps because there is no one left of their kinship group to care about them. Or they may be prison inmates kept in solitary confinement.

Such prisoners may become so distraught that they either take their life or renounce it by going mad. Or we may hear about children who for one reason or another are reared in isolation, growing into beings who only physically resemble humans; in all other ways they are simply live organisms who become human only when they are exposed to other humans.

[A Life Lived in Groups]

All these examples of the importance of groups tell us about ourselves and the human species, and suggest the extent to which we need one another. In no part of the world do people live absolutely alone by choice. Isolation is universally considered an extreme punishment, and it can be a brutalizing experience. The child sent to his room, the prisoner condemned to a special cell where he remains totally alone, the deportee or exile, are all examples of individuals expelled from a group as a form of punishment. When people do seek isolation voluntarily, they are usually pursuing some ideological principle or symboli-

Would you like to have less or more interaction with other human beings? How do you react to being alone for long periods of time?

Keeping Your Distance

> *Sociologists have always had a vested interest in pointing to the ways in which the individual is formed by groups, identifies with groups, and wilts away unless he obtains emotional support from groups. But when we closely observe what goes on in a social role, a spate of social interaction, a social establishment—or in any other unit of social organization—embracement of the unit is not all that we see. We always find the individual employing methods to keep some distance, some elbow room, between himself and that with which others assume he should be identified.*

This is the conclusion sociologist Erving Goffman reached after noting the diverse ways inmates in a mental hospital attempted to escape the stigma of their institutionally defined roles and the persons who, in the hospital's eyes, they were supposed to be. These are arrangements of self-defense, Goffman said; although they perhaps find more fertile grounds for development in "total institutions"—places like prisons or mental hospitals where inmates are cut off from the larger society and subjected to a set of imposed rules—they are evident in all types of social organization. We need groups to attain a sense of ourselves as persons, he suggested, yet we resist total submersion in groups in order to gain a sense of self-identity.

Erving Goffman, *Asylums: Essays on the Social Situation of Mental Patients and Other Inmates* (Garden City: Doubleday & Company, Anchor Books, 1961), p. 319.

cally rejecting society. But isolation has never been considered a natural way of life.

Yet it is doubtful whether many of us realize the extraordinarily pervasive nature of group life. The individual human being is created by a group, and he remains under the influence of innumerable

Isolation from society is one of our most extreme punishments.

groups from the time he is born until he dies. From the moment of conception, the biological being about to become an individual is hardly ever alone. In the womb, he forms a strong, physical bond with the mother; his life depends on her body. Even after he is born, his survival depends on a group, usually his immediate family.

The child's development as a human being, as well as his survival, depends on continued interaction with other people. A constant relationship with those around him teaches him the foremost characteristic of humanness: language. Soon after, again from interaction with others, the child develops a concept of self. All other social characteristics, from the most elementary group habits of our society to the most complex attitudes, are learned through observation of, and association with, others. As a young child, the individual belongs to a peer group of playmates. Later, he forms friendship groups at school and then at work. Finally, he may be a member of a family group of his own creation, and his children, if he has any, repeat the cycle of maturation and socialization through interaction in groups.

Throughout his life, the individual belongs to temporary and permanent groups, organized for specific or general goals. What kind of person he becomes depends greatly on the groups to which he belongs and on the quality of relationships these groups provide. The individual is an individual only in contrast to groups that have formed his individuality. There is no such thing as a total individual, as no one lives totally alone all of his or her life.

[The Nature of Groups]

The sociological definition of the word *group* is different from the common definition of "a number of people congregated at the same time, in the same place." In the context of sociology, fifteen students cramming for an exam in a student lounge are not necessarily a group. Twenty commuters on the morning train into town are not necessarily a group. Nor are eight salesmen eating lunch at the counter of Moe's Delicatessen. If we know nothing else about these people except that they are in the same place at the same time, we call them *aggregates,* not groups.

There are many individuals, across the nation and across the world, who share the same specific characteristics. There are, for example, millions of people who were born on the Fourth of July of a particular year, who have flaming red hair, who are lefthanded, or who part their hair in the middle. We cannot say that these people make up a group, either. Instead, we say that they form a *category.*

Are the relationships in your class of the type that would characterize you as an aggregate? Are there any groups in formation or already formed in the class?

Suppose, however, that three of the fifteen students cramming in the student lounge have been studying there since the beginning of the school year. What's more, they have an English class together, and they eat lunch at the same time. Because they are human and, there-

Social Action: The Operational Approach

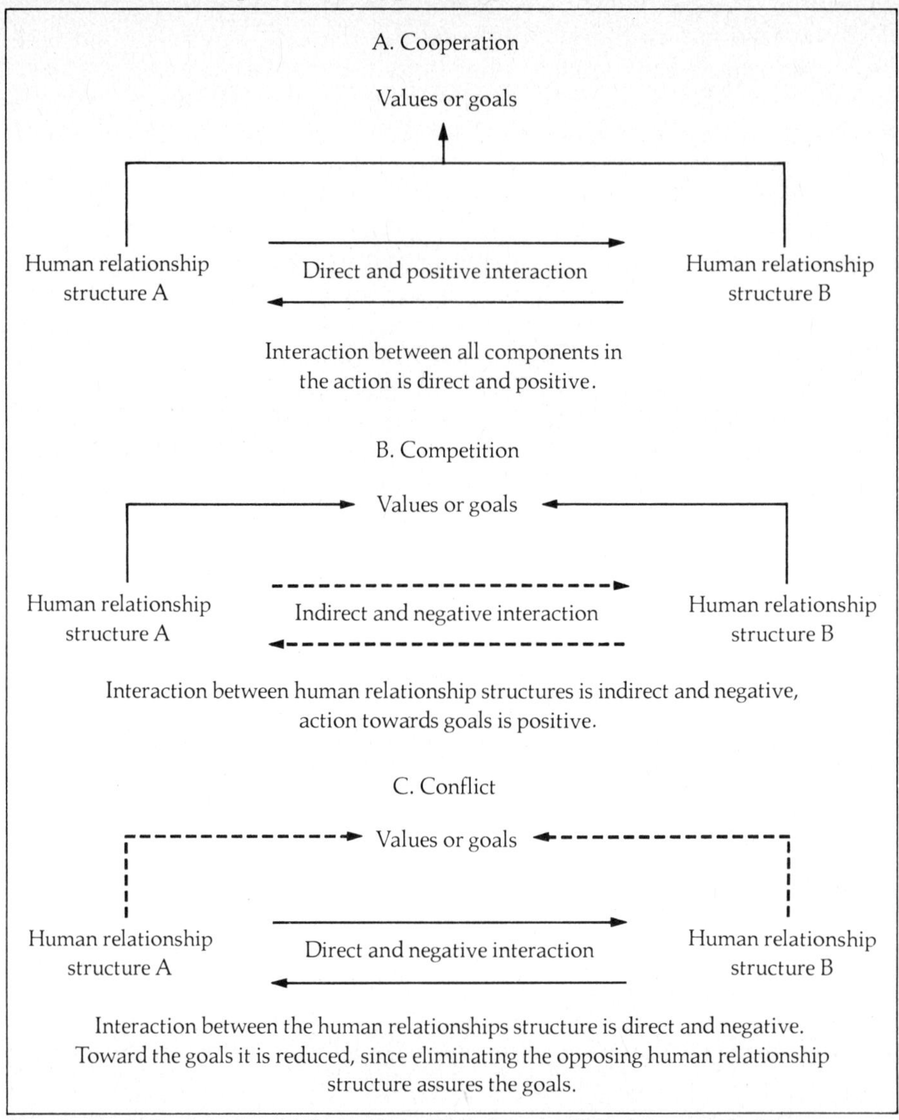

From *Society Its Organization and Operation*, by W. Anderson and F. Parker, © 1964 by Litton Educational Publishing, Inc. Reprinted by permission of Van Nostrand Reinhold Company.

fore, social beings, at first the students only exchange greetings. Later they sit together in English class and in the cafeteria, talking about the difficulty of the courses, the excitement of life, and the beauty of the local scenery. Out of an aggregate of fifteen, then, three have formed a group. By the same token, suppose that all the redheads who were born on the Fourth of July in 1945 organized a club. The members of the club corresponded regularly and met periodically for the purpose of setting up a scholarship fund for redheads born on the Fourth of

July of subsequent years. The redheads, then, would have ceased to be a category and would have become a social group.

The Sociological Definition of a Group

In sociological terms, a number of people is not a group, regardless of its size, goals, or origin, unless it meets the following conditions:

1. There is physical and, more important, symbolic interaction among the members. (*Symbolic interaction* is communication through speech, gestures, writing or even music. In this kind of communication, members are aware of one another; mutual awareness causes them to respond, or behave, in particular ways and, thus, to influence one another.)
2. Each member recognizes that he is part of the group. Conversely, the group also recognizes him as a member.
3. Members are aware of the roles, duties, and obligations, as well as the privileges, resulting from group membership.

In short, physical interaction alone is not sufficient to generate a group; when you bump into several people in a crowded elevator, you are still only part of an aggregate. For sociologists, symbolic interaction is the vital prerequisite for determining whether a collection of people is a group.

Symbolic interaction need not involve face-to-face communication. If relatives and friends who live at opposite points of the earth are still able to affect one another through correspondence, they remain a group. Moreover, members of a group need not be personal friends. As long as there is some kind of communication among people that results in mutual adjustment of behavior, the people make up a group. In this sense, citizens of a nation, who are united by common political processes and who share a number of similar loyalties, a common history, and the sense of a common future, are considered a group.

Classifications of Groups

There are an extraordinarily large number of groups and great diversity among them. Groups vary in size from two members to several hundred million, as the chapter title suggests (from a pair of individuals to a whole society). The number of groups in every society is countless; it surpasses the number of individuals, because each individual belongs to more than one group. Small wonder, then, that researchers find classification of groups to be problematic. A researcher must decide whether to categorize groups according to size, interests, duration, type of organization, quality of interaction, and so on, in an infinite variety of ways. None of these classifications is right or wrong; classification depends on the purpose in examining the group.

Primary and secondary groups and relationships. Sociologists invariably classify groups into primary and secondary groups. The term *primary group* was coined by Charles Horton Cooley (1864–1929), a pioneer American sociologist. Cooley designated primary groups as groups in which members engage in intimate interaction and cooperation, the influence of which is basic to the development of an individual's personality.

Later sociologists decided that additional characteristics distinguished primary from other groups. Among these characteristics are relatively small group size, physical nearness of members, intense interaction among members, group stability, and relatively long duration of group existence. In addition, interaction in primary groups occurs informally and spontaneously, as individuals begin to know and deal with one another on an individual, personal, and total basis. The family provides the foremost example of a primary group. However, a clique of friends, a circle of playmates or fellow students, and even one's neighborhood or community may also be considered primary groups.

If we imagine a long, straight, horizontal line called an *ideal continuum,* and if we place primary groups on one end of this continuum, the other end will be occupied by *secondary groups.*[1] Secondary groups tend to be large and to exist for a short period of time. Interaction among members is formal, utilitarian, specialized, and temporary. In a secondary group, the members are not interested primarily in one another as persons but are interested in one another in terms of the roles and functions they perform in society. If you have to ask yourself "What's in it for me?" you are probably involved in a secondary relationship.

Take the list you developed of groups you have been or are a member of, and divide the groups into primary and secondary groups. How did you decide which groups were primary?

To illustrate the difference between primary and secondary groups, let's assume that you and Mary, the owner of a pizza parlor, have known each other since kindergarten. Suppose that you and she have some of the same friends, bowl on the same team, confide in each other, and frequently visit each other's homes. You and Mary, then, form a primary group, and the two of you interact in a primary relationship. On the other hand, suppose that you remember Mary only when the craving for pizza overtakes you, and the only dealings you have with her are to order and pick up pizzas. Regardless of how friendly you are during the transaction, you and she form a secondary group and interrelate in a secondary relationship.

Although some relationships may be recognized as purely primary

---

[1]The ideal continuum is part of the concept of ideal type, a form of sociological methodology developed by Max Weber as an aid to the analysis of social phenomena. The ideal type is an abstraction, a conceptual model or construct, a hypothetical idea in which the object is to exaggerate a phenomenon's most characteristic features so that a standard may be established against which to measure reality. The ideal type, then, is constructed from the combined observed features of a specific phenomenon, but it never corresponds exactly to the phenomenon as it appears in real life. In this case, for instance, no primary group that exists in reality has exactly all of the characteristics we have just attributed to it, but most primary groups have most of these characteristics. The same is true for the secondary groups.

This group of Bolivian schoolchildren probably began as an aggregate; both secondary and primary relationships may be formed from prolonged interaction among the children and their teacher.

and others as purely secondary, most relationships fall somewhere between the two extremes. Moreover, some primary relationships may in the course of time slide into secondary relationships, and very often secondary relationships become primary ones.

Another way of looking at primary and secondary groups is in terms of what they *do* for us. The secondary group satisfies a particular goal, whether it is the taste for pizza or the need to make a living. But we judge the primary group by the emotional satisfaction it affords us and not by useful functions that it performs for us.

Primary groups are universal and have probably existed since the beginning of mankind. When an individual is totally removed from primary relationships, the spirit is soon broken, and mental health may be severely affected. Even so, not all primary relationships are of a harmonious nature, nor are they always satisfying to the individual. Primary relationships may involve a large amount of conflict or the enforcement of conformity, which stifles individuality.

Why, do you suppose, would a person's mental health break down if removed from all his or her primary groups?

Primary groups are of tremendous importance to individuals. We may even say that primary relationships are necessary to the well-being of most people. Where primary relationships are lacking in what we would generally consider a "natural" primary group—the family, say—people go out of their way to create such relationships in other groups.

As we will see in a later chapter on personality development, the emotional rewards that a satisfactory primary relationship offers are indispensable if the human infant is to grow into a self-confident, loving, and fulfilled adult. The fact that there are so many people who are unhappy and frustrated, who hate themselves and others—and who often take out their feelings by antisocial and even criminal actions—suggests that the primary relationship is increasingly absent or unsatisfactory in our society.

Do you feel that the quality of your group contacts is satisfactory? How would you improve them, if you could?

Later in the chapter we will discuss the fact that urban, industrial societies are characterized by secondary relationships. Therefore, many of the functions that at one time were performed by primary groups, are now carried out by secondary groups. When we were a predominantly agricultural society, the sick were cared for by the family, not by paid nurses and doctors in an expensive hospital. Parents and grandparents lived with their sons and daughters until they died, and did not spend lonely days and nights in commercial convalescent homes. If someone needed a loan, they appealed to a rich uncle rather than to a bank. Hospitals, convalescent homes, and banks are very efficient. But you can hardly have the same feelings toward a hospital or bank—or the strangers that run these institutions—as you do toward your parents and relatives. The hospital and bank are *impersonal;* they treat *you* the same way they treat every other patient or customer. To your parents and relatives, you are special and unique. They care about what happens to you, and their caring makes you feel worthwhile.

In our society, people move among only a few primary groups. Even the family has shrunk to only a nucleus, and often grandparents, aunts and uncles are only seen at Christmas or Thanksgiving, if at all. And so people hold the few primary relationships they do have very dear. All their love is concentrated on their mates and children. But when people invest all their love in so few people, they may expect too much. They may expect their loved ones to fulfill all their emotional needs. When these people fall short of expectations, or when they die, the experience is traumatic and some people never adjust. Any bereaved or elderly person who lives alone, and most of those recently divorced, will tell you that their most frequent companion is loneliness.

Other classifications of groups. In examining groups, we find the concepts of in-group and out-group useful. These concepts describe the "we-as-opposed-to-they" feelings of which every group member is at least somewhat conscious. Such feelings are a universal feature of group formation. Their advantage is that they produce a feeling of unity within in-groups. But such feelings can disrupt a society, especially when out-groups are perceived as enemies by in-groups. Racial conflicts, for example, may arise from such feelings. Each side perceives itself as the good guys, and the out-group as the bad guys.

Groups can also be classified into reference groups and membership groups. *Membership groups* are the formal or informal organizations to which an individual belongs. For example, the YWCA is a formal membership group, while a clique of friends is informal. *Reference groups* are groups to which an individual aspires to belong and on which he patterns his present behavior. A reference group may be a political, economic, religious, ethnic, kinship, or social organization. The individual may already be a member of it, and participate in its activities, or he may not. As sociologist Robert Nisbet says, the important point is that the individual refers to and accepts its values so thoroughly that its influence on him is more *apparent* than the influence of any other group.[2]

What are the most influential reference groups in your life? Why might the family be more important, in the long run, than any single reference group?

Table 2-1 Primary and Secondary Relationships

	Primary	*Secondary*
Typically found in Such groups as:	family playmates clique village	nation religious denomination trade union professional association
Such dyadic relationships as:	husband-wife parent-child teacher-pupil friend-friend	officer-subordinate clerk-customer performer-spectator congressman-constituent
Social characteristics	informal feelings of freedom and spontaneity inclusive knowledge of other person identity of ends other-oriented personal	formal feeling of external constraint specialized and limited knowledge of other person disparity of ends self-oriented impersonal
Physical conditions	small number long duration physical proximity	large number short duration physical distance

Source: Adapted from Kingsley Davis, *Human Society,* 1949, p. 306. Reprinted by permission of the Macmillan Company, New York.

[2]Robert A. Nisbet, *The Social Bond* (New York: Afred A. Knopf, 1970), pp. 107–108.

(However, the family group has more *actual* influence in the long run.) The reference group provides a model for the individual, on which he patterns his opinions, convictions, and actions, and to which he continually compares himself. We tend to see "the way things are" according to how our reference group sees them. However, our reference group need not remain the same forever. The young boy whose reference group was conservative Republicanism because his father was a conservative Republican may switch to a liberal or even leftist reference group once he is in college and trying to loosen family ties.

Do you think of yourself as a "joiner"? What, in your opinion, would make a person a "joiner"?

Some groups are of a voluntary and others of an involuntary nature. We cannot choose the kind of family into which we are born. This primary group, then, is an *involuntary group.* Secondary groups may also be involuntary. Young men who are drafted into the armed forces are usually not able to select their favorite branch of service or the location of their tour of duty. Conversely, there are hundreds of thousands of organizations, ranging from fraternities to political parties and from fan clubs to bridge clubs, that an individual may join entirely of his free will—or sometimes for reasons of social and economic expediency. Such groups are called *voluntary groups.*

The Size of Groups

Sociologists also consider groups from the standpoint of their size. Small groups such as the family, a circle of close friends, a clique within a large organization, and a committee formed for specific problem solving share several common characteristics:

1. Relations among members are usually on a face-to-face basis.
2. In general, members share common values.
3. The group is usually durable.
4. Members exhibit feelings of identification with the group and group loyalty.
5. In general, members accept one another.
6. Members perceive the group as a separate entity.
7. Members perceive the group as striving to fulfill definite goals.

In addition, small groups usually value stable membership; the difficulty of joining them enhances membership; they greatly influence the behavior of their members; and within them, democratic leadership is more effective than it is within large groups.

Large groups, of necessity, have characteristics that differ from those of small groups. Above all, they tend to be much more highly organized, often assuming the proportions of formal organizations and bureaucracies. These large groups will be discussed in more detail later in this book. Right now, however, we will give a brief description of how formal organizations and bureaucracies work.

Formal organizations usually possess some kind of definite structure because their goals, programs, and the roles of their personnel are fairly specific. When formal organizations reach large-scale dimensions—as in the case of complex corporations, state and federal governments, and multicampus university complexes—their form of organization is called *bureaucratic.* A *bureaucracy* is a formal organization characterized by:

The word *bureaucracy* is derived from the French word *bureau,* meaning 'desk'. What relationship might there be between a desk and the formal type of organization we call *bureaucracy?*

1. Job specialization or division of labor.
2. A set of rigid rules and standards designed to promote uniformity.
3. An attitude of impersonal impartiality.
4. A hierarchical arrangement of officials.
5. The use of rationality in reaching organizational objectives.

We are all familiar with some facets of bureaucracy because in large, complex societies bureaucracy becomes, to a great extent, a way of life. Our bureaucratic way of life has been undergoing criticism for quite some time. Many critics maintain that overorganization stifles creativity, and is generally dehumanizing. Yet bureaucratic organization is also largely responsible for our high standard of living, including high productivity, rapid transportation, and the advances in medical science. By organizing our lives so efficiently, bureaucracy can give us more time to pursue our creative impulses. In the end, it may actually enhance our personal freedom.

It is important to remember, too, that primary groups continue to be formed within the confines of secondary groups. Successful primary interaction in large formal organizations and in bureaucracies is vital to the organizations' success. If the interests of a large organization are perceived as running counter to those of the primary groups in it, the large organization may fail. This is so because an organization's success is measured by its productivity. Productivity, in turn, depends, to a large degree, on the attitude of employees. Successful primary group interaction in a large organization may lead to satisfied employees, who produce well. If, however, employees are dissatisfied with the goals of an organization, this same successful primary group interaction will strengthen them and encourage them to sabotage the organization.

A school organization is usually bureaucratic. In what ways does the functioning of this bureaucracy depend on successful primary relationships within it?

Finally, the largest group to which people belong is one with which we all are familiar—society. This group is discussed in detail in the following chapter. For now, it is enough to know that, in general, societies are examined from the standpoint of their attributes—whether they are urban or rural, traditional or modern, Gemeinschaft or Gesellschaft.

Gemeinschaft and Gesellschaft Societies

Have you ever had contact with a Gemeinschaft society? How did it compare to our own?

German sociologist Tönnies, in examining different kinds of societies, arrived at concepts similar to those of primary and secondary groups. He noted that in small, homogeneous (made up of people with similar life-styles) societies members interacted with one another on an informal, personal, face-to-face basis, and that tradition dictated behavior. Tönnies called this kind of society a *Gemeinschaft,* which is roughly translated from German as "a communal, or traditional, society." Certain isolated Eskimo communities are Gemeinschaft societies.

Relationships are very different in societies that are large and heterogeneous (made up of people with diverse life-styles) such as modern industrial societies. In these societies, relationships among members are impersonal, formal, functional, and specialized. Furthermore, they are often contractual—dealings are spelled out in legal contracts rather than being governed by tradition. Tönnies called these societies *Gesellschaft,* or "associational societies." The United States is an example of a Gesellschaft society.

In the modern world, there has been an easily observable shift from Gemeinschaft to Gesellschaft societies. The large size of the societal group and the complexities of a technological economy require secondary groups, which are dedicated to efficiency rather than sentiment. Therefore, in Gesellschaft societies, many of the tasks of pri-

This rural village shelters a typical traditional or Gemeinschaft community in Kenya.

mary groups, such as education and economic transactions, have passed to secondary groups.

The great reliance in Gesellschaft societies on secondary groups has both disadvantages and advantages. Many behavioral problems—even the high incidence of suicide—have been blamed on the breaking of primary group ties. On the other hand, the large-scale impersonal organizations we call *corporations* have greatly improved our physical standard of living because they handle economic matters efficiently. Furthermore, secondary groups, by taking into account a wide range of interests, counteract some of the narrow interests and viewpoints often found in small, tightly knit groups.

In the second part of this book, when institutions are discussed, we will be examining some of the problems created by the change from Gemeinschaft to Gesellschaft societies. What kinds of problems would you anticipate being caused by this change?

[Social Interaction and Social Processes]

The various kinds of groups that exist in societies—as well as societies themselves—are not static. They change and are constantly modified. Interaction among members of a group and among groups is continually taking place. In a sociological sense, *interaction* refers to behavior, or action, that is *symbolic*—verbal or gestural. The behavior is directed toward others, and the individual is aware of how others will probably respond. Interaction is reciprocal; each person is aware of and responsive to the actions and reactions of others. If you say "Hello" to an acquaintance, you expect a "Hello" in return. If you open the door for a person carrying packages, you expect that person to say "Thank you."

Although interaction is not governed by rigid rules, it is not completely haphazard, either. There are enough patterns and repetitions for us to study and predict human behavior in given situations. Many of these patterns were established long ago. We, and others in our society, follow these patterns to simplify our lives. It would be ridiculous for us to have to decide every moment of the day how to behave in a given situation. In small, nontechnological, homogeneous societies, most interaction is structured in this way. In complex societies, however, we also face situations for which we do not have established patterns of behavior.

What kinds of experiences did you have in the process of learning our patterns of dating and mating behavior? Was it easy to find out what was expected of you?

Whether established long ago or fairly recently, a number of key patterns of interaction are present in all societies. These key patterns constitute, in the words of Robert Nisbet, "the microelements of the social bond, or the molecular cement of society."[3] One or more of these patterns, also called *social processes,* are at work any time interaction takes place.

Cooperation, Competition, and Conflict

A great many social processes may be discerned when we observe so-

[3]Nisbet, p. 50.

cial interaction, whether it occurs on a primary or secondary group level. Sociologists, however, focus on three primary social processes—cooperation, competition, and conflict—and two secondary social processes—accommodation and assimilation. All the other processes are really combinations of, or derivations from, the primary processes.

What other organisms beside the human species may be successful because of their ability to cooperate? What goals influence your decisions to cooperate or not in a given situation?

Cooperation. Cooperation is a primary social process involving two or more persons or groups working jointly in a common enterprise for a shared goal. Cooperation is often considered the most basic of the social processes because without it life would be difficult, if not impossible. Some social thinkers maintain that the human species, as well as other organisms, has been able to survive only because individuals were able to cooperate, integrating their activities in such a way as to benefit the group. According to this view, evolution, or survival of the fittest, is actually survival of the most cooperative.

We need not look far for evidence of cooperation. On the primary level, a family does not for long remain a pleasant, functional group unless members cooperate. When father is willing to start dinner if he is the first to come home; and mother is willing to stop at the store for soft drinks; and the teen-age daughter is willing to put a load of laundry in the washing machine—then we can be reasonably sure that the household will run at least with a certain degree of harmony. If members do not cooperate, the household may be chaotic, with no one eating regular meals or wearing clean underwear.

On a secondary group level, an obvious example of cooperation is represented by a loaf of bread bought at the supermarket. The cooperative effort of many people has gone into that loaf: farmers and farm workers, bakery workers, truck drivers, wholesalers and retailers—all cooperate, using techniques of merchandising, advertising, mathematics, business, and so on. And the web of cooperation around a loaf of bread is extended a million or more times for each product or service you use.

The traditional children's story of *The Little Red Hen* is one way that children in our society are socialized to cooperate. How does the story accomplish this goal?

However, even though we, as a group, benefit from this social process, each group member does not benefit to the same degree. Corporation managers and workers cooperate in producing a number of objects, but their rewards are unequal. Even among the workers on an assembly line who cooperate to put together a finished product, some will earn more than others either because of the nature of their jobs, or because of seniority.

Competition. Competition is a form of interaction that occurs when two or more individuals try to take possession of the same scarce object, such as gold, or intangible value, such as love. Competition is a basic process because most living organisms must compete for limited resources necessary to their survival. Plants, for instance, compete for sunlight, water, and food. Animals, including humans, compete for food, shelter, and sex gratification. But whereas plants and animals limit their competitiveness to things needed for survival, people also compete for things that are not needed for sheer survival, but that they have been *taught* to need by their culture. Although the high school coach may try to convince the basketball team that they *must* win the game against a rival school, no one on the team will die if they lose. You will not stop living if the man you desperately want to go out with decides to date your friend instead. Winning athletic contests or mates of our choice are not indispensable needs, but we perceive them as such because we have internalized them so well from our culture.

Our society and the culture it has created determines which things are desirable and worthy to compete for, and which are undesirable and need not be competed for. For instance, we usually consider it appropriate to compete for profits from a business enterprise, but we do not usually consider it appropriate for one man to compete for another man's wife. Society and culture determine also who can and who cannot compete for specific items. Only a licensed dentist can compete for patients. Finally, society and culture have worked out certain rules to prevent competition from becoming outright conflict. Competition is regulated in marketing, for example, so that the conflict is contained and does not break out into violence.

Of course, competition is very much a part of our society. Competition is essential to the operation of our economic system, and plays an important part in many other facets of our lives. But competition would have long ago hurled us into ruthless conflict if it had not been always tempered with cooperation. Which social process is preferable as a mode of interaction? Can we be sure that cooperation is always the process that works best for the group?

Do you feel this society is overly competitive? What types of competition should be encouraged, and what types discouraged?

On the one hand, it seems obvious that competition creates a certain hostility, whereas cooperation encourages friendliness. But on the other hand, competition does seem to stimulate great achievements. There have been experiments made that indicate that when employees are asked to compete for higher income and promotions, their overall productivity does increase. That is not the whole story, either, because in some instances cooperation is more important in increasing individual productivity (one employee working faster than others on an assembly line slows productivity rather than increasing it because his finished work piles up too fast and disrupts the tempo). Sociologists and other social researchers have not been able to come to hard-and-fast conclusions regarding which basic social process is most beneficial to the group. In some cases, competition works more to the ultimate advantage of the group than cooperation. Still, in competition one individual is always a loser. Losing is unpleasant and creates anxiety and feelings of insecurity. Consequently, many people prefer to withdraw from competition altogether in order to avoid frustration and disappointment. When they withdraw, they also give up on an opportunity

How does competition affect our educational institution? Do you feel that competition among students is beneficial or harmful? In what ways?

Contrasting Styles of Competition

What is competition like in a cooperative context? An Odawa Indian, in describing how the cooperative traditions of his community were disrupted when the Canadian Department of Indian Affairs attempted to restructure his society, gave this example:

> *None of the kind of play we had was really structured and organized. That came after the recreation directors from the outside world came in and told us that we had a problem in the community, that we were not organized, and they were going to introduce some.*
>
> *They introduced them all right, and the tremendous competitiveness that went with them. It's not as bad on Manitoulin Island, where I'm from, as it is a lot of other places where competitiveness is rolling in. I'm glad I can remember that as a kid I was able to become involved with a community with others and nobody was competing. Even if we did formally compete in the games we did, no one was a winner though someone may have won. It was only the moment. If you beat someone by pulling a bow and arrow and shooting the arrow further, it only meant that you shot the arrow further at that moment. That's all it lasted. It didn't mean you were better in any way whatsoever.*

Wilfred Pelletier, "Childhood in an Indian Village," *This Magazine Is About Schools* (Spring 1969).

to obtain the rewards of competition. These considerations suggest we need to include both competition and cooperation in our society.

Conflict. Conflict is diametrically opposed to cooperation. That is, conflict is a hostile struggle between two or more persons or groups for an object or value that each prizes.[4] Conflict is also the process in which opposing parties attempt to injure, harm, or destroy one another in order to achieve a certain goal.

The society of the Senoi of Malaysia is based on the daily discussion of dreams, their meaning, and how to deal with dream monsters and friends. How might this orientation dramatically reduce conflict in everyday life?

Like cooperation and competition, conflict is also present in most facets of life. Some social thinkers of the past believed that conflict was a universal characteristic of humans, but this belief has been largely disproved by the discovery of societies where conflict is kept at an absolute minimum, such as the Senoi of Malaysia. Although conflict is a very prevalent social process, it is intermittent. That is, sooner or later one of the opposing parties emerges victorious, and

[4]Nisbet, p. 75.

Conflict is a form of human interaction that appears in all aspects of our lives.

conflict ceases, at least temporarily.

Conflict does not necessarily involve violence, although very often it does. People can engage in conflict through words that can ruin reputations or careers, or destroy sensitive personalities.

Conflict may be observed in every group, from the most intimate to the most impersonal. It may revolve around societal rewards that are in short supply—physical things such as food, or intangibles such as respect—or around ideological disagreements.

The effects of conflict are not always disruptive and negative. Although conflict and competition both tend to divide people and groups, in the face of a common antagonist, group unity is greatly enhanced. During World War II, for instance, Americans felt very friendly toward the Soviet Union because that nation was our ally against a common enemy. In addition, conflict often leads to social change, and some social changes are ultimately beneficial to society. A certain amount of conflict, then, is actually a creative and dynamic force in society. But conflict can be very damaging to a society if it results in violence and psychological harm.

Can you cite some events characterized by conflict that have had a creative and dynamic effect on our society? Would cooperation have had a similar effect under the circumstances?

Although we have discussed the three basic social processes separately, it should be clear that the processes are in reality not so distinct, and that they often occur in the same interactive situations. For example, when two gas stations on opposite sides of the street agree to charge the same price, they are cooperating and competing at the same time. Two opposing teams compete for victory, but the members of each team cooperate among one another. And cooperation can also easily change into conflict, although the reverse may be somewhat more difficult.

Accommodation and Assimilation

Two social processes that are by-products of conflict and cooperation are accommodation and assimilation. We have already called attention to the temporary, or intermittent, nature of conflict. After one or the other of the antagonists in conflict emerges as victor, there is a peacemaking, conflict-settling period called *accommodation.*

Accommodation does not permanently settle issues. It simply keeps things cool, in a state of temporary, peaceful coexistence. Conflict remains present under the surface and may eventually erupt again. But the stage is also set for cooperation and the ultimate solution of conflicts.

To what extent have accommodation and assimilation characterized relations between blacks and whites in America? Between men and women?

If two groups formerly in conflict cooperate and arrive at an ultimate solution of the conflict, the process is called *assimilation.* Assimilation is essentially a process of fusion, in which one individual or group becomes completely accepted as part of another group. This fusion is usually a slow process, whereby the group that is being assimilated adopts the culture of the other group, becomes a part of all social systems within the society, and attains equal opportunity and life chances. Chapter 6 illustrates how these two social processes function in the context of our multigroup society.

[Social Organization]

Interaction in terms of the social processes we have described is thought to occur within the framework of a social system. A *social system* is an imaginary model, or the sociologist's conceptualization, of how social relationships work. Every social group is considered a social system, within which each part is interdependent and interconnected to the other parts and to the whole. The elements of this system are individual group members relating to one another to attain a specific goal. (For analytical purposes, and not because it is so in reality, the social system is viewed as a unit that is distinct from the individuals who make it up.) In their effort to reach their goal, the members of the social system are guided both by actual behavior and by shared, patterned, and recurrent expectations of behavior. These guides—in the form of patterns resulting from constant repetition of the social processes we have just examined—form the *social structure.*

The network of patterned behavior that both guides and is the product of interaction is called *social organization.* Some sociologists do not distinguish between social organization and social structure. Others interpret structure as the ideal pattern of behavior and organization as the way people actually behave.[5] Still others view structure as one dimension of organization, which also includes function (division of labor) and process (adaptation to change).

For our purposes, such distinctions are unnecessary. We may redefine social organization as the patterned and recurring manner in which individuals and groups interact. This does not mean that social organization is necessarily a fixed set of rules. It is instead a dynamic process in which stable and predictable patterns are continually redefined and changed to fit the changing conditions of the social and physical environment.

Levels of Social Organization

What is the basic difference between the interpersonal and the intergroup level of social organization? Why might psychologists be more interested in the former, and sociologists in the latter type of organization?

Social interaction occurs on three levels of social organization. The first is the *interpersonal,* or *social relationship,* level. Relationships at this level occur when two persons occupy definite positions in relation to each other: husband to wife, father to son, teacher to student, girlfriend to boyfriend, and so on. These relationships constitute the basic elements of social structure and underlie all other social relationships.

The second level is the *group, intergroup,* or *organizational,* level. Relationships at this level occur within and between organized groups. Sociologists are particularly concerned with the process and structure of intergroup relationships.

Some sociologists include an additional level, an abstract *social reality* level that emerges as a result of the features that groups develop as they become organized. This social reality is external to the individual and is not merely a total of interpersonal relationships. In other words, even though the relationship at the interpersonal level is the basic unit of social structure, additional group laws, actions, and patterns of organization develop in relationships at the group and society levels. These laws, actions, and patterns are independent of those emerging at the interpersonal level. Groups, in short, are not simply individuals multiplied by numbers: they become something more than the sum of their parts.

Role and Status

Status is relative, and depends on the milieu in which the person or the observer operates. In what kind of milieu would the status of banker be high? Low? In society as a whole, would the banker's status be high or low?

The fundamental elements of social organization are norms, roles, and statuses. Here, we will discuss only roles and statuses, postponing the discussion of norms until the next chapter, so that norms can be analyzed in the context of culture.

Role and status are different aspects of the same idea. In its sim-

[5]Robin H. Williams, Jr., *American Society,* 2nd rev. ed. (New York: Alfred A. Knopf, 1960), pp. 22–38.

plest definition, a *status* is a position in a social group (teacher, banker, senator, plumber, and so on). It generally implies ranking (high or low), or value rating according to the prevailing values of the group or society. A *role* is the carrying out of the status—its dynamic aspect (what the teacher, banker, senator or plumber *does*). Role guides the occupant of a status in behavior befitting that status. For example, a comedienne's role is to entertain people. Depending on what milieu she is in, and how successful she is, her status may be perceived as high *or* low.

Each society is faced with an immense number of functions that must be performed if the society is to operate effectively. Efficiency is improved when specific tasks, rather than being performed haphazardly by everyone, are allocated to particular individuals. The allocation of tasks leads to division of labor, which, in turn, creates statuses. As ways of behavior begin to cluster around allocated tasks and become crystallized, transmittable, and to a great extent predictable, roles are developed.

Statuses and the roles that grow up around them are not static. They are continually subject to change, growth and replacement by the individuals involved in them. In addition, social change and daily interaction constantly serve to redefine roles.

What statuses have been ascribed to you? Are you comfortable fulfilling the roles for these statuses?

Ascribed and achieved status. Some statuses and their satellite roles are ours at birth; we cannot avoid occupying them. A newborn child is either a male or a female; it belongs to a racial group; and its family already occupies the status of banker or farm laborer, or of whatever jobs the parents may have. Such statuses are called *ascribed* because they are not attained through any individual effort or merit.

The family group makes sure that the child behaves in accordance with his status—in other words, that he fulfills his role. If the child is a male, the family may provide him with toys and other objects that are often associated with masculinity in our society—baseballs, bats, football helmets, and guns. Moreover, he may be taught values that are generally associated with maleness in our society: big boys do not cry; they stand up for their rights and do not run home to mother; and so on. Parents also prepare the child to act according to his other statuses. If, for example, he is the son of a banker, he may be expected to attend a prep school and an Ivy League university and to engage in specific kinds of interaction with the "right" people.

Do you feel that sex should be a prime determinant of your status in society? In what ways?

If the child is a female, she may be presented with a different set of toys and values to prepare her for her role. Women's roles are, however, changing. In increasing numbers women are expressing dissatisfaction with the roles they are asked to assume and with the status society assigns them. The growing popularity of the Women's Liberation movement, particularly among white, middle-class women, is evidence of this dissatisfaction. There are many causes for women's

Retiring from Status

What status is granted retired people? While great age brings high prestige in many primitive societies, in the present-day societies surveyed by Simone de Beauvoir, the elderly are by and large forgotten. In capitalist countries like the United States where economic function is so important in defining a person's overall status, retirement means an abrupt reclassification from the status of the useful and the active to the status of the useless, the inactive, and the old. These changes in status reflect a change in social role. "The role of the retired person," one commentator has said, "is no longer to possess one." Or, as Beauvoir contends: "A man defines his identity by his calling and his pay: by retiring he loses this identity. A former mechanic is a mechanic no longer—he is nothing. . . . [Retirement] therefore means losing one's place in society, one's dignity and almost one's reality."

Loss of status in one sphere often has consequences in other spheres of life. In families where the man has been the sole breadwinner, wives often dread their husband's retirement, Beauvoir reports. Not only does income fall, but now the man is home all day, disrupting the established rhythms of domestic life. Husbands often feel ashamed of no longer supporting the family and fear a loss of status within the family. A drastic reduction in income threatens isolation and a loss of sociability as well, especially among the poorer classes. As one French worker expressed it: "Once I have no money, who do you suppose will bother with me? . . . When you are down and out, you don't find people anymore . . . . I don't want anybody to stand me a drink because I can't pay my round."

Simone de Beauvoir, *The Coming of Age,* trans. Patrick O'Brian (New York: G. P. Putnam's Sons, 1972), pp. 262–277.

discontent; but perhaps the broadest goal of the movement is to eliminate sex as a primary determinant of role. The women's movement is pressing for equal socializing and educational experiences for both boys and girls in the hope that as adults they will share equally in the functions of breadwinning, parenthood, and housekeeping. The goal is to raise fully developed *people,* not males and females each restricted by social roles to inadequate, limited experiences of life.

Ascribed statuses are involuntary and depend on gender, age, race, ethnic group, and, to an extent, on the social position of one's family. But there are also statuses that are achieved through individual effort

What statuses have you achieved? Are there other statuses that you would like to achieve? What will you have to do to achieve them?

and choice. For example, the statuses of husband and wife are *achieved statuses,* as are those of father and mother, and certainly those of teacher and plumber.

At first glance, our ascribed gender statuses—maleness and femaleness—and their consequent roles may seem more or less predetermined by physical and hormonal factors. After all, since only females have a uterus, they must be predetermined to play the role of mother. And since only males secrete testosterone, they must be predetermined to play the role of aggressors. This view, also called the "anatomy is destiny" view, was prevalent for many, many years. But recently, social scientists have been rethinking this view. Events such as the transsexual operation undergone by British author James Morris—born a male in full possession of a male sexual organ, a husband and father of five who is now Jan Morris—made many wonder if biology is indeed as important a determinant of sexual roles as we had thought. Morris had an ascribed status as male; an achieved status as female.

As it turns out, whether we consider ourselves male or female depends more on our cultural learning and experiences than on the anatomical and hormonal equipment with which we are born. Our parents begin the process of gender identification when they prepare us, from infancy on, to play the different roles that fit our sexual differences. And still other factors—personal impressions and social learning, which vary according to our social class, religion, family life-style, and the acquired concepts of masculinity and femininity—influence what we think our gender status is and how we carry out the role we think befits our gender.

What kinds of behavior would you expect from a man who has been described to you as being *macho,* in this society?

All of us who have been raised in this society are aware of how the statuses of males and females are ranked, and what the role expectations are for each (although, as we have said, these do vary according to class, religion, life-style, and so on). Other societies have different ways of ranking the statuses of male and female, and therefore have different expectations as to the roles that males and females play in their societies. For instance, most of us are familiar with the term *machismo,* which refers to a type of behavior culturally expected from a Latin American male. Machismo involves a whole set of characteristics, including aggressive behavior toward both men and women. We may not have heard the term *marianismo,* which refers to the role of Latin American females. Because of the gratification that women, in their later years, receive from their status in Latin America, they seem to be willing to put up with a passive and subservient role in their youth.

In traditional, preindustrial societies, ascribed status is a much more prevalent condition than is achieved status. In feudal Europe, for instance, society was actually divided into *estates*—a kind of permanent and rigid social class—and mobility from one estate into another was difficult or impossible to achieve. In preindustrial India people were similarly divided into *castes,* with members of each caste pledged to a specific job or profession for generations. Obviously, in such societies the scope of individual choice was small. Even if a person had ability and talent, he could seldom rise above the occupation and social class of his father.

Do you think there might be social advantages in a system that rigidly prescribed statuses and roles? What benefits might such a society offer the individual?

Industrial societies, on the other hand, have by and large made a philosophical commitment to individualism and personal achievement. Freedom of choice is jealously defended, and individual accomplishments are ardently applauded. As a consequence, industrial societies tend to support achieved, as opposed to ascribed, status. In the United States ascribed status, whether high or low, is often officially considered unfair. We disapprove of the fact that sons and daughters of the super rich can enter a life of comfort and leisure without having worked for it. And we decry the fact that the children of the poor similarly are introduced into a life-style of poverty for no fault of their own. However, we still do act on ascribed status, as when we buy fake coats of arms.

Finally, we must be aware that the categories of ascribed and achieved status are not rigid. They, too, may be thought as the two poles of a continuum represented by the availability of choice. Is the status of high school dropout, for instance, ascribed by virtue of membership in a low socioeconomic class, or achieved as a result of free choice? In the same way, the status of husband or wife may be ascribed or achieved, depending on the amount of pressure to marry that is involved.

The multiplicity of statuses and roles. Each person occupies a large number of statuses in society and is expected to perform the roles associated with them. The president of a huge corporation occupies not only a high status in the corporation, but probably also occupies the status of son, brother, husband, and father. He may also be a trustee on the board of a university, a member of an exclusive country club, an elder in his church, and an official in the Republican party. On occasion, he is also a patient in a doctor's office and a client at his stockbroker's. All these are temporary statuses.

These statuses are not equally important, and in our society, the corporation president will probably be best known for his status as president of a corporation. His status may also vary, according to the group that is ranking him. He may have a very high status in the corporation of which he is president, a very low one in his family, and a status equal to that of the other elders in his church.

Do you have some conflicting statuses and roles? What kinds of behavior are expected of you in each status?

No one performs all his roles equally well. The corporation president must be good at playing the role attached to his main status or he would not remain in his position very long. But if, as in the stereotypical image of the suburban, upper-middle-class family, his wife is undergoing psychiatric treatment and his children are chronic runaways, perhaps he leaves much to be desired in his roles of husband and father.

Finally, people select the roles they consider important. In other words, there is a relationship between a person's self-image and the role he or she chooses to play. Possibly the corporation president sees himself as a great American business leader. Consequently, he may play his role as corporation president well, but may neglect many of his other roles—for instance, those of husband and father. Should he ever lose his status of corporation president and be forced to abandon the corresponding role, he may experience a traumatic loss of identity. This feeling is at the bottom of much of the unhappiness that men often experience on retirement and that mothers often experience when their children become independent and leave home (the "empty

Identifying with Roles

Imagine a waiter in a cafe whose mannerisms appear self-conscious and stilted, who appears a little too eager in the performance of his duties, taking orders, carrying trays, setting tables. Each of his movements appears carefully calculated and executed with almost mechanical precision. He is playing a game, the philosopher Jean-Paul Sartre says, playing at being a waiter in a cafe. Why? For whom is the waiter performing? Other people? Himself? Sartre thinks he is performing for both. He is performing for others, says Sartre, because this is what society expects of him. Like the gestures of the waiter, "there is the dance of the grocer, of the tailor, of the auctioneer, by which they endeavor to persuade their clientele that they are nothing but a grocer, an auctioneer, a tailor. A grocer who dreams is offensive to the buyer, because such a grocer is not wholly a grocer."

The waiter is performing for himself, says Sartre, because he is trying to convince himself that he really is a waiter, and to do this he tries to act as "real" waiters do. But you can never really *be* a waiter, Sartre believes; you can only represent yourself as one.

When sociologists talk about roles they often use the language of the theater. The words "performance," "playing" a role, even the word "role" itself all remind us of a drama. Are we, then, just pretending when we "play" roles? Are we like the actor who plays Hamlet but can never actually *be* Hamlet?

Jean-Paul Sartre, *Being and Nothingness*, trans. Hazel E. Barnes (New York: Philosophical Library, 1956), p. 59.

nest" syndrome). The same loss of identity can occur when a husband or wife dies or when an individual who thinks of herself as a poet is forced to make a living pushing buttons on an assembly line. Later we will deal more specifically with the problems that result from the loss of identity caused by limited role commitments.

Have you ever been faced with conflicting roles that are attached to the status of student? How have you handled such conflicts?

Role conflict. A person performs one role better than another partly because certain facets of his personality affect him and partly because he may have learned his role imperfectly. Role conflict may also contribute to the problem.

Frequently, our society prepares us for roles that in real life we do not have the opportunity to play. The young are often taught ideal, rather than real, patterns of behavior. This disparity leads to role conflict and disillusionment. Sunday school may teach young people to love their neighbors, turn the other cheek, and to be honest, fair, and peace-loving. But these qualities are hardly descriptive of our society. Instead, our neighbors are confined to ghettos; injury is repaid with worse injury; pacifism may lead to a jail sentence; and honesty and fairness, particularly in business, may very well lead to bankruptcy. This is not to say that we should stop teaching ideal patterns of behavior. All societies have such unmet ideal patterns and they are not always hypocritical. Ideal patterns serve a necessary function, acting as a brake on real behavior patterns and practices that may decline to an undesirable level without the example of the ideal societal goals. They may also affect individual behavior patterns in some who see the discrepancies between the real and ideal patterns and who therefore attempt to change the real patterns. These ideal patterns also serve to upgrade social behavior patterns. For example, a person who sees the discrepancy between "All men are created equal" and current inequality, may learn to fight for the ideal.

Such role conflicts are almost nonexistent in small, nontechnological, homogeneous societies. In such societies, the young live near their elders and learn from them exactly what they are expected to do as they grow up. Our kind of society, however, has a complex economy in which most tasks are performed outside the home. Rapid social change makes it impossible to predict future life-styles. For these reasons role expectation is, at best, fuzzy and, at worst, causes serious personality disorders.

We are also often expected to play several demanding roles simultaneously. The corporation president's role demands that he spend an unusually large proportion of his time on business connected with the corporation. To be an effective husband and father, however, he should also spend enough time in family activities so intimate interaction can occur. Which of these roles should take precedence?

Sometimes role conflict exists within the limits of a single role. Anyone in a position of leadership faces such a conflict. A leader can

What roles do you most want to fulfill? Do you anticipate any conflicts between these roles and those society may want you to fill?

uphold discipline and increase the chances that the group will reach its goals. But in the process he may become so disliked by his subordinates that the group has difficulty following him. Or he can slacken discipline and be well liked, at the possible expense of an efficient attainment of goals. A leader must constantly weigh possible behavior in terms of the role of leading.

Role confusion and role performance. Role confusion often follows a change of status. A man who has spent most of his life behind a desk and is suddenly faced with retirement at age sixty-five may find that he cannot fill the leisure hours at his disposal. He does not know what his new role should be. A young college-educated woman who has begun a promising career and who is suddenly confronted with motherhood and the drudgery of housekeeping is ill prepared to cope with this new role. And in a changing society, she may not be able to decide which role should predominate.

Faulty role performance is another problem, which can result in mental illness, maladjustment, or general frustration. For many rea-

Methodology: Participant Observation

To gain a fresh understanding of black, lower-class men, Elliot Liebow, armed with a notebook but no hypotheses, began by getting to know the men who hung out at a corner carry-out shop in a black neighborhood of Washington, D.C. He was using the method known as "participant observation"—joining in the activities of the group under study. For more than a year, Liebow accompanied about two dozen men as they hung out on "Tally's Corner," shot pool, drank coffee or beer, went to movies or to court, visited relatives, Liebow all the while participating in conversations, trying to see the world through the eyes of the men themselves. He tried to act as another friend might, offering opinions, helping out in time of need. With one man, Tally, he became close friends. As his purpose was exploratory, Liebow let himself be guided by the men's rhythms of daily life and his own good sense. He responded honestly when asked why he was there, a practice often but not always followed by researchers. Each night he recorded his observations and the day's conversations.

As Liebow shared in the men's activities, trust and acceptance grew—crucial elements in any participant observation study. Degrees of participation and acceptance vary widely in such studies. Liebow did not accompany the men to work, live in their neighborhood, gamble, or form sexual attachments. His acceptance by

sons—sometimes simply by chance—people fail in the roles for which they have been prepared. Sometimes they never even achieve the status of the role, and do not have the chance to even try the role. What is more, in our highly competitive economic system, people frequently fail in their professions and businesses. The high incidence of divorce demonstrates that large numbers of people fail in their marital roles. However, many people who seem to fail in one role may actually be fulfilling a conflicting role very well. For example, a woman who divorces her husband in order to better fill her role as mother cannot be considered a failure as a mother.

Why might faulty role performance lead to mental illness? Which group type would have more influence over role decisions, primary or secondary groups?

Many people, especially today, are dissatisfied with the roles they are expected to perform. The current generation seems determined to break the bonds that have for so long held us so rigidly to our roles. Today, in our society, blacks are refusing to be limited to their inferior status, with its consequent role. Women, too, are rebelling against their status as second-class citizens—sex objects who are expected to assume the role of housekeeper without pay. Many young men are not permitting themselves to be trained for occupations they consider

the men was limited by his differences from them. He had more income, more education, more saleable skills than they; he was white, the men of the streetcorner, black. Within these limits, however, Liebow was able to learn how the men felt about their situation and see their lives from both inside and outside their own experience.

Using his field notes as a guide, Liebow tried to make sense of what he had found. He organized his findings around the main roles of the men—as breadwinners, as fathers, as husbands or lovers, as friends—because this would allow comparability with other studies and because this is how the men looked at themselves. Participant observation allows the researcher to compare what people say with what they do, and Liebow used this virtue to show a process by which the streetcorner men, defeated in their attempts to achieve the goals of the larger society, pretended to others that they had never desired them in the first place. Sons acted like their fathers, Liebow said, not because of the cultural transmission of roles, but because their experiences of failure were so similar. The low self-esteem, persistent failure, and unstable family relationships characteristic of the streetcorner men, he concluded, stemmed primarily from their impoverished circumstances.

Elliot Liebow, *Tally's Corner: A Study of Negro Streetcorner Men* (Boston: Little, Brown and Company, 1967).

irrelevant and dehumanizing. The battle to break traditional roles and role stereotypes promises to be lengthy and uphill, but it can be won.

[Summary]

Given the statements made in chapter 1 about the sociologist's role, is it proper for a sociologist to encourage certain types of role change, such as are advocated by the women's movement?

People everywhere are members of some group at almost all times in their lives. Through interaction within a group, the human organism becomes a human being. Seldom does anyone choose isolation as a way of life voluntarily, and isolation is often used as a means of punishment.

In the sociological sense, not all aggregates and categories of people constitute groups. A group must have the following characteristics: (1) it must display symbolic interaction among the members; (2) each member must know that he is part of the group and the group must recognize him as a member; and (3) members must be aware of both the roles, duties, and obligations and the privileges resulting from membership.

There is a great number of groups in society, varying in size from two to several hundred million. One way of classifying groups is into primary and secondary. Primary groups are relatively small, stable, and durable groups, in which members engage in intimate, intense, informal, and spontaneous interaction. Members of primary groups know and deal with one another on an individual, personal, and total basis. Secondary groups display opposite characteristics: they tend to be large, of short duration, and the interaction among members is formal, utilitarian, specialized, and temporary. Relationships in primary groups are of the utmost importance to humans, even though they may not always be harmonious or satisfying to the individual. Our society is increasingly characterized by secondary groups and relationships, which are much less satisfying to individuals although they are more efficient. For this reason, primary relations develop even within secondary groups.

In addition to their primary or secondary classification, groups are also categorized (1) according to whether they are small or large; (2) according to the concept of in-group and out-group; (3) according to whether they offer membership or reference; and (4) according to whether they are voluntary or involuntary. Large groups tend to be highly organized and often assume the proportion of formal associations with bureaucratic forms of organization. Features of bureaucracies include (1) job specialization (division of labor); (2) rigid rules and standards; (3) impersonality and impartiality; (4) a hierarchical arrangement of officials; and (5) the use of rationality in attaining goals.

The largest group to which people belong is society. Societies that are relatively small, in which members are homogeneous, in which behavior is dictated by tradition, and in which members interact on an informal, personal, face-to-face basis are called *Gemeinschaft societies.* Societies that are large and heterogeneous, in which relationships among members are impersonal, formal, functional, contractual, and specialized (as in industrial societies) are called *Gesellschaft societies.* The trend in the modern world has been a transition from Gemeinschaft- to Gesellschaft-type societies.

The reciprocal relationships that take place within and among groups are called *interaction.* Interaction consists of several social processes, the most basic of which are cooperation, competition, and conflict. Cooperation and conflict sometimes lead to the social processes of accommodation and assimilation. Whatever the type of relationship—primary or secondary—one or more of these social processes are at work.

The structure, or social organization, of the social system is made up of shared and repeated patterns of behavior that have emerged, and continue to emerge, as a result of the interaction of group members. Social organization is a dynamic process rather than a rigid set of roles; it contains both stable and changing elements.

Interaction occurs on three levels of organization: on the interpersonal level (relationships between two persons who stand in a definite position to each other), on the group level (within and between groups), and on the community level (within a community or a society).

Interaction always occurs within a context. We relate to others from the standpoint of our own position (status) in our group, while we carry out behavior befitting that position (role). Status and role are basic elements of social organization, directing interaction within and between social systems.

We occupy some statuses involuntarily. Our ascribed statuses are those over which we have no control: our sex—male or female—our age, our racial and ethnic origin, and the economic standing of our families. Throughout our lives, we achieve other statuses as a result of our own efforts or merit. Both these kinds of statuses have attendant roles that we are trained to fulfill.

In modern societies, many people face role conflict. Our society prepares us for some roles that we never have an opportunity to play. *Frequently, we are expected to perform satisfactorily in roles that make contradictory demands upon us.* Then, too, we ourselves sometimes fail in the roles we have assumed.

Today, many groups are dissatisfied with their statuses and the roles they are expected to play. The changes that will probably occur in some stereotyped statuses and roles will have a definite effect on the social organization of our society.

In the next chapter, we will examine a social system in which we all participate—society. We will consider the normative structure of its social organization, as well as the product of the interaction within it—culture.

Terms to Remember

Aggregate. A number of people who are in the same place at the same time but who do not interact with one another.

Category. A number of people who have some characteristics in common but who do not interact with one another.

Symbolic interaction. Communication through speech, gestures, writing, or even music. In this kind of communication, members are mutually aware of one another, and awareness causes them to behave in a particular way.

Group. A number of people who engage in symbolic interaction. The members of a group are mutually aware of and influence one another; they recognize their membership in the group, and are, in turn, recognized by the group as members; and they recognize the roles, duties, obligations, and privileges that result from group membership.

Primary group. A relatively small group of people who live physically near one another and who interact intensely. Primary groups tend to be stable and of relatively long duration. Interaction is informal and spontaneous; members deal with one another on an individual, personal, and total basis.

Secondary group. A group that is, in general, larger and of shorter duration than is a primary group. Interaction among members is formal, utilitarian, specialized, and temporary. Members are interested in one another mainly in terms of the roles and functions they perform.

Bureaucracy. A hierarchical system in an organization. The hierarchy depends on job specialization—or division of labor—on a set of rules and standards designed to promote uniformity, and on an attitude of impersonal impartiality.

Society. The largest social group analyzed by sociologists.

Gemeinschaft. A small, homogeneous, communal, and traditional society. Relationships among members are personal, informal, and face-to-face, and behavior is dictated by tradition.

Gesellschaft. A large, heterogeneous society, such as modern industrial societies. Relationships among members tend to be impersonal, formal, contractual, functional, and specialized. Also called an *associational society.*

Social processes. Key patterns of interaction common to all human societies.

Cooperation. A basic social process involving two or more individuals or groups working jointly in a common enterprise for a shared goal.

Conflict. A hostile struggle engaged in by two or more persons for an object or value that each prizes.

Competition. A social process that occurs when two or more individuals try to obtain possession of the same scarce object or intangible value. A form of oppositional interaction.

Accommodation. The peace-making, conflict-settling period following the victory of one antagonist in conflict.

Assimilation. A process of fusion in which one individual or group becomes completely accepted into another group.

Social system. A conceptualized group in which each part is interdependent and interconnected to other parts and to the whole. The elements of this system are the individual group members relating to one another.

Social structure. The shared, patterned, and recurrent expectations of behavior that guide members of social systems in their relationships with one another.

Social organization. The network of patterned human behavior that both guides and is the product of interaction. Sometimes considered as the real, as opposed to the ideal, way people behave. It is not necessarily a stable set of rules but a dynamic process in which stable and predictable patterns are continually redefined and changed to fit the changing conditions of the environment.

Status. A position, including ranking and rating, in a social group.

Role. The carrying out of a status. A way of behaving that befits a status and is transmittable and, to a great extent, predictable.

Ascribed status. An inherited position—one that is not attained through any individual effort or merit.

Achieved status. A position attained through individual effort or merit.

Suggestions for Further Reading

Blau, Peter M. *The Dynamics of Bureaucracy.* Chicago: University of Chicago Press, 1963. A distinguished sociologist illustrates the social processes that lead to change in a bureaucracy.

Cooley, Charles Horton. *Social Organization.* New York: Schocken Books, 1962. First edition, 1909. One of the classics of sociology, containing the original definition of a primary group, as well as other pertinent discussions of social structure and social organization.

Gans, Herbert J. *The Urban Villagers.* New York: The Free Press, 1962. An interesting analysis of primary groups and interpersonal relationships in an Italian, working-class community.

Gross, Edward. "Some Functional Consequences of Primary Groups in Formal Work Organizations." *American Journal of Sociology* (August, 1953), pp. 368–373. Reprint S-106, The Bobbs-Merrill Company, Indianapolis. The effect of primary groups on formal organizations from the viewpoint of the positive support they engender.

Hinton, Bernard L., ed. *Groups and Organizations.* Belmont, Calif.: Wadsworth, 1971. A collection of essays dealing with the formation of, and processes within, small groups flourishing within the context of formal organization.

Howton, William F. "Work Assignment and Interpersonal Relations in a Research Organization: Some Participant Observations." *Administrative Science Quarterly* (March, 1963), pp. 502–520. A more recent analysis of a phenomenon similar to that discussed in the article by Edward Gross.

Mills, Theodore. *The Sociology of Small Groups.* Englewood Cliffs, N.J.: Prentice-Hall, 1967. A brief compendium of small-group theory, including the findings of numerous experiments in social psychology.

Olmstead, Michael S. *The Small Group.* New York: Random House, 1962. A readable paperback describing research on both primary and secondary groups and stressing the fact that not all small groups are primary.

Presthus, Robert. *The Organizational Society.* New York: Random House, Vintage Books, 1962. This paperback emphasizes the conflicts between the aims of large-scale organizations and the needs for personal growth and creativity of the individuals who constitute them.

Redfield, Robert. *The Little Community and Peasant Society and Culture.* Chicago: University of Chicago Press, 1960. A classic description of the traditional Gemeinschaft society.

Shils, Edward A., and Janowitz, Morris. "Cohesion and Disintegration in the Wehrmacht in World War II." *Public Opinion Quarterly* (Summer, 1948). Reprint S-263, The Bobbs-Merrill Company, Indianapolis. A somewhat old but still valid study illustrating that morale remained high in the German army as long as primary groups remained operative.

Suttles, Gerald D. *The Social Order of the Slum.* Chicago: University of Chicago Press, 1968. A description of the differences in social organization among four ethnic groups in Chicago.

Warren, Roland. *The Community in America.* 2nd ed. Chicago: Rand McNally, 1972. A discussion of how communities may be studied and a sociological perspective on the processes affecting American communities.

Society and culture

GROUP LIFE IS the subject matter of sociological inquiry. Sociologists do not focus on the individual in isolation. They center their research around questions involving the individual's relationships in his or her physical and social surroundings. Each of the following chapters will analyze some aspect of these relationships. In this chapter, we will discuss the widest frameworks in which these relationships take place, namely society and culture.

We have already mentioned many different kinds of groups within which people interact. We have said that society was the largest of these groups. But why is the entire population of our planet taken together not considered a group? We suppose that the whole world could be considered a group, in relative terms, if we needed to differentiate humans from Martians or Saturnians. But we have not met any Martians yet. Furthermore, we are still very far from being a global community. Our diplomats do interact with people from other societies, as do some tourists, journalists, and just plain adventurers. But for most of us, the world might as well begin and end in our own town or at most in our own nation. Therefore, society is usually the largest group whose interaction sociologists study.

How would you describe human beings and the ways they interact to a Martian? What problems arise in trying to communicate our ways of life? Do these problems suggest ways in which sociologists study different groups among human beings?

We all have common human ancestors. But we are scattered throughout different parts of the world, and we have bred within restricted groups. These facts make one group different from another both in appearance and life-style. Anyone who has traveled even a few hundred miles away from home—or who has watched travel shows on television—is aware of the differences among human groups. For instance, our neighbors to the north, the Canadians, are very much like us. They make up a multigroup society, as we do, and most of them are descendants of immigrants, as we are. Yet a perceptive ob-

These Mexican musicians are members of a society that is culturally different from, but in close proximity to the United States.

What kinds of differences in life-style have you noticed within the United States? What might cause these differences?

server will notice a number of differences. The Canadians speak English with a slightly different accent from ours, and in one of their provinces, Quebec, French is the predominant tongue. The Canadians have retained not only an anglicized spelling system, but also many more political and social traditions of England than we have. Life in their large cities is much like life in our large cities. If you were to spend time in a smaller, provincial town, however, you would note that Canadians phrase things differently, think somewhat differently, and cook differently from the way we do.

What of our neighbors to the southwest of us in Mexico? Here we have a people who speak a different language from ours and whose traditions are quite different. Many Mexicans even look different from many of us, since they are a mixture of European, Indian, and black people. Rather than eating the beef stew and biscuits traditional among our largest group—the descendants of English settlers—the Mexicans eat tacos and tortillas and many dishes based on beans and ground corn. More importantly, many of their societal and personal values, as well as their ideas concerning the roles of men, women and the institutions of marriage and family, are quite distinct from our own.

Still, the differences we find among societies so near us are comparatively subtle. You, though an American, could live in Canada or Mexico without having to make big adjustments in life-style. You might have to learn a new language, or you might have to change some of your attitudes, or you might be forced to alter your diet slightly. But Canadians, Mexicans, and residents of the United States are all part of a wider group whose traditions are largely derived from Western civilization. Although we are different, we have many similarities. In fact, the mass media tend to spread and publicize the customs and traditions of societies all around the world, and many societies are beginning to resemble one another. But what if an American some fifty years ago had been thrust into, say, an Eskimo society? How would he have reacted to the Eskimo custom of offering the guest a choice morsel of raw meat? And how graciously would he have accepted the offer of his Eskimo host's wife for the night? Even the most broad-minded American would no doubt have experienced some cultural shock, although the Eskimo might have been even more confused by the American's reactions. The Eskimos were the original inhabitants of Canada, as the Indians were of the United States. Culture shock has wiped out most of these native Americans, who could not withstand the technologically superior Europeans.

The example of Eskimo culture is taken from a life-style that existed half a century ago. What changes may have taken place since then among the Eskimos? Would Americans today be equally shocked by such a cultural difference?

Whether subtle or shocking, differences do exist among groups of people in the world. Since our society, too, is made up of differing groups of people—or the descendants of differing groups—we can find variety in our own midst. We, too, speak with different accents, according to the region in which we were born. We, too, eat different foods, according to what is available or what our parents taught us to like. We, too, have different attitudes, believe in different gods, vote for different parties, live in different kinds of houses, have different ambitions and goals.

Differences among people are almost without limits. At the same time, we must not forget that people share significant similarities. No matter how far and wide we travel in the world, we will find that sooner or later all people must eat—though how and what they eat will differ from place to place. All people eventually must sleep, though some sleep in beds and others on mats on the floor. All people have some sort of dwelling for shelter. All classify themselves according to some sort of kinship system. All organize themselves according to some type of social system. All make their economic decisions according to some kind of economic system; and so on.

What "significant similarities" can you add to this list of human universals?

The question, then, arises: In what ways are people similar, and in what ways are they different? We can also ask: What is responsible for differences and similarities among human groups? To answer these questions with any degree of precision, we must understand two central concepts of the social sciences: society and culture. For it is in the context of society and according to the patterns of culture that human life unfolds.

[Society]

We can define *society* as the largest group of people inhabiting a specific territory. The people in a society share a common culture as a re-

How does the sociological definition of *society* differ from definitions implied by such phrases as "high society," "society woman," "Society of Engineers," and "the society of one's friends"?

sult of interacting on a regular, continuous basis, and as a result of interacting according to patterns of behavior on which all, more or less, agree. Like all sociological definitions, the definition of society stresses social relationships, or interaction, rather than individuals. Society differs from many other kinds of groups because within this group people can live a total, common life. Society is not an organization limited to a specific purpose as, for example, the American Medical Association is. It is the most self-sufficient group, and its independence is based on the techniques developed for fulfilling the needs of its members.

From a sociological standpoint, society is the interrelated network of social relationships that exists within the boundaries of the largest social system. In the past, the largest social system was a clan, a tribe, or simply a family. Today, the largest social system is the nation-state. In the nation-state, individuals are grouped and interrelated as families, communities, racial and ethnic groups, political parties, social classes, and so on. When we speak of American society, we are referring to the more than 200 million individuals (grouped in families, communities, and countless other classifications) who inhabit the United States, and whose social relationships occur within its boundaries.

Every society organizes representative groups and positions to which it gives the power of making decisions and settling conflicts. Each society requires that its members feel greater loyalty to it than to any other group. Such loyalty is possible partly because the members share a language and a culture uniquely their own, even though a number of groups within the larger society have cultures and languages that differ significantly from those of the majority.[1]

Kinds of Societies

Why would a sociologist find it most useful to classify a society by its mode of subsistence or basic pattern of social organization? How are the two characteristics related?

Throughout history, societies have assumed a number of different forms. As is true of other groups, societies can be classified in countless ways. For purposes of analysis, societies are generally classified according to either their chief mode of subsistence or their basic patterns of social organization.

Sociologist Gerhard Lenski distinguishes among eleven types of societies according to their mode of subsistence—the way they provide their members with food, shelter, and clothing. The most common of these societies are listed below.

The hunting and gathering society. The earliest and the least complex society is the hunting and gathering society, formed by people thousands of years ago. This kind of society is characterized by: (1) a small, no-

---

[1]Marvin E. Olsen, *The Process of Social Organization* (New York: Holt, Rinehart & Winston, 1968), p. 96.

madic population, with an uncomplicated technology; (2) almost no division of labor or any kind of specialization; and (3) particular stress on the importance of kinship ties. A few such societies still exist in the modern world: the Bushmen of southern Africa, some Eskimo tribes, and the Stone Age societies being discovered in Brazil and the Phillipines. However, unavoidable contacts with modern societies doom all these comparatively simple societies to extinction or to marked change.

Why would a society with an uncomplicated technology be likely to have little or no division of labor? Do you think this would also apply to the division of labor between men and women? Why or why not?

The horticultural society. The second simplest society—the horticultural—appeared in history after people discovered how to cultivate grains. In the horticultural society, the cultivation of wheat, rice, and other grains was the chief means of sustenance. Hunting and gathering were secondary. In this kind of society, domestic artifacts first appeared, and tools were more sophisticated than those of hunters and food gatherers.

The horticultural society contained reasonably large, settled communities; developed the basics of trade; and produced, for the first time, a surplus that had the consequence of dividing members of the society into social classes. The production of surpluses, or extra supplies of food, laid the foundation for social inequality, a condition that has existed in all later societies. Surpluses eventually led to a situation in which some people were rich and others poor, some led and others followed, and so on.

The agrarian society. The next milestone in the development of human societies was reached around 3,000 B.C., following the invention of the plow. The plow led to the formation of the agrarian society. In this type of society, even greater surpluses were produced, and people no longer had to move about to search for fertile soils. People became even more differentiated into landholders and landless peasants, and social stratification deepened. To maintain the system and to oversee the increasingly complex economy, members of the society developed a bureaucracy. The agrarian society also developed the initial stages of a money economy; gunpowder; iron smelting; and the use of windmills as a source of power.

Other preindustrial societies and industrial societies. Other preindustrial societies classified by Lenski are the fishing, maritime, and herding societies. All exhibit features that are similar to those of agrarian societies. The most revolutionary change in the form of societies occurred with the emergence of the industrial society. Most societies in the world today are either already industrial or are trying to attain the industrial stage. Such societies are characterized by: (1) urbanization (growth of cities at the expense of rural areas); (2) massive mechanization and automation (the substitution of machines for human labor and the human brain); (3) complex bureaucratization (organization into formal groups for greater efficiency); (4) separation of institutional

Why might fishing, maritime, and herding societies develop features that are similar to those of agrarian societies?

The plow that this Tunisian peasant is using is part of an agrarian tradition that reaches back thousands of years.

forms (the development of schools, hospitals, stores, factories, to perform functions formerly performed by the family); and (5) the substitution of impersonal ties for kinship ties.[2] The transition from agrarian to industrial society brings havoc to most societies and ours is no exception. Many of our chapters will deal specifically with these problems industrialization creates for group interaction.

Classification According to Social Organization

Societies are more often classified according to their basic patterns of social organization than according to their mode of subsistence. To analyze organization, sociologists place societies on two extremes of an ideal continuum, Gemeinschaft and Gesellschaft. As we said in Chapter 1, Gemeinschaft societies are communal, or traditional, whereas Gesellschaft societies are modern industrial, or associational.

Much of the turmoil of our times is the result of a trend, begun in the late Middle Ages, away from the communal and toward the associational type of society. Even partially industrialized societies, and particularly those of the Third World, are in the throes of this transi-

---

[2]Gerhard Lenski, *Human Societies* (New York: McGraw-Hill, 1970), pp. 118–142.

tion. And the transition has not yet been completed even in the industrial societies of the world.

Traditional, or communal, societies. Gemeinschaft societies have the following characteristics:

1. They are usually small in size.
2. There is very little division of labor, or role specialization.
3. The family is the focal unit of society—on it, all social organization hinges. If groups larger than the family exist, they are kinship groups—clans and tribes.
4. Social relationships are of a primary nature—durable, personal, and emotional.
5. Patterns of behavior are dictated by custom and tradition, and expectations of behavior are specific and well defined.
6. Lacking groups other than the family, clan, and tribe, the society is homogeneous and acts as an integrated social unit.

How might Lenski's classification of societies by mode of subsistence be related to Tönnes' classifications of Gemeinschaft and Gesellschaft? What modes of subsistence do Gemeinschaft societies probably have?

Modern industrial, or associational, societies. Gesellschaft societies display characteristics that are almost the direct reverse of the characteristics of Gemeinschaft societies:

1. They are usually large in size.
2. There is a complex system of division of labor, or role differentiation.
3. The family's position as the essential social unit is eroded by social institutions and occupational, political, and social groups. Other kinship groups also lose importance.
4. Social relationships are of a secondary nature—transient, impersonal, and unemotional.
5. Formal and informal laws regulate patterns of behavior, whereas behavioral expectations are unclear and ill defined.
6. Because the society is heterogeneous and multigroup, unity diminishes.

How might each of the characteristics listed for associational societies be related to the mode of subsistence in these societies? To the technology?

[Society and Culture]

The purpose of our discussion up to this point has been primarily to prepare you for a clear understanding of the principal and vital product of societies—their culture. *Culture,* like society, is a frequently misunderstood word. In everyday conversation, *culture* is used in general and sociologically incorrect terms. For example, we tend to think of "cultured" people as individuals who have good manners, who attend concerts and symphonies, who go to art shows, and who have read the classics of world literature.

As a matter of fact, any individual who has been reared in a social group is cultured. *Culture is the way of life of a people.* Any part of the way of life, whether it concerns philosophy or theology, garbage collection or waste disposal, is part of culture.

Society and Culture

Why is it impossible to speak of an "uncultured person," in sociological terms? What does the phrase mean, in popular usage?

We mentioned that culture is the product of a society. We should add that culture and society are two aspects of the same phenomenon, that they are interrelated and interdependent. Culture cannot exist without a society—or, at least, without a social group—and it would be impossible to conceive of a society without a culture.

The interdependence of culture and society is understandable in terms of what was said in Chapter 2. No social group is immune to interaction, which takes place through a number of social processes. Furthermore, interaction is not entirely haphazard but is guided by recurring patterns of behavior. These patterns of behavior are not simply set up but emerge as a result of the continued interaction of the members of a group. The outgrowth of interaction, then, is culture, which dictates further interaction.

For purpose of contrast, we can view culture and society in a theatrical context. Society can be considered a group of actors who play roles befitting their statuses. The script that the actors use in playing their roles is culture. This script has been written for the actors by generations of their predecessors. Each generation, including the present, has added, deleted, changed, or modified some parts of it.

A Definition of Culture

Culture is a central concept of sociology—and more importantly, of human life. It has many facets and includes many things. It is not enough to define it simply as a way of life of a people, nor as the product of and guide for social interaction. On the other hand, it is equally senseless to pile definition on top of definition.

The difficulty of defining culture is apparent when we consider that anthropologists A. L. Kroeber and Clyde Kluckhohn, in their extensive investigation of culture, found no less than 164 definitions of the concept.[3] Perhaps we can obtain a composite view of culture by pointing out some of its fundamental characteristics:

1. Culture is that product of social interaction that is uniquely human.
2. Culture includes all the accumulated knowledge, ideas, values, goals, and material objects of a society that are shared by all the members of the society and that have been passed from generation to generation by individual members.
3. Culture is learned by each member of a society during socialization—the process through which the individual learns to become human. Cultural learning takes place through symbolic interaction, a kind of communication in which language or gestures are used.
4. Culture provides each member of a society with ways of satisfying biological and emotional needs in a manner approved by the soci-

---

[3]A. L. Kroeber and Clyde Kluckhohn, "Culture: A Critical Review of Concepts and Definitions," *Papers of the Peabody Museum of American Archaeology and Ethnology,* vol. 47 (1952), Parts II and III, pp. 3–223.

ety. Culture does this by supplying people with systems, or patterns, or organized behavior.

5. Each human society develops a culture that is distinct from other cultures. Yet all cultures share similarities, because they deal with biological and emotional needs that are universal.
6. Culture, as well as society—of which culture is both a product and a guide—is in a constant state of flux. It changes either imperceptibly or rapidly, according to the circumstances.

In capsule form, we may define culture as the totality of what is learned, shared, and transmitted by the members of a society through interaction.

Given this list of characteristics of culture, would you say that any culture is *innately* human? Would you say that any culture is better than any other? Explain your reasoning.

The Human Quality of Culture

We have noted that culture is the product of *human* social interaction. We emphasize the human aspect because animals also engage in social interaction. They live in groups, form more or less transient families, and even have basic forms of social organization and systems whereby members are divided into something akin to social classes. Yet, as far as we can determine, they have no culture.

Animals lack culture mainly because they lack the ability to communicate *symbolically.* Animals communicate through a system of *signals* that are biologically determined and genetically transmitted responses to outside stimuli. An animal yelps in response to pain, runs in response to fear, and kills in response to hunger. These basic forms of communication are very limited in scope.

Biology and instinct determine how animals behave in particular situations. Genetically transmitted instinct tells salmon to return to fresh waters to spawn and die. Instinct tells some birds—and not others—where and when to migrate. It tells bees and ants how to organize themselves efficiently, including what tasks each must perform.

Animals can be taught to act in ways that are not instinctual. We can teach a dog many tricks—how to lie down, sit up, and roll over. Unfortunately, the dog will never be able to tell his newborn pup how to perform these tricks. The owner will have to teach the young dog the same tricks over again.

Humans, on the other hand, communicate through *symbols.* Symbols, essentially, are signs that can be used in an abstract manner and whose meanings are communally agreed upon. All English-speaking people agree what the sound of the word *bread* stands for—a type of food made out of flour, water, and other ingredients. The sound of the word *flag* brings to our minds the concept of country; the sound of the word *map* represents a place. Language is the most effective system of symbols used by humans. In language, symbols are employed to name things, individuals, and categories. Gestures, music, and art are also communicated by symbol systems.

Have you ever experienced culture in which the symbolic use of gestures was substantially different from our own? What differences did you notice?

Language plays a particularly important role in the development and transmission of culture. It does not seem possible that culture could grow without language, which is the most obvious *product* of culture. Language has made communication easy and has allowed people to engage in coordinated group activities that helped them survive. With cooperation in the hunt (aided by language) came the establish-

Those Who Stand and Wait

What codes of behavior grow up around standing in line? In 1967 a group of researchers observed and interviewed a sample of the 10,000 people waiting for tickets to the final series of Australian football. Although officials set the terms of ticket-buying—how many were available, when they would go on sale, that tickets would be distributed on a first come, first serve basis—people each year developed a spontaneous social system and culture around standing in line.

Melbourne's official ticket line began at 3 P.M. the day before the box office opened, and to enforce this rule the police set up barricades around the stadium. Hundreds of people came to the park early and formed themselves into a line. When the barricades were removed, they filed in their original order to the beginning of the official line. The crowd had developed their own norm, which they followed throughout: that those who wait longest should have the first opportunity to buy tickets. Belief in this code was unanimous, the researchers found; no one approved of butting in.

Belief in this general rule still allowed for variations in practice, which, pushed to excess, tended to subvert the norm. The time for waiting was long, seventeen hours in many cases. Queuers developed two systems in response to this. They organized shift systems whereby one person would hold the place for a time while friends took a break. Another practice was "staking a claim"—leaving a possession in your place while you went off to get something to eat or play a game. "During the early hours of waiting," the researchers noted, "the queues often consisted of one part people to two parts inanimate objects." Once in 1966 late-comers, seeing that the middle of the line had consisted of such symbols for most of the day, burned all the objects and took their places. They "were protesting the violation of the principle of serving time to earn occupancy of a position," the researchers said.

Leon Mann, "Queue Culture: The Waiting Line as a Social System," *American Journal of Sociology* 74 (November 1969): 340–54.

ment of communities and a more efficient division of labor. Language allowed people to share, remember, and pass on references to both objects and abstractions. The importance of symbols, as compared to signals, is that they are not biologically determined and genetically transmitted. They are learned from others, and they can be changed, modified, combined, and recombined in an infinite variety of ways.

The Effects of Biology on Culture

Biology is at the root of many human, as well as animal, limitations. In many respects, biology has limited our effectiveness in living on our planet. We cannot live in a vast part of the earth because we cannot breathe in water. Because we have a thin layer of skin, with very little hair on it, we need protection from the elements. We are comparatively small and defenseless, lacking the claws and fangs of many animals, as well as their sharp sense of smell and sight.

These shortcomings are more than made up for by the qualities we do possess.

1. A grasping hand with a thumb that can be opposed to the other four fingers, which enables us to handle and make even the most delicate objects.
2. An upright posture, which frees the forelimbs for handling objects.
3. Binocular vision, which enables us to focus far or near.
4. Highly complicated vocal equipment, which enables us to speak.
5. An extremely well-developed brain, part of a complex nervous system, that makes it all possible.

Our upright posture is considered one of the biological characteristics that enabled us to become "human." Why might upright posture have this effect? How does it relate to the characteristic of an opposable thumb?

The biological equipment of humans has enabled them to create culture, with which they adapt to their physical environment. Before people could create culture, however, they had to develop language. After the development of language, each member of a society was able to communicate his personal experiences. These experiences were then shared by the whole society and eventually transmitted to the new generation. The members of the society could then respond to an experience they had not personally faced. They could learn from it, consider it good or bad, dismiss it as irrelevant or remember it as useful, or do whatever they chose with it. It is much easier to acquire and accumulate knowledge in this manner than if each individual had to acquire it personally!

[Cultural Content]

Culture is not visible or tangible in and of itself. We can't see it, touch it, nor sell it over the counter. Nevertheless, culture is very much present among us. When we analyze its content, we find that culture consists of many elements.

Material Culture

One part of culture is both visible and tangible because it is made up of the huge numbers of products conceived and manufactured by humans. All material objects, from a primitive stone ax to a complex guided missile, belong to the category of material culture. Material objects are created to fill a shared need. They develop when one individual has an idea that is seized upon by other individuals, who add, modify, change, and put the idea to use.

The automobile, the foremost symbol of modern material culture, is an example of a product that is the result of the interaction of countless generations of people. The originator of the automobile owed much to those prehistoric cave dwellers who first honed stones into circular shapes (or found some ready-made by nature), who saw how rapidly they rolled down inclines, who stuck sticks through their middles, and who attached to them heavy objects that they wanted moved. They, and the other members of their social group, must have been elated to realize that they only had to push or pull, rather than carry the weight.

Generations later, after people had domesticated several animals, other ingenious (or lazy) individuals carried the idea further. They attached wheeled equipment, such as a cart and a plow, to animals. Now humans did not need to use their own energy to push, pull, carry, and work the soil, but could use animal power.

What kind of nonmaterial culture might a sophisticated society have in which all material aids to communication were obsolete?

Much later inventions, including the steam engine and the internal combustion engine, made it possible for people to sit safely in a train or a car, going wherever they wanted to go rapidly and in comfort. Henry Ford, at the beginning of the century, and the automobile industry, today, applied the finishing touches to an idea born of the human brain and produced by human hands thousands of years ago.

Nonmaterial Culture

Another part of culture consists of rules for human behavior. Nonmaterial culture is made up of behavioral expectations and ideas. Material and nonmaterial culture do not exist separately from each other. Sociologist Francis Merrill points out that material and nonmaterial are not different kinds of culture but merely different levels: "The basis of culture is found in the human mind, and the physical manifestations have meaning only in terms of these mental patterns. Ideas are the real foundation of culture. Material objects are useless without the knowledge of how to use them."[4]

What development would be suggested by the absence of telephones, radios and so on, in a highly developed society?

Human behavior is shaped by the knowledge, beliefs, and values of a society and by a system of rules that regulates behavior. This system is called the *normative system.* The normative system did not de-

[4]Francis E. Merrill, *Society and Culture* (Englewood Cliffs, N.J.: Prentice-Hall, 1969), p. 85.

velop in a day, a year, or even a generation. Each society arrived at this normative system in a cumulative fashion.

The normative system. A large part of a society's nonmaterial culture is dedicated to regulation of and prescriptions for behavior, called *norms.* Norms cover a wide range of behavioral standards. They dictate conduct in informal and formal situations and in insignificant and serious ones. Different categories of norms tell when it is right to shake hands with the left hand or with the right. Norms also tell when it is permissible to kill someone.

Under what circumstances, according to our norms, is it permissible to kill someone? How are the norms governing such behavior changing in our society?

Norms emerge when a society, through experience, finds a particular act to be either harmful or beneficial to the society. If the act is to be harmful, the society gives it negative value and forbids its performance. If the act is found to be beneficial, the society gives it positive value and encourages its performance. These ideas of right and wrong become the norms of the society. They are general clues as to how to behave in specific circumstances. Norms are internalized; in other words, they become part of the individual's ideas of right and wrong. People do not follow norms only because they fear punishment, but also because they believe it is right to do so. People who act contrary to norms usually feel guilty.

Pitfalls for the Unwary

One way folkways are transmitted is through books on proper conduct. These have ranged from a sixteenth-century Italian classic on proper decorum for courtiers to modern guides for those in search of respectability. Here is a recent sample, drawn from Emily Post's book of etiquette:

> *If food is too hot, quickly take a swallow of water. Never, NEVER spit it out! It is offensive to take anything out of your mouth that has been put in it, except dry fish bones and equally dry fruit pits or seeds. If you choke on a fish bone, cover your mouth with your napkin and leave the table quickly. To spit anything whatever into the corner of your napkin is not permissible. It is unpleasant to see anyone spit wet skins or pits on a fork or onto the plate, and it is excusable only if you get a bad clam or something similar into your mouth. Even then the best—because it is the least noticeable—method is to take it from your mouth in your fingers: thumb underneath and four other fingers forming a screen over whatever it is from lips to plate. And then wipe off on your napkin any moisture still on your fingertips.*

Elizabeth L. Post, *Emily Post's Etiquette,* 12th ed. rev. (New York: Funk & Wagnalls, 1969), p. 552.

There is disagreement over the origin of norms. Some social scientists and thinkers believe that norms, or rules of behavior, emerge first and then values grow out of them. Others believe that a value, or distinction between that which is good and that which is bad, emerges first and norms develop around it. Such speculation is best left to social philosophers. What is important to remember is that cultural norms are essentially a set of behavioral expectations, a system that tells a member of a society how his society expects him to behave in specific circumstances.

Whether values are derived from norms or the other way around, they may be defined as widely accepted beliefs or feelings that specific actions, relationships, sentiments, or goals are necessary for the society's well-being. Values are often held unconsciously by individuals, but they can often be detected as cultural themes that cut across more specific attitudes. Even in heterogeneous societies with many subcultural groups (discussed later in this chapter) a majority of people share a common core of experiences and traditions. The specific value orientation of a people is what makes American culture distinct from, say, Chinese culture. Value orientations are sometimes expressed in terms of a people's ethic. Sociologist Max Weber described two major cultural themes in his work *Protestant Ethic and the Spirit of Capitalism.*[5] In this work he compared the religious and economic institutions of Eastern and Western societies. He showed how the value orientations of some Western societies, derived from Calvinism and stressing individualism, hard work, rationality, and frugality, led to the spread of capitalism. The absence of many of these values in Eastern societies, on the other hand, maintained them in a feudal economic system for a much longer period of time.

What values might Eastern societies have that conflict with the adoption of an ethic prescribing hard work and rationality?

Folkways. Because it is easier to examine a phenomenon if it can be viewed from different vantage points, sociologists have categorized cultural norms according to their importance and function. One such category is *folkways,* a term first used by the early American sociologist William Graham Sumner (1840–1910).[6] Folkways are those norms that specify expected behavior in everyday situations. How many times a day members of a society are expected to eat, what types of food are eaten, how food is obtained, what types of clothes are worn to different social functions, and how people behave at a funeral—all these customary and habitual ways of acting are guided by folkways. Every culture develops a great number of folkways, but complex societies display an extraordinarily large number of them. Some folkways become permanent features of a society—celebration of holidays, for in-

---

[5]Max Weber, *The Protestant Ethic and the Spirit of Capitalism,* tr. Talcott Parsons (London: Allen and Unwin, 1930).

[6]William Graham Sumner, *Folkways* (New York: New American Library, 1960). First published 1907.

stance—but others are transitory, such as fashions in clothes, furniture, or automobiles.

People do not find it easy to ignore folkways. The violation of a folkway can cause great embarrassment to both the violator and those around him. Deliberate and repeated violation of folkways may cost a person his job or his reputation. Nevertheless, violation of folkways will not bring about severe punishment from the society, because folkways do not dictate behavior in the truly significant areas of human life.

How might folkways be related to values? If it is a folkway to eat turkey on Thanksgiving, what kind of value is expressed in maintaining this tradition?

Mores. Some behavior is considered either extremely harmful or extremely vital to society. The patterns that guide such behavior are called *mores.* Mores define the rightness or wrongness of an act, or its morality or immorality. People who consistently violate folkways may be excluded from some groups, but people who violate mores are punished by the whole society. Violation of mores is considered a crime against the whole society.

Mores are perceived by members of society in terms of absolutes of right or wrong. In reality, mores are relative to time and place. As Sumner maintained, mores can make any act right or wrong because the society in which they exist believes the act to be right or wrong.

In many societies, at one time or another, mores permitted ritual murder, infanticide, cannibalism, incest, and other practices that we consider horrible today. But who are we to say that such actions are indeed horrible? Who is to judge whether killing an infant at birth is more cruel than exposing a whole society to starvation because of overpopulation? Often, we consider attitudes in India irrational and ridiculous because Indians refuse to kill their sacred cows even though people are starving. But a member of a society in which mores permit cannibalism as a means of survival would find our revulsion at the thought of eating human flesh equally irrational and ridiculous.

Even within a society, mores are not absolute. Child labor was considered perfectly justifiable in the United States only a century ago. Today, we think of it as cruel. Mores concerned with the treatment of minority groups, capital punishment, and especially sex roles are in a state of change at the present time.

Mores that are couched in negative terms and that revolve around acts considered extremely repellent to the social group are called *taboos.* The biblical command "Thou shalt not kill" is an example of a taboo; other taboos forbid incest and cannibalism. Both mores and taboos are deeply etched on the members of society. Some people actually become physically powerless to perform a forbidden act. Counterinfluences can, however, weaken the hold of mores and taboos on a substantial number of societal members, a fact that prompts the adoption of laws.

Why do you think our mores governing child labor have changed so much in such a relatively short time?

Laws. Mores sometimes fail to draw a clear distinction between acts that are forbidden and those that are permitted. Furthermore, mores are frequently violated. To define and reinforce the most important mores, most societies find it necessary to resort to laws. *Laws* are formal codes of behavior that are binding on a whole society. They specify both the behavior that deviates from norms and the punishment appropriate for each kind of norm-deviating behavior. The punishment is meted out by representatives of society.

Laws are particularly necessary in a complex, heterogeneous society that is experiencing rapid social change, because many norms are not clear enough for all groups to understand or accept. In simpler societies, which have stronger kinship ties, a smaller number of norms are sufficient to prevent chaos and maintain order.

What values are expressed by the laws against the smoking of marijuana? What contrary values are held by the violators of these laws?

Whereas most norms tend to be internalized by the members of a society in the course of socialization, laws may not be. Thus, the more nearly laws reinforce mores that are universally accepted in a society, the more successful are the laws. In the United States, it is difficult to enforce the law against the smoking of marijuana. Enforcement is unsuccessful partly because many people do not accept the norm forbidding its use. Another law, prohibition of alcohol, was so unpopular and difficult to enforce that it finally had to be repealed. Laws, then, can be repealed or modified. This gives laws an advantage over folkways and mores, which tend to persist as habits.

Sometimes, people hope that by passing laws they can change mores and folkways that lead to injustice and cause conflict in a society. The civil rights legislation enacted in this country has made specific forms of racism illegal. Although this legislation did not eliminate racism, the attitudes of which are functions of folkways and mores, it at least defined and reinforced certain values. Folkways and mores will probably eventually change to meet the conditions of the law.

Many critics of our penal system maintain that imprisonment and other forms of restrictive punishment are not a useful means of social control. Why might this be so? Do you agree? Why or why not?

Norms and social control. Every society must make sure that its members conform to most of its expectations. Otherwise, anarchy and disorder would prevail and the business of the society could not go on. How would we ever drive home at rush hour if people refused to obey the norms governing driving? How would we keep alive if we could not trust the driver in front of us to stop at the red light? Society therefore tries to exert *social control* on its members.

There are many ways in which a society exerts social control. The ultimate form of social control is physical force. If you drive your car at 75 miles per hour in a 35-miles-per-hour zone, you will have a heavy fine. If you fail to pay the fine you will be arrested. If you offer resistance, you will be bodily subdued and handcuffed. Physical force is at the core of political power and authority. But a society that depends on force alone to exert social control is a harsh one indeed. Most often, societies depend on more subtle methods of social control.

Social control can be exerted through economic pressures. Few persons will walk around the office in their bathing suits, because they know they may lose their jobs for doing so. Social control can also be exerted through occupational pressures. These pressures ensure that the majority of people occupying specific statuses play the roles appropriate to them and expected of them. The president of General Motors is not likely to be found in a corner tavern, drinking a shot

Keeping Telephone Workers in Line

The responses of some telephone workers are standardized through an elaborate system of social control, reports Elinor Langer, who worked as a customer's service representative in 1969 for the New York Telephone Company. It begins in the training program where service representatives are taught in detail the responses and procedures they should use in dealing with customers. The program's purpose, Langer believes, is to standardize responses and remove any possibility of a human transaction between representatives and customers. Langer gives this example: a customer calls to say: "My wife is dying and she's coming home from the hospital today and I'd like to have a phone installed in her bedroom right away." A correct response is: "Oh, I'm very sorry to hear that, sir, I'm sure I can help you, would you be interested in our Princess model? It has a dial that lights up at night." Simultaneously the representative writes: "Csr wnts Prn inst bdrm immed."

The uniformity of responses learned in the training program is maintained by a system of observers. The conversations of each unit (five to six women) are monitored by the unit's supervisor. (Representatives are aware of the system, but not whose conversation is being monitored). Meanwhile, a second level of eavesdroppers listen in at random to conversations, checking the accuracy of the information representatives give out. In turn, they are monitored by a third group. "One result of the constant observation," Langer says, "is that one can never be certain where the observation stops." Some workers told her they feared it extended to their own home phones.

Linked to the system of observers is the "Service Index"—comparative performance ratings for each unit. Langer's unit once received the best rating in Manhattan. Company officials presented the manager with a plaque. As a positive sanction for their good performance, the representatives were given free coffee and Danishes.

Elinor Langer, "Inside the New York Telephone Company," ed. William L. O'Neill, *Women at Work* (Chicago: Quadrangle, 1972), pp. 307–360.

and a beer, on a Saturday night. Such behavior would be considered undignified in his position, though it is considered acceptable for the factory workers.

Perhaps what keeps us in line more than any other societal pressure are the gossip, ridicule, disapproval, ostracism, and punishment heaped on us when we defy our society's folkways, mores, taboos, and laws. In our daily interaction, our behavior is constantly evaluated by others. When we behave according to the norms of our group, we receive positive sanctions. Positive sanctions consist of rewards. These rewards can be official—a judge may be named to the Supreme Court because of his outstanding performance. Rewards can be informal—someone who matters to us may give us a pat on the back, a smile, or a kind word.

Would you expect positive or negative sanctions to be most effective in social control? Is there evidence to support your view?

When we behave contrary to the norms of our group, we receive negative sanctions. Negative sanctions consist of punishment. Punishment, too, can be official—a person may be jailed as a result of breaking a federal, state, or local law. It can be unofficial—we may receive a stern look or an unkind word, be shunned, avoided, ridiculed, or lose prestige.

The unofficial sanctions we receive within our primary groups, especially within the family, have the most impact on us. This is because our families and our friends are part of our self-identification. We know who we are in terms of our relationship to them, and they are part of our self-image. When these people criticize us—or worse—our very self-image is attacked. Official sanctions, particularly the negative ones, can also be very significant. They may relieve us of our freedom, and even of our lives.

Another way of seeing how our behavior is continually weighed by others according to the prevailing norms, and how sanctions are distributed, is to look at our actions on a continuum, shown as follows:

Can you give an example of an undefined act, an act that is not governed by folkways, mores, or laws? Are any of our acts completely free of cultural influence?

Undefined Acts — Folkways — Mores — Laws

⟵——————————————————⟶

Suppose you are writing down what your instructor is saying with your left hand. Today, our society has no norm regarding left- or right-handedness. Your behavior is an undefined act. It is of no importance to society, and neither negative nor positive sanctions are exerted upon you.

But suppose that you are at a funeral, and just as the minister is praising the dead person, you start screaming: "Baloney! He deserves to be dead!" You would have violated a folkway that prescribes you to speak no ill of the dead, even at the cost of being a hypocrite. No doubt, the minister would give you a stern look, all the people would turn around to look at you with furrowed brows (negative sanction) and some might even say "Quiet!" or "Get out!" At any rate, you would probably be embarrassed and would feel more comfortable leaving.

Now, say you are a young minister, newly married, and in your first assignment. You like the people in your congregation, and you want very much to do a good job. But the youth group organizer, a woman you are forced to see and work with every day, is in your thoughts constantly. Even though you love your wife, you have never before seen anyone as interesting as the organizer is. What is more, she seems to like you too. So, one day you give in to temptation. Unfortunately, you are caught by the senior minister "in the act," as they say. You have violated one of our society's mores, or, in the view of the senior minister, a taboo—"Thou shalt not commit adultery." There will most certainly be negative sanctions. You may be fired or you may be disgraced in front of the congregation. And you will have to face the hurt look in your wife's eyes. Not only will you be embarrassed, but also you actually may have a difficult time getting another position. Adultery is not considered a serious violation of mores among all groups in society. Sexual fidelity is a value in transition. But a member of the ministry would still be expected to respect the mores pertaining to marriage.

Finally, if you kill someone in a fit of rage or in the course of a more deliberate transaction, you will have violated a mos (*mos* is the singular form of *mores*) of such importance that it has been codified into a law. The negative sanction in this case is life imprisonment, or in some states, death. Laws prohibit behavior that is considered extremely harmful to the society.

Occasionally you may hear a person described as *amoral.* How would a sociologist explain such a characteristic? How does *amoral* differ from *immoral?*

The desire to belong. Norms, and the positive or negative sanctions that follow our obedience or disobedience of them, are powerful mechanisms of social control. What makes them so powerful is the fact that we are tremendously anxious to be accepted by almost any group in which we find ourselves at any particular time. Researchers have found that in group discussions, individual members tend to eventually change their minds to conform to the consensus of opinions expressed by other members. In a group of twenty, if fifteen argue one point and five argue the opposing point, chances are good that, in time, the five opponents will come to agree with the majority. Demagogues, on the one hand, and group therapists, on the other, have long been aware of this deep desire of the individual to be accepted by the group, and have used this desire to change behavior.

The changing nature of norms. Most norms change with time and circumstance. During colonial times, a man found kissing his wife in public was subject to imprisonment. At that time, there was a law against kissing in public. In the late nineteenth century, kissing one's wife in public may have been disapproved of, but not punished by law. At the beginning of the twentieth century, the same act may have

Have you ever been involved in a conflict caused by the changing nature of norms? Was it easy to decide how to behave under those circumstances?

raised some eyebrows, but it was no more than a violation of a folkway. Today kissing one's wife in public disturbs very few people. There are other intimate practices between spouses whose performance is still prohibited by law and that would violate important societal norms.

[Culture as Structure: An Organized System of Behavior]

We stated earlier that culture is a patterned system of behavior, rather than a haphazard collection of folkways, mores, laws, and so on. (Remember, culture is a conceptual system—an imaginary model.) To examine the various parts of this system—the structure of culture—sociologists find it helpful to divide culture into several components.

A *trait* is the smallest element, or unit, of culture. In material culture, every single object that society uses is a trait. In nonmaterial culture, every single idea, symbol, or belief existing in a society is a trait. Thus, a nail, a brick, and a house are all traits of material culture. Saluting the flag (patriotism), kissing (a symbol of affection), voting (a belief in democracy), or praying (a belief in a god) are all traits of nonmaterial culture.

Develop a list of culture complexes all of which are involved in a single institution, such as the family for example.

A number of related traits that accumulate around an activity form a *culture complex.* Football is a culture complex. It consists of material traits—the football itself, uniforms, helmets, a field—and nonmaterial traits—the knowledge and ability of the players, a set of rules, a belief in winning, and team spirit. All areas of human life display numerous culture complexes.

When a number of culture complexes cluster around a central human activity, an *institution* emerges. Institutions are formal systems of beliefs and behavior, composed of interrelated norms and culture complexes.

Institutions primarily center on and help to fulfill universal human needs. Sociologists usually consider that there are five basic institutions, which arose from five fundamental human needs:

1. The need to regulate sexual interaction and care for the helpless newborn human being gave rise to the institution of the family.
2. The need to provide food, shelter, and clothing resulted in the emergence of the economic institution.
3. The need to maintain peace and order within a society led to the formation of the institution of government.
4. The need to transmit culture and train the young gave rise to the institution of education.
5. The dread and fear of the unknown created the institution of religion.

Could you envision a society in which one or more of the five listed institutions no longer was needed? What kinds of changes would be required to make an institution obsolete?

Although these basic institutions are common to all societies, the forms they assume vary from society to society. In following chapters,

Methodology: The Laboratory Experiment

Will people defy an apparently legitimate authority when his commands contradict a person's conscience? This is the question social psychologist Stanley Milgram tried to answer in a controversial and now famous laboratory experiment. In the laboratory experiment the researcher controls the environment. This allows him to alter at will the conditions, the setting, and the subjects in order to systematically observe the effect each change has on the results of his experiment.

Milgram's initial experiment went like this: subjects, all males, were told they were participating in an experiment on the effects of punishment on learning. Each subject was instructed to administer an electric shock to a "learner" every time he answered a question incorrectly, increasing the voltage with each wrong answer. The "learner," a willing participant, was strapped to the electric chair to prevent his escape once the test began. As the shocks increased beyond 300 volts, the "learner" writhed in pain and begged for release. As the subject hesitated, the experimenter would repeatedly command him to continue. The subjects, upset and confused by the choice between conforming to the dictates of an authority in the cause of science and responding humanely to the suffering of the victim, began sweating, groaning, or breaking into nervous laughter. Three subjects had uncontrollable seizures.

None of the forty subjects tested defied the experimenter before the shock level reached 300 volts; twenty-six obeyed orders to the end, administering the most potent shock possible. After the experiment the subjects were, in Milgram's phrase, "dehoaxed": the shock apparatus was declared a fake, the "learner" revealed as the experimenter's accomplice, and the true purpose of the experiment disclosed.

The question that inevitably arises in any laboratory experiment is whether the artificiality of the setting distorts the way people are likely to behave in the real world. This is one reason why the laboratory experiment is not one of the research methods most frequently used in sociology. Milgram's experiment, in addition, reopened a debate on the morality of some social science research designs. Critics questioned the morality and significance of Milgram's experiment because he had obviously tricked and provoked his subjects. By causing severe emotional stress to the subjects, critics said, Milgram himself had violated the very norm he was testing, that of not hurting a person against his will.

Stanley Milgram, "Behavioral Study of Obedience," *Journal of Abnormal and Social Psychology* 67 (1963): 371–378.

we will discuss, in detail, these and other institutions important to American society. For now, it is enough to look briefly at how institutions relate to the actions of individuals.

We can think of institutions as doing for people what instinct does for many animals. Institutions supply people with procedures detailing how to act in specific circumstances in a way the society desires them to act. In addition, people become convinced that the behavior outlined by the institutions is the only alternative open to them.

Sociologist Peter Berger illustrates the way institutions function with a clear and humorous example. He says that when a cat sees a mouse, the cat instinctively chases and eats the mouse. It is as if the cat heard the imperative: "Eat, eat!" The cat's behavior is nothing the cat *chooses* to do; it is somehow programmed to do so.[7]

We are also programmed, like the cat, but by institutions and society, rather than by genes. For example, social programming may seem to suggest that there are no alternatives to getting married. For some of us, there may seem to be no alternatives to going to college. Some people move down the paths society has programmed for them, without ever perceiving other possibilities.

Should we feel angry that our society suggests there are no alternatives when in reality there are? Perhaps we should. On the other hand, the belief that there are no alternatives often works to our own advantage, saving us time and trouble. What if the educational institution were completely open to all possible alternatives? Everyone would be learning totally different facts, ideas, and skills, perhaps by different methods, and pretty soon no one would understand anyone else. So, while it is true that many societies have been too heavy-handed in their demands for institutional conformity, they have made it possible for people to exist and flourish in groups, which is the way we must live.

[Cultural Differences and Uniformities]

Have you ever traveled abroad? What institutional differences from your own society made the most impression on you? Were there features that you would favor incorporating into our own institutions?

If you have ever traveled abroad, you must have personally observed things that are done differently in other societies than in your own. The degree to which societies differ depends partly on the distance between them. Canada will not greatly disorient an American, whereas China probably will. Societies also differ according to their cultural heritage and technological development.

Ethnocentrism Versus Cultural Relativity

Why societies differ has bothered thinkers and spawned theories throughout history. Unfortunately, judgments of particular societies

---

[7]Peter L. Berger, *Invitation to Sociology* (New York: Doubleday, 1963), pp. 87–90.

have tended to be made from the viewpoint of *ethnocentrism,* an attitude whereby one judges other societies by the standards of one's own. In the spirit of this attitude, the ancient Greeks called *barbarians* all those foreigners who did not speak Greek. The same attitude often leads an American tourist today to call *immoral* and *lazy* a people whose goals differ from those of his own culture.

Cultural Differences and Uniformities

Why would an American be likely to view other peoples as *lazy?* What impression might the same American make on those people? How might they describe him?

Ethnocentrism is present, to some degree, in all social groups. It is reinforced by many of our institutions—the family and education, in particular—and by the "we-against-they" feeling that characterizes every group. In moderation, ethnocentrism has the positive value of promoting unity and loyalty within a group. On the social order level, cohesiveness and loyalty lead to patriotism. In excess, ethnocentrism acts like blinders on a horse, hiding from view all the good features of other cultures. The slogans "America, right or wrong;" "America,

How Ethnocentrics Live: An Example

Our solid American citizen awakens in a bed built on a pattern that originated in the Near East but that was modified in Northern Europe before it was transmitted to America. He throws back covers made from cotton, domesticated in India, or linen, domesticated in the Near East, or wool from sheep, also domesticated in the Near East, or silk, the use of which was discovered in China. All of these materials have been spun and woven by processes invented in the Near East. . . . He then shaves—a masochistic rite that seems to have been derived from either Sumer or ancient Egypt. . . . He puts on garments whose form originally derived from the skin clothing of the nomads of the Asiatic steppes, puts on shoes made from skins tanned by a process invented in ancient Egypt and cut to a pattern derived from the classical civilizations of the Mediterranean, and ties around his neck a strip of bright-colored cloth that is a vestigial survival of the shoulder shawls worn by the seventeenth-century Croatians. . . .

When our friend has finished eating, he settles back to smoke, an American Indian habit, consuming a plant domesticated in Brazil in either a pipe, derived from the Indians of Virginia, or a cigarette, derived from Mexico. . . . While smoking, he reads the news of the day, imprinted in characters invented by the ancient Semites upon a material invented in China by a process invented in Germany. As he absorbs the accounts of foreign troubles, he will, if he is a good, conservative citizen, thank a Hebrew deity in an Indo-European language that he is 100 percent American.

Ralph Linton, *The Study of Man: An Introduction* (New York: Appleton-Century-Crofts, 1964).

love it or leave it;" and the inscription "God is with us" that German soldiers wore in their belts are examples of extreme ethnocentrism.

Ethnocentrism can also be directed against groups within a society. Such internal ethnocentrism is extremely divisive. Americans are facing racial turmoil partly because of ethnocentrism.

To counter the subjectivity of an ethnocentric approach, social scientists have suggested the alternative concept of *cultural relativity.* According to this concept, each culture is analyzed on its own terms, in the context of its own societal setting. No one has the right to use the values and norms of his own culture to judge any trait of another culture. There are no universal norms, or moral absolutes. Under specific circumstances, any act can appear good or bad. Therefore, any judgment we make of the act must be based on the context of the specific circumstance. Cultural relativity requires that any act, even if it is completely contrary to one's own norms, should be regarded positively if it fulfills the needs or satisfies the goals of the society in which it is performed.

Some implications of cultural relativity are troublesome. If we accept this concept, are we to condone Nazi Germany's attempt to annihilate millions of people simply because the Nazis believed that the mass murder of people they considered inferior would benefit their society? Isn't the act of annihilating millions of people wrong under any circumstances?[8]

One way of solving problems raised by cultural relativity would be to develop a world nation or society. What advantages and disadvantages would such a unification have?

Problems like these appear to be insoluble. All we can say is that cultural relativity requires its followers to display understanding of cultural features as they appear in societal settings. It does not require its followers to agree that a feature is good or to condone it in any way. Tolerance, respect, and understanding of cultural values, not their acceptance, is the objective of cultural relativity.

No amount of cultural relativity can spare us from experiencing a kind of culture shock when we are suddenly brought in contact with a culture quite dissimilar to our own. This is often the experience many Americans report when they first visit the ancient culture of India. Some never recuperate from the shock, are repulsed by their experience, and never want to go back. Others overcome their initial reaction and reach varying degrees of understanding of the culture.

Less shocking, but nonetheless somewhat bewildering to those of us reared in American society, is the culture of the Abkhasians, a group of Caucasian peasants living in the Soviet Union. While Abkhasians display a number of cultural customs similar to our own, it is the cultural differences that fascinate us. The most obvious difference is their longevity, and the way it is taken for granted. Other differences include (1) their attitudes toward work, sex, and food; (2)

[8]Robert Redfield, *The Primitive World and Its Transformations* (Ithaca, N.Y.: Cornell University Press, 1953), pp. 139–164.

their ideas of what constitutes beauty in women, and what erogenous zones are; (3) their beliefs concerning obesity and their antipathy toward smoking and excessive drinking; (4) their kinship structure; (5) the high status they attribute to people with increasing age; and (6) the comparatively unchanging nature of their cultural norms.

Theories of Cultural Differences

Early adventurers, missionaries, and even some anthropologists, unaware of the dangers of ethnocentrism, brought home tales of the fantastic and savage customs of the peoples they encountered in their travels. Not until social scientists used the scientific method in their research did they construct theories that attempted to solve the puzzle of cultural differences.

Some of these early theories were based on a racial explanation of cultural differences. But we now know that race is the result of biological differences and that we cannot explain a social product such as culture on the basis of biology.

Other theorists gave a geographic explanation of cultural differences, claiming that climate, elevation, topography, nearness to or isolation from other societies, and kinds of foods available were responsible for cultural variations. Much of the variation among cultures is, in fact, the result of geography. Obviously an Eskimo child will not be taught to build dwellings made out of palm fronds. Nor will an inhabitant of the Amazonian region learn how to build igloos.

How might theories of cultural differences based on geography have led to either conscious or unconscious racism?

Yet not all cultural variation can be explained by geography. Societies located at great distances from each other have developed a number of cultural similarities. And societies located in the same area have often developed very dissimilar cultural patterns. For instance, although the Hopi and the Navaho are neighboring tribes, the Hopi devoted their time to peaceful pursuits, whereas the Navaho were warlike; the Hopi were sedentary and agricultural, the Navaho nomadic and pastoral; Hopi men had one wife, and Navaho men many wives. Allowing for the obvious influences of geography, then, cultural variations to a large extent remain an enigma.

Culture, like an individual, is not changeless. Culture is an ongoing process, in which new elements are continually being added on to the elements already possessed. If a culture has adopted a given characteristic—peacefulness, violence, creativity, or whatever—that trend is not easily reversed.

Cultural Universals

As striking as some cultural differences appear to us, a close examination of cultures shows us that there are also remarkable similarities.

Abkhasia: The oldest residents of the village of Achandara, Lit Kvareliya (left) and Samson Dzheliya, like to smoke their Abkhasian tobacco.

The similarities are particularly apparent in institutions, for institutions arise in response to biological and emotional needs shared by all humans. As an example, all social groups regulate sexual relations to prevent haphazard reproduction and to provide for the welfare of offspring. Consequently, the institution of the family exists in all known cultures.

The form that institutions assume varies greatly from society to society. In some societies, marriage takes a polygynous form (the male is permitted many wives); in others, a monogamous form (males and females are permitted only one spouse at a time); and in still others, it is polyandrous (the woman is permitted more than one husband at a time). Kinship is traced through the father in some societies and through the mother in others. In preindustrial societies, the family institution performs almost all functions—including those of education, economics, and social control. In other societies, separate institutions perform these functions.

Not only do institutional forms vary but all the other culture traits and complexes surrounding the institution also vary. The countless traditions and rituals that have developed around the family institution—puberty rites, marriageable age, the value placed on women and so on—differ greatly from society to society.

Cultural norms, values, and beliefs are also unexpectedly similar. All people enjoy adorning themselves, whether they wear a ring through their nose or on their little fingers. All people seem to have some taboos regarding particular foods, whether pork or dog. All people have some form of music and dancing and some form of art or handicraft. All people indulge in superstitious beliefs of one kind or another; and so on. The social anthropologist George P. Murdock compiled a long list of elements common to all known cultures. The list is long and includes such widely differing elements as age-grading and weather control.

If you leaf through a magazine devoted to travel you frequently see photographs of people carrying out folkways that are quite different from our own. What essentials of human culture, shared with us, underlie these different folkways? Give some examples.

Similarities common to all cultures are called *cultural universals.* They are general themes on which each culture develops its own variations. For example, Murdock includes hospitality on his list of cultural universals. Until quite recently, in the Eskimo culture, a hospitable host loaned his wife out for the night. In the Chinese culture, a host felt obligated to give away any object admired by his guest. In the Arabic culture, no host was satisfied until his dinner guest approved the meal with a hearty belch. What is significant, however, is that the cultural universal of hospitality is present in all societies.[9]

[Ideal Versus Real Culture]

Ideal Versus Real Culture

We must realize that although culture guides and directs our everyday behavior through its normative and institutional systems, it does not guide everyone's behavior. Some individuals never internalize the cultural norms. Others deliberately reject norms. But no individual—whether he is considered a deviant or simply a nonconformist—ignores or rejects *every* cultural norm. Such an individual could not exist among members of a society.

We often hear a person described as a *nonconformist;* usually such a person is valued quite differently from someone who is described as a *deviant.* What differences are implied by these two terms, in everyday usage?

More importantly, we should be aware that there exist, in every society, behavioral patterns that are not condoned by the culture, yet that are widely practiced. The term *overt* culture describes officially accepted patterns, while *covert* culture describes unofficial rules for behavior. For instance, many people who vote to keep their states "dry"

---

[9]George Peter Murdock, "The Common Denominator of Cultures," in Ralph Linton, ed., *The Science of Man in the World Crisis* (New York: Columbia University Press, 1945), pp. 123–142.

Have you ever encountered and had to deal with a double standard that applied to a decision you had to make? What factors were involved in your decision?

You may have heard the statement, "Do as I say and not as I do." How does this statement reflect real and ideal culture? How effective is a command to live ideally, if it comes from someone who does not live ideally?

(to forbid the sale of alcohol by the glass) rather like the stuff in private, and drink it regularly. Others subscribe to a rigidly moralistic system of sexual behavior in public, while promiscuous in private. Long lists of such double standards could be drawn up.

The fact is that we can recognize in each society an *ideal culture* (the formally approved folkways, mores, and laws) and the *real culture* (what people really do, how they really behave). When we speak of cultural norms we are usually speaking of the ideal cultures. When we refer to the real culture, we speak in terms of statistical norms—how many people actually behave in specific ways. For example, it is a cultural norm in a democracy that everyone is equal before the law. But the statistical norms show that members of minority groups are less equal than members of the dominant majority. Minority members are arrested more frequently, sometimes for minor infractions, and they receive longer sentences. In other words, there is a discrepancy between the ideal and real patterns of behavior.

The existence of many such discrepancies in a society may indicate that social control has not been sufficiently developed among members. Or it may indicate that for some reason the mores in question are too difficult for a majority of people to uphold. In the long run, patterns tend to catch up to the ideal ones, or the ideal tends to catch up to the real. The process of transformation, in any case, takes many generations. Needless to say, only the ideal patterns are taught formally by church or school. The real ones are picked up informally, generally through primary group relationships. They are consequently often more effectively learned than the ideal patterns.

[Subcultures and Countercultures]

So far, we have discussed culture on a societal level, noting uniformities and variations among whole societies. However, uniformities and variations also occur among the groups that make up a society. This is especially true of the heterogeneous, technologically developed societies that are beginning to predominate in the modern world.

Subcultures

In our society, which is extremely heterogeneous, groups are formed according to the members' race, ethnicity, religion, and numerous other distinguishing features. Even in homogeneous societies, in which members belong to the same ethnic and religious groups, people form additional groups based on the region in which they live, their occupation, their social class, their sex, and their age. Such groups are called subcultures. A *subculture* has distinctive features that set it apart from the wider culture of the society, yet it retains the principal features of the general culture.

Subcultures and Countercultures

The word *subculture* never implies any inferiority to the larger culture. It simply distinguishes a subdivision. As a matter of fact, membership in a subculture enriches an individual's life because it provides him with additional alternatives—with other ways of doing things—with which he can reach society's goals.

Because our society contains a number of subcultures, almost all of us have been brought up within one. For example, American teen-agers form a subculture. They remain within the general framework of the overall culture and are guided by its patterns of behavior. At the same time, some of their interests and behavior are peculiar to their age group. Teen-agers have a special language, a distinctive manner of dress, a taste for particular kinds of music, and a fondness for specific foods.

In some instances, a single family may develop patterns of behavior that are sufficiently distinctive to qualify it as a subculture—for example, some of the families described in William Faulkner's novels and Tennessee Williams's plays. In other instances, a subculture may consist of people forgotten by time (or people who have forgotten time). For example, the Amish and the people of Appalachia speak, behave, and hold the values of their pioneer predecessors.

Often, subcultures arise around a particular occupation. The families of professional military men, astronauts, ministers, and university professors (especially in small university towns) may, in some cases, be considered subcultures. Musicians, whether of the jazz, rock, or classical variety, form subcultures, too. Institutions—the school, the military, the government—develop behavior patterns and a language that may be considered subcultural. The world of entertainment—show business—is yet another example of a subculture.

The relationship between the overall culture of a society and its subcultures is, therefore, not static. There is a continuous flow of influence from culture to subcultures, and vice versa. For example, the jargon of the jazz musician eventually found its way to the general public, just as the jargon of the rock musician is doing today.

What subcultures, if any, can you identify with? What have these subcultures contributed to the culture of our society as a whole?

Most of us are members of a religious subculture. If we are Catholics, we are familiar with the names of many saints and what their special areas of concern are; we know what the Feast of Ascension celebrates, or what the meaning of the Lenten season is. If we are Jewish, we will at least know what the term *kosher* signifies and that we are supposed to fast on Yom Kippur.

Religious groups are obvious examples of subcultures, as are racial and ethnic groups. But we seldom think of long-settled Americans as "ethnic" or even as subcultural groups. Still, the Appalachians—those to whom many an ethnocentric city dweller refers as "hillbillies"—constitute a subcultural group. Because of long isolation in their mountainous regions, they have developed a culture that touches the culture of the society in general, but that also possesses many elements all its

These Hasidic scholars, who live in Brooklyn, New York, are members of an American subculture.

own—from differences in language to values and goals.

Countercultures

Some groups within a society adopt a value system and goals that are in direct opposition to those of the larger culture. Such groups may or may not have other distinguishing features. In any case, many sociologists consider these groups not merely as subcultures, but as *countercultures.* Some criminal groups may be considered countercultures, although not all, for many criminals accept the final goals of our society and reject only the means of attaining them. However, a gang of delinquent boys or girls, for example, is usually considered countercultural. Although such a gang has a definite set of values and standards of behavior, they are not the same values and behavior accepted by society at large. In fact, they tend to challenge or run counter to the values and behavioral standards of the larger society.

In recent years, the term *counterculture* has been used to refer to a movement springing from some young people—the so-called flower children, or hippies, or simply those in search of alternative life-styles. Today, this movement has lost much of its initial momentum, perhaps

Subculture, Counterculture, or Mainstream?

How would you classify groups like those headed by the famous gangster of the 1920s, Al Capone? Here is an interviewer's account of what happened when he made a sympathetic remark about Capone's hard beginnings growing up in the slums of Brooklyn:

> *"Listen," he said, "don't get the idea I'm one of these goddam radicals. Don't get the idea I'm knocking the American system. The American system—" As though an invisible chairman had called upon him for a few words, he broke into an oration upon the theme. He praised freedom, enterprise and the pioneers. He spoke of "our heritage." He referred with contemptuous disgust to Socialism and Anarchism. "My rackets," he repeated several times, "are run on strictly American lines and they're going to stay that way. . . .*
>
> *"This American system of ours," he shouted, "call it Americanism, call it Capitalism, call it what you like, gives to each and every one of us a great opportunity if we only seize it with both hands and make the most of it."*

Claud Cockburn, *I, Claud* (Baltimore: Penguin Books, Harmondsworth, Middlesex, 1967), pp. 118–119.

because as a society, we have partly adopted some of the attitudes and values previously considered countercultural. For example, long hair, once strictly a mark of countercultural youth, is today an almost universal mark of the youth subculture. The same is true of informal, utilitarian attire. On a more important level, living together without institutional marriage or outside a nuclear family, also once typical of counterculture members, is becoming commonplace among a substantial number of young people.

What values are at stake today in conflicts between society as a whole and the youth subculture? Are these conflicts as sharp today as they were a decade ago? What events may have affected the counterculture of the hippies?

The basic difference between subcultures and countercultures lies in their attitude toward society. Subcultures, for the most part, reinforce the cultural patterns of the larger society, while allowing loyalty to a smaller group. The newly-arrived immigrant may feel more at ease living among other immigrants in a "little Italy" or "Chinatown." But basically his goals are the same as those of a native: to get a good job, to save money, to buy a house, to educate his children, to attain a higher standard of living, and so on.

Countercultures, on the other hand, reinforce their members' rejection of the goals, values, and norms of the society at large. Members of countercultural groups may think it foolish to work for wages when there are other ways of making money; or to buy a house when they can "crash" in someone else's "pad"; or to try for a higher material standard of living when happiness can be obtained in other ways. They defy the conventional norms of society, but remain faithful to the norms of their own countercultural group. In this way they are able to rationalize their deviation from conventional norms and are strengthened in their resolve to continue defying dominant patterns of behavior.

One of our laws, the Constitution, guarantees the right to the pursuit of happiness. What values does this law embody? What different ways of achieving the same value may be expressed by a society and its countercultural subgroups?

Finally, subcultures flourish in our society because we are a multigroup society to begin with, with many racial, ethnic, and religious backgrounds. The fact that we are a highly specialized, industrial, technological society also adds to the variety of our subcultures. Perhaps even the fact that there are so many of us forces us to depend on a subculture. In general, however, countercultural groups usually appear in response to people's frustrations with the dominant society.

[Summary]

Interacting human groups that provide the basis of social structure are usually examined in the context of the largest social order, society. A society is a large group of individuals who interact with one another on a regular, continuous basis and according to patterns of behavior on which all more or less agree. It is also an interrelated network of social relationships that exist within the largest social system. The members of a society lead a common, total life. In other words, of all groups, a society has the highest degree of self-sufficiency, or the least degree of dependence on other groups. Today, most societies correspond to the nation-state.

Sociologists usually classify societies according to either their chief mode of subsistence, or their basic patterns of social organization. For several hundred years, societies have been moving from the traditional model toward the modern industrial model, which is characterized by great numbers of people, heavy reliance on secondary relationships, and emphasis on institutional forms.

The most important product of the interaction occurring in societies is culture. Culture is both the way of life of a people and the product of and guide for further social interaction. Culture has both material content (tangible objects) and nonmaterial content (ideas, values, knowledge, and beliefs). Much of a society's nonmaterial culture is made up of norms, rules of behavior that are learned and shared by each member of the society through interaction. Norms include folkways, mores, and laws.

To examine culture as a structure, we may divide it into traits (the smallest units of culture), culture complexes (a number of related traits), and institutions. Institutions are formal systems of beliefs and behavior, composed of interrelated norms and culture complexes. Institutions primarily center on and help fill universal human needs. Five basic institutions are common to all human societies: the family, the economy, education, government, and religion.

At a societal level, cultures display differences. Foreign cultures may appear irrational and silly if they are judged by the standards of one's own culture. This way of judging is called *ethnocentrism* and is practiced, to some extent, by all social groups. The concept of cultural relativity counteracts ethnocentrism by requiring that each culture be analyzed in its societal context and on the basis of how well it fills its members' needs.

Cultural differences among societies are the result of geographic and other factors, of which little is known. The similar characteristics displayed by cultures arise because all cultures must help to fulfill universal human needs, both biological and emotional. Characteristics common to all cultures are called *cultural universals.*

Because societies are made up of varying groups, culture also varies within a single society. Groups within a society may be formed on the basis of geographic location, social class, occupation, race, ethnicity, religion, and so on. Individual groups may have their own culture, including their own language or jargon, customs, traditions, and ritual. If the principal values of such a group are the same as those of the general culture, the group is called a *subculture.* If the principal values are in direct opposition to those of the larger culture, the group is called a *counterculture.*

Terms to Remember

Society. A fairly large group of individuals who interact with one another on a regular, continuous basis and according to patterns of behavior on which all more or less agree. A society is also an interrelated network of social relationships that exists within the boundaries of the largest social system.

Culture. The life-style of people in a society. Culture is both the product of social interaction and a guide for further social interaction. It is the totality of all that is learned and shared by the members of a society through their interaction.

Signals. Biologically determined and genetically transmitted responses to outside stimuli.

Symbols. Genetically independent responses to stimuli. Symbols are learned and can be changed, modified, combined, and recombined in an infinite number of ways. Language, music, and art are common symbol systems.

Normative System. A system of rules regulating human behavior.

Norms. Behavioral standards that dictate conduct in both informal and formal situations; a set of behavioral expectations.

Folkways. Norms that direct behavior in everyday situations; customary and habitual ways of acting.

Mores. Norms that direct behavior that is considered either extremely harmful or extremely helpful to society. Mores define the rightness or wrongness of an act, or its morality or immorality. Violation of mores is punished by society as a whole.

Taboos. Mores stated in negative terms. Taboos center on acts deemed extremely repellent to the social group.

Laws. Formal codes of behavior. Laws, which are binding on the whole society, outline norm-deviating behavior and prescriptions for punishing it.

Social Control. The process by which order is maintained within society through obedience to norms—folkways, mores, taboos, and laws.

Sanctions. Rewards (positive) or punishment (negative), directed at individuals or groups by either legal and formal organizations (official sanctions) or the people with whom we interact (unofficial sanctions) to encourage or discourage some types of behavior.

Culture Trait. The smallest element, or unit, of culture. In material culture, it is any single object. In nonmaterial culture, it is every single idea, symbol, or belief.

Culture Complex. A number of related traits that accumulate around an activity.

Institution. A number of culture complexes clustering around a central human activity.

Ethnocentrism. The attitude by which one assumes that one's own culture is right and that cultural patterns different from it are wrong.

Cultural Relativity. An attitude by which each culture is analyzed on its own terms, in the context of its own societal setting.

Cultural universals. Similarities common to all cultures.

Subculture. A group that has distinctive features setting it apart from the wider culture of the society, but still retains the general values of the wider culture.

Counterculture. A group that possesses a value system and goals that are in direct opposition to those of the larger culture.

Suggestions for Further Reading

Barnouw, Victor. *Culture and Personality.* Homewood, Ill.: Dorsey, 1973. A definitive text on culture that includes the various ways in which the concept has been defined, as well as a survey of the numerous studies and methodological approaches to the subject of culture.

Benedict, Ruth. *Patterns of Culture.* Boston: Houghton Mifflin, 1961. A classic work in which a well-known anthropologist shows how different cultures function to produce useful members of their societies.

Hall, Edward T. *The Silent Language.* New York: Doubleday, 1959. Also, "Our Silent Language." *Americas,* 14 (February, 1962): 5–8. A description of nonverbal actions and behavior, showing the differences between the cultural norms of North and South America.

Suggestions for Further Reading

Kluckhohn, Clyde. *Mirror for Man.* New York: Fawcett World Library, 1964. A famous anthropologist writes about the value of studying cultures and offers numerous examples of ethnocentrism and culture shock.

Linton, Ralph. *The Study of Man.* New York: Appleton–Century–Crofts, 1936. A classic of anthropology, in which the role of culture in human societies is analyzed.

Linton, Ralph. *The Tree of Culture.* New York: Alfred A. Knopf, 1955. A posthumous work delineating the development of culture in various parts of the world and presenting a theory of cultural development and cultural change.

Lipset, Seymour Martin. "The Value Patterns of a Democracy: A Case Study in Comparative Analysis," *American Sociological Review* 28 (August, 1963): 515–531. The value systems of four major contemporary societies are examined and compared by an eminent political sociologist.

Miner, Horace. "Body Ritual Among the Nacirema." *American Anthropologist* 58 (June, 1956): 503–507. Reprint S–185 by Bobbs–Merrill Company, Indianapolis. A humorous description of a familiar culture as though it were seen through the eyes of an anthropologist from another culture.

Roszak, Theodore. *The Making of a Counter Culture.* Garden City, N.Y.: Doubleday, 1969. An examination of the forces leading toward the establishment of a culture opposed to the dominant values of a technological society and with alternative cultural patterns.

Shapiro, Harry L., ed. *Man, Culture, and Society.* New York: Oxford University Press, 1956. A collection of essays providing examinations of various aspects of culture from the viewpoints of physical, cultural, and archaeological anthropology.

Slater, Philip. *The Pursuit of Loneliness.* Boston: Beacon Press, 1970. Facets of American culture, particularly the values and norms surrounding the issue of individualism, are criticized by a contemporary sociologist.

Sumner, William Graham. *Folkways.* New York: Mentor, 1960. A reprint of a classic and definitive work. Subjects include customs, folkways, and mores, and the emergence of the normative system.

Wolfe, Tom. *The Pump House Gang.* New York: Bantam Books, 1968. A view of the subcultures formed by surfers, teenagers, motorcyclists, and others who have chosen to drop out of the dominant culture.

Yinger, Milton J. "Contraculture and Subculture," *American Sociological Review* 25 (October, 1960): 625–635. An essay clarifying the two important concepts in the title.

The individual in society: socialization and deviance

The situation described is typical of the bureaucracy that characterizes our society. (Bureaucracy will be more fully discussed in a later chapter.) What, in your opinion, is the advantage of a system that so frequently frustrates the individual?

IMAGINE FOR A moment, a situation that is probably familiar to you. It is a hot day in early fall. You, and a long line of other students, are waiting to register for the next academic term at your college or university. For forty-five minutes you stand in a small, airless room, pushed from behind and shoved from in front. Finally you are at the head of the line. You hand in a number of different forms, and after a lengthy examination, the registration assistant tells you that Form XX is not in order. You will need another signature, for which you will have to track down the professor. He might be in his office two blocks away, in the cafeteria having lunch, in the library doing research, or perhaps at home. After you have obtained the signature, you can return to the registration area. You wait in line a second time, to find out whether all your classes are still available. Then, maybe—but only maybe—you will be registered.

What is your reaction to this situation? Do you swallow hard, turn around, and leave muttering under your breath? Do you smile angelically, say thank you, and go to look for the professor whose signature you need? Do you slam the forms down on the table and scream that you don't have the time to go chasing after absent-minded professors? Do you try to threaten or coax the assistant into registering you immediately?

All these reactions, and many more, are within the realm of possibility. People react differently to the same situation because personalities differ. Why do they differ? What makes one person pleasant and optimistic, and another unpleasant and sullen? Why is one person generous to a fault, the other miserly? Why is one person courageous,

People react differently to the same events, depending on differences in personality. What do you think these people are reacting to?

the other a coward; one person peaceful, the other belligerent? Are people born with temperaments that determine how they behave? Or are temperaments molded by the learning that takes place in society? Do personalities develop by chance or by design? Are they formed by heredity or by environment?

So far we have been emphasizing the group aspect of human existence—the importance of group life and of social interaction. We have discussed how social interaction leads to the organization of a social system in which members behave in a patterned, fairly predictable way, according to the statuses they occupy and the roles they fulfill. We noted that interaction within our largest social system, society, creates the peculiarly human phenomenon called *culture.* Culture is the basic factor differentiating humans from animals.

We must not lose sight, however, of the fundamental element of groups—the individual human being. It is individuals who, in their interactions with one another, develop patterns of behavior for society. To understand how groups function, we must understand how the individual functions. We must examine human personality, including the forces—biological, psychological, and social—that create it and affect it.

What do people mean when they comment that "so-and-so really has personality"? Do you think this usage is acceptable to sociologists? Why or why not?

[What Is Personality?]

Personality is a familiar word. We all know what is meant by such expressions as "What a nice personality she has!" and "He has no personality at all!" From a scientific point of view, however, such statements are nonsense. Every human being has a personality. Whether a person is "nice," "not nice," or "insignificant" is part of the whole personality. *Personality* is a complex and dynamic system that includes all of an individual's behavioral and emotional traits—his attitudes, values, beliefs, habits, goals, actions, and so on. Of course, the term *personality* is an abstraction, a construct used by social scientists to refer to what appears to be fairly consistent behavior and emotional traits characterizing a specific individual.

The study of personality involves examining the motivation for behavior. It involves investigating the reasons why two people behave differently in the same situation. To understand why we behave as we do, we must look at ourselves in our physical and social environments, and our culture structure. We must try to understand ourselves from the point of view of how biological, psychological, and social factors affect us.

How would you describe your own personality? Do you perceive your personality to have changed as the result of specific events? In what ways?

Personality is a *dynamic* system. That is, personality continually changes as a result of specific events that affect the person, and in accordance with how the person perceives these events. We can also look at personality as a *circular* system. Our personalities dictate how we see our roles in society and how we fulfill these roles. At the same time, our roles in society, and the way we fulfill them, affect our personalities. Finally, each of us has a *distinctive* personality, because, while each of us is born with a specific set of inherited traits and potentials, each of us has nevertheless had experiences that have been exclusively ours. Even identical twins whose biological heredity is the same have different life experiences. These different experiences modify their personalities enough to make them distinct from one another.

Researchers involved in the study of personality include psychologists, sociologists, anthropologists, and even ethnologists, who study animal behavior in natural surroundings. Most of the research in the area of personality has consisted of speculations about what proportion of human personality is made up of inherited traits and what proportion consists of learned behavior. Basically, then, scientists are still trying to answer the question of whether we are predominantly biological or predominantly cultural creatures. There is evidence to support either view.

How would you set up a controlled experiment to find out what part of a human personality is inherited? Are there other ways to investigate this area?

Sociologists take all views into consideration when they speculate on how a new biological organism—the human infant—becomes a human being with a unique personality. But since sociologists stress the importance of interaction and the group nature of human life, these are the elements sociologists consider most important in personality formation. The bulk of our discussion of personality formation and deviation will be based on the sociological concept of socialization and internalization of norms. We will also present several personality theories with a biological, cultural, and behavioristic orientation.

A Social Product on a Biological Basis

Since human infants cannot survive in isolation, they cannot grow into mature beings unless they interact with others. Human personality develops only as a person relates to the people around him. This kind of relating is called *socialization,* a learning process during which members of society transmit to the new individual the social and cultural heritage of his group. At the same time, the new individual acquires a personality.

However, while personality is chiefly a social product, the process through which it develops—socialization—is facilitated, perhaps even necessitated, by a number of human biological characteristics. In the first place, humans generally lack strong instincts. Consequently, they are not programmed to behave in certain ways. Birds know instinctively that they must build nests at a certain time of the year. And they instinctively know how to build nests. But humans do not know instinctively that they must build houses. Nor do they know instinctively how to build houses. People must learn, through experience or from others, that without shelter they might freeze. And, if they are not told how, they learn how to build shelters by the process of trial and error, using whatever materials are available.

Of course, humans do have biological drives, such as hunger and sex. These drives are perceived as tensions or discomforts in the organism that cry out for some sort of relief. What action for relief should be taken is up to the individual to figure out, and he figures it out through learning. Learning how to satisfy biological drives is made much easier by culture, which represents the accumulated learning of countless preceding generations of people.

Why might the absence of instincts in human beings lead to creativity? How could you define and test creativity?

The absence of instincts is at the basis of human creativity. Faced with a biological imperative that he must somehow satisfy, the individual is open to direction by his group. He can also refuse direction, and find a better way of satisfying the drive, thus setting new patterns of behavior for future generations. Because of this freedom, humans are not uniform and totally alike. Each individual is unique.

Another human characteristic of biological origin is the human need for social and physical contact, which can be interpreted as the need for love. Children deprived of loving human contact—those institutionalized or simply neglected—do not develop normally either physically or mentally. Many grow up to be functional mental retardates (if they grow up at all, since death rates among such children are very high).[1] Although we do not know quite why and how, it seems that an absence of body contacts and stimulation in infancy inhibits the development of higher learning functions.

Our biological cousins, the monkeys, show a similar need for body

[1]René Spitz, "Hospitalism," in R. S. Eissler et al., *The Psychoanalytic Study of the Child,* vol. 1 (New York: International Universities Press, 1945), pp. 53–72.

Feral Children

Children who have grown up isolated from human contact are known as *feral* children—*feral* meaning untamed or wild. They are of special interest to sociologists and psychologists because they provide some case studies of the independent effects of socialization on human development. One of the more recent American examples is that of Isabelle, a child of about six years, discovered in Ohio in 1938. The illegitimate daughter of a deaf-mute, she was secluded with her mother in a dark room by her mother's family. When found, she could communicate only by gesture and shunned strangers, particularly men. Like many feral children, she was at first considered retarded and completely uneducable. Under intensive care, however, she developed at an amazingly rapid pace. By the age of fourteen she had graduated from the sixth grade.[1]

The most famous case is that of Victor, a child found in the forests of France at the close of the eighteenth century. Discovered at the age of eleven living on berries and capable of uttering only a single sound, Victor attracted the attention of Jean Itard, a psychologist eager to show that culture was a fundamental determinant of humans. Under Itard's tutelage, Victor grew from being totally uninterested in humans and incapable of imitation to a point where he desired to please his teacher and could grasp the rudiments of speech and writing. Itard's account inaugurated an historic debate over whether there is such a thing as "human nature" and has become a classic in educational literature.[2]

[1]Kingsley Davis, "Final Note on a Case of Extreme Isolation," *The American Journal of Sociology* 3 (March 1947): 432–437.

[2]Lucien Malson, *Wolf Children and the Problem of Human Nature,* and Jean Itard, *The Wild Boy of Aveyron* (New York: Monthly Review Press, 1972).

Speculate on why we may need body contact in order to develop fully. What kinds of parental behavior might help an infant develop its full potential?

contact. In experiments with rhesus monkeys, researchers found that although baby monkeys received food from a cold, wire surrogate "mother," in times of stress they ran to a soft and cuddly terrycloth "mother." They also preferred to spend most of their time with the soft surrogate mother.[2]

The fact that human infants are dependent on adults for a long time also predisposes them to accepting socialization. During this period of helplessness, infants are at the mercy of others. Babies *have* to accept socialization efforts in order to survive. At the same time, in-

[2]Harry Harlow, "Learning to Love," *American Scientist* 54 (September 1966): 244–72.

fants establish emotional bonds with those who care for them, so that infants eventually *want* to accept socialization.

Finally, the human animal has a high potential for learning and has the ability to use a symbol system such as language. The capacity for language is ultimately what makes us human. Through language we not only are able to transmit knowledge, but we can also express emotions, convey feelings, and acquire values and attitudes. Since we can communicate ideas, our interaction does not revolve around biological functions alone, but is of a symbolic nature. This symbolic interaction makes us capable of creating culture. In turn, culture facilitates our lives in society.

If someone says that he does not communicate well with his parents, what kind of relationship do you suppose he has with them?

Socialization: A Two-Way Process

Socialization begins when the infant, tense from an imbalance in his organism—revealed by hunger, thirst, cold, discomfort, pain—discovers that someone helps him relieve his tensions. The child soon comes to associate that someone—usually the parents but, later, other members of the household—with pleasure and the relief of tension. The presence of those persons becomes a goal in itself and does not simply represent a means of being fed and comforted.

In accepting the parents as pleasure giving, the infant takes the first step toward accepting all others as necessary to his comfort. In tending to their newborn in culturally prescribed ways, the parents, in turn, encourage the child to solve biological needs in socially approved ways. They also introduce him, through gestures and language, to human communication. From this time on, the new individual learns to take others into account and to define himself in terms of them.

It is often pointed out that human beings have the longest maturation period of any animal. How might this length of maturation encourage socialization of the individual?

Socialization is a two-way process. It permits society to mold each new generation of biological beings into human beings who accept the culture of their elders. It permits the infant born into society to familiarize himself with and learn how to behave in an environment already prepared by countless preceding generations. In the process, it permits the individual to develop a unique personality.

Social interaction, as you can see, is a human necessity. Without it, society cannot pass culture from generation to generation, and the individual cannot develop a self and a personality. Social interaction takes place through the use of symbols, the chief of which is language. Sociologist Robert Nisbet suggests that:

The whole experience of growing up is essentially the assimilation and internalization of values, ideas, techniques, and ways of behavior that are already in existence when each of us comes into the world. But we must think of symbolic interaction as forming the very stuff of human personality, character, self, and identity. Only through communication in terms of shared symbols is it possible for each of us to acquire his sense of self, character, and identity.[3]

[3]Robert A. Nisbet, *The Social Bond* (New York, Alfred A. Knopf, 1970), p. 59.

Aims of socialization. The specific aims of the process of socialization may be stated as follows: (1) teaching the fundamentals of life in society; (2) instilling societal aspirations; (3) transmitting skills important in the society; and (4) teaching to fulfill social roles.[4] A person's identity—who he or she is—is also largely provided by socialization.

Were there any attitudes that your family managed to transmit to you without openly expressing them? How did you figure out what attitudes were being suggested?

Socialization occurs on both a conscious and an unconscious level. While children may deliberately be taught particular behavior, attitudes, and values, whether at home or at school, other behavior, attitudes, and values—especially of the society and of in-groups—may not be deliberately taught. But from the conversation and actions of the adults around him, a child may deduce what they are. Ethnocentric and racial feelings are often transmitted in such a manner.

Agents of socialization: the family. Obviously, the attainment of human personality ordinarily takes place in the context of the family. The family plays a crucial role in the process of socialization for a variety of reasons. First, the family influences the child in the earliest stage of development. Second, the family attempts to meet all of the child's needs, both physical and emotional. Third, the family is the most constant influence in an individual's life, because he usually maintains a relationship with it from infancy into adulthood. Fourth, the family is a primary group and the individual learns most readily from persons with whom he has close personal and emotional ties. Finally, the child is born into the same racial group and social class to which his family belongs. His class position determines to a great extent what he internalizes—that is, what becomes a part of him—from the culture. Members of different social classes have different socialization experiences.

Make a list of major attitudes that you hold. How many do you attribute to the influence of your family? To the influence of a peer group? Which do you feel has had more impact in shaping your personality?

The family, of course, is not the only influence on human social development. The school—beginning with nursery school or day-care centers—peer groups, occupational or recreational groups of which the individual becomes a member, and the mass media also have a great impact on the socialization of the individual.

In *The Lonely Crowd,* David Riesman and his coauthors suggest, in fact, that in modern societies the peer group is more important in socialization than are the parents. According to Riesman, the personality type that emerges from modern methods of socialization is "other-directed." That is, unlike the individual who lives in less populated, nonindustrial societies, the other-directed person does not act primarily according to well-defined internal standards, but behaves in ways that make other people like and approve of him. The peer group is very important to the child. And parents, instead of instilling strict standards of behavior, accept the influence of the child's peer groups and instill values of popularity and approval.[5]

---

[4]Frances E. Merrill, *Society and Cultures* (Englewood Cliffs, N.J.: Prentice-Hall, 1969), pp. 99–100.

[5]David Riesman et al., *The Lonely Crowd* (New Haven, Conn.: Yale University Press, 1961).

The peer group may indeed play a more important part in socialization than it did in the past. Generally, however, the peer group and the institutions and individuals who strongly influence socialization act upon foundations already instilled within the family.[6]

Socialization: The Acquisition of Self

How far back do your childhood memories go? What kind of personality did you have as a child? To what extent was that personality a reflection of how others saw you?

Following birth, the infant is totally unaware of self. He is a living bundle of drives that create tensions unless they are satisfied. He does not know that he is human, or that he even *is.* At first, the infant is unable to distinguish between parts of his body and other objects in his environment. Eventually, he notices that others act toward him in a specific manner, distinct from the manner in which they act toward

According to Cooley's looking-glass theory, we develop our self-image by seeing how others see us.

objects and other people. From this realization the new individual recognizes that he is separate, distinct, and different. The self—the awareness of one's distinctiveness—emerges as a result of interaction with others. Through interaction, the individual learns from others who and what he is in relation to them, and how he should feel toward himself as a result of this relationship. The individual's behavior also follows the clues given by those around him. Socialization is generally consid-

[6]Kingsley Davis, *Human Society* (New York: Macmillan, 1949), pp. 405–406.

ered successful when the individual behaves as he thinks those around him want him to behave.

Cooley and the looking-glass self. Many theorists have attempted to describe the processes through which the self emerges. The most accepted sociological theories on the subject are those of Charles Horton Cooley and George Herbert Mead, two pioneer American sociologists.

Cooley believed that the development of human personality, and particularly the development of a socially defined self, must begin in the early stages of human life. In interaction with his immediate family and, later, with peer groups, the maturing individual learns that he is distinct from others and his needs are satisfied because he is loved. He learns that he stands in a particular relationship to others and they continually make judgments about his appearance and behavior according to standards, or norms, with which he soon becomes familiar.

We sense the opinions of others from their reactions to us. On this basis, we determine whether our self is "good" or "bad," pleasant or unpleasant, and we behave accordingly. Cooley thought that this process, which he called the "looking-glass self," consisted of three elements: (1) we imagine how our behavior appears to others; (2) we imagine how others judge our behavior; and (3) we feel pride or shame about others' judgments of us.[7]

In short, we look into an imaginary mirror. The mirror reflects back to us our image as others see us. If the image is good, we are satisfied with ourselves. If the image is bad, we feel ashamed. We all know the feeling. When we dress for an important occasion, we wear our most becoming clothes because we anticipate other people's reaction to our attractive appearance. The imagined judgment of others is what, in reality, creates us. Throughout our lives, we continually present ourselves to others in the hope of making a favorable impression. When a favorable impression is reflected back to us, only then do we feel good about ourselves.

To emerge and develop, the human self must have a mirror that reflects its image. It must have other people who react toward it, although others need not be physically present at all times—the individual soon generalizes others as "they," and perceives "their" reaction and judgment even in their absence.

Mead: mind, self, and symbolic interactionism. The theory that social interaction is the basis of the emergence of self and personality was further developed in the work of George Herbert Mead (1863–1931). Mead is responsible for a school of social psychology called *symbolic interactionism.*[8] There are many complex ideas embodied in symbolic

---

[7]Charles Horton Cooley, *Human Nature and the Social Order,* 1st ed. 1909 (New York: Schocken Books, 1964), p. 152.

[8]George Herbert Mead, *Mind, Self, and Society* (Chicago: University of Chicago Press, 1934).

interactionism, but they all center around the interrelationship of *mind* (the abstract whole of a person's ideas); *self* (the individual's self-conception, or self-awareness); and society. Symbolic interactionism clarifies the process whereby the biological organism becomes an actual human being through interaction of a symbolic nature—gestures and language. It explains the procedure by which the agents of socialization accomplish their work.

Mead maintains that the first prerequisite for personality formation is social, and especially symbolic, interaction. Such interaction precedes the acquisition of language, mind, and the consciousness of self. Symbolic interaction is at first nonverbal—the infant cries and the parents respond to it—and sets the stage for more meaningful communication through language. At first, when the infant cries, he is not deliberately trying to communicate hunger, thirst, or wetness. He does not know that he is experiencing hunger, thirst, and wetness. But when his parents routinely respond to his crying with a bottle, or a breast, or a fresh diaper—or just some cuddling—these answering actions assume a meaning for him. In the future, he will cry to elicit a response, conveying a fairly clear meaning to his parents as to the nature of his complaint.

What are some of the advantages of being able to use language in situations where an animal would use instinct or experience? Why do you think communication skills are stressed in school?

Mind and self do not emerge until language is present, because they involve manipulating and communicating through ideas. Actions are replaced with ideas once language is acquired. Mind and self are social products because the individual internalizes, or makes his own, the attitudes of those around him through the medium of language.

Mead suggested that we develop personality by imitating the behavior of people around us.

The child learns not only what the word *fire* stands for, but also people's attitudes toward fire (it is dangerous). Not only does the child learn to take on the attitudes of others toward objects in his environment, but he also learns to take on the attitudes of others in regard to himself. The new individual thus becomes capable of thinking about himself as he thinks about others. He becomes an object to himself.

Sometimes you may hear of a person described as being alienated from himself. How might such a process relate to Mead's analysis of self-objectification? Would such a person be likely to develop warm relationships with others? Why or why not?

This ability, apparently peculiar to humans, becomes evident as soon as the child begins to realize the distinctions among *I*, *me*, and *you*. Then he begins to treat himself as he treats others. He thinks about himself, hates himself, loves himself, communicates and relates with himself. Most importantly, he learns to control his own behavior and direct it into meaningful channels. The new individual becomes self-critical because others are critical of him. This is how society begins controlling the individual.

The uniquely human quality of being able to get outside ourselves and to see ourselves as others see us—and in so doing, to define our self—is possible because of role playing. Children dress up as, and pretend to be, mothers, fathers, policemen, mailmen, and so on. During such games, each child speaks to himself and answers himself both in his own role and in the role of the person he is playing.

Mead believes that adult roles are learned through a three-stage process. In the first, preparatory stage (ages one to three), children imitate adult behavior, but do not really understand it. In the second, or play stage (ages three to four), children have more understanding of the behavior, but do not carry out the roles consistently. One minute the little girl is a witch and the next she is an explorer. The last stage is the game stage (ages four to five and on) where the roles played assume consistency and purpose, and where children sense the roles of other players and their mutual relationship.

By taking the role of others the child learns how others feel about him and how he must act in order to receive the desired response from them. Because he can put himself in the position of others, he learns how to anticipate their actions and reactions. This learning guides his behavior in his interaction with others.

At first, others whose role the individual takes are members of his family and of his peer group, or as Mead calls them, *significant others.* At a later stage in the development of the self, the individual learns to take the role of society as a whole. In Mead's terms, he takes into account the *generalized other.* This change occurs when the individual realizes that there are some situations in which he must take, at the same time, the role not only of one significant other but of several people. As in a ball game, the individual must take the role not simply of Bobby, Susan, or Billy, but of the whole team as a unit. He must take into account not only mother, dad, and Aunt Patricia, but all his friends, his whole age group, his whole community, and eventually his whole society. The change from taking the role of significant

Make a list of major rules for behavior that you try to follow. Can you identify the person or persons who first instilled these rules in you? Are any of them contradictory?

others to taking the role of the generalized other is complete when the individual, in considering an action, no longer thinks, "Mommy says I must not do it," but rather, "It's not right to do it."

When we begin to act with the idea in mind that we ought or ought not do some things because "It is not right," we have internalized—made a part of ourselves—the folkways, mores, values, and other norms of society. We no longer refrain from some actions out of fear of punishment or the displeasure of others but because we want to avoid blaming ourselves or suffering in our own self-esteem. We have acquired a conscience, which tells us what we ought or ought not do. No longer do we need the physical presence of others to direct our behavior. This internalized understanding of the attitudes of the generalized other controls the behavior of individuals sufficiently to permit the existence of a relatively free society such as ours, which is not totalitarian, but which does impose restraints on the individual.

What kind of personality would be formed if it were dominated by what Mead calls the *me* aspect of a person?

Although the self that emerges as a result of the internalized attitudes of others is principally of a social nature, it has another, more creative and spontaneous element. This element, which Mead calls the *I* emerges before the social element, which he calls the *me*. The *I* is the subjective, acting, natural, uninhibited part of the self. The *me*, in contrast, is the objective representative of cultural and societal expectations that have been made part of his personality by the individual. The *I* is unique to each individual; the *me* is conventional in that it is shared with others.

According to sociologist Erving Goffman, nearly all of our behavior is an act for other people. If this is so, how do you explain the development of people who continually elicit unfavorable reactions from other people?

Although the self is social, then, it is not entirely social. We are not just what others want us to be by virtue of having internalized the attitudes of others. These internalized attitudes are the demands that group life makes on the individual. Still, the individual is not bound to them alone. He is also free to act without taking the group expectations into consideration. Human behavior consists of varying amounts of the *I* and *me*. When the *me* is totally lacking, behavior is impulsive, irrational, and may be contrary to the welfare of the group. When the *I* is totally dominated by the *me*, social control operates at its most effective level.

Some individuals are controlled by the *I* to a greater extent than by the *me*. Their behavior often becomes troublesome to the group. Other individuals are said to be *over-socialized* in the sense that their *me* is always in command. Such individuals tend to lack spontaneity and creativity. The ideal situation for human behavior is one in which the demands of the *me* allow the expressions of the *I*.

As we said at the beginning of this chapter, personality theories abound because people tend to be fascinated with themselves and want to find out what makes them tick. Unfortunately, a theory that would explain it all has eluded us. The behavioral scientists who have studied personality formation and have come to theoretical conclusions about it have surely hit on some aspects of the truth.

Resocialization

In addition to acquiring the culture of his society as part of his personality the individual must sometimes undergo a drastic form of resocialization. Resocialization may be needed when an individual moves to an entirely new culture or subculture. Most often it is necessary when an individual joins a "total institution." In such institutions, the individual lives with a number of people who, cut off from the rest of society for a period of time, reside and work in a controlled, rigidly structured environment. The armed services, convents or monasteries, mental institutions, prisons, and prisoner-of-war camps are examples of total institutions.

Have you ever experienced life in a total institution, or known anyone who has? What was that life like?

The resocialization that takes place in such situations involves a definite set of procedures. First, the institution's representatives try to

Breaking Down Prisoners

The degrading practices employed by prison officials in their attempts to resocialize inmates tend to be of two sorts, says Jessica Mitford in a recent book on prisons. As one professor of criminology told her: "In 'good' prisons, like those in California, physical degradation is replaced by psychological degradation. I call these 'pastel' prisons; they look good, shiny, sanitary. But inmates will tell you thousands of ways in which they are psychologically degraded."

Here for example is how one ex-convict described his stay in a "good" prison's reception and guidance center:

> *During the initial six- to twelve-week quarantine period, which each man undergoes when he first enters prison, his manhood and individuality are subtly vitiated. The inmate may have less than a sixth-grade education. Yet he is subjected to a barrage of questionnaires, it's a painful and embarrassing experience. He'll be asked about "sibling rivalry" although he won't have the faintest idea what that means. And "Are you obsessed with fears of latent homosexuality?"*
>
> *It's vicious, attritional. The whole point of the psychological diagnosis is to get him to go for the fact he's "sick," yet the statement he's sick deprives him of his integrity as a person.*
>
> *Most prisoners I know would rather be thought bad than mad. They say society may have a right to punish them, but not a hunting license to remold them in its own sick image.*

Jessica Mitford, *Kind and Usual Punishment* (New York: Vintage Books, 1974), pp. 108, 113–114.

destroy the individual's present identity, substituting for it feelings of inadequacy and dependence on the institution. They do this through isolating the individual from the outside world, by having him give up his personal possessions for a standardized uniform, by calling him by a number or a status rather than by his name, and by taking away his freedom. If these methods are insufficient for a speedy erasure of personality, other techniques are attempted. These techniques include degrading and humiliating the individual by forcing him to perform menial and meaningless tasks. The individual, no longer "what he used to be," is further made to feel inferior, insignificant, and inefficient. The individual's superiors claim absolute authority over him. The individual is more or less severely punished for the slightest disobedience to the rules. Finally, any independence left in the individual is quickly stamped out by his peers, who put pressure on him to conform so they can avoid punishment to themselves.

Through such procedures—and in extreme cases, through additional techniques of brainwashing—it is possible to cause the individual to deny his personality and to acquire a new one acceptable to the institution. There is, however, evidence that even under conditions of extreme stress (for example, brainwashing), some individuals cling stubbornly to their identities, literally refusing to accept the new identities being forced upon them.

Have you ever succumbed to pressure of the sort being described here? How did you feel about yourself in the process?

From this, we must conclude that whereas some aspects of personality are susceptible to change, others resist it. Moreover, individuals react differently to attempts at resocialization.

[Cultural Determinism]

Since socialization experiences differ in each society, it seems logical that each culture stamps its members with some specific personality features that differentiate them from members of other societies. For example, if a certain society values, let's say, punctuality, it is reasonable to expect that most members of that society will be punctual and will demand punctuality in others. That trait will have been stressed in their socialization process. Punctuality will become an individual personality trait of most members. It will also be recognizable as a societal trait. A number of anthropologists and sociologists have emphasized the impact of a society's culture on individual and collective human personalities. The theories they have developed are grouped under the term *cultural determinism.*

In what cultures is punctuality a recognizable trait? What forces might encourage the development of punctuality as a societal trait?

For instance, the early sociologist Emile Durkheim (1858–1917) saw culture in terms of *collective representations,* which result from the collective consciousness of a society. Collective representations are what a cultural group accepts as true and valid. They are then internalized by members of the group. Each member of a society is coerced into conformity by these collective representations, which are unchangeable.

Later anthropologists reflect similar views. For example, Leslie White, writing in the forties, conceived of culture as an irremovable force created for an individual by his ancestors. White felt that culture manipulates the individual in the same way that a puppeteer controls a puppet. Humans must exist if a culture is to emerge, but they are merely the instruments through which cultures express themselves. Culture exists separately from humans, shaping them into what they are and, in the process, creating itself.[9]

Another anthropologist, Margaret Mead, does not place quite as much emphasis as White does on culture's function in molding human personality. Nevertheless, she maintains:

Have you ever experienced another culture? How might your personality have been shaped by that culture in ways that differ from your personality as it really is?

We are forced to conclude that human nature is almost unbelievably malleable, responding accurately and contrastingly to contrasting cultural conditions. The differences between individuals who are members of different cultures, like the differences between individuals within a culture, are almost entirely to be laid to differences in conditioning, especially during early childhood; and the form of this conditioning is culturally determined.[10]

Mead is, in short, saying that the culture of a society and the culture of groups within a society are the forces most responsible for personality. The anthropologist was led to this conclusion by her study of three nontechnological societies. The different cultures of these societies apparently molded their members into entirely different kinds of human beings.

Socialization as Role Learning

The basic elements of the social organization of groups are roles, statuses, and norms. In order for groups to operate efficiently, the members of the group must individually play the roles that befit their statuses according to the norms of the group. How do we learn to play our roles? Through socialization. How do we know which roles to play and which statuses befit us? Some roles are imposed on us by virtue of our gender, our age, our race, our nationality, and, when we are children, by virtue of our religion and social class. These are our ascribed statuses. Other statuses we achieve through our own efforts. These are our achieved statuses. Whether ascribed or achieved, the roles that go with our statuses must be learned.

When you were a child, what roles did you aspire to fill when you grew up? Do you still aspire to fill those roles? Why or why not?

We have also seen that an important part of socialization is our ability to take the role of the other. Essentially, that is how we learn all our roles. Of course, we do not acquire all the specialized skills of a role by simply pretending to be someone. These skills come much later, if the role really becomes ours. But we do acquire the values, at-

---

[9]Leslie White, *The Science of Culture* (New York: Grove Press, 1949), pp. 340–353.

[10]Margaret Mead, *Sex and Temperament in Three Primitive Societies* (New York: William Morrow, 1963), p. 280.

titudes, motivations, and emotions that go with a given role. The little girl who imitates her mother and treats her dolls as her babies certainly is not learning all there is to know about housekeeping and child care. But she is learning that it is a value in our society for women to become wives and mothers, and that children should be loved and disciplined. She is learning what her society will be expecting of her once she grows up and becomes a wife and mother. A similarly rigid—but different—set of role expectations is imbued in the little boy. Sex role expectations are changing, so these examples will eventually be obsolete.

In our specialized modern societies, we are expected to learn many roles throughout our lives. The most influential ones are the so-called *general roles,* based on age, sex, and occupation. Less influential, but still of some significance, are the *segmental roles* that we only play occasionally, as patients in a hospital, customers in a beauty shop, members of the PTA, and so on. The point is that every time we learn a new role, it alters our outlook on life and affects our patterns of behavior. Each new role influences our personality and demands some resocialization. When individuals marry, they must be resocialized to fit their new roles of husband and wife in society. The success or failure of the marriage will largely depend on how well they play their new roles, or at least on how well they play them according to each other's expectations. When a couple have a child, a similar role readjustment is required of the new parents. With each readjustment in roles, the personality is modified.

Have you ever tried to change the way a role is played out (for example, teaching your teacher something)? What was the reaction of other people to the change? How could you explain their reaction?

Socialization as Internalization of Norms

The socialization process can also be viewed as the internalization of norms. A child who has learned how to dress and feed himself, how to wash and brush his teeth, what to say when he sees someone, and who regularly follows thousands of similar patterns of behavior, has adopted the behavior patterns of the group that has socialized him. He has internalized the norms of that group. We can be fairly certain that he will behave according to these norms even when he is alone, out of reach of the group. When you are home alone, you may forego some manners that you would observe if others were there. You may not cover your mouth when you yawn. Or you may not bother setting the table when you eat. But in most respects you act pretty much the same way as when your family *is* home. Your personality, then, is also a reflection of the norms you have internalized.

No one internalizes every norm of the society, nor even every norm of the socializing group. Because each individual has unique socialization experiences, even within the same family, only some norms are internalized by most individuals.

What is even more important is the fact that we belong to a

Children often look forward to the day when they can do as they like, and imagine that they will want to stop observing certain norms. What is likely to happen to such urges before they reach maturity?

Double Standards in Two Cultures

Differences in culture account for a difference in the experience of adolescence for French and American males, Laurence Wylie, a specialist in French community life, believes. While he makes no pretenses of having made a thorough study, his ideas illustrate the possible fruits of cross-cultural research. Compared to most American children, he says, the French child is more restricted in early life. French children are taught to respect the limits imposed by others from an early age. Life is compartmentalized, the child learns, and rules are artificial, man-made conveniences that he must follow. Limits are also set for American children, but the emphasis here is on teaching ideal codes which the child will come to accept as his own and which appear as a part of reality itself.

The French child is more likely to be upset by the intensity of his feelings at the onset of puberty, but he is more accustomed than the American child to exercising self-control. The American child is suddenly confronted with a new set of limits. Adult attitudes change from encouraging his self-expression to expecting him to control his impulses. At the same time he learns that how people actually behave is far different from the ideal codes he has been taught. This double standard and the restrictive codes come as no surprise to the French child because this is what he has been taught all along. The problem for the French child becomes learning to live within clearly imposed limits; the problem for the American child becomes discovering behind the bewildering facade of ideal codes the real limits society imposes.

Laurence Wylie, "Youth in France and the United States," in Erik H. Erikson, ed., *The Challenge of Youth* (Garden City: Doubleday, 1965), pp. 291-311.

number of groups, each with its own set of rules. Sometimes the rules of one group conflict with the rules of another. In this event, we must choose which set of rules we will take as our own. This choice is hardly ever a conscious one. We are most likely to choose the rules of the group that provide us with the most satisfaction, or the group that has become most important for us—our primary and our reference groups. Generally we internalize some norms from each group, but the effect of our primary groups remains more influential than that of secondary or more impersonal groups.

What if our primary groups—our family, our friends—exhibit norms that are *not* shared by the society at large, but that actually run counter to them? More than likely we, too, would internalize at least some of these norms, a fact that could make us deviant in the eyes of society. The process of personality acquisition, then, includes the learning of both conformity to most societal norms, and conformity to some group norms that may conflict with societal norms. This conflict exists whether we are members of a subcultural group that is considered deviant by other members of society, or whether we are "normal," middle-class Americans who must choose between the norms of our parents, friends, professional colleagues, or our husbands or wives.

Do you feel that you have internalized any forms of deviant behavior? According to whose standards is this behavior deviant?

The National Character, or Modal Personality

The point made by Margaret Mead's study is that the culture of each society creates a specific personality type. This finding has been labeled the theory of the *modal personality,* or national character. For example, Mead, as well as other anthropologists, found that a culture that stresses competitiveness and one-upmanship—or success at the expense of others—and the importance of magic, produces a personality characterized by traits such as hostility, suspicion, secretiveness, jealousy, and distrust.[11]

Many people feel that common stereotypes such as "English humor," "Latin lover," and "Irish temper" are somewhat true. The basic personality type of Americans, at least in the mind of Europeans, is represented by an individual who is brash, loud, optimistic, and unconventional. The basic personality type of Englishmen, at least in the mind of Americans, is represented by a person who is reserved, unemotional, distant, traditionalist, and methodical.

Objections to Cultural Determinism

Unquestionably, culture and personality are deeply intertwined. In fact, because the individual acquires his personality while he learns his culture, personality formation and cultural absorption are really not two different processes, but two facets of the same process.[12] But culture alone cannot be responsible for the development of human personality. To say that is to ignore the differences among individuals. Furthermore, it discounts the individual's ability to interpret events and choose alternative courses of action.

The theory of national character is also increasingly coming under attack. For example, in heterogeneous societies like the United States there are a large number of subcultures, each of which has its own cultural traits. It is therefore unwise to make sweeping generalizations about national character.

Can you identify cycles of liberalism and conservatism in our history? What kind of period do you expect between now and the year 2000?

[11]Ruth Benedict, *Patterns of Culture* (Boston: Houghton Mifflin, 1934), chapter 5.

[12]Melford E. Spiro, "Culture and Personality: The Natural History of a False Dichotomy," *Psychiatry* 14 (1951): 19–46.

Theories involving cultural determinism are based on the assumption that culture does not change. However, there is ample evidence that the favored cultural traits of societies are not deep-rooted and can change with time and circumstances. These changes explain the cyclical nature of history—periods in which mores are liberal, relaxed, and permissive seem to be followed by periods in which mores are conservative, rigid, and highly controlled. Following this line of reasoning, we can say that whereas the "typical" American is probably still materialistic, the emergence of a countercultural movement seems to indicate that a reversal of materialism could be in progress.

[Normal Versus Abnormal Personality]

Why does the term *normality* generally carry a value judgment of "good," while *deviance* carries a value judgment of "bad"? How do such judgments affect the self-image of exceptionally creative people, for example?

Our discussion of the human personality would be incomplete without reference to what is commonly called the *normal* personality and to what constitutes deviation from it. The concept of normality is extremely difficult to define, primarily because it varies not only from culture to culture but within cultures. In our culture, for example, if a man shows fear of a menstruating woman, we would probably consider his behavior abnormal or neurotic. Yet in many nontechnological cultures, such fears are common and are considered perfectly normal.

Within cultures, the definition of normality varies according to time, class membership, and sex. Today, for instance, if a person tells us that sex is evil and the work of the devil, most of us would say that the person was greatly disturbed. Yet in Victorian times, that was a common view of sex. For another example, the conviction that hard work is a virtue is not completely shared by members of all classes or age groups. Members of the counterculture, in fact, may actually consider avoidance of hard work a virtue. Finally, worrying about wrinkles and impending old age is unfortunately considered normal for a woman. But men are not supposed to express worry about such things, at least publicly.

What is a victimless crime, and why are some people advocating that such acts be decriminalized? Why might society at one time have been threatened by such acts? Why is deviance on such issues no longer so threatening?

The problem of defining normality is further complicated by the changes taking place in our society today. We live in an era of social and cultural turmoil, publicized by the mass media. Social and cultural norms are changing more rapidly than ever before. Thus, a definition of normality based on "standards acceptable to the community" leads to the question: Standards acceptable in *which* community or to *which* members of the community? Smoking marijuana, for instance, is both illegal and unacceptable in most communities. But it is acceptable behavior in some groups and in other communities. Homosexual behavior is frowned on in most places. But gay communities, with their own churches and other institutions, are springing up in most large metropolitan centers. And unmarried women who live with men are certainly not considered "fallen women" as they may have been a generation or two ago. With societal and cultural norms in such a flux, def-

Methodology: The Field Experiment

In the field experiment the researcher meets an existing group on its own turf (in contrast to the laboratory experiment), but manipulates the conditions of the group to suit research purposes (in contrast to participant observation). The most famous research done in this way was a series of experiments conducted at Western Electric's Hawthorne plant in Chicago between 1927 and 1932 by a team of researchers headed by Elton Mayo.

In one experiment the working conditions of six women were varied to see what effect these changes would have on productivity. Regardless of the changes the researchers made, productivity rose. An informal group had developed among the women. They liked working in the test room away from their usual supervisors and believed their performance might lead to permanent changes in factory conditions. In other words, the experiment itself was the major cause of changes in productivity. Sometimes known as the "Hawthorne effect," the results have alerted subsequent researchers to the influence their own presence may have on the group under study.

In a later experiment the investigators explored what kind of informal organizations already existed among workers. For this purpose, fourteen men from one department were placed in a separate room. No other conditions were altered. The plant operated on a group piece-rate system whereby individuals were paid on the basis of how many pieces their group produced. The researchers expected the group to coerce its slower members into producing more. Instead, the workers censured deviance from the norm of what they considered a fair day's work. Particularly singled out were those "rate busters" who produced too much.

Interpretation of these findings has differed. Many have followed Mayo's lead in emphasizing this "restriction of output" as part of a process by which the group solidified itself in order to maintain its own equilibrium and protect itself from management. Others have seen in this process of censuring deviance a rational content. Workers, they say, restricted their output in response to the threat of layoffs and employer practices of reducing the piece rate when productivity increases significantly. Mayo's experiments demonstrated the existence of primary groups in bureaucratic institutions and showed the importance of social relationships in what had appeared to be only matters of fatigue and economy.

F. J. Roethlisberger and William J. Dickson, *Management and the Worker* (Cambridge: Harvard University Press, 1941); and Henry A. Landsberger, *Hawthorne Revisited* (Ithaca: Cornell University Press, 1958).

initions of normality are almost nonsensical. Behavior must therefore be judged on the basis of the effect it has on others.

Deviations from the Norm

Find out what the definitions of *normal* and *abnormal* are in a statistical context. How do these definitions relate to the sociological ones given here?

Even though normality is extremely difficult to define, it is usually necessary to make some distinction between behavior that is acceptable and behavior that is unacceptable. Unacceptable behavior harms both the individual and society. Keeping in mind the problems we have discussed, then, we shall use the definitions commonly accepted by social and behavioral scientists. *Normal* refers to behavior that is approved by our society and culture. *Abnormal* or deviant refers to behavior that is not approved. Abnormal behavior may consist of psychological life-adjustment problems or neuroses. Or it may consist of more severe personality disorders and psychoses, as well as of outwardly directed, antisocial behavior.

"Deviant" Behavior

We have enclosed the term "deviant" in quotation marks to remind you that it is a relative, not an absolute description. As we have said, this term may be defined broadly as behavior that does not meet the expectations of a group. In the eyes of the beholders—the members of the group—such behavior is usually considered undesirable. Naturally, a member who does not behave as other members expect him to represents a threat to the stability of the group. Not only is such a member likely to create disorder and disrupt the smooth functioning of the group, but he may also incite the remaining members to question or challenge group norms. For instance, say you live in a small, rural, midwestern community, in which the people are for the most part hardworking, God-fearing, and otherwise imbued with the values of the Protestant ethic. You may decide that you do not like to work and go to church, but would rather ride your motorcycle all day. You may decide to survive by breaking into the homes of others, stealing their valuables, and then selling them to a "fence." But you should not be surprised that the members of your community will consider you deviant and will try to punish you. You represent a threat to them in the sense that you steal their hard-earned valuables. And you are also a threat because your way of life challenges everything they hold dear. Your example may tempt their own children to stray from a path that they consider righteous.

Despite a general tendency to support normal behavior, our society also supports deviant behavior to some degree. What kinds of deviance do we occasionally encourage? If it is supported, can it still be defined as deviant? Why or why not?

Of course, quite often the definition of what constitutes deviant behavior depends on how much power the person making that definition has in the community or society. In other words, if the local drunk accuses you of deviant behavior, chances are no one will pay attention. But if the minister or the local banker accuse you of deviance, it is more likely that others will follow their lead.

It is important to realize, however, that deviant behavior is not always, nor is it necessarily, "bad" for the group. As one sociologist puts it, deviant individuals become examples of behavior outside the group, allowing group members to see why they are different from other groups, or special. For example, a thief in our midst helps us feel that we are better because we are not thieves. Being able to see this specialness helps members of a group retain an identity, and gain cohesion and solidarity that are beneficial to the group. "Thus deviance cannot be dismissed simply as behavior which *disrupts* stability

How might the existence of teen-age delinquents contribute to the stability and solidarity of their communities?

Who Is Crazy?

One experiment in the effects and often arbitrary nature of the labels "sane" and "insane" was conducted by D. L. Rosenhan of Stanford University. Rosenhan and seven other researchers secretly gained admission to different mental hospitals scattered across the country. Each was admitted with a diagnosis of schizophrenia after complaining that he or she had been hearing voices that seemed to be saying "thud," "empty," or "hollow." Aside from this initial statement and falsifying their names and occupations, the researchers fabricated nothing about their personal lives and acted as naturally and compliantly as possible while confined. The researchers were kept in the hospital from 9 to 52 days—the average length of confinement was 19 days. All but one were released with a diagnosis of "schizophrenia in remission." While in the hospital, the researchers were treated like all the other patients; the staff operated under the assumption that since a person was in the hospital he or she must be disturbed, and the most normal of actions and explanations were interpreted as manifestations of this disturbance. One nurse, seeing a researcher often taking notes, recorded that the "patient engaged in writing behavior." Although about a third of the regular patients discovered the researchers to be interlopers almost immediately, none of the staff members recognized the new "patients" to be sane.

Hearing of this study, one hospital's staff boasted that such errors were unlikely to occur at their hospital. Rosenhan replied that sometime during the next three months one or more pseudo-patients would attempt admittance. Of the 193 patients admitted during those three months, 41 patients were judged imposters by at least one staff member—though Rosenhan sent no one.

Rosenhan, D. L. "On Being Sane in Insane Places," *Science*, January 19, 1973, pp. 250–258.

in society, but may itself be, in controlled quantities, an important condition for preserving stability."[13]

Another long-range, positive effect of deviance is that it contributes to social change. After all, the first individual who challenges the status quo always disobeys a norm and is therefore considered deviant. In the early years of this century, women who staged demonstrations and picketed the White House in an attempt to obtain the vote were certainly considered deviant—especially by the men. Had women remained perfectly conforming creatures, they might have prevented some temporary disorders in society, but they would still be unable to vote. Since then, every adult's right to vote has become a value of the whole society. Clearly, some types of deviant behavior eventually work to the benefit of the group.

Can you list further examples of behavior that, although deviant at first, helped society develop positively and that also became normal? What conditions would you expect to be necessary in a society to encourage this process? What is meant by the phrase "An idea whose time had come"?

Limits of deviance. We all deviate, to some degree, at some time, from societal norms. When we speak of deviance, we are referring to behavior that passes the limits of what the group will tolerate. The limits of tolerance differ in various groups. They vary according to the importance of the norm and the circumstance under which it is violated. The limits also vary according to any special attributes of the norm-violating individual—his age, his mental and psychological state, and so on.

We already know that norms are ranked according to their importance. At the societal level, for instance, they are arranged into folkways, mores, and laws. A society tolerates violations of folkways much more readily than it tolerates violations of laws. Norm violation is also tolerated under some circumstances, and not others. For example, drinking to excess may be tolerated on New Year's Eve or on a particularly happy occasion. Killing is tolerated (even encouraged) in a war. People are more tolerant with a child or a foreigner who violates some norm than they are with a native adult. We also still tolerate some types of behavior from boys that we do not tolerate from girls, and vice versa. And—contrary to our best democratic intentions—we tolerate more norm violations from the advantaged in our society than from the disadvantaged. (For example, the mayor's son may get a suspended sentence on a major traffic violation, but the janitor's son is likely to spend some time in jail.)

The Roots of Deviance

The principle of cultural relativity (which, as we have suggested, is a common sociological approach to the analysis of societies and their cultures) is equally appropriate to the analysis of deviance and conformity in our own society. Our society consists of a variety of subcul-

[13]Kai T. Erikson, "Notes on the Sociology of Deviance," in *The Other Side: Perspectives on Deviance,* Howard S. Becker, ed. (New York: The Free Press, 1964), p. 15.

tures and countercultures. Conformity in one group sometimes means deviance in another. To middle-class Americans, members of motorcycle gangs seem deviant. To the gangs, the members appear conforming, whereas middle-class Americans seem deviant. Members of such gangs find themselves in a stressful and conflict-producing situation. If they conform to the norms of the general society, they are ostracized by their peers. If they conform to the norms of their gang, they are considered deviant—and sometimes punished—by the society.

What constitutes conformity or deviance is also subject to changes in time. At one time, for a woman to go out on a date with a man, unchaperoned, marked her as a woman of "ill repute." Today, unmarried singles spending weekends together are quite widely accepted. Nonetheless, there remains a central core of norms to which most citizens of each society and subculture are expected to conform. Deviation from that core constitutes the focus of the sociological analysis of deviance.

Theories of Deviance

The layman's explanations for deviant behavior generally revolve around psychological causes, or mental "illness." In many instances of deviant behavior, some sort of psychological impairment may indeed be at work. However, most deviant acts are committed by clinically "normal" people. In addition, sociologists feel that all human behavior—including deviant behavior—is a product of the type of social organization in which we live, of the social structures we erect, and the social processes in which we take part. Sociological theories of deviance reflect this bias.

When you read about a murderer in the newspapers, what kinds of explanations for his or her behavior do you tend to formulate? To what extent do you tend to see sin, mental illness, or environmental conditions as the cause for such behavior?

Anomie theory. One of the best-known attempts to formulate a general theory of deviance has been made by sociologist Robert K. Merton. Merton notes that our society sets forth certain cultural goals toward which all members are expected to aspire. But the institutionalized means for reaching these goals are not available to all societal members. For instance, becoming wealthy is a widely acclaimed cultural goal in our society. Every child knows that it is desirable to live the "good life," to have a large house, to drive an expensive car, to wear attractive clothes, and so on. But how many people can actually become rich by the means that are available to them? Can an unskilled, uneducated, underemployed urban slum dweller get rich by legitimate means? Only if he wins the first prize at the state lottery, or inherits a large sum from a long-lost grandfather who found gold in Alaska. The chances of becoming wealthy, for a large segment of our population, are slim indeed. Such people—if pressured enough to "succeed"—will use illegitimate, or deviant, means to achieve wealth. If they do, however, the disharmony between the culturally approved goals and the disapproved means will produce the strains characteristic

To what extent do thieves fulfill approved goals of our society? How might our societal goals have to change to reduce incidents of robbery, embezzlement, and so on?

When Is Deviance Respectable?

Murder, rape, burglary, espionage. In thrillers of a former age only villains indulged in such activities. In today's thrillers like those of Mickey Spillane and Ian Fleming, the hero himself often commits these deviant acts. We come to accept the deviance of the hero, one analyst of deviance in popular fiction, Jerry Palmer, believes, because of the context in which it occurs. Conspiracies that threaten world order, masterminded by the cruel and the criminal, suffuse the world of the thriller. In the face of the underhanded ways of the villain we are led to accept the hero's actions as the only effective way to fight the conspiracy. In this context, deviance appears justified because the ends—world order and peace—appear justified. What is important about these novels, Palmer believes, is the type of personality it portrays as heroic.

In the world of the thriller there are typically three sorts of people, says Palmer. There is the well-intentioned but bungling amateur. There is the villain, the "bureaucrat of crime" who, like Ian Fleming's Dr. No, is rigidly wedded to his grand plan. The hero is the happy medium of these extremes. He shares with the amateur a capacity to improvise, making him superior to the evil bureaucrat who is lost when his plan is disrupted. He shares with the bureaucrat skill and experience, qualities the amateur totally lacks. He is, in short, a professional, competitive and isolated. He is socialized, but retains his individuality. He asserts his individuality through initiative, competition, and deviance, and his sociability through his end of saving the world. The effect of this, Palmer maintains, is to bolster our belief that only by being competitive can we be individuals. Meanwhile, the reader can take pleasure in deviance while resting assured that it is all in a good cause.

Jerry Palmer, "Thrillers: The Deviant Behind the Consensus," ed. Ian Taylor and Laurie Taylor, *Politics and Deviance* (Baltimore: Penguin Books, 1973), pp. 136–156.

of a state of normlessness, or *anomie.*

Merton listed a typology of the modes of adaptation that individuals choose in order to avoid anomie and still deal with conflict between cultural goals and institutionalized means. The first mode of adaptation is *conformity,* that is, acceptance of both the cultural goals and the institutional, culturally approved means for achieving them. The majority of societal members choose this mode of adaptation, which means that they either have access to legitimate means, or they are resigned to forego the goal.

Another mode is *innovation.* Here the individual accepts the cultural goals but not the institutionalized means for achieving it. Instead, other means for achieving cultural goals, sometimes norm-violating means, are employed. Much crime and delinquency in our society may be attributed to the innovative mode of adaptation.

Recently it was discovered that people who were good at mathematics were able to manipulate the telephone system to place calls free of charge. Can you think of other innovative ways "to beat the system" that border on the criminal, while accepting the general goals of society?

Ritualism is a third type of adaptation in which the individual subscribes to a rigid set of rules that prescribe the "correct" and "proper" way of doing things. The emphasis here is not on the cultural goal, which has been abandoned or rejected, but on a technique that detracts attention from goal achievement. The most common example of this mode of adaptation is provided by bureaucrats for whom following even the most ridiculous rules becomes more important than accomplishing the ultimate goal of the organization.

Retreatism is the kind of adaptation in which both the cultural goals and the institutionalized means for attaining them are abandoned. Retreatist individuals become the aliens of a society, being "in it but not of it." Alcoholics, drug addicts, hoboes, hippies, and some types of skid row residents illustrate this mode of adaptation.

Finally, *rebellion* represents a form of adaptation consisting of the rejection of existing cultural goals *and* means. New or altered goals and means for achieving them are substituted for the old norms. Rebels are often the instigators of new social movements that present an alternative to existing cultural norms.[14]

Merton's theory is quite general and covers a lot of territory. It is an influential theory, and has been the starting point for a number of more specific theoretical constructs, particularly in the field of criminology.

Which of Merton's types of adaptation apply most closely to your own behavior? Do you use all of them at one time or another? How do you choose which adaptation is best under specific circumstances?

Labeling theory. This theory is still in the developmental stage. It provides a startlingly new conception of what constitutes deviant behavior. Instead of focusing on the actions that are generally thought of as deviant, the theory concentrates on the individuals involved, and on how these individuals perceive one another. The questions asked by labeling theorists include: How does the group come to define a specific individual as deviant? How do the members of the group modify their reactions and interaction with an individual defined as deviant? And what are the consequences of the changed behavior of group members on the deviant individual?

Howard Becker, a sociologist who was instrumental in developing the labeling theory, explains that once we define someone as deviant, even on the basis of only one antisocial or criminal act, our attitudes toward this individual and our expectations for him are totally

[14]Robert K. Merton, *Social Theory and Social Structure* (New York: The Free Press, 1956), p. 140.

changed. We believe and expect that he will continue to commit such acts. For example, Becker says that:

A man who has been convicted of housebreaking and thereby labeled criminal is presumed to be a person likely to break into other houses; the police, in rounding up known offenders for investigation after a crime has been committed, operate on this premise. Furthermore, he is considered likely to commit other crimes as well, because he has shown himself to be a person without respect for the law.[15]

In other words, we attach labels to people and then treat them as if they were nothing but what the label implies. If a person has had a mental breakdown, or has been institutionalized in a hospital or prison, we expect him to act criminally or in a deranged manner. And we stand ready to blame any norm-violating action on him.

The tragic thing is that such a person usually lives up to our expectations. We noted that the process of personality formation included the acquisition of a self that is largely a reflection of what others think of us. If an individual realizes that others believe him to be a criminal, and expect him to act criminally, he comes to think of himself as truly a criminal. Sooner or later, he develops patterns of deviant behavior, even if those deviant patterns were not his initially. He becomes subject to a self-fulfilling prophecy.

According to sociologist Erving Goffman, we are constantly playing roles for approval. What kinds of approval might be elicited by criminal behavior?

Neither the anomie nor the labeling theorists pretend to have all the answers to the reasons for the formation of deviant personalities. They simply indicate the relationship between an individual's social environment and culture and the structure of personality. While the social environment and group culture exert a heavy influence on each individual, each individual responds with different behavior patterns. These patterns are prompted by the unique experiences of his socialization process. Inherited temperament may also affect deviance. The two theories represent sociological attempts to explain why and how specific deviant patterns of behavior emerge in a society, and in what ways some individuals learn to play deviant roles. In addition to these two general theories, sociologists also try to set forth theories that explain specific deviant actions of the sort that are most troublesome to societies. Crime and delinquency, for instance, are areas of great concern to our society today.

Crime and Delinquency

Some types of actions are easily defined as criminal. When someone breaks into your home when you are asleep, steals all your silver, jewelry, and other valuables, and shoots you if you wake up, no one will deny that a criminal act was committed against you. But many other

[15]Howard S. Becker, *Outsiders: Studies in the Sociology of Deviance* (New York: The Free Press, 1963), p. 33.

types of behavior have been, at one time or another, defined as criminal by our legal system, and yet are so frequent, that the definition of criminality becomes a hollow legality. We have already mentioned that many states, or counties, prohibit the sale of liquor in spite of the fact that many of their residents are drinkers in the privacy of their homes. Similarly, the consumption of marijuana is considered a felony in most states, defining marijuana smokers—even one-time users—as criminals. Both patterns of behavior, although officially considered criminal, are not believed to be seriously deviant by those who perpetrate them and by many others in the society. Clearly, there are behavioral areas that can at best be defined as "gray": neither criminal nor noncriminal.

Are laws applied uniformly? How do societal norms affect the enforcement of laws? Are there ever discrepancies between laws and norms? How does society handle such discrepancies?

Since we need a working definition of crime, however, we may state that a criminal action is one that violates formal criminal statutes. We use our legal codes to determine what constitutes criminal behavior. These codes, in the United States, are not uniform. Local communities, states, and the federal government all have their own codes. These codes, however, are differentiated from the unwritten societal norms in that: (1) they are put into effect by political authority; (2) they are specific rules instead of informal understandings; (3) they are supposed to be applied uniformly to every deviant; (4) they carry specific punitive sanctions; and (5) they are administered through official agencies of the society.

A distinction is also made between criminal behavior on the part of adults and on the part of juveniles, or those under 18 years of age. This distinction is based on recognition that minors may not yet be fully socialized. If the crime is particularly serious, however, a juvenile may be treated as an adult and tried under laws that govern adults.

What social changes may be involved in the increase in women criminals? What norms and roles are being affected to produce these changes?

Who and where are the criminals? We need only to listen to the news on the radio or television, or look at the headlines of newspapers and magazines, to know that crime and delinquency are on the rise everywhere in our society. Social scientists who have studied the statistics have made certain conclusions about what proportion of which groups commits the majority of criminal acts. For example, more males than females commit criminal acts, although the proportion of women criminals is growing. More blacks than whites are arrested and prosecuted. But we must remember that blacks are, disproportionately, members of the lower socioeconomic groups, whose involvement in criminal acts is generally higher, regardless of race. The black criminal rates can be explained by both the anomie theory (blacks search for illegitimate means to achieve cultural goals) and by the labeling theory (there is more discrimination against blacks than whites in the society at large and in the system of justice). Finally, statistics also indicate that the largest proportion of criminals and juvenile delinquents originate in low socioeconomic classes. The crimes poor people commit tend to be against property. That is, the crimes are various kinds of theft. Here too we must remember that the statistics count only those arrested and convicted. People from higher socioeconomic backgrounds may commit just as many criminal acts, but since they have greater access to attorneys and to the system of justice, they may be better able to avoid arrest or conviction.

Geographical area also influences the data. Urban areas, particularly the centers of large cities, are much more crime-ridden than are rural areas and suburbs. As suburban areas become more citified, however, and as urban values begin to pervade the rural areas, crime invades the country in the same forms it shows in cities.

Personality: Conforming or Deviant?

People are social animals, living and constantly interacting in groups. Therefore, it is to the advantage of each society if a degree of social order can be maintained. One way to ensure social order is to socialize each new generation in such a way that members will *want* to behave in a manner beneficial to the society. The majority of people in each society are indeed socialized to behave in this way. But the same process that is at work in our acquisition of personalities conforming enough to be supportive of the society, is also at work causing us to deviate from some of its norms. We learn to conform, and we learn to deviate, through the same process of socialization. But the exact mechanism that determines who learns what and why still escapes us. Why is it, for instance, that in one family the less favored child refuses to accept parental norms and becomes a deviant adult, whereas in another family, a similarly less loved child decides to "try harder," becoming in the process a highly conforming adult? Much remains to be learned about how we become distinct individuals. All we can say is that we always seem to need others to show us the way.

[Summary]

Each human being resembles *all* other human beings, resembles *some* other human beings, and resembles *no* other human being. Each human resembles all other humans because we are all members of the same biological species, and thus are all born with the same basic drives and needs. We all share physical needs for oxygen, warmth, food, and the avoidance of pain, and we all share emotional needs for affection and security. Each human resembles some other humans because as a member of a particular society, he shares in the culture of that society, having been socialized into its norms by a fairly standard process. And each human resembles no other human because experiences unique to each individual, and operating on an equally unique set of inherited potentials, create a personality that is like no other. Personality develops on the basis of (1) a unique genetic heredity; (2) a unique physical environment; (3) socialization into a shared culture; (4) common, or group, experiences; (5) unique, or individual, experiences.

Sociologists, who believe that the individual develops and functions primarily within a group, almost universally agree that socialization is the determining factor in the development of personality. A belief in socialization, unlike a belief in cultural determinism and behaviorism, does not lead to the conclusion that the individual can be molded into almost anything, provided the right environment or training is available. On the contrary, the individual is believed to come into the world equipped with inherited traits and potentials—and perhaps with a specific temperament, as suggested by recent studies. He is also equipped with definite, powerful drives and a strong desire to have them fulfilled. Socialization, therefore, does not only give the individual identity, it also teaches him how to satisfy his biological drives through social channels and how to fit into the fabric of society.

Socialization is a two-way process in which the newborn accepts the care of a significant other in exchange for having his biological needs satisfied in culturally approved ways. The chief agent of socialization is the family, although the peer group and the mass media grow in importance. One result of socialization is that the biological organism develops a personality—therefore a mind and a self—of its own. The individual begins to look in the imaginary mirror presented by significant others and learns how they see his self. The self is also helped to emerge when the individual becomes capable of thinking about himself as he thinks about others, and when he can take the role of the other.

Resocialization involves the breaking down of old patterns and the building up of new ones. Personalities are continually resocialized as we learn to play new roles that befit new statuses. Sometimes total resocialization is attempted, as when an individual becomes a member of a "total institution"—a military service, jail, or hospital.

The emergence of a personality also depends on culture. Members of specific societies tend to develop a type of personality that reflects certain cultural characteristics. Some behavioral scientists insist that there are indeed national, or modal, personalities. But these characters are difficult to define in culturally heterogeneous societies such as ours.

Socialization, and consequently personality formation, takes place as we learn to play certain roles befitting statuses that we acquire at different times in our lives, or that are related to our gender, race, age, and so on. Furthermore, socialization and personality reflect our internalization of societal norms, specifically the norms of the primary groups with which we interact most. Not everyone internalizes every societal norm: we tend to pick and choose, internalizing most often the norms of the groups that give us the most emotional satisfaction. When we internalize certain norms that conflict with the norms of society at large, we may be viewed as deviant.

Abnormality, or deviation from the norm, is a very relative concept. We all deviate, more or less, at one time or another, from some norms. Even the most hardened criminal deviates only from a few of the many thousands of norms society teaches. Deviations may consist of psychological problems or antisocial behavior. Sociologists are concerned with deviant behavior that goes beyond the tolerance limits of society.

Deviation from norms on the part of some societal members is not necessarily bad. For one thing, group identity and cohesiveness tend to increase when the members can see what happens to those who violate norms. Deviant individuals, in addition, often initiate social change that in the long run is beneficial to society. Deviance is tolerated in different degrees, according to the kind of norm violated, to the circumstance under which it is violated, and to the characteristics of the person violating it.

Most deviant acts are committed by clinically normal people. Therefore, something other than mental illness is usually at work. Deviance has been explained by sociologists primarily in terms of two theories. The anomie theory suggests that people deviate in response to the normlessness that results when cultural goals cannot be reached through legitimate institutional means. The labeling theory maintains that an individual deviates because of the way people react to him when he has been labeled a deviant because of one norm-violating act.

There are numerous forms of deviance in society, but the most worrisome today appear to be crime and delinquency. Criminal or delinquent actions violate formal, criminal statutes, although there is a vast gray area of acts that are sometimes considered criminal by some people. Statistics show that males, blacks, and the poor commit the majority of crimes. However, these statistics may hide the fact that white, middle-class people may commit just as many crimes, but are better able to avoid arrest or conviction.

Every society needs a certain amount of social order to function smoothly. Consequently, new generations are socialized to uphold a number of societal norms. In the process of socialization, each individual acquires a personality, which is a unique self combined with the shared characteristics of his culture. But the same process that teaches us to behave in a constructive way to benefit society, sometimes teaches us to be deviant and destructive.

Terms to Remember

Cultural determinism. A theory in which human personality is viewed as being basically the product of the individual's culture.

Looking-glass self (Cooley). The process of personality formation, in which an individual's self-image emerges as he perceives the observed attitudes of others.

Mind (Mead). The abstract whole of a person's ideas.

National character, or modal personality. A basic personality type developed by each society. It reflects the specific culture of that society.

Personality. A complex and dynamic system that includes all of an individual's behavioral and emotional traits, his attitudes, values, beliefs, habits, goals, and so on.

Self (Mead). The individual's self-conception, or self-awareness.

Socialization. The learning process by which a biological organism becomes a human being, acquires a personality with self and identity, and absorbs the culture of his society.

Symbolic interactionism. A sociological school of thought established by George Herbert Mead whose theoretical speculations in the area of personality formation centered around the interrelationship of mind, self, and society and included the belief that society and the individual give rise to each other through the process of symbolic interaction.

Resocialization. A process in which the individual's existing self-concept and identity are erased in favor of a new personality more in keeping with the total institution of which the individual has become a member.

Deviance. Norm-violating behavior beyond the society's limits of tolerance.

Anomie. Normlessness. As used here, the term refers to the theory of anomie with which sociologist Robert Merton attempts to explain deviance as a reaction to the stress on cultural goals for which no legal institutional means exist.

Labeling. A major theory of deviance that attempts to explain deviant behavior as a reaction to the group's expectations of someone who has once been decreed as deviant.

Suggestions for Further Reading

Benedict, Ruth. *Patterns of Culture.* Baltimore, Md.: Penguin Books, 1946. An interesting account of the emergence of modal personality, by a renowned anthropologist.

Blumer, Herbert. "Sociological Implications of the Thought of George Herbert Mead." *American Journal of Sociology* (March 1966): 525–544. A restatement and clarification of Mead's theories regarding the social self.

Elkin, Frederick. *The Child and Society.* New York: Random House, 1960. An interpretation of the socialization of children and personality formation according to the precepts of role theory.

Erikson, Erik. *Childhood and Society,* rev. ed. New York: W. W. Norton, 1964. A well-known psychologist speaks on socialization and personality formation.

Eysenck, Hans J. *The Biological Basis of Personality.* Springfield, Ill.: Charles C. Thomas, 1967. The biological factor in personality development is skillfully and exhaustively analyzed.

Fromm, Erich. *Escape from Freedom.* New York: Avon, 1965. A classic on personality, among other things, from a philosopher of psychology.

Ranking and stratification

WE USUALLY DEFINE history as the record of the past deeds of humanity. When we examine the record, however, we note that there is hardly any mention of most of humanity. The only people we read about were kings and queens, popes, presidents, prime ministers, prophets, and demagogues. These people are credited with discovering continents, building nations, and shaping the destinies of the rest of mankind. Some wore brilliant headpieces, while their subjects wore a single gray feather. Some were buried with costly jewels in elaborate tombs, while their servants were buried in earth. Some even ate with golden utensils, while the masses scavenged for scraps.

Why do you think there is a tendency for the upper classes to dominate the record of humanity's past?

In all known societies except the very simplest ones, there has always been a division between the few and the many. The few have led and the many have followed. The few have had much and the many have had little. The few have been powerful, and the many have been powerless. Why are there such differences among people? Are some individuals born with special talents for leading and for accumulating wealth and power? Is the majority, on the other hand, born without such talents? Or are these talents acquired through a special set of circumstances?

American ideology and our system of values are based on the principle that all people are created equal. This principle simply means that all of us (at least in theory) have an equal voice in making the decisions by which we govern ourselves. In most other respects, we are quite unequal. We are all born in the same way—naked and dependent for survival on those around us—and we all eventually die. But between birth and death, there is a world of difference between the life of one individual and that of another. Part of this difference is caused by factors we have already discussed. For example, each of us comes into the world with a specific genetic inheritance unlike that of anybody else. Each of us is socialized in a small group, by a relatively small number of people. And each of us has different everyday experiences, so that even two identical twins develop distinct personalities. So we are naturally unequal to begin with.

To what extent do you feel you choose your friends according to what social class they are in?

But differences in personalities resulting from distinct genetic traits and socialization experiences are not the only evidence of inequality. More obvious, and often more tragic, are the social inequalities: the fact that people have unequal amounts of wealth, of prestige, and of power. Even if you look around your classroom, you will see evidence of such inequalities. Some of you will have come to school in a Corvette, others on the public transit system. Some will be sporting a suntan in January. Others will be pale and sniffling from breathing the polluted air of the city. Some will earn high grades, while others will fail the course. Some have educated parents and others come from homes in which education is not particularly valued. Some of you have always been leaders, whether in the games you played as children, or in school as outstanding students, or in life in the positions you obtain. Others have always been followers.

What is it that makes some of you leaders and others followers, some of you rich and others poor, some of you successful and prominent, and others insignificant? Is the ability to obtain success, wealth, and power an inherited talent? Is it personally achieved through hard work? Or are there still other, more subtle ways of obtaining these desirables? Is inequality ever justifiable? Would it not be more equitable to divide our society's resources equally among all, rewarding no one and slighting no one? Would such a solution kill all motivation and stop the progress of civilization, as some say? Or would it bring us heaven on earth?

Kurt Vonnegut, an American writer, has written a powerful short story in which he describes a society in which total equality is rigorously enforced. The norms of this society are set by the average people: average in intelligence, in looks, in physical strength, and so on. People who are above average in anything must subject themselves to a system of handicaps that makes them equal to the average citizen. Those with above-normal intelligence must wear radio transmitters in their ears that emit different kinds of sounds at set intervals, to disturb any serious thinking the person may be indulging in. ("Average" people only think when absolutely necessary!) Those of above-normal appearance must wear masks and other devices that ruin their good looks. Those of above-normal strength must wear weights around their necks. No one is allowed to do anything better than anyone else: ballerinas must dance as awkwardly as any normal person would, musicians must play as people with no particular musical talent do, television announcers must have at least a little speech impediment, and so on. The hero, a superior human being whom none of the handicaps

Are there any ways that society really does handicap talented people in the way Vonnegut suggests? Do you think such handicapping is ever intentional?

What Equality Means in China

The ethic that is instilled in the People's Republic of China and the social system that supports it are worlds apart from Kurt Vonnegut's vision of absolute equality. The Chinese ethic is not that you should be the same as everyone else, but that you should use your talents to benefit the group rather than to increase your own wealth and prestige at the expense of others. This is maintained by limiting opportunities for private accumulation, group norms that enforce the notion of a common dignity of persons and their labors whatever their differences in talent, and by encouraging individuals to satisfy their needs through collective action. The result, many observers have noted, is a high level of team spirit. Here, for example, are the reflections of Felix Greene during his visit to China:

> *The Chinese recognize that every human being needs an adequate standard of food, shelter, and clothing. But they are aware, I think, that ownership above these minimal real needs leads to competitiveness and rivalry and that everything above the simplest personal possessions can much more happily be held in common. The result is that the element of personal acquisitiveness here appears to be reduced almost to a vanishing point. This is no 'me first' economy; it is a 'we' economy that is growing here. They are really not interested in making more money for themselves. . . . Economically, they are already looking (though it is still a long way off) for the day when the work week will be very greatly reduced and are in a thousand different ways encouraging the development of personal creativity. But on a deeper level the Chinese have long been aware . . . that personal rivalry and personal protectiveness both lead to alienation. The Chinese appear to be finding their basic psychological security not in the search for personal possessions, but in the quality of their relationship with each other, and the implications of this are enormous.*

Felix Greene, *Awakened China: The Country Americans Don't Know* (Garden City, Doubleday, 1961), p. 189.

can make "normal," prefers to commit one act of beauty and then be killed rather than continue to live in such a society. Vonnegut suggests that the kind of equality in which everyone is exactly alike is not only inconceivable, but must also be a dreadful bore.[1] The point Vonnegut is making is that, while differences among people often make for

[1]Kurt Vonnegut, Jr., "Harrison Bergeron," in *Welcome to the Monkey House* (New York: Dell, 1970), pp. 7-13.

tragic inequality, the same differences also make for a rich and varied society. Sociologists are, of course, intensely interested in differences among people and in the causes and results of such differences.

[Stratification]

Differences among people are so important that everyone tends to look for and find the variations and ranks that help define oneself. Sociologists are especially interested in the tendency of people to rank themselves according to specific criteria, with the result that human societies are stratified, or divided into a number of layers. The criteria used include: (1) wealth, or how much of the societal resources they own; (2) prestige, or the degree of social honor their position in soci-

How would you rank yourself in our society—high, middle, or low? What are you basing your judgment on?

The Other Bohemians: A Study in Ruling-Class Cohesiveness

Every year over one thousand men from all over the United States journey to a retreat set among a forest of redwoods in a secluded area north of San Francisco for two weeks of elaborate rituals, relaxation, expensive entertainment, and fireside chats. Those who gather at the Bohemian Grove are members and guests of an exclusive West Coast social club comprised mostly of leading industrialists, bankers, politicians, lawyers, and other professionals.

Fraternization at exclusive retreats like the Bohemian Grove is evidence of "ruling-class cohesiveness," says G. William Domhoff in a recent study of three such retreats. By "ruling-class" he means the top 1 percent of the population who own a substantial portion of the privately held wealth in America—the owners and managers of large corporations, together with foundation and government leaders. The rich and the powerful do not live as strangers to one another, argues Domhoff, but move in the same social circles, interacting, and often intermarrying. The function of exclusive social clubs, retreats, and other informal gatherings is to create stronger social bonds among the upper class. At such gatherings, members can exchange views on the important social and business problems of the day, often leading to some form of consensus on general strategies. The similarities of position and frequencies of contact among this top 1 percent, in Domhoff's view, make of this group a definite social class.

Domhoff, G. William, *The Bohemian Grove and Other Retreats* (New York: Harper & Row, 1974).

ety evokes; and (3) power, or the degree to which they can direct others as a result of the preceding factors. People not only rank themselves, but they rank one another according to the same criteria.

What kinds of changes would have to occur to allow a society based on superabundance rather than on scarcity? What social changes might then take place?

This phenomenon of *stratification* occurs in every society that has produced a surplus. For this reason, social scientists assume that stratification is a consequence of the way resources are distributed in a society. A society that produces no surplus gives little opportunity to acquire wealth or prestige and power based on wealth. The division of people into social levels results from attempts to answer the question: Who gets what, and why?[2] This question is answered differently in different societies. Therefore, the stratification systems of different societies vary according to the values and goals predominant in each.

Inequality

What conditions of the modern era might prompt people living now to question inequality, even though in the more distant past inequality was unquestioned?

No society has as yet invented a system that prevents some inequality in the distribution of scarce and desirable things such as wealth, prestige, and power. Some always seem to get more than others. Social inequality is as old as the world itself. In the past, most people accepted such inequality as an inevitable fact of life. More recently, people have questioned inequality, and have attempted to remedy some aspects of it. The ideology of communism—though not its current reality—has as its ultimate goal a classless society in which desirable things are owned collectively. Our own democratic ideology, using the capitalistic economic system, seeks to give every member of society the equality of opportunity to compete for scarce resources. This goal too, however, is still an ideal rather than a reality.

Sociologists believe that some social inequality is inevitable. Their theories of social inequality are derived from opposing philosophical positions—conservative and liberal—that are centuries old. The classical conservative position holds that inequality is part of the law of nature, and that it is a product of the gross selfishness and greed of humans. These attitudes must be curbed by society through some of its institutions, a process that may also result in inequality. But such inequality is the price we must pay for the smooth functioning of society. Charles Darwin's biological theory of the survival of the fittest was applied socially to this philosophical tradition. Those who accepted this view maintained that since the resources of society were scarce and people had to compete for them, only the strongest, the most intelligent or the most virtuous would attain them. This situation would make for inequality, but at the same time would ensure that only the "best" people in a society rose to positions of power and privilege. Ultimately, their rise would benefit society, for they would provide enlightened leadership.

[2]Gerhard Lenski, *Power and Privilege: A Theory of Social Stratification* (New York, McGraw-Hill, 1966), p. 3.

In the classical liberal view, humans are basically good—not selfish and greedy. It is society that makes them evil. In society, each individual or group must struggle to get a share of the scarce goods and services that society values. This struggle becomes divisive and ends with the domination of one group over other groups. The victorious group, with the help of institutions the society has established, exploits the other groups, and forces them to accept the status quo. Once the winning group ascends to power, it imposes its will on the remainder of society by claiming authority over it. Therefore, because members of a society struggle for scarce resources, the stratification of that society and its resultant inequality are unavoidable.

Do you tend to take a conservative or a liberal attitude toward human nature?

Functionalist Theory

The intellectual descendants of the conservative viewpoint are the contemporary thinkers of the functionalist school of thought. (We have already discussed functionalism as an important theoretical model of sociology in chapter 1.) Functionalists emphasize the needs of the society instead of the needs of individuals. The existence of every society depends on the regular performance of specific tasks that are difficult and require special intelligence, talent, and training. Since people are basically selfish, society must institute a system of rewards with which to lure the most talented, the most intelligent, and the best-trained individuals to perform these tasks. The positions most essential to the welfare of a society must be the ones most highly rewarded. In addition, those positions for which there are few qualified personnel should be highly rewarded. It may be argued that collecting garbage is almost as vital to the health of a society as practicing medicine, since uncollected garbage is a threat to public health. But collecting garbage requires little training, or talent, or even intelligence. Therefore, there are many individuals who can perform this function. Practicing medicine requires a long period of study and training. Not all individuals are capable of undergoing the discipline of such training. Therefore, there are fewer potential doctors than there are garbage collectors, and consequently doctors are much better rewarded.

Which factor do you think contributes more to the fact that fewer people can become doctors than can become garbage collectors: the money to go to school, or the ability to finish school?

Functionalists stress the need for order, stability and balance in a society. A system of stratification, they say, even though it produces some social inequality, has a stabilizing influence on society. It prevents conflicts among individuals competing for scarce resources from erupting and disrupting the orderly functioning of society. Because of the functionalists' beliefs in the need for harmony, functionalism is also called the *equilibrium theory.*[3]

Critics argue that functionalist theory is not entirely valid. They point out that societies do not always reward the members who fulfill

[3]In the United States, the best-known followers of functionalist theory are sociologists Kingsley Davis, Wilbert Moore, and, with variations, Talcott Parsons.

essential roles. In our society, for instance, although physicians are well rewarded for their vital role, other professionals whose function seems equally vital (teachers, nurses, social workers) are notoriously ill rewarded. In addition, we seem to reward sports and entertainment personalities very well for the few hours of entertainment they provide us.

How might a functionalist respond to the objection that entertainers may be disproportionately rewarded in our society?

Furthermore, stability is not sufficient to overcome the many disadvantages of stratification. For instance, the existence of a stratification system prevents many talented people who do not have access to training from developing their talent. Only through extreme good luck do many talented people in various fields eventually rise to the top. The biographies of famous people provide countless examples. Millions of people live on the edge of survival and are condemned to gray, uninteresting existences, simply because they were born into a social class in which the chances of attaining "the good life" are slim or nonexistent.

Conflict Theory

The conflict theorists of today are the intellectual descendants of a more liberal view of human beings. Conflict theorists, as opposed to functionalists, stress the fact that, as a result of conflicts and dissension, the natural condition of society is constant change. Such change, even though it is the result of continuous struggle, may be creative. It can lead to progress and can prevent the stagnation of a society. At the same time, however, conflict theorists view stratification systems as mechanisms of coercion. Those in positions of power impose the stratification system on the rest of society because the system works to their advantage.

What aspects of life in communist countries today suggest that these countries are trying to break the power that the family has to transmit ascribed status?

The best-known conflict theorist was Karl Marx. He believed that all of history was a record of class struggles caused by the unequal distribution of rewards in societies (dialectical materialism). Marx saw all societies as stratified. He specifically suggested that the institution of private ownership of the means of production led to the modern division of society into the present social classes. These classes are in conflict with one another because the owners (the bourgeoisie) have, and want to keep, a monopoly of power over the nonowners (the proletariat). The bourgoisie tries to obtain and keep this power both by force and by instilling values that encourage people to accept the stratification system they are trying to impose. Once in control, and with a system of stratification in operation, they perpetuate the system through various institutions, particularly the family, which transmits either wealth, education, and prestige, or poverty and ignorance, from one generation to the next.

Marx further believed that, even though stratification was a technique of oppression of one social class by another, it also was the mechanism for the development of a classless society. This kind of society would come about when the proletariat developed a class consciousness, realized its own self-interest, and finally rebelled against the bourgeoisie. Ultimately, he theorized, there would be an end to political power and class distinctions and antagonisms. People would live in an association in which the free development of each person would be the condition for the free development of all people.

Marx has had a deep influence on the study of social stratification. Most theorists either agree or disagree with his premises on the subject. Contemporary conflict theorists, such as C. Wright Mills and Ralf Dahrendorf, agree with the notion of class conflict, although not necessarily with the idea that such conflict results from the ownership of the means of production. Conflict theorists emphasize that inequality in society generates conflict and is the result of struggles for power among various groups. They also stress the role of certain institutions (family, education, government, and economy) in maintaining social inequality.

Neither the functionalist nor the conflict theories of social stratification are mutually exclusive. That is, we have evidence that societies exhibit both stability and consensus, and conflict and dissension. The two theories simply suggest two different views of looking at the stratification systems of societies.

Can you construct a theory of stratification that includes both stability and consensus, and conflict and dissension?

Must There be Inequality?

In the end, neither of the two theories gives us definitive answers as to the causes of stratification in society, nor does either suggest methods for doing away with social inequality. In fact, almost every human society, and most animal species, has some sort of hierarchical arrangement of members. Chickens have a definite "pecking order." Baboons and many other animals live in social groups with a ranked system of leadership. Are we to assume, then, that biological differences are the basis for stratification and inequality? Do the biggest, the strongest, and the smartest inevitably become the richest or the most powerful? Do accidents that handicap our ability to compete automatically put us in an inferior position in society?

There is no doubt that both biology—or genetic inheritance—and chance play significant parts in the system of stratification. But basically the system is a human device, a social form of organization that societies employ because it has seemed to be the most effective way to ensure survival. In a society that has an inadequate surplus, and limited resources, the survival of the society as a whole is ensured by unequal distribution to the most powerful members.

Will stratification systems and their inherent inequality ever be completely eradicated? Probably not. It seems inconceivable that a society could ever exist in which every member would possess exactly the same number of goods as his neighbor. It is also unlikely that each person could be regarded in the exact same manner as his neighbor and possess the exact same amount of power as his neighbor. In addition, many people doubt that an unstratified society would even be desirable. Such people feel that all aspirations toward excellence would be squelched, and mediocrity would reign supreme. Nevertheless, there is much room for improvement in existing stratification systems.

Would you like to see changes in our stratification system? What kinds of changes? How do you think they could be effected?

[Class, Status, and Power]

All systems of stratification are constructed in the same basic way, no matter in which society they appear. They all display such characteristics as (1) differentiation (people identify with different social groups); (2) ranking (people are ranked in hierarchical order, from the bottom to the top); (3) institutionalization (people come to accept the system as the normal pattern of behavior); and (4) influence on individual personalities (people's personalities reflect their positions in the system). Moreover, social stratification systems are all based on the possession of things that are scarce, and therefore prized, which are popularly categorized as *wealth, prestige,* and *power.* Sociologists prefer to speak of these categories, or dimensions, of the stratification system as *class, status,* and *power.* It is according to these categories that people are assigned a rank in society and relegated to a stratum or level with others who are similarly ranked.

Do you think that stratification has affected your personality? In what ways?

Class

We all speak of *social classes*—the easy life of the upper classes, the poverty of the lower classes, the moral values of the middle classes—but few of us could define the term with any degree of accuracy. We have difficulty determining how many classes there are, and who belongs to exactly which class. We also have difficulty saying exactly what social class is. Class is an important concept in sociology, however, and sociologists have therefore developed more exact ways of defining the term.

Class in the United States. Many Americans, when asked about social classes in the United States, will answer that there are none. Or they say that they, and almost everyone else they know, belong to the "middle class." This belief prevails as a result of a mistaken interpretation of the democratic principle of equality. As we mentioned earlier, many think that because the Declaration of Independence states that "all men are created equal," they are equal in all ways, including having an equal opportunity to acquire wealth, prestige and power. But we only need to look around at the different life-styles of the various segments of our population to see that classlessness is a myth.

At the same time, the nature of our society provides no definite way to define membership in a specific social class. The population of the United States is extremely heterogeneous and is spread over a large geographic area. For these reasons, local stratification systems, which conflict with nationwide data concerning social classes, tend to form. For instance, the richest farmer in a rural community in Kansas may belong to the upper social class in that community, but on a national level we would certainly have to classify him as belonging to a lower social class.

In what sense is rank in a class system relative?

Definitions of class; Marx and Weber. We have mentioned that Karl Marx viewed classes as resulting from the unequal distribution of scarce resources in society. Specifically, he maintained that classes are determined by the relationship of a group in society to the *means of production.* Groups that own a large proportion of the society's wealth—as well as the tools and capital necessary to produce that wealth—have control over groups that own little of either the wealth or the means of producing it. Marx's approach to stratification and his concept of class are essentially economic in nature. Classes, in his view, are basically composed of the *haves* who want to maintain their privileged positions; and the *have-nots* who eventually revolt against the exploitation and oppression imposed on them by the haves.

Another approach to stratification and the concept of class was proposed by Max Weber. Weber thought the Marxist view was too simplistic. He proposed a threefold approach to stratification. He agreed with Marx that one phenomenon of stratification was class, which had a predominantly economic foundation. However, Weber expanded the concept of class to include the dimension of *life chances,* which we will discuss in the following section.[4]

A second phenomenon of stratification, Weber said, was based on status. *Status* is used to refer to the degree of social esteem that an individual or group enjoys (or fails to enjoy) in society. As we will see when we analyze the several facets of stratification separately, there frequently is an overlap between class and status. But the overlap between class and status does not always, nor necessarily, occur. There are instances in which people hold a high position in the class system without holding a comparably high status.

Finally, Weber felt that stratification is also based on power. Power, or the capacity to carry out one's wishes in spite of resistance, also may or may not be related to class and status. Stratification based on power is essentially political, rather than economic, in Weber's view. In fact, Weber uses the term *political class* or *party* to mean an elite, a group that is more powerful than other groups in society.

Can you give an example of stratification based on power rather than on wealth? How are the two bases related?

---

[4]Max Weber, *The Theory of Social and Economic Organization* (New York: Free Press, 1957). First ed., Oxford University Press, 1947.

Life chances. One of the concepts useful in discussing stratification first suggested by Weber, and further developed by later sociologists, is that of life chances. The term *life chances,* as conceived by Weber, refers to the opportunity of each individual to fulfill or fail to fulfill his or her potential in society. Because some people share the access to scarce resources, and others share the lack of such access, there is a strong probability that people in each class will have similar achievement experiences in the society. An individual's life chances include his opportunity to survive during the delicate years of infancy and to reach full potential in physical appearance and health. They include the opportunity to obtain an education equal to his desire and talents, as well as the opportunity to be exposed to all the things that the culture has to offer. Finally, life chances include the individual's right to live in circumstances that prevent him from becoming a deviant. Life chances also include the individual's inability to fulfill all these potentials.

How does Weber's theory of life chances cover facts that are not covered by Marx's theory of stratification?

A person's life chances are determined by his position within the stratification system. The higher that position is, the more positive his life chances are. The lower his position, the more negative his life chances. One life chance tends to determine another. A favorable location on the stratification ladder almost guarantees the fulfillment of most life chances. A low location almost guarantees that life chances will not be fulfilled and that they will be repeatedly denied even to future generations.

Life chances exist in and influence all spheres of human life. They are especially apparent in the stratification system, because they are linked to class. If we compare the life chances of an individual born into an upper-upper class family with the life chances of an individual born into a lower-lower class family, the differences become strikingly apparent. Statistics indicate that, as of 1972, 41.4 percent of the total national income was received by the richest 20 percent of the families in the population, whereas only 5.4 percent of the total national income was received by the poorest 20 percent of families in the population. Obviously the richest 20 percent were able to afford to buy 36 times as many life chances as the poorest 20 percent.[5]

In addition to differential life chances between rich and poor, there are differences in life chances between whites and other racial groups. A white male with 17 years or more of education, could expect to earn 53 percent more income than a nonwhite male with the same amount of education about a decade ago. Today, this gap may have narrowed somewhat.[6] Life expectancy, mortality rates of mothers and babies, incidence of heart disease, and malnutrition are all related to color and

[5]U.S. Department of Commerce, Bureau of the Census, *Statistical Abstract of the United States, 1974* (Washington, D.C.: Government Printing Office, 1974), p. 384.

[6]Herman P. Miller, *Rich Man, Poor Man* (New York: Thomas Y. Crowell, 1964).

Americans do not all have equal life chances. How are these Americans trying to improve their opportunities in life?

class. In addition, members of the lower class are, according to statistics, more frequently the victims of accidents and criminal acts and are punished more severely by the law when caught breaking it than are members of higher classes. Also, lower-class members join fewer organizations and have fewer friends than do people in higher social classes.

Thus, unequal distribution of income is not simply an economic matter. It results in inequalities that spread into all areas of life. The primary inequality of income and the other inequalities that spring from it are extremely difficult for an individual to overcome, notwithstanding our society's reputation as "the land of opportunity." The worst aspect of the problem is that a vicious circle exists. The individual who, through sheer accident of birth, begins his life in a lower-class family, is socialized into accepting a particular set of values that do not help him become upwardly mobile. Living in an environment hostile to him, he develops a type of personality that does not aid him either, and his life chances become still further impaired. It takes a truly extraordinary person to break such bonds.

Who would be more likely to define himself by class—someone from the upper or from the lower classes? Explain your answer.

What is class? The Weberian concept of class has predominated among sociologists. Gerhard Lenski defines *social class* as "an aggregation of persons in a society who stand in a similar position with respect to some form of power, privilege, or prestige."[7] In other words, some people, because of a similarity in occupation, income, education, or life-style, set themselves apart from the rest of the population. In time, they become sufficiently differentiated from others, and unified—sometimes unknowingly—among themselves, to constitute a separate social level, or stratum, or class.

People who are ranked as belonging to a specific social class display similarities in how they handle the experiences of life. They tend to have similar values, live in similar neighborhoods, bring up and educate their children in similar ways, have occupations with approximately similar incomes and prestige, and so on. In short, they display a similarity of life-styles.

Status

Status is the second important category or dimension of social stratification. It is a way of ranking people according to the prestige evoked by the roles they perform in society. We have defined *status* as *the position of the individual in relation to other individuals,* or as *the position of the individual within the social system.* Applied to stratification, status is a ranked position—high, middle, or low. The rank is determined by how the role attached to the status is valued. For instance, because the role of physician, particularly that of a specialist in a difficult field, is valued in our society, that position has a high status.

Why, do you think, is the role of physician highly valued in our society? How do we reward physicians for their role?

The possession of a high status is a value in our society. The desire to obtain a high status in a group and in society is therefore built into the individual as part of his socialization.

The importance of status. Status is very important to most people.

[7]Lenski, pp. 74–75.

Lenski comments that the concern for status "influences almost every kind of decision from the choice of a car to the choice of a spouse. Fear of the loss of status, or honor, is one of the few motives that can make men lay down their lives on the field of battle."[8] The desire for status heavily colors many decisions of daily life, particularly the important ones. You can make an interesting study of your own status striving by analyzing the status motives behind each of your actions, over a period of just one day.

Class, Status, and Power

Choosing about twenty actions from one day of your life, analyze the status motives behind each one. What conclusions do you develop from the analysis?

We have already noted in preceding chapters that some of our statuses are ascribed and others achieved. In our society, high status is officially considered to be more often achieved than ascribed. But, as we will see later, certain features of ascribed statuses can help or hinder achieved statuses. For example, ascribed power and a wealthy family gave Nelson Rockefeller the opportunity to achieve status as vice president of the United States.

A single status, of course, does not describe our total position in society. Each of us has many statuses in society. We are daughters, mothers, wives, doctors, chairpersons, and so on. The combination, or totality, of all of our known statuses makes up our *social status.* Our social status defines our total position in society.

Determining status. Most people become quite adept at obtaining information and interpreting clues to determine the social status of someone they have just met. In the United States today, people first try to learn the nature of an individual's occupation. If we want to judge a new acquaintance's social status, we first ask "What do you do?" The answer is a good indication of income and education. We also note how our new friend dresses, how he or she speaks, what kind of car she drives, where she lives, what clubs she belongs to, what church she is a member of, what school she attended, what schools her children attend, and so on. Before long, a fairly clear picture of the individual's social status emerges.

What categories do you use to judge a person's status?

In assigning a particular social status to an individual, the members of society who are ranking him or her must be aware of what determines high, middle, or low status in that society. The standards by which social status is assigned are widely publicized and therefore generalized by the mass media, although statuses do vary from community to community and certainly from society to society and from era to era. A penniless nobleman has much less social status in the United States, where we value money and achievement, than he may have in Great Britain, where aristocracy is still highly regarded. However, certain subgroups in the United States may assign a higher social status to the nobleman than would our society as a whole. Likewise, subgroups in Great Britain may assign a lower social status to him, be-

[8]Lenski, pp. 37–38.

cause they value aristocracy less than does the majority.

Social status is also determined by family. In our society, the social status of a family still derives from that of male breadwinner, although this situation is slowly changing as a result of the women's movement. His social status is, in turn, determined chiefly by his occupation. A child acquires his social status from his family and keeps it until he is an adult, when he may have to achieve his own social status.

Cultural values may also help to determine an individual's status. In the United States today, we officially value high intelligence, efficiency, and productivity above all. People who have such characteristics are often rewarded with highly prized social positions. But such positions are often not awarded on the basis of merit or achievement alone. Many intelligent, efficient, and productive people are kept out of rewarding social positions because they have a low ascribed status from membership in particular racial, ethnic, religious, and regional groups. The total social status of a black person may thus be low, despite a high achieved status (for example, physician).

In the composite of a high-status individual presented here, what are the various indicators of status?

The variables that determine social status are occupation and source of income, color, education, sex, age, religion, and ethnic origin. A composite, or a model, of a high-status individual in our society would present the following picture. The individual is likely to be a white male in his late thirties who was educated at Harvard and is a corporation lawyer, with a fairly high income. He is probably also a member of the Episcopal Church; is active in state politics and civic groups. He may also be a descendant of early settlers of the American colonies.

Status inconsistency. We might conclude that variables directly opposed to those associated with high social status would determine low status. Increasingly, however, in studying industrial societies, sociologists have become aware of *status inconsistency.* In this phenomenon several of the variables traditionally associated with high social status may be lacking, yet the individual still enjoys high status. Likewise, the variables associated with low status may be lacking, yet the individual is ranked as having low status. For instance, a Puerto Rican immigrant does not have the color, income, education, religion, and ethnic origin usually associated with high status. If he becomes famous and wealthy, he is said to be *status inconsistent.* The same may be said for the descendant of rich industrialists who loses his entire fortune and his status. Although certain characteristics primarily related to ascribed statuses serve to indicate social status, many people in our type of stratification system are able to rise above or fall below these indicators.

One way of dealing with inconsistencies is to make an exception to the rule. Another way is to develop a theory that explains both the rule and the exceptions. Can you develop a theory of stratification that explains why a Puerto Rican immigrant who has "made good" might have a high status in spite of his or her origins?

Status inconsistency also occurs when an individual has a position that ranks high in status, but that provides him with a comparatively low income. His income does not allow him to have the life-style of other members of his *status group.* A status group consists of all indi-

Status Groups: Some Examples

When the classical sociologist Max Weber came to define status groups, he said such groups "usurp" or appropriate, status honor by setting themselves apart from others on the basis of some characteristic or badge that they attempt to monopolize. What Weber suggested was that status is something that is originally appropriated and later defended, rather than just a social ranking. As an example of a status group, Weber used the FFV (the First Families of Virginia), whose prestige was not based on any economic function they performed (though these families were wealthy), but on their claim to be descendants of the first white settlers. The DAR (Daughters of the American Revolution) could also be considered a status group.[1]

When conflict theorists use the concept of status groups, they emphasize the appropriation and defense of group privileges. Sociologist Robert Blauner, for example, believes racial groups are status groups in Weber's sense. Whites have set themselves apart from other racial groups (making of race a special issue) and attempted to monopolize prestigious roles (along with wealth and power), on the basis of their skin color.[2] Do you think males form a status group in this sense? Do you think you could create your own status group by emphasizing some special characteristic you share with a few others and by convincing others that it is desirable?

[1]H. H. Gerth and C. Wright Mills, ed. and trans., *From Max Weber: Essays in Sociology* (New York: Oxford University Press, Galaxy Book, 1958), pp. 186–194.

[2]Robert Blauner, *Racial Oppression in America* (New York: Harper & Row, 1972), pp. 27–28.

viduals who are ranked similarly and who tend to associate with each other, developing common life-styles. A writer or artist may have high status, but be miserably paid.

Status inconsistency is also frequently found among black professionals. A black executive may not be admitted to a golf club because of his or her skin color. In such situations, the individual tends to be judged by his *master status*—the status that society considers the most important of several alternatives.[9]

Pretend that you are writing and directing a soap opera in which a high-ranking society businessman must give a dinner party for a black woman scientist. What kinds of conflicts may arise? How might the businessman defend his action to his fellow businessmen?

[9]Everett Hughes, "Dilemmas and Contradiction of Status," *American Journal of Sociology* 50 (1945): 353–359.

Power

The third most important category of stratification is power. *Power* is defined as the ability of one individual or segment of the population to control the actions of another individual or segment of the population, with or without the latter's consent. Power is the capacity to get other people to do what you want them to do. Power is exercised in all social systems, from the simplest to the most complex.

Power is multifaceted and elusive. Thus, it is frequently difficult to make definitive statements about its nature, source, and location. As applied to stratification, power can be divided into personal power and social power. *Personal power* is the freedom of an individual to direct his own life in any way he chooses, without much societal interference. In our society, great personal freedom is frequently tied to possession of wealth. If a person is rich enough, he is free to do almost anything he wants to do and can obtain "anything money can buy."

Social power is the ability to make decisions that affect entire communities or even the whole society. Social power may be exercised legitimately, with the consent of the other members of society. In this case it is called *authority.* Different levels of authority are represented by parents, teachers, and the government.

Power may also be illegitimate—exercised without the official approval of society. Organized crime, for example, exercises power illegitimately. This use of power was vividly portrayed in a fictionalized account of underworld operations, Mario Puzo's *The Godfather.* The underworld coerces an individual by threats of violence into acting as it wishes. Members of the underworld simply "make him an offer he can't refuse." The offer, of course, involves the threat of violent death.

Location and use of power. Although we tend to think of power as a political phenomenon, it affects all areas of human life. Most observers agree that the manner in which a society's goods and services are distributed chiefly depends on who has power. Lenski wrote, ". . . power will determine the distribution of nearly all of the surplus possessed by a society."[10] This is expressed in the folk wisdom of the saying, "Money is power."

Power is deeply interwoven with the other dimensions of stratification, class and status. The individual who has power can control decision making so that decisions are favorable to him. In this way, he can obtain wealth. Wealth puts him in an upper social class, which gives him a high status. In traditional nonindustrial societies, religion and traditions have supported the idea that the rich are powerful and are entitled to rule, whereas the poor are powerless and are in need of being ruled. Even in modern, industrial societies, religion and tradition have tended to support the stratification system.

[10]Lenski, p. 44.

Methodology: The Interview

Floyd Hunter's classic study in the 1950s, *Community Power Structure,* commenced the American debate over the concentration of power on the local level. To find the real decision makers of "Regional City" (thought to be Atlanta), Hunter interviewed selected members of the community. He asked fourteen "judges"—long-time residents knowledgeable in the city's affairs—to select the most influential leaders from among lists he had gathered of people active in the city's business, government, civic, and "society" affairs. Hunter then interviewed the 40 people the judges selected most frequently.

Hunter used a combination of structured and unstructured interview techniques. He asked each person a predetermined set of questions about their institutional affiliations, who *they* thought were the city's most influential people, and about how important issues were decided. When the occasion arose, Hunter would depart from his questionnaire to explore other issues and experiences. In this way, he was able to discover relationships among the reputed leaders and gain a picture of the city's power structure.

Hunter found a high frequency of contact among the forty people he interviewed, especially among an even smaller elite. They met in the same places, he found; they belonged to the same clubs, and lived near one another. They chose each other as community leaders and worked together deciding community projects. Among this group, those who owned or controlled large amounts of capital predominated. Of the forty, twenty-three were industrialists, financiers, or executives of commercial enterprises. These were the real policy-makers of the community, Hunter argued, the power behind the throne of official government. They left policy execution, however, to the elected officials. Regional City's mayor and the county treasurer, former businessmen themselves, served primarily in the interests of this elite group, Hunter concluded.

Critics of Hunter have said that he discovered only people's image of the power structure, not necessarily its reality—a criticism that could be made of the interview method in general. Hunter's supporters have replied that the formal leaders (like everyone else) act on the basis of their images, and would therefore consider the views and power of those they thought most influential before making any decisions.

Floyd Hunter, *Community Power Structure: A Study of Decision Makers* (Garden City: Doubleday, 1963).

In modern industrial societies, the naturalness of such a system has long been questioned. In these societies power has been spread among many people, rather than being concentrated in the hands of a very few individuals. Because of universal suffrage, political power has been diffused; decision making is no longer in the hands of one or a few people. Furthermore, local power groups such as the urban political machines or the family businesses that dominated small towns have, in general, disappeared because of increasingly centralized decision making. Centralization, in turn, is a result of "big government," "big industry," and "big labor," phenomena that are discussed in later chapters.

The division of power on a national level has been viewed in various ways. Sociologist C. Wright Mills suggested that decisions having a crucial impact on national and international affairs were being made by no more than 300 corporate, military, and political leaders.[11]

On the other hand, David Riesman believes that a number of interest groups compromise on major decisions, attaining a balance of power. The power each group has is the ability to veto decisions that go entirely against its interests. To a lesser extent, each group also has the ability to initiate some decisions.[12] The American Medical Association, for instance, has often vetoed medical legislation.

What examples of shifts in power might a follower of Talcott Parsons offer to support his theory that power circulates in our society?

Economist John Kenneth Galbraith thinks in terms of "countervailing" powers. According to Galbraith, big labor, big government, and big business are in a constant tug-of-war; the power of each is somewhat offset by the power of the others.[13] Talcott Parsons, an adherent of functionalist stratification theory, believes that power in our type of economy is not fixed, but circulates like money, changing hands frequently.[14]

Regardless of the way social scientists conceptualize power, the average member of society feels that his fate is controlled by a small number of individuals in positions of authority. He senses that he lacks both personal and social power because of his low status in society.

We will see in later chapters whether indeed some segments of society hold sway over others; who are those in power and who are the powerless; and on what basis power or the lack of it are distributed in the society.

---

[11]C. Wright Mills, *The Power Elite* (New York: Oxford University Press, 1956), chapter 12.

[12]David Riesman et al., *The Lonely Crowd* (New Haven, Conn.: Yale University Press, 1961), pp. 245–255.

[13]John Kenneth Galbraith, *American Capitalism* (Boston: Houghton Mifflin, 1956).

[14]Seymour Martin Lipset and Reinhard Bendix, *Social Mobility in Industrial Society* (Berkeley, Calif.: University of California Press, 1959), p. 261.

[How Sociologists Determine Social Class]

Class, status, and power can be roughly determined by any member of society. Sociologists, however, need more accurate ways of describing our stratification system. Social scientists have used a number of approaches in categorizing social classes. In *Middletown*, a classic study of stratification, Robert and Helen Lynd divided the population of a representative Midwestern American town into two classes: the business class and the working class.[15] Another classic set of studies by W. L. Warner and Paul Lunt, the Yankee City Series, examined the stratification system of a New England seaside town. Classifications were made according to a six-class division; upper-upper, lower-upper, upper-middle, lower-middle; upper-lower, and lower-lower. These divisions are the ones most frequently used in the literature dealing with stratification.[16] However, some researchers use the white-collar, blue-collar, and professional middle-class classifications.

How would Marx have described the difference between what the Lynds call the business class and the working class?

Sociologists disagree not only about the number of classes in existence but also about the standards that determine who belongs in which class. The categories used by researchers to pigeonhole people into social classes are arbitrary and artificial. They do not occur naturally in society, but are simply a device researchers use to simplify their work. A researcher may decide that an individual whose salary has increased by $1,000 per year belongs not only in a different income category than before but also in a higher social class. There is no law, either of nature or of society, that supports such a classification. In preindustrial societies, on the other hand, such natural divisions did exist. In feudal Europe, for instance, the social distance between the nobility and the serfs was so great that the existence of the two categories could be considered natural.[17]

In general, researchers determine social class by using one of the following approaches:

1. *Life-styles approach.* Researchers observe and question people about their life styles—whom they interact with, what types of material objects they possess, what types of recreational activities they engage in, what organizations they belong to, what speech mannerisms they have, and so on.[18]
2. *Reputational approach.* Researchers ask people to act as judges in ranking others in their community. This approach sometimes presents problems because it is difficult for a judge to know everyone

---

[15]Robert Lynd and Helen Lynd, *Middletown in Transition* (New York: Harcourt, Brace & World, 1937).

[16]W. L. Warner and Paul Lunt, *The Social Life of a Modern Community* (New Haven, Conn.: Yale University Press, 1941).

[17]Leonard Broom and Philip Selznick, *Sociology* (New York: Harper and Row, 1968), p. 154.

[18]Harold M. Hodges, Jr. and W. Clayton Lane, *Social Stratification* (Cambridge, Mass.: Schenkman, 1964), pp. 79–81.

in his community. Furthermore, a judge's biases may influence the way he ranks a person.

3. *Subjective approach.* Researchers ask people to rank themselves. This approach has been found unreliable chiefly because the average person often has gross misconceptions both about the stratification system of his society and about his place in it. Many people cling to a belief in classlessness. Others see only a clear-cut division between the rich and the poor. Still others conceive of classes in strictly Marxist terms. To them, society is divided into those who own the means of production and those who labor for them.

Using your class as the sample population, develop class categories by one or more of the approaches described here. Which approach do you find most suitable? Why?

4. *Objective approach.* Researchers use indicators such as income, education, occupation, and position of authority without relying on the feelings, evaluations, and perceptions either of the individuals who are being examined or of a panel of judges. The researchers, as impartial and objective scientists, develop categories based on income, education, occupation, and so on, placing people into the appropriate category. Objective methods permit significantly more exact measurements than do the subjective and reputational approaches. Nonetheless, they too fail to describe reality in all cases. A researcher following this approach would put into the same category a retired postal worker living on a pension of $10,000 a year and a cub reporter working for the first time on a big city newspaper. Yet $10,000 is the highest income the postal worker will receive during the remainder of his life, whereas it is the lowest amount the reporter will receive during what he hopes will be a prosperous career.
5. *Occupational prestige approach.* Researchers ask people which occupations and sources of income are the most prestigious. This approach is sometimes considered part of the reputational approach. However, it depends on a much larger—usually on a national—sample. The true reputational approach is most effectively used in a small community, where people know each other well. The occupational prestige approach has proved to be the best index of social class in the United States because of its practicality. Occupation determines the amount of money that is earned, and the amount of money possessed determines, in many instances, the amount of power wielded and the prestige held. But money alone does not determine social class. Some occupations are rated very high even though the pay for them is relatively low.

In your choice of occupations, do you feel you are guided more by the status or the wealth and power that is associated with an occupation? Are you using any other considerations? If so, what are you using?

Systems of Stratification

To simplify analysis, we study stratification as an interconnected system. A *stratification system* is the overlapping manner in which societal members are ranked into classes, status groups, and hierarchies of power. In analyses of stratification systems, the following elements are

Middle Americans Describe Themselves

The "subjective approach" to class, though it may give a misleading picture of the overall stratification system, allows people to describe their class situations in ways that the categories of most sociologists fail to capture. Here is how some people surveyed in Boston responded when asked what came to mind when they heard the phrase "the Middle American":

"Me, I'm the Middle American. People who are in the $7,000–$15,000 income group. People who are working average blue collar jobs making do with what they have. People who vote regularly, take care of property, and are fairly responsible. To lower income families, I would be out of reach. To richer people who don't pay income tax, I am someone to be ignored." (35-year-old working-class woman).

"Joe Average. A guy who must work for a living, puts in his 40 hours a week, and makes $9,500 a year. He has a wife and two kids, an overpriced car and a house that he is still paying on. The low man is on relief, the high man is making lots of money. People would think of me as a Middle American. For the same reasons. I've got an overpriced car, house, wife, and two kids—all of that. Actually, we are lower-middle. We haven't made it to middle." (45-year-old lower-middle-class man).

"The Middle American would be the average in my mind. They're making enough money to generally get by, but just to get by, like me. Maybe one car, enough to eat. Well, a few extras. I think he's the backbone of the country. He pays all the taxes and doesn't squawk. He doesn't get anything for nothing. He gets hurt. Other people would generally consider me a Middle American because my views are what people consider to be Middle American . . ." (40-year-old working-class man).

Lee Rainwater, *What Money Buys* (New York: Basic Books, 1974), p. 120.

generally examined: (1) the number and size of the social classes in a society; (2) the degree of *social mobility*—the ease with which an individual is able to change his class membership by moving up or down the ladder of social stratification; (3) the differences in life-styles among social classes; (4) the conditions leading to class divisions; and (5) the distribution of power among classes and status groups.

Why would the degree of social mobility be an important factor in describing a social stratification system? How would mobility affect life chances?

By considering these elements, especially social mobility and life-styles, we can distinguish among different models of stratification systems. Sociologists analyze stratification systems as if they were placed on an ideal continuum. (We must remember that these systems, as analyzed by sociologists, are simply abstract constructs, or models.) The two extremes of the continuum are represented by the *open* and the *closed* stratification systems, while the middle is represented by the *estate* system. The stratification system of each society fits somewhere along this ideal continuum.

The closed society, or caste system. Whether a society has an open or closed stratification system depends on the way its members obtain wealth, prestige, and privilege (also called *class, status,* and *power*). In *closed societies,* class, status, and power are ascribed, determined strictly on the basis of family inheritance, rather than on personal effort. In such societies, the individual is born into a specific social stratum, called a *caste.* Because the social system is extremely rigid, the individual has no opportunity to move in or out of the caste.

One feature of India's caste system was the existence of a class of outcastes, who were at the bottom of the social pyramid. What kind of function might such a class of "untouchables" serve for the society as a whole?

Classical India offers a good example of a closed society. The caste system that flourished in India for hundreds of years was distinguished by several features. Castes were arranged in order from high to low. These castes represented areas of service to society and were ranked according to their importance to it. Some ranking also resulted from struggles for power or of conquest by other groups. Religion and tradition usually forbade members of one caste to intermarry or to interact in any way with members of another caste. Each caste was restricted in occupation: priests could not become political leaders, and political leaders could not become priests. The status of each individual in a caste was ascribed. He inherited his social position and was unable to change it. Even if an individual accumulated a great deal of wealth and wisdom, he could not enter a higher caste. The caste system was justified by the religion and the traditional mores of the society.

Today, India is considered a democracy and is slowly becoming industrialized. Industrialization will eventually doom the caste system. Traditions will break down as more and more people live in cities, work in factories, and are given the opportunity to obtain an education. The caste system has already been legally abolished, but many Indians, particularly those living in rural areas, are still influenced by it.

To someone reared in the United States, the Indian caste system may seem stifling and antilibertarian. However, it provided the Indian citizen with certain satisfactions. The Indian almost always had underdogs—members of lower castes—against whom he could discriminate, and so increase his status in his own eyes. Permanent membership in kinship and religious groups also furnished a great deal of security. The individual may have experienced greater peace of mind and fewer frustrations than those who are free to compete for a high social standing.

What advantage, if any, might the members of the lowest classes in India have derived from their low status?

The social and philosophical traditions of a caste system are, of course, in direct opposition to the values of our own society. Nevertheless, many social thinkers have likened our treatment of certain minority groups—especially blacks—to that given people in a caste system. In the United States, a person who is born black is limited as to where he or she can live, how well he or she will be educated, and what jobs will be available. Social interaction is usually limited to members of the group. But in closed societies the caste arrangement is sanctioned by society and tradition, is reinforced by the institutions, and accepted by the majority of the people. In our society such an arrangement defies official societal values. It causes frustration and resentment in the group delegated to caste status, and feelings of distrust in those who see the difference between the ideals and the reality.

The estate system. Less rigid than the caste system is the estate system, the economic and social system of feudal Europe. The estate system also has characterized many nations in Asia, though in different form. In the estate system, societal positions were ranked according to their functions. Although the estates were ranked from low to high in order of importance, they were all theoretically considered to be of equal importance—"Some fight, some work, some pray." (At least, this is how members were encouraged to remain in their social position).

Why would a stratification system based on occupation and land ownership be somewhat less rigid than a caste system?

The three main social divisions, called *estates,* were the nobility, the church, and the peasants. Within each estate there was a stratified hierarchy of positions. Among the nobility, the hierarchy ranged from the king and his family down to lesser nobles and, finally, to local administrative officials. Among the military, whose leaders were recruited from the ranks of the nobility, the hierarchy reached from the commanding staff down to the officer corps and to common enlisted men. Among the churchmen, the hierarchy was based on a similar arrangement, with the pope at the top and, beneath him, cardinals, archbishops, bishops, and parish priests. The peasants were divided into villeins, who were semifree, emancipated tenant farmers, and serfs, who were not free.

Support for the system came from religion and tradition, as in the caste system. However, the estate system permitted quite a bit more mobility among social strata than did the caste system. As a matter of fact, the second- and later-born children of the nobility had to enter one of the other estates, because according to law, only the firstborn son inherited his family's possessions and rank. Occasionally serfs who had distinguished themselves in some way were freed and given land. Villeins were also often allowed to enter the lower ranks of the clergy.

In estate systems, serfs were considered to be tied to the land. What function might this restriction have served, say, in seventeenth-century Russia? What do you think happened to the system when the serfs were freed?

Because of the vow of celibacy, the estate made up of churchmen (clerics) had to be periodically replenished from outside the church. Additional churchmen came from both higher and lower estates, although the sons of noblemen and military men tended to become cardinals and bishops, whereas the children of peasants tended to become parish priests and monks. Nevertheless, it was not unusual for an ambitious parish priest to rise within the church hierarchy, and for a simple foot soldier to achieve a position of leadership.

From your knowledge of American history, what facets of the estate system are recognizable as having existed in the pre-Civil War South?

The remnants of this system are still visible in some modern societies, in which there are landed gentry and inherited titles of nobility. Such a system is also the essence of stratification on the vast ranch empires of South America, called *latifundia.* And some facets of the system are easily recognizable as having existed on American plantations a century ago, although plantations had a predominantly caste system of stratification.

The open society, or class system. At the other extreme of the continuum we find the open society, or class system. In theory, such a society should offer each member equal access to material resources, equal access to power, and equal access to prestige. In reality, of course, such ideal open societies do not exist. The closest examples would perhaps be the Israeli kibbutzim or similar utopian communities. These, however, are small communities, not whole societies. On a societal level, modern industrial societies such as the United States most nearly approximate the model of an open society. Open societies have several characteristics in common: (1) classes do exist, but they are not institutionalized to the same degree that castes and estates are; (2) because class lines are unclear, members of society do not display excessive class consciousness, although inequality stemming from class divisions is apparent; (3) status usually is achieved; however, there is a great deal of evidence to indicate that status tends to be ascribed in the lowest and the highest social classes; (4) social mobility is possible and occurs frequently.

In an open, or a class system, members of society are not ranked according to their functional specialization. Doctors, for instance, do not make up a social class because of what they do. But *wealthy* doctors, lawyers, and industrialists, who have status and power because of their important positions, do form a social class. Their occupation does not determine their social class. It is merely an indication of and a channel for the attainment of wealth, power, and prestige, according to which they are socially ranked.

Why might it have been important, for our development as an industrialized nation, to free the slaves?

Open stratification systems work best in industrial societies that have market economies. Such societies offer more opportunities for social mobility than do societies in which the market is controlled by the government. In controlled economies, people may not have the opportunity to choose their jobs and to increase their wealth.

Although social mobility is possible and is even encouraged in open systems, it is not evenly distributed throughout such systems. Limitations of a racial, religious, ethnic, and regional nature restrict mobility. However, the individual is permitted much more leeway for

In the United States, the general tendency to value achieved status is limited by status ascribed according to sex, age, and ethnic origins. Cesar Chavez (center left) is a union organizer who has tried to help Mexican-American farm workers break out of a low ascribed status.

social as well as physical movement than in a closed system.

The spectrum from caste to class is a measure of the value placed on ascribed or achieved characteristics. Americans, whose dogma includes equality and importance of the individual, value achievement more highly than ascription. In terms of age, sex, and race, however, ascription continues to play a heavy role. Consequently, our own society, which is a fairly representative example of an open, or class system, is theoretically considered more open than it is in reality, a fact that is often forgotten even by the most 'objective' sociologists.

[Social Mobility]

We have seen that one of the principal differences between open and closed societies is that there is social mobility in open societies, and none or very little in closed societies. We said that the term *social mobility* refers to an individual's ability to change his social class membership by moving up or down the ladder of his stratification system.

Many of us can trace our family history back for one or two generations. What evidence of social mobility do you find in your family history? Is primarily vertical or horizontal mobility involved?

Sociologists, however, usually distinguish between *vertical mobility,* which occurs in an upward or downward direction, and *horizontal mobility,* which occurs when there is a change of status without a consequent change of class. To illustrate, the secondary school teacher who is made principal is upwardly mobile. The department chairman who is demoted to teacher is downwardly mobile. And the school superintendent who becomes an executive of an insurance company at no greater salary and with no greater or lesser prestige than he had as a superintendent is horizontally mobile.

The Upwardly Mobile Individual

Not all individuals take advantage of the opportunities for upward mobility. According to studies in the field, those who are upwardly mobile frequently display the following traits: (1) they are urban residents; (2) they are only children, or one of two children; (3) they are influenced by ambitious parents; (4) they acquire more education than their parents did; (5) they marry later than others of their generation and usually a partner of higher status; and (6) they wait to establish a family, limiting its size to no more than two children.

It is easy to figure out why such traits are associated with upward mobility. Most industries and businesses are located in urban centers. Thus, urban residence provides an individual with many more chances to obtain a good job than does rural residence. An only child, or one of two children, has more opportunities for higher education than do children who come from large families. Not only is it financially easier for parents to send one or two children to school, but it is also possible to give a great deal of time and attention to a small number of children.

How do you relate to the traits described as characterizing the upwardly mobile? Do you see yourself as upwardly mobile? If so, has this caused any interfamily conflicts for you? Why?

Ambitious parents are able to influence their children to become upwardly mobile because parents are chiefly responsible for socialization in our society. People who acquire a better education than their parents did take the first step toward a job that is better than their parents'. Consequently, upward mobility is furthered. Marrying relatively late in life makes it possible for an individual to delay the assumption of responsibilities. He or she can spend time in school, obtaining the education that may lead to a good job. Because they are well educated and have good jobs, upwardly mobile individuals are able to marry people from higher social classes than their own. Finally, by waiting to establish a family, such individuals make sure that they are able to care for their offspring well. By limiting family size to no more than two, they repeat the cycle, which leads to upward mobility for their children.

In sociological terms, individuals like those we have just described display *intergenerational mobility.* In other words, they belong to a higher social class than did their parents. They also display *intragenerational mobility,* in that they do better in their careers, and consequently belong to a higher social class, than do other people of the same generation.[19]

Social Mobility in the United States

It is widely believed that upward mobility is the pattern in the United States and other industrial nations. Advanced technology has freed workers from many unskilled manual jobs and forced them to train

[19]Lipset and Bendix, pp. 73–74.

for more highly skilled, better-paying jobs. Education has been extended to include the formerly uneducated masses.

However, the assumption that upward mobility is a trend may be open to question. It may well be true that the upward mobility of professionals and technical workers, managers and executives, and clerical and service workers has become so great that these people will someday form the basis of the upper-middle and upper classes.[20] But uneducated and unskilled workers now have less opportunity to become upwardly mobile than they had in the past.

One study of mobility suggests a trend toward downward mobility. Researchers used the transition from a manual to a nonmanual job as an indicator of upward mobility. They found that 28.8 percent of the sons of manual workers became nonmanual workers, whereas 29.7 percent of the sons of nonmanual workers became manual workers.[21] Of course, this percentage difference is small, and in terms of money, manual jobs are sometimes better rewarded than nonmanual ones.

The highest degree of mobility seems to occur within, rather than between, categories of jobs such as blue-collar and white-collar. In short, an assemblyline worker can more easily become a foreman than he can become a junior executive. The point of breakthrough from manual to nonmanual jobs lies in clerical and sales positions and in small businesses. However, special talents, if allowed to flourish, are often the key to spectacular upward mobility. Consider the case of boxing champion Joe Frazier, who made the ascent from penniless sharecropper to millionaire. Thousands of others have made a similar ascent.

Social mobility seems to be insignificant at the extremes of the stratification system. At the very top and at the very bottom of the system, mobility is virtually replaced by a caste system. At the very top, upward mobility is a matter of more and more accumulation of wealth—status and power are already there, and there is nowhere else to go. Downward mobility at this level becomes improbable because status is a function of lineage, which is stable. At the very bottom, socialization tends to impede learning the skills or obtaining the education that would help improve social position. Horizontal mobility, then, seems to be the norm at both extremes of the stratification system.

It has been suggested that education may no longer be the force for upward mobility that it once was. Do you feel that an education will ensure a job in this economy? Why or why not?

Have you ever heard the saying, "The rich get richer and the poor get poorer"? What does this saying suggest about life chances for the upper-upper and lower-lower classes? How does this cycle operate?

An Evaluation of Social Mobility

We tend to assume that social mobility is a positive rather than a negative value and that an open society is preferable to a closed one. But

---

[20]Peter Berger and Brigitte Berger, "The Blueing of America," *The New Republic* (April 3, 1971).

[21]S. M. Miller, "Comparative Social Mobility," in *Structured Social Inequality: A Reader in Comparative Social Stratification*, ed. Celia S. Heller (Macmillan, 1969), p. 329.

Up and Down the Class Ladder

The rates of occupational mobility for males have remained remarkably constant over the past century, despite important shifts in the composition of the work force. This is the conclusion of Stephan Thernstrom, comparing data he gathered for Boston to mobility patterns since 1880 in diverse cities and towns throughout the United States.

About 25 percent of the men who began their careers as manual workers in each generation since 1880 ended in white-collar jobs, while about 16 percent of those who started as white-collar workers fell into blue-collar positions. Those whose lives were disrupted in mid-career by the Depression of the 1930s formed the only significant deviation from this pattern.

Approximately 40 percent of the sons of manual workers in each generation moved into white-collar jobs, while about 20 percent of the sons of white-collar workers fell into working-class jobs by the end of their careers. Chances for upward mobility appear less for those born in 1930, but these sons, Thernstrom argues, were only in mid-career when the sample was taken in 1963. Only about 5 percent of the sons of unskilled or semi-skilled workers have become professionals or prosperous businessmen in each generation over the past century, but among the same group, over half obtained skilled worker or white-collar positions.

Stephan Thernstrom, *The Other Bostonians: Poverty and Progress in the American Metropolis, 1880–1970* (Cambridge: Harvard University Press, 1973), pp. 45–110, 232–261.

we cannot flatly state that social mobility is "good" and that lack of mobility is "bad." A closed society, in which there is little social mobility, shelters the individual from the frustrations of unsuccessful competition. It does not encourage expectations that cannot be fulfilled. Furthermore, it protects a person from the strain of adjusting to unfamiliar surroundings. The mobile individual must constantly adapt to socially unfamiliar situations—a new class, new norms, new values. A member of a closed society spends his life in an environment that is familiar to him. In other words, an open society, with its high degree of mobility, does not guarantee happiness. The belief in competition and achievement takes a heavy toll in suicides, neuroses, and psychoses, broken homes, alienated youth, and physical illness.

On the other hand, a closed society, in which there is little social mobility, is not very likely to become a world leader. Heredity does not guarantee that the son of a capable and wise father will be equally capable and wise. A society that does not give talented people from the lower strata an opportunity to advance into positions of leadership will not fare well for long. What is more, such a society becomes marked by hopelessness and despair, for many of its members live without even a glimmer of hope for a better tomorrow.

What are we to conclude, then? Which system is preferable? Would you prefer being born into a permanent social stratum? Or would you prefer being born into a society that is *completely* open? In such a society, any citizen could rise to any height through sheer merit. Those who did not achieve great heights—and there would always be some—would have only themselves, and their inadequacies, to blame. Does this kind of society seem desirable to you? There is no absolute answer to these questions, of course. But it is worthwhile to remember that a completely open society, in which achievement is based solely on merit, would not be a Garden of Eden.

Would you prefer a closed system to an open system for any reason? What classes, in a closed system, would be most likely to benefit from its advantages?

[Summary]

Stratification is a phenomenon present in all societies that have produced a surplus. Stratification is the process by which members of society rank themselves and one another in hierarchies (from low to high) with respect to the amount of desirable goods they possess.

The existence of stratification has led to the centuries-old problem of social inequality. In societies that have closed stratification systems, such inequalities are institutionalized and rigid. An individual born into a particular economic and social stratum, or caste, remains in this stratum until he dies. Most modern industrial societies have open, or class, stratification systems. In open stratification systems, social mobility is possible, although some members of the population do not have the opportunity to fulfill their potential.

The three categories of stratification—status, class, and power—are closely interrelated. In the United States, occupation or source of income almost always determines status. In turn, status is related to class membership. Finally, the degree of power held by any one individual depends, to a great extent, on his status and class. Other variables that determine a person's position in the stratification system of the United States are color, sex, age, religion, region, and ethnic origin.

An individual's life chances—his opportunity to become a complete human being and reap the satisfactions that his society has to offer—are greatly diminished if the individual belongs to a low social class or to a nonwhite group. Although American society has been sufficiently open to permit considerable upward mobility, attained primarily through education, it has remained obstinately closed to the lower strata of society. Members of lower classes are further hampered by being socialized to hold values that do not help them become upwardly mobile. In addition, they develop a type of personality that discourages mobility. Spending their lives in a hostile environment, they lack the life chances that many other people have.

Stratification and social inequality may always be a part of human societies. However, modern industrial societies have the affluence and the knowledge, and, we think, the moral obligation, to narrow the gap between those at the top and those at the bottom of the stratification system.

Terms to Remember

Authority. Social power exercised with the consent of the members of society. Different levels of authority are represented by parents, teachers, and the government.

Closed, or caste, stratification system. A system in which class, status, and power are ascribed; mobility is highly restricted; and the social system is rigid.

Conflict theory. A theory of stratification according to which the natural condition of society is constant change and conflict resulting from class struggles. Stratification systems, and consequent social inequality, are considered evidence of such conflict.

Functionalist theory. A theory of stratification in which social inequality is viewed as inevitable because society must use rewards to make sure that essential tasks will be performed by the most talented and most highly trained individuals. Functionalists maintain that the natural condition of society is order and stability.

Life chances. The opportunity of each individual to fulfill or fail to fulfill his potential as a human being in society.

Open or class society. A society in which the stratification system allows for social mobility and in which a person's status is achieved rather than being ascribed on the basis of race or birth. Open systems are characteristic of industrial societies.

Power. A category of stratification. The ability of one individual or segment of the population to control the actions of another individual or segment of the population, with or without the latter's consent.

Social class. A category of stratification. An aggregate of persons in a society who stand in a similar position with respect to some form of power, privilege, or prestige.

Social mobility. An individual's ability to change his social class membership by moving up or down the ladder of the stratification system. Upward or downward mobility is called *vertical,* whereas mobility that results in a change of status without a consequent change of class is called *horizontal.*

Social status. A category of stratification. The individual's ranked position within the social system, the rank being determined by the role the individual performs.

Social stratification, or ranking. A process existing in all but the most simple societies, whereby members rank one another and themselves hierarchically (from low to high) with respect to the amount of desirable goods and services they possess.

Stratification system. The overlapping manner in which societal members are ranked according to classes, status groups, and hierarchies of power.

Estate system. The prevailing economic and social system of feudal Europe, consisting of three estates of functional importance to society. The estates were hierarchically arranged and permitted a limited amount of social mobility.

Suggestions for Further Reading

Bendix, Reinhard, and Seymour Martin Lipset, eds., *Class, Status, and Power.* New York: Glencoe Free Press, 1966. This collection of essays has become a classic in the field of social stratification.

Dahrendorf, Ralf. *Class and Class Conflict in Industrial Society.* Stanford, Calif.: Stanford University Press, 1959. A clear and well-reasoned statement of the conflict theorist's position.

Heller, Celia S. *Structured Social Inequality: A Reader in Comparative Social Stratification.* New York: Macmillan, 1969. A comprehensive reader in the area of stratification.

Hollingshead, A. B. *Elmstown's Youth.* New York: John Wiley, 1949. A classic in the field of social stratification, this book examines the influence of social class on the young people of a midwestern community.

Jencks, Christopher, *et al.*, *Inequality* (New York: Basic Books, 1972). A controversial study that overturns many assumptions on how to reform some facets of inequality.

Lenski, Gerhard. *Power and Privilege: A Theory of Social Stratification.* New York: McGraw–Hill, 1966. Power as the basic manipulative force of social life underlies this theory of a renowned sociologist.

Lipset, Seymour Martin, and Reinhard Bendix. *Social Mobility in Industrial Society.* Berkeley: University of California Press, 1966. A comparative approach, the results of which refute the notion that industrial societies are as open as they seem to be.

Mills, C. Wright. *The Power Elite.* New York: Oxford University Press, 1959. A polemical book by a well-known conflict theorist, asserting that power in the United States is the property of an interlocking directorate of top corporate, military, and governmental leaders.

Warner, W. Lloyd. *Yankee City,* abridged edition. New Haven, Conn.: Yale University Press, 1963. An interesting and readable analysis of the social system of a New England community seen as a microcosm of the larger American society.

We and they: majority and minorities

Given the fact that intolerance becomes sharper the greater the differences between people, do you think we would be able to avoid conflict with vastly different beings from outer space? Why or why not?

IF SPACE TRAVEL ever became a concrete reality, and if we ever met beings similar to humans, we would be very curious to learn how they organized their lives. We would be especially interested in finding out whether they had succeeded in eliminating conflict on their planet (if they were ever faced with it). We would also want to know what the chief causes of their conflict had been. We on earth are very far from having resolved conflict. Conflict has been a part of every society recorded in history. It seems that in their need to cling to others like themselves, humans develop such an intense loyalty for their own group that they cannot tolerate groups formed by others. Intolerance appears to become sharper the greater are the differences in skin color, language, religious beliefs, customs and gender. Intolerance is also expressed in the stratification system of a society. Specific qualities of groups—their race, their national background, their sex—are perceived by the dominant group in the society as indications of inferiority. This assumed inferiority becomes the rationalization for keeping the "different" groups down, especially in the area of competition for the scarce resources of the society.

What function might intolerance serve in a stratification system linked to an economy based on scarce resources?

Why do different groups seem unable to live in harmony with one another, to respect one another's opinions, and to tolerate one another's differences? Are we innately unable to get along with each other? Or are we socialized toward ethnocentrism and the value of competition?

Such questions cannot be answered categorically. Much of the problem of majority and minority, of oppressor and oppressed, of those who are in and those who are out, revolves around our basic way of life, our human characteristics, and our social system.

Humans are social beings—that is, they live in groups. Groups are necessary to people, and without some groups most people could not survive. But group life produces conflict. We disagree and quarrel with members of our own group. And groups disagree and quarrel with one another. Almost all of history is a record of groups fighting each other. Today too, in many parts of the world, conflict rages—between Catholic and Protestant, between Arab and Jew, between communist and capitalist, between white and black, between rich and poor, and between man and woman.

In our own society, the conflicts among groups appear to have destructive consequences in spite of the fact that conflict can be creative and can lead to important changes in society, as conflict theorists maintain. Conflicts threaten our image not only as a stable and secure nation, but as one of the foremost examples of a democracy. This nation was theoretically founded as a haven for the oppressed of the world. But the many groups that reached our shores never quite melted into the "melting pot" as they were supposed to. Many Americans today remain hyphenated—Black-Americans, Italian-Americans, Japanese-Americans—either because they want to retain their distinctiveness, or because they are forced to retain it. In an ideal democracy the retention of one's group identity is a matter of choice, and is not forced on anyone. Group identity, however, has been used to relegate members of certain groups to the bottom of the stratification system in our society. This is contrary not only to our moral values, but to the ideology of our political system. Whether done by a numerical majority, or by a majority based on power, the domination of one group over other groups is never tolerable. Oppression and the resentment it creates keep us from accepting an idea that we will all have to embrace if we are to survive: that is, the universality of humankind.

Why, in your opinion, might the universality of humankind be an idea we will have to accept in order to survive?

Sociologists approach racial, ethnic, and sexual conflicts from various directions. Some sociologists study such conflicts as products of the system of ideas that is racism and sexism and trace the development of racism and sexism throughout history. Others view racial, ethnic, and sexual conflicts as phenomena related to personality. They examine the character structure of particular types of personalities and the channels and agencies through which intolerant attitudes are acquired and spread. Finally, a third group of sociologists is interested in the social structure in which such conflicts occur—in the factors in a society that are responsible for conflicts. All three approaches offer insight into the problems of racial, ethnic, and sexual oppression in our society and in the world.

[Minorities]

The word *minority* has referred to different kinds of groups at various times in history. Today, a minority group is any group in society that is forced to remain at the bottom of the stratification system—or that has a low status in spite of adequate income—because of discriminatory practices of the wider society based on differences in culture, race, religion, or sex. Specifically, minority groups are "categories of people that possess imperfect access to positions of equal power and to the corollary categories of prestige and privilege in the society."[1] Imperfect access is ensured by the power of the dominant group—a power that the subordinate group lacks.

How is the term *minority* derived from our belief in democratic processes? How does current usage of the term conflict with our belief in such processes?

The term *minority* does not necessarily connote numbers. Minorities are not always small groups. They can even exceed 50 percent of the population, as women do. Minorities are relegated to a lower position in the stratification system as a result of membership in a group that differs from the majority in race, culture, religion, or sex.

In the United States the English settlers subdued the native populations and set out to establish and control government and the economy. Having control of these key institutions, the original settlers were able to acquire important positions and pass them on to members of their own group. Later groups of immigrants, particularly south and east Europeans, received less desirable positions. Africans who came as slaves received the least desirable positions of all. Women consistently received less status and power than men, whatever their social status.

In such a situation some conflict is unavoidable. The dominant group guards its privileged status and thwarts attempts by subordinate groups to take some of it away. Subordinate groups eventually decide that their inferior status is unsatisfactory and demand a "piece of the action." Conflict, nonetheless, is not always apparent. In stable, primarily agricultural societies, conflict tends to remain beneath the surface. The dominant group is able to control the subordinate groups by convincing them that it is responsible for them in a fatherly way. In other words, members of the dominant group look upon themselves as kindly masters who take care of their less fortunate "children." In dynamic, urban, industrial societies, conflict is much harder to contain. All groups desire scarce goods, and the competition for them brings conflict into the open. The present racial situation in the United States is an illustration of fairly open conflict.

Two of the words used to describe class relations in agricultural societies are *paternalistic* and *patriarchal*. Both of these words are related to the Latin word *pater*, father. In what way might such class relationships resemble those of a family?

Kinds of Minorities

Minorities come into existence when two or more groups occupy the same territory. This situation can arise from political subdivisions following wars. It can also come about because people migrate to improve their lives or are forcibly removed from their native lands to other territories.

---

[1]Norman R. Yetman and C. Hoy Steele, eds., *Majority and Minority* (Boston: Allyn and Bacon, 1971). p. 4.

The United States has minorities that were formed on each of these bases. The Indians had their land seized by the conquering Europeans. Ethnic minorities immigrated to seek political and religious freedom and because they wanted to improve their standard of living. Black people were brought here and made slaves. The Chinese and other peoples came or were brought in as a source of cheap labor.

Minority groups differ from the dominant group and from one another primarily with respect to race, culture, and sex. *Racial minorities* differ biologically. Their skin color, hair texture, head shape, and eye color or slant sets them apart from others. Blacks, American Indians, and Asians are the predominant racial minorities in the United States.

Ethnic minorities differ culturally. Their language, customs, religion, food habits, child-rearing practices, values, and beliefs differ from those of the dominant group. Immigrants, most of whom came in the nineteenth and early twentieth centuries, and their descendants make up ethnic minorities. Their status has varied according to the extent to which their appearance and customs differed from those of the dominant group. Immigrants from the British Isles and northern Europe resembled members of the dominant group in appearance and had similar cultures. Consequently, they were accepted and some were able to attain high status. Immigrants from eastern and southern Europe—Russians, Poles, Italians, Greeks, and Jews—have not been as readily accepted, nor have recent immigrants from Puerto Rico and Mexico.

Religion may be a significant cultural difference between ethnic groups and the dominant group. For some ethnic minorities, religion has been the primary factor in determining low status. This has been true of Jews, Roman Catholics, the followers of Asian religions, and various small sects.

To what minorities, if any, do you belong? How has your membership in such groups affected your life?

The term *sexual minority,* of course, refers to women. Although numerically women constitute a majority, and although economically many belong in the ranks of the upper class, the status of women still greatly depends on their fathers and husbands. Their attempts to attain equal power and privilege in society are as blocked as those of other minority groups.

Common Features of Minorities

Whatever their differences in appearance, culture, or goals, all minority groups have some features in common: (1) they are usually subordinate groups within complex societies; (2) they have specific physical and/or cultural traits that the majority group considers undesirable; (3) they are aware that they differ from the dominant group and tend to stick together because they feel more secure when they share their differentness; (4) for the first few generations, and sometimes much longer, members of minorities tend to marry within the group; (5) descent determines membership in a minority group, and membership is

What pressures might cause members of different minorities to conflict with each other rather than to cooperate to achieve equality?

sometimes retained despite the disappearance of obvious physical or racial distinctions.[2]

But even though their general situation is the same, the various minorities in our society are quite different from one another. They have not usually banded together to create alliances and pressure groups that would strengthen their position in society. On the contrary, many ethnic and racial minorities harbor deep feelings of resentment against one another, as well as against the dominant majority. Separation, rather than cooperation, has been their method of existence, and self-interest their concern. This policy of separateness may now be changing, however.

Goals of Minorities

Not all minorities have wanted to join ranks with the dominant group, though all have desired equal treatment. Some have wanted to keep their own cultural heritage, including religion and language, while coexisting in peace and harmony with the dominant group and with any other minorities in the society. Such minorities are called *pluralistic.* Switzerland is an example of a pluralistic society—one in which various minority groups, each with its own culture, live together in peace.[3] Pluralism is also sometimes expressed as being the goal of the United States.

Other minorities have preferred to absorb completely the culture of the dominant group, hoping in this manner to gain status as part of the majority. Such minorities are termed *assimilationist.* Assimilation was the goal of many early European immigrants to the United States. In recent years, however, assimilation has lost its appeal for members of many minorities, particularly for blacks and Chicanos.

Do you feel that groups who wish to secede should have the right to do so? Why or why not?

Some groups have wanted cultural and/or political independence from the majority. They seek self-determination. These minorities are called *secessionist.* Nations such as Bangladesh were created out of the demands of secessionist minorities. French Canadians have been thwarted in a similar attempt, and Ireland is still trying.

Finally, still other minorities have claimed as their goal not merely equality with the dominant group but a reversal of status with it. They have wanted to become the dominant group. These are called *militant* minorities, found in a number of African nations that recently gained their independence—Algeria, Ghana, and Libya, for example.[4] Such

---

[2]Charles Wagley and Marvin Harris, *Minorities in the New World* (New York: Columbia University Press, 1958), p. 10.

[3]Of late, however, as new minorities (chiefly from southern Europe) have become more visible, the dominant Swiss majority has begun to practice prejudice and discrimination against them.

[4]This typology of minorities appears in Louis Wirth, "The Problem of Minority Groups," in *The Science of Man and the World Crisis,* ed. Ralph Linton (New York: Columbia University Press, 1945), pp. 347–372.

groups, usually numerically superior to begin with, remain minorities only during their struggle to become the dominant group. They abandon militancy and minority group status once their goal is attained. Another goal, migration, may be included as a solution to the intolerable treatment of minorities by a dominant group. The most recent example of migration is that of Soviet Jews who are willing to exchange their minority status in the Union of Soviet Socialist Republics for a similar status in the United States or Israel.

What Problems Do Minorities Face?

The presence of minorities within a society tends to produce conflict. This conflict occurs not only because minority groups are perceived as different by the majority, but also because they perceive themselves as different. Minority members traditionally have been given a special kind of treatment. They have been victims of prejudice, discrimination, and unequal opportunities in the economic system, and their life chances in all areas of life have been affected.

In dealing with the problems of minorities, we must concern ourselves with the majority as well, for this group controls the economic and political mechanisms of the society and most of its mechanisms for change. Sociologist Robert Bierstedt makes this same point:

It is the majority which confers upon folkways, mores, customs, and laws the status of norms and gives them coercive power. It is the majority which guarantees the stability of a society. It is the majority which . . . penalizes deviation —except [deviation] in ways in which the majority sanctions and approves. And it is the inertia of majorities, finally, which retards the processes of social change.[5]

In other words, the problems of minorities do not necessarily stem from their own inadequacies or their deviation from the standards of society. Instead, problems may stem from the social institutions supported by the majority. This view is not readily accepted by the majority, which prefers to blame features that many minorities display—high crime rates, high school dropout rates, unstable marriages and broken homes, and the inability to rise socially—on the lack of intelligence and laziness of the minority group members.[6] Thus, the solutions majorities use to overcome problems arising from the existence of minority groups are often misdirected and are sometimes horribly cruel.

In different societies, the dominant group uses different methods of dealing with minorities. Some majorities welcome assimilation, and others force it under penalty of expulsion. Most preach pluralism, but

---

[5]Robert Bierstedt, "The Sociology of Majorities," *American Sociological Review* 13 (December 1948): 709.

[6]Yetman and Steele, pp. 7–9.

We and They: Majority and Minorities

In what ways can our society be perceived as organized around the exploitation of minorities? What social function does the existence of minorities serve?

only a few attain it. Some get rid of an undesirable minority by wholesale population transfers. Others exploit minorities economically, keeping them in a state of ignorance and submission. The American South was one such society and today South Africa is another. We may also argue that our own society and way of life is organized around the exploitation of some minorities, including women. A change in the character of exploitation must, therefore, lead to revolutionary changes in our society as well as in our economy.

If all other methods fail and conflict seems unsolvable, recourse is sometimes made to genocide—the killing off of all members of the unwanted group.[7] As horrible as such a so-called solution sounds, it is employed often enough. The murder of six million people by Nazi Germany and the massacre of millions in Bangladesh are only some of the most recent examples of this solution.

Misconceptions About Race

The largest minority group in the United States—with the exception of women—is a racial minority. Racial minorities, partly because of their visibility, have traditionally evoked the strongest reactions from the dominant group. For these reasons, the concept of race and the system of beliefs it spawns are worth careful analysis.

The word *race* is subject to much misinterpretation. Originally, it was a concept that scientists used to describe specific biological differences occurring in the human species. But the word soon became part of the lay person's vocabulary, acquiring meanings it was never meant to have. It is common to hear people speak of a Latin, Jewish, or Irish race, when, in reality, *Latin* refers to a language group, *Jewish* to a religious and cultural group, and *Irish* to a nation group.

The word *race* is misused because the concept is misunderstood. People have observed the *cultural* differences among groups and have interpreted them as being *biological*, which would make them hereditary and unchanging. Thus set apart by differences, real or imaginary, each group is called a *race*.

You may have heard the term *human race*; what is meant by this usage, and is it scientifically accurate? Why or why not?

Some people believe that the way an individual thinks, feels and behaves is determined by his physical appearance. In some societies, this belief has become so ingrained that even though no essential biological differences are apparent, people perceive them as existing and as being important. For example, in South Africa, a nation that practices open racism, many of its citizens appear to be, for all intents and purposes, white. Yet if it can be proven that their ancestry includes blacks, they are treated as if they in fact were completely black.

In reality, ". . . all men share innumerably more physical traits than they differ on. In comparison to what they share, genetic dif-

[7]Wirth, pp. 347–372.

ferences among human groups are almost negligible. Genetic variations *within* groups, psychological and behavioral predispositions in particular, are far larger than variations *between* groups."[8] And, of course, physical appearance has nothing to do with behavior, unless it becomes a case of a self-fulfilling prophecy. In other words, if members of a racial group are constantly told that they are inferior and will never rise socially, eventually they may come to believe these charges about themselves and behave accordingly.

What Is Race?

The term *race* is coming into disfavor even among scientists because of the confusion and misconceptions it has created. Nevertheless, most scientists would agree on the following statements regarding race.

All of mankind is descended from the same common stock, the species *Homo sapiens.* This species is classified into a number of populations representing variations within the species, which are called *races.* We can liken this relationship between the species *Canis familiaris* (dog) and its variations: German shepherds, poodles, Great Danes, and Chihuahuas are all dogs, but they visibly differ in appearance. Their differences are caused by inbreeding that crystallized certain traits that may have appeared randomly in individual ancestors. In the same way, some of us have dark skins, wide lips, and broad noses, and others have light skins, thin lips, and narrow noses. Some of us have tightly curled hair, others have perfectly straight hair. But we are all humans. Classifications are made on the basis of differences in the frequency with which certain genes occur among the populations. And genes, because they transmit hereditary traits, determine what physical traits will be concentrated in the population.

What kinds of dangers are involved in inbreeding? What conclusions might we therefore draw about the benefits of intermarriage?

The classification of people into races is artificial and does not correspond to definite distinctions among humans. Because of frequent intermixture, differences in physical traits can be measured only in relative terms. For instance, if we say that a group can be distinguished because of skin color, we must be aware that skin color is a trait that runs through the entire species and is measured on a continuum from almost colorless to very dark. If we tried to show every degree of skin color on the continuum, the divisions would reach astronomical numbers.[9] We are all aware that some black people have very light skin and that some white people have very dark skin. We run into problems when we try to set up the boundaries at which "black" and "white" begin and end.

You may, at one time or other, have been asked to fill out a form stating your racial or ethnic background. What categories were used? Did you find it easy to categorize yourself? Why or why not?

In addition, racial classifications do not correspond to national, religious, linguistic, cultural, and geographic groups, although geographic

[8]Charles H. Anderson, *Toward a New Sociology* (Homewood, Ill.: Dorsey, 1971), p. 262.
[9]Melvin M. Tumin, *Comparative Perspectives on Race Relations* (Boston: Little, Brown, 1969).

isolation in the past may have been responsible for different gene pools. That is, frequent inbreeding may have led to the distribution of a limited number of genes among the population. A gene pool is the combined sum of all genes present in all individuals in a given population.[10] Nor do any social traits or behavior of these population groups have a connection with inherited racial traits. Finally, there is no scientific support for the idea that differences in personality, temperament, character, or intelligence are based on race.[11]

Racism

Another word that is used imprecisely today is *racism,* often interpreted as meaning "hatred toward members of other racial groups." In sociological terms, *racism* is a belief that racial groups display both physical *and* behavioral differences, and that both physical traits and behavior are inherited. Related to this belief is the idea that the physical and especially the behavioral traits of some groups are inferior or undesirable. Racism is the basis for prejudice and the unequal treatment of some racial groups—segregation, discrimination, hostility.[12]

These demonstrators are protesting discrimination against homosexual people.

[10]Marvin Harris, *Culture, Man, and Nature* (New York: Thomas Crowell, 1971), p. 635.

[11]The controversial findings of some researchers, such as Arthur Jensen, who claim that intelligence is genetically transmitted and cannot be socially improved have not been universally accepted as valid. In addition, these findings link lower IQs to lower social class levels, and not necessarily to race.

[12]Paul B. Horton and Gerald L. Leslie, *The Sociology of Social Problems* (New York: Appleton-Century-Croft, 1970), p. 354.

The basis of racist thinking is stereotyping, a process by which we assign common, uniform characteristics to an entire group of people, without allowing for individual differences. These characteristics may portray the entire group as either inferior or superior. We are familiar, for instance, with the stereotype that blacks are intellectually and morally inferior, but athletically and musically superior to whites. We have also heard of the "natural intellectual superiority" of Jews and of the "naturally passionate temperament" of Latins. An evening with Archie Bunker shows us how extensive these stereotypes are, and reminds us how well acquainted we are with them: homosexuals are effeminate, women are dingbats, blacks are criminals, Catholics do whatever the pope tells them, Jews are shrewd, and so on.

What stereotypes of racial or ethnic minorities have been applied to you? Do you identify with these stereotypes? How do these stereotypes affect your self-image?

History of Racism

Racism is not new and was not invented by white supremacists. It probably began when our early human ancestors, moving from place to place, met other groups of humans who not only looked odd to them but whose behavior was also different from theirs. Lacking any knowledge of culture-building processes, one group assumed that the other group's odd appearance and behavior were inherited traits belonging specifically to that group. Because of the universality of ethnocentrism—a belief in the superiority of one's own group—each group assumed that it was better than the other.

As old as racism may be, however, most societies, though definitely ethnocentric, are not racist. In the West, racism did not begin to assume the proportions of a full-fledged ideology, or system of beliefs, until the middle of the nineteenth century. At that time, justifications for racism began to be built on misconceptions of new scientific knowledge.

Charles Darwin's theory of evolution, with its concepts of the survival of the fittest and hereditary determinism, was applied to human groups. Darwinian theory was interpreted as meaning that the Anglo-Saxon and Nordic "races" were the fittest peoples—the most highly evolved and civilized. The development of self-rule and representative government among these groups was cited as partial proof of their superiority. The genetic laws discovered by the Austrian monk Gregor J. Mendel were interpreted as meaning that the "purity" of the white race must be maintained, so humans would not revert to a more primitive form. At the same time, the belief persisted that cultural differences were hereditary.

Why might racism have developed into a full-fledged system at about the time the Anglo-Saxon peoples were embarking on a course of imperialism?

Eventually, racism became a rationalization for the imperialism practiced by nations that were enriching themselves at the expense of other peoples. Colonialism and other forms of imperialism were explained away by the belief in the "white man's burden." According to this belief, whites had an obligation to hold the reins of political and economic power, so the progress of the world would not be blocked. The implication was, of course, that inferior races were unable to govern themselves.

Racism Today

Ideas die slowly. Racism seems to be taking a particularly long time to die. Nonetheless, research indicates that racism as an ideology has

What Is Institutional Racism?

Racism, sociologist Robert Blauner believes, like all social oppression should be studied as the attempt to create and defend group privileges. To see racism only as a function of prejudice, he argues, makes it appear that racism would end with changes in white attitudes and ignores the material and status privileges whites gain from the oppression of blacks. The defense of these privileges, he contends, is no longer dependent on individual prejudice and intentional discrimination for its continuance. Racism, he says, is now institutionalized: the domination and control of nonwhites is maintained through the normal procedures of the major social institutions.

How does institutional racism work? Most obviously, Blauner says, it works by the denial of equal participation in the society's institutions, such as the exclusion of blacks from skilled trade unions. Second, the interrelation of institutions makes it possible for a pattern of racism to be maintained while each institution can deny its own responsibility for oppression. Thus employers blame schools for inadequate preparation of blacks, while schools blame employers for creating poverty conditions. Third, institutional racism arises out of indirect processes such as those involved in jury selection. Juries are chosen from voting lists; black people are underrepresented on such lists; therefore blacks tend to be underrepresented on juries. Another aspect of institutional racism is that the requirements of institutional roles or social positions have more effect on a person's actions than his or her racial attitudes. For example, the prosecuting attorney in the 1968 trial of Black Panther leader Huey Newton had a reputation for being relatively unprejudiced, Blauner says, but in his role of prosecutor he excluded black people from the jury, defended the actions of the most racist police officers and fought for a conviction that carried the death sentence.

Robert Blauner, *Racial Oppression in America* (New York: Harper & Row, 1972).

declined markedly among Americans in recent years. As of the late 1950s, 80 percent of the whites in the United States had officially rejected the idea of black inferiority. However, many whites have substituted a new belief for their former belief in inferior traits transmitted through heredity. Many whites now feel that blacks are free to better themselves but lack the ambition to do so. Such a belief, though not racist according to the former definition of the word, is racist in the sense that there is a refusal to place the blame where it belongs. The blame is placed on blacks who are still considered inferior because they have not bettered themselves. What is ignored is that blacks have not bettered themselves because racism has seeped so deeply into our institutions that the cards have been stacked against them.[13]

To a racial minority such as blacks, racism is viewed primarily as the action—as opposed to the ideology, or beliefs—of the dominant group in exerting its power to maintain a system of white domination. Therefore, many blacks deny that they are guilty of "racism in reverse" when they express hostile sentiments against whites, because they do not have the power to impose their views on the white majority. As sociologists Norman Yetman and C. Hoy Steele note, "Racism in its most inclusive sense must refer . . . to actions on the part of a racial majority that have discriminatory effects—i.e., that effectively prevent members of a racial minority from securing access to prestige, power, and privilege.[14] Many people feel, however, that racism in reverse does exist, although it may not be technical racism. Open rebellion is the healthy response to oppression. When open rebellion is impossible because the odds are too unfavorable, the hostility goes underground. The response becomes one of superficial, passive submission to the dominant group, while hostility is expressed only to oneself, or to other minority members.

Unsophisticated whites frequently make antiminority jokes, offering as an excuse that minority members frequently make similar jokes about themselves. What kind of self-image is expressed when a minority member makes such a joke? How did that self-image develop?

Sociologist Daniel Thompson has identified three forms of leadership among blacks as a reaction to white racism. The first form is the "Uncle Tom." This type of leader deals best with white supremacists and segregationists. He accepts their definition of the status quo but obtains some benefits for his group by flattering members of the dominant group. In their own way, Uncle Toms manipulate whites for their own interest. This type of leadership was prevalent in the period from 1870 to 1930.

The term *Uncle Tom* is derived from a character in an Abolitionist novel, *Uncle Tom's Cabin.* Today the term has been applied first to blacks and then to any minority member who behaves in a certain way. How would you expect the female equivalent of an Uncle Tom to behave?

The second type of leader is the "diplomat." These individuals act as if they were white. They are often professional people or labor leaders who interact with white bureaucrats. This type of leader uses governmental agencies, lawsuits, and deals to obtain benefits for his people. Black leaders in the period from 1930 to the 1950s could be characterized as diplomats.

---

[13]Yetman and Steele, p. 361.
[14]Yetman and Steele, p. 362.

The third form of black leader is the "race man," who developed in the sixties. Race men are not necessarily black racists, but they are proud of being black. They interact most effectively with white liberals, using the techniques of passive demonstration or militant activism.[15] The era of passive demonstration ended in the mid-sixties. Ever since, militant activism has been the stance of many blacks. This stance is likely to be continued because a technologically and bureaucratically complex society such as our own can be easily disrupted and its activities brought to a halt by strikes and other acts of sabotage. In the 1970s, however, we are seeing a new style of leadership in the growing political activism of a number of black leaders. This activism is being expressed by involvement in national bipartisan politics rather than by the earlier forms of third party and civil disobedient politics.

Which type of leadership that has been described would you judge as the most effective? Why?

[Ethnicity]

Because of the inexactness of the word *race* in distinguishing groups of people, the relatively new term *ethnicity* is gaining increasing popularity. *Ethnicity* refers to a group's distinctiveness based on social and cultural factors, rather than on biological ones. In other words, the members of an ethnic group share common cultural traits, such as language, religion, values, beliefs, food habits, tribe or national membership, and so on.

What benefits might an entire society reap from the trend towards groups emphasizing and retaining their ethnic identity? What benefits do such groups reap?

On the basis of such commonly held traits, in heterogeneous nations, they have developed a subculture within the larger society. This subculture is recognized as being distinctive both by the members of the ethnic group and by society at large. The feeling of peoplehood, or oneness, shared by members of an ethnic group is rooted in a common national origin or historical tradition. It is maintained by a strong "we" as against "they" feeling, of in-group loyalty against out-group encroachment. And it implies a belief in a common destiny.

For most of human history, the feeling of oneness on which ethnic groups depend was based on membership in a common tribal unit. When nation-states emerged, they became the focus of ethnicity, although the feeling of oneness was sometimes additionally supported by a common religion. Membership in a nation-state remains the basis of ethnicity in small, homogeneous countries. In large, heterogeneous countries, the basis of ethnicity is varied and overlapping. Race, religion, or national origin may determine ethnicity. Historically, in such large nation-states, the dominant group attempts consciously or unconsciously, to assimilate all other ethnic groups.[16]

A by-product of the feeling of oneness shared by members of eth-

---

[15]Daniel Thompson, *The Negro Leadership Class* (Englewood Cliffs, N.J.: Prentice-Hall, 1963), chapters 5 and 7.

[16]Anderson, pp. 232–233.

nic groups is varying degrees of ethnocentrism. Ethnocentrism is the price a member of an ethnic group pays for the emotional satisfactions—an identity and a way of life—such membership affords him. We say "the price he pays" because, carried to extremes, ethnocentrism becomes the basis of racism, prejudice, and discrimination. It is important to remember that ethnocentrism is found in all groups. Among primitive tribes, for example, the name members very often give themselves is "the people." This implies that others outside their tribe are not really "people."[17]

[Prejudice]

Conflicts do not inevitably erupt simply because different ethnic and racial groups live in the same society. In many places around the world, ethnic and racial groups live together in comparative harmony. And even in racially and ethnically homogeneous societies, conflicts of a political, social, or economic nature—rather than an ethnic nature—arise. Sometimes these conflicts result in violence. In our own society, some social scientists even suggest that ethnic and racial groups have actually prevented conflicts of a political and economic nature from erupting into violence.[18]

Prejudice comes from a Latin word meaning to prejudge. Prejudgment is making up your mind about someone before you examine the evidence. Prejudgments are based on stereotypes and hearsay. Some amount of prejudgment is necessary in everyday life. When moving to a new town, we have to take other people's word about the best neighborhood or the best store to shop in. Prejudice, on the other hand, is not only making a judgment before you have the facts, but also refusing to change your mind even when confronted with unassailable evidence that your premises were false.

Characteristics of Prejudice

What are the characteristics of prejudice? First of all, feelings of prejudice are encouraged by insecurity, social isolation, frustration, and the need to rationalize personal failure.

Why might prejudice arise from the need to rationalize personal failure?

Second, prejudice is learned behavior. When children observe their elders' prejudices, they imitate them and develop prejudices of their own.

Third, prejudice seems to be largely unconscious. People who harbor many prejudicial feelings tend not to be aware of them. But those who have almost no prejudicial feelings are deeply aware of the few they have. Part of the explanation for this is that prejudiced people accept their prejudices as facts.

---

[17]Ruth Benedict, *Patterns of Culture* (Cambridge, Mass.: Houghton Mifflin, 1959), p. 7. First edition, 1934.

[18]Anderson, p. 234.

Through White Eyes

One way in which racial stereotypes are perpetuated is through the mass media. In a study of "Westerns" and other American movies about the Third World, Tom Engelhardt analyzes how this works. The paradigmatic scene, says Engelhardt, begins with a wagon train full of white settlers invading Indian territory. Through the focus of the camera we come to identify ourselves with the whites and see the world sympathetically through their eyes. As the wagon train advances through Indian territory it pulls up for the night, forming itself into a circle that defines "us"—a small innocent white community of warmth and humanity in an alien land. Invariably, the Indians, with whom we are given no opportunity to identify, attack. Faceless hordes sweep down over the plains, hordes that far outnumber our tiny band of women, children, and men, hordes who have no regard for their own lives or ours, intent only on massacre with no apparent reason. In self-defense we fire back.

What is missed in this scenario, says Engelhardt, is that it is the whites who are invading. In American movies about the Third World, the structure of the film and the focus of the camera transform white invasion, imperialism, and colonialism into what appears as an act of white self-defense. Like American Indians, Chinese and Japanese people are portrayed either as subhuman, irrational, and hostile, or as children ripe for well-intentioned ministrations by whites. Villains are the only Third World people who appear in any other but dependent roles. Most recent films that are supposedly sympathetic to Third World peoples fail to escape this pattern of seeing the world only through white eyes. What these movies do, Engelhardt contends, is to encourage us to see Third World peoples as less than human creatures, and as such, at least expendable, if not fit for extermination—before of course they exterminate us.

Tom Engelhardt, "Ambush at Kamikaze Pass," *Bulletin of Concerned Asian Scholars* (Winter–Spring 1971).

Fourth, prejudice does not originate through contact with the group against which it is directed. An individual need only be exposed to the prejudices of those around him to become infected himself. Prejudice has little connection to reality. If you have been taught that the Chinese are shifty, you may see them as shifty whether your experience bears this out or not. If a Chinese acts in a way that seems to prove he is not shifty, you may interpret this action as further proof of Chinese shiftiness. This ability of prejudiced people to interpret all facts in the light of their prejudices enables some of them to hold opposing prejudices. For instance, many people who are prejudiced against Jews are convinced that Jews are rich and interested only in money. But the same people will often blithely declare that Jews are Communists and radical subversives, working against capitalism.

How is it possible for an individual both to be prejudiced against Jews and also to declare that "some of my best friends are Jews"?

Fifth, prejudice is generally directed toward groups, not toward individuals. This is probably true because many people have interpersonal relations with members of racial or ethnic groups that are pleasant and that deny the truth of the prejudiced stereotypes. But prejudice is irrational; it remains unchanged in spite of such positive personal relationships.

Finally, prejudice persists because it is emotionally satisfying to the individual. Some people may experience guilt feelings about their prejudices. But, usually, prejudice is ego-satisfying. It gives the individual a feeling of superiority and a chance to blame his failures on someone else. It also provides him with an opportunity to relieve his personal tensions. For most people, the satisfactions derived from prejudice more than make up for an occasional pang of guilt.[19]

Who Is Prejudiced, and Why?

Researchers have found that some individuals and some groups in our society are more prone than others to hold racial and ethnic prejudices. Several theories have been constructed in attempts to explain why this is so and to distinguish among different kinds of prejudice

In one theory, a distinction is made between culture-conditioned prejudice and character-conditioned prejudice.[20] In culture-conditioned prejudice, an individual, in displaying prejudice, is merely reflecting the norms of his community. This kind of prejudice is found mainly among middle-aged and old unskilled laborers and farmers, religious fundamentalists, inhabitants of small towns, and the least educated, poorest members of the lower class. The prejudices of these people may stem, to a large degree, from fear of competition on the job market. Upper-class people may be less prejudiced because their social positions are secure enough not to be threatened by members of minorities.

In character-conditioned prejudice, the source of prejudice is within the personality of the prejudiced person. In his now classic study, *The Authoritarian Personality,* T. W. Adorno found a high correlation between the development of prejudice and a type of personality that he

[19]Horton and Leslie, pp. 356–359.

[20]Gordon Allport, *The Nature of Prejudice* (Reading, Mass.: Addison-Wesley, 1954), p. 282.

called authoritarian.[21] Some of the features of an authoritarian personality include submission to authority, admiration of power and toughness, conventionality, condescension toward inferiors, insensitivity to relationships with others, and a deep-rooted and partly subconscious sense of insecurity. In such persons, prejudice is merely part of a total outlook on life in which situations and problems are perceived in terms of absolutes—good or bad, right or wrong—and in which people are either heroes or villains.

Other theories of prejudice formation place the blame for one group's prejudices against another group on the psychological mechanism of scapegoating. *Scapegoating* is a term that refers to the tendency of frustrated individuals to respond with aggression. If the source of the frustration cannot be directly attacked, then a third party may become the object of aggression. People obtain the same relief by blaming a conveniently close group for an unpleasant event or situation that they cannot resolve. Using this technique, Hitler was able to blame the Jews for the loss of World War I and for the disastrous financial condition of Germany. Many people in our own society blame members of minorities for whatever unpleasantness they themselves are experiencing—unemployment, inflation, high crime rates, and so on.

Why might it be true that some members of minorities are among the most prejudiced people in society, given what you know about the formation of prejudice?

Still other theories are based on the assumption that prejudice is, in a way, symbolic—that we see in other groups specific traits that on the surface we hate or fear but that we really envy and would like to imitate.[22]

We must keep in mind that none of these theories claim to supply all the answers to questions concerning the causes of prejudice. Nonetheless, it is probable that each explains some facet of prejudice.

[Discrimination]

Whereas prejudice is an attitude or a feeling, *discrimination* consists of actions taken as a result of prejudicial feelings. For example, the belief that all black people are violent is a prejudice, but the formation of a committee to prevent them from moving into a neighborhood is discrimination.

The Relationship Between Prejudice and Discrimination

Prejudice and discrimination usually go hand in hand. But they can also occur independently of each other. For instance, you may retain your belief that all blacks are violent. If, in spite of this belief, you let them move into your neighborhood without interference, you are displaying prejudice without discrimination. On the other hand, you may think your neighbors are bigots for believing such a ridiculous thing

[21]T. W. Adorno et al., *The Authoritarian Personality* (New York: Harper & Row, 1950).
[22]Horton and Leslie, pp. 359–367.

about blacks. However, because you don't want to make enemies of your neighbors, you sign a petition to keep a black family from moving into your neighborhood. Now you are displaying discrimination without prejudice.

In general, though, prejudice and discrimination are mutually reinforcing. If there are strong prejudices against a minority group in a society, these prejudices will be acted upon and will result in discrimination. The denial of the vote to blacks and women, the refusal to permit members of particular racial and ethnic groups to live in some neighborhoods and hold some jobs are all examples of prejudice-inspired discrimination. Today, most forms of discrimination are illegal. But because there are ways of getting around the law and because these ways are widely used, discrimination still flourishes among us. Some forms of discrimination will be described later in this chapter in our discussion of individual minority groups.

Are there any ways in which you have benefited from the existence of prejudice and discrimination?

Kinds of Discrimination

Discrimination, not prejudice or a racist ideology alone, is the principal method used by the powerful majority to protect its privileged status, thereby ensuring that minorities have unequal status. Discrimination appears in several forms, each of which seldom appears alone. Sociologists Yetman and Steele distinguish between attitudinal discrimination and institutional discrimination, categories that are further elaborated in accordance with the sources of discriminatory behavior.[23]

Attitudinal discrimination in general refers to a situation in which the rewards of society are arbitrarily withheld from minority group members whose qualifications are equal to those of the majority group. The most obvious form of attitudinal discrimination is individual discrimination, which refers to discriminatory behavior that is prompted by the personal prejudice of a majority group member. The basis of individual discrimination is often character-conditioned prejudice. If a white landlord refuses to rent an apartment to a Puerto Rican couple who can afford the rent simply because he thoroughly dislikes Puerto Ricans, he is displaying individual discrimination. According to statistics, instances of such discrimination are on the decline in America.

Have you ever experienced or witnessed an act of individual discrimination? How did you react to the situation? What attitudes were involved?

But discrimination need not be occasioned by individual prejudice. An individual may discriminate simply by conforming to existing cultural patterns that are discriminatory in nature. Adaptive discrimination refers to discriminatory behavior prompted not particularly by personal prejudice but by the knowledge that such prejudice exists on a societal level. An individual who fails to discriminate may feel that he is endangering his own interests. The white landlord who has noth-

[23]Yetman and Steele, pp. 361–373.

ing against Puerto Ricans but who is consciously or unconsciously afraid that his other tenants will move out if he rents to a Puerto Rican couple is displaying adaptive discrimination.

The two forms of attitudinal discrimination are ultimately psychological in nature: either the discriminating individual is himself prejudiced, or he submits to, and is influenced by, the sanctions of a prejudiced society, or a reference group in it.

The category of *institutional discrimination* is not attributable to prejudicial feelings. Institutional discrimination refers to the system of inequalities at work within a society, separate from the prejudices and attitudes of majority group members. Because of institutional discrimination in our society, most Puerto Rican couples do not have the qualifications necessary for obtaining a good job. Therefore, most Puerto Rican couples do not usually have the money to rent an apartment in a nice, quiet, middle-class neighborhood. Institutional discrimination denies minority group members the opportunity to become qualified in ways the majority group considers essential to the attainment of a high standard of living.

To what extent do you feel that your life chances have been affected by structural discrimination?

The category of institutional discrimination can be further analyzed as consisting of two additional kinds of discrimination. *Structural discrimination* is the kind of discrimination that follows from the operation of such social structures as the political and economic institutions. Historically, the source of social inequality is rooted in the castelike system that ensured the majority its dominance. Although caste distinctions are diminishing today, the effects of such a caste system continue to persist. Because of structural discrimination inequality is maintained and could continue to exist even if adaptive and individual discrimination suddenly disappeared. Structural discrimination is the most pervasive in our society. Because of the way our economic structures work, for example, there is no longer a need for a large force of unskilled laborers. Consequently, we have a large reservoir of unemployed—overwhelmingly made up of blacks and other minorities—who are fated to remain locked in a condition of poverty until the economic institution is somehow changed.

The last element of institutional discrimination, *cultural discrimination,* is a result of the fact that we are a multicultural society. We are composed of a number of groups which, because of ethnocentric feelings, consider their own values, norms, attitudes, and interpretations of reality as the only valid ones. Such ethnocentrism, normal in all groups, becomes cultural discrimination in our society because the majority group has the power to define its own values, norms, attitudes, and interpretations of reality as the standards for the entire society. Because of cultural discrimination, members of minority groups must live up to the standard of the white majority in order to gain entrance into the economic and social mainstream of the society. Even though the values of the majority may not be in themselves discriminatory, then, they have the result of excluding minorities and legitimizing the system of racial and ethnic stratification. Structural discrimination in particular is so closely tied to the social system of a society that it may take generations to eradicate.

[The Struggle to Belong]

Three major ideologies in regard to minorities have been accepted at different times in the United States. Each provided guidelines for the way minority groups were thought of and treated in this country. An examination of these ideologies helps to show how a largely Anglo-Saxon, white, Protestant nation has absorbed—or failed to absorb—over forty-one million immigrants from various parts of the world. We should note that these ideologies have not been equally applied. European immigrants have been the most favored, and blacks and Asians have been the least favored. Women are a special case, which we will discuss more fully later in this chapter.

Anglo-Conformity

The ideology that has historically had the greatest following in the United States originated in this country. *Anglo-conformity* represents an attempt to superimpose WASP (white Anglo-Saxon Protestant) values on all immigrants. The basic principle of Anglo-conformity is that the institutions, language, and cultural patterns of England should be maintained. This attitude stems from the belief of the early settlers that even though their new nation had been born of a struggle with England, English institutions were basically sound and might be endangered by immigrants accustomed to other political systems. Anglo-conformity naturally led to discrimination. Immigrants from countries that had close cultural ties with England were given preference over other people immigrating to the United States. Generally, though, all immigrants who agreed to embrace Anglo-Saxon customs and language—and who looked like their hosts—were accepted.

Why might English settlers in this country have been satisfied with English political institutions, although unable to function within them while still in England?

Anglo-conformity resulted in many attempts to Americanize the immigrant. Federal, state, and local agencies together put pressure on the immigrant to learn English, abandon his customs, and ultimately become a naturalized citizen. The final victory of Anglo-conformity was the passage of laws establishing quotas for immigration—laws that discriminated sharply against immigrants from eastern and southern European countries as well as from Asia, because they were "least like us."

The Melting Pot

The *melting pot* ideology developed during the nineteenth century when Americans began to think that many immigrants could make important contributions to the new nation. The idea then took root that rather than clinging to strictly English institutional and cultural forms, the United States could fuse, both biologically and culturally, all the various stocks within it. The result of such a fusion would be "the New American." This viewpoint received dramatic expression in a play that was popular at the turn of the century. Written by a young Jewish immigrant, Israel Zangwill, the play was entitled *The Melting Pot.* In it, the hero expresses his belief that the ideal of the brotherhood of man will finally be realized in this country.

The melting-pot ideology and Anglo-conformity were both widely accepted during the first half of the twentieth century. Then, the melting-pot view became modified by the findings of a sociologist who studied patterns of intermarriage. Ruby Jo Reeves Kennedy found that British-Americans, Germans, and Scandinavians tended to intermarry with one another, thus creating a Protestant "pool." Irish, Poles, and Italians also intermarried, creating a Catholic "pool." Jews married other Jews, creating a Jewish "pool." In other words, although intermarriage was occurring among people of different nationalities, it tended to be restricted by religion. It was realized that we were melting not in a single pot, but that we were becoming a triple-melting-pot nation. The latter paved the way for the ideology of cultural pluralism.[24]

What three "melting pots" symbolize the relationships established by ethnic minorities in this country?

Cultural Pluralism

The ideology of *cultural pluralism* is the one that is most widely accepted today. It stresses the desirability of each ethnic group's retaining its cultural distinctiveness, rather than being assimilated into the dominant American culture. One of its earliest spokesmen, Horace Kallen, suggested that the highest achievement of democracy would be to permit the people of the nation to exist in a federation, or commonwealth, of national cultures.[25] Of course, the ideal of cultural pluralism is very far from having been attained. Only the European immigrant—whether he gave up his native heritage to become an Anglo-conformist, whether he gave up some of it and retained some of it in the melting pot, or whether he still lives in an ethnic enclave—has, to a great extent, entered the mainstream of American society. His children have college educations, have joined a higher socioeconomic class than his, and have penetrated all levels of the economy and government. The Kennedy family (Irish-Catholic), Henry Kissinger (German-Jew), Edmund Muskie (Polish), and Joseph Alioto (Italian) prove that ethnic groups derived from European cultures are represented in the political structure of the nation.

[24]Ruby Jo Reeves Kennedy, "Single or Triple Melting Pot? Intermarriage Trends in New Haven, 1870–1940," *American Journal of Sociology* 49 (January 1944: pp. 331–339).

[25]Yetman and Steele, pp. 264–278.

The fate of other ethnic and racial minorities has been less satisfactory. These minorities are made up of people who differ greatly from other Americans in appearance. Or they are made up of people who arrived late in the country and lack the skills necessary for functioning in an urban, industrial society. We turn now to these "visible" minorities and their situation today.

[Black Americans]

Making up 11 percent of the population of the United States, black Americans are this nation's second largest minority group after women. Black immigration was not, of course, voluntary, but a result of slavery. Therefore, the history and nature of discrimination against blacks is unlike that of discrimination against other minorities.

The Different Minority

The civil rights movement of the fifties and sixties—as well as the violent eruptions in several of our urban centers—brought the plight of the black minority to national and even world attention. Members of other ethnic groups have asked, "Why all the fuss? We had the same problems, but we worked hard and pulled ourselves up by our bootstraps." Such people fail to consider that blacks are very different from other ethnic groups.

Why has visibility played such a crucial role in the history of antiblack discrimination?

First, the black has had to contend with the matter of visibility to a much greater extent than members of any other group. The second- or third-generation Jew, Pole, or Italian, with education and with perhaps a slight change of name, is no longer noticeable as a minority member. He blends in with the dominant group. Such invisibility has been out of the question for the black.

No other ethnic groups—including Asians, who are also visible—were cut off from their cultures on their arrival here. But slavery destroyed the blacks' cultural ties with Africa. Many were brought to this country as individuals and did not even have family ties to fall back on. The culture that blacks eventually developed reflects their peculiar situation in this society. This culture even includes a particular way of speaking, in addition to customs and traditions that vary from those of the dominant majority. The speech of many blacks, although based on English, can be virtually unintelligible to other cultural groups, perhaps intentionally so.

Why might blacks have found it useful to develop speech patterns that the majority finds difficult to understand?

Living in an alien culture but not a part of it, blacks could hardly fail to accept that culture's negative attitude toward themselves. As social psychologist Kenneth Clark writes:

Since every human being depends upon his cumulative experiences with others for clues as to how he should view and value himself, children who are consistently rejected understandably begin to question and doubt whether they, their family, and their group really deserve no more respect from the larger society than they receive. These doubts become the seeds of a pernicious self-and-group-hatred and the Negro's complex, debilitating prejudice against himself.[26]

According to Cooley's looking-glass concept, the individual sees himself reflected in others. Mead, too, maintains that we develop a self and identity by taking the role of others. The type of personality the individual develops is based on his perceptions of what other people think of him. If significant others—parents, adults, relatives—have a low regard for themselves, they will relay their self-image to the child in the process of socialization. Thus, a vicious cycle has been established.

It has been said that black self-hatred is a response to discrimination by the majority. Are there any positive aspects of the self-image suggested by the stereotyped way blacks are often seen by whites?

Clark also says that black self-hatred is expressed in black adults' lack of motivation and fear of competing with whites for jobs. It is expressed in a feeling of helplessness in political and civic affairs, as shown by lack of black participation in voting and in community affairs. Finally, it is expressed in family instability created by lack of hope. Examples of such family instability presented by Clark are the large number of fatherless homes, in which the woman has either been abandoned by the man or has never been married at all. Fatherless homes were frequent during slavery. In more recent times, they have resulted from the black male's lack of opportunity to be an adequate wage earner and provider. Some people have characterized the black family as a virtual matriarchy—a mother-dominated household—with a consequent distortion of the male role.

Other social scientists assert that households headed by mothers are characteristic of the poor in general, not of blacks in particular. In addition, they point out that women do a very good job alone; that fatherless homes are not necessarily unstable. Clark, of course, was speaking of the period preceding the mid-sixties. Since then, many changes have taken place, and the self-concept of blacks has increasingly given way to the new motto: "black is beautiful." Social scientists, consequently, have begun to reevaluate their observation of the black family, particularly in the light of the women's movement, with the result that fatherless homes are no longer considered necessarily unstable or personality distorting.

Some Factors in Black History

Many of the other problems that plague the black minority, particularly the large segment still forced to live in central city ghettos, can be traced to the effects of slavery and to the continued lack of representation in the power structure. Drug addiction, criminality, suicide, homicide, emotional illness, and juvenile delinquency may all be

[26]Kenneth B. Clark, *Dark Ghetto* (New York: Harper & Row, 1965), as reprinted in *Change* (Del Mar, Calif.: CRM Books, 1972), pp. 105–106.

partly explained as escapist responses to intolerable circumstances. In addition, such deviations may be more apparent than real. That is, deviant actions on the part of minorities and of the poor in general tend to be reported with much more zeal than the deviant actions of the majority. Such zeal is, again, partly due to prejudice and discrimination: it makes us see in every black or minority face a potential criminal. And it makes the system of justice work to the advantage of the affluent members of the majority.

Sociologist Melvin Tumin lists the following unique factors in black history that still exert a negative influence in the present:

You have already seen that social mobility is related to education (this relationship is more fully discussed in the chapter on the educational institution). Why, then, might whites have deliberately prevented blacks from obtaining education?

1. Most Blacks came into the United States as slaves. Identified as something less than full human beings, they were powerless to prevent Whites from imposing that identity upon them.

2. Blacks were forcibly assigned to the most dishonored and unrewarding occupational roles, almost always involving hard manual work, and presumably requiring little or no intelligence, from which no escape was possible.

3. As slaves they were not allowed to accumulate financial resources with which to strive for socioeconomic improvement.

4. Whites perpetuated these dishonored identities, roles, and sparse resources by deliberately withholding genuine education in the language and culture of the United States.

5. At all times, skin color served as immediate identification and hence as a mechanism of social control.

6. In Africa the basic unit of social organization and group security had been the extended family. But slave owners deliberately separated Black adult males and females, preventing any possible unified action and promoting the pattern of fatherless, mother-ruled families that persists to this day.

7. Family fragmentation also made each individual totally dependent on his owner, preventing indigenous social organizations from reaching any effectiveness. Such organizations have served as crucial facilitators of socioeconomic mobility for almost all other ethnic or nationality groups that have entered the United States.[27]

Some of these conclusions have been recently challenged by two economic historians. Robert William Fogel and Stanley L. Engerman maintain that the institution of slavery was both profitable and efficient. More importantly, they continue, there is no evidence that black families were split up or that slaves were specifically bred for the market. On the contrary, the stable, nuclear, black family, with a Victorian morality, was more often the norm than the exception. In addition, the black labor force did not perform exclusively menial tasks. Over 25 percent of the males were managers, professionals, craftsmen, and semiskilled workers, while on a majority of the large plantations, the overseers were black. In short, according to the authors, slavery

[27]Melvin M. Tumin, *Patterns of Society* (Boston: Little Brown, 1973), p. 168.

Why is the Fogel-Engerman theory so startling in the context of traditional interpretations of black history? What basic traditional assumptions have these two historians challenged?

did not turn blacks into pitiful victims; it did not destroy their family or their sense of achievement; nor did it undermine their independence of judgment or their self-reliance. Slavery was an economic success, and as such it is a measure of black achievement.[28] The Fogel-Engerman thesis involves a somewhat startling correction of the traditional historical view, and justifies the assertions by many black Americans that its accuracy is supported by the strength and morality of black people today.

Whether the movements preaching complete separation of the races will lead to a positive solution or whether a pluralistic approach will hasten full equality is a question no one can answer with any degree of certainty. What is certain is that the black minority no longer tolerates its inferior position. On the other hand, the white majority—especially those whites who have little else but their color to value—will not easily give up its superior position. The two segments of society—black minority and white majority—seem to be currently suspended in an impasse.

Does your experience of black-white relations today support the suggestion that hostility is more characteristic of blacks and of whites now than in preceding decades?

If we are to believe statistics, relations between blacks and whites do not look encouraging. Studies sponsored by the Institute for Social Research found that black attitudes towards whites have changed in the period from 1968 to 1971 in the direction of increased hostility and suspicion. Many blacks who were interviewed saw "most whites" as hostile and oppressive and were willing to use extreme measures, including violence, to achieve their own rights. This survey also indicated that blacks may prefer black residential separation. Other questions on issues of separatism and job discrimination showed no appreciable change. The interviewers concluded that although black attitudes are not totally negative toward the white majority—blacks are still willing to fight for the United States in a major war—young black adults (ages 21–29) display much higher scores of hostility and suspicion than do older blacks.[29] Black attitudes toward whites have been affected by two developments. First, incidents such as the bussing riots in South Boston have impaired hopes for black-white unity raised by successes in the 1960s. Second, the black civil rights movement has raised black consciousness and helped decrease self-hatred. Hostility is therefore less likely to be directed towards oneself, and more likely to be directed outward, at whites.

[Jews]

The third largest minority group in the United States consists of six

---

[28]Robert William Fogel and Stanley L. Engerman, *Time on the Cross: Evidence and Methods—A Supplement* (Boston: Little Brown, 1974).

[29]Howard Schuman, and Shirley Hatchett, *Black Racial Attitudes: Trends and Complexities* (Ann Arbor, Mich.: Institute for Social Research [The University of Michigan], 1974), pp. 117–128.

Methodology: The Sample Survey

To find out whether black attitudes towards whites had changed significantly between 1968—the time of the ghetto rebellions and the assassination of Martin Luther King—and 1971, Howard Schuman and Shirley Hatchett utilized one of the most popular methods of sociological research, the sample survey. The sample survey involves polling a "representative" sample of a population on its social characteristics and, usually with the aid of a computer, relating these characteristics (such as age, sex, income, and so on), to attitudes or behavior patterns. A well-known example of the sample survey is the Gallup Poll.

In their analysis of black racial attitudes, Schuman and Hatchett used three Detroit area surveys, one conducted slightly before and one conducted shortly after the assassination of King in 1968, and one conducted in 1971. The researchers used as their population a sample of people who were representative of Detroit's black household heads and their wives, aged twenty-one to sixty-nine. By asking the same questions at three points in time, the researchers could measure quantitatively attitude changes that had occurred. As in most surveys, the researchers asked highly structured questions and allowed for only a multiple-choice type of response. This makes possible standardized comparisons among large numbers of people (the sample survey's great virtue), but it misses the nuances of feeling and the reasoning behind the answers people give (its great drawback).

Schuman and Hatchett found no significant evidence of attitude change between the two surveys conducted around the time of King's death. Between 1968 and 1971, however, attitudes changed significantly. Among blacks polled after King's death, 10 percent felt they could not trust any white person; by 1971 the figure had risen to 16.4 percent. Whereas in 1968 22.7 percent thought whites wanted to keep blacks down, 40.9 percent felt that way in 1971. Willingness among blacks to use violent means to attain their rights (if other methods failed) rose from 23.5 percent to 44.4 percent. Preference for living in an all-black neighborhood rose from 6.6 to 9.9 percent. Younger people, the researchers found, were more likely to feel whites were hostile towards them. Not surprisingly, those who felt this way reported fewer friendly encounters with whites.

These Detroit results, the researchers suggested, might be representative of attitude trends among blacks in other cities. "The riots," they concluded, "*crystallized* the belief among many blacks that progress was too slight and their status in American society still basically frustrating."

Howard Schuman and Shirley Hatchett, *Black Racial Attitudes: Trends and Complexities* (Ann Arbor: Institute for Social Research, University of Michigan, 1974).

Why might the Jews' desire for a separate identity alienate them from the majority? Do you think there is any way to be different and yet to avoid discrimination? How?

million Jews. American Jews have suffered from prejudice and discrimination in the past, and to some extent still do. But as a group, they have attained a rather high social status. Although some political offices and some professions—not to mention some neighborhoods and country clubs—remain closed to the Jewish minority, the group's status as a minority does not include a position at the bottom of the stratification system. In addition, many Jews seem to desire no further assimilation but prefer to maintain their own cultural and religious identity.

Perhaps it is this wish for a separate identity that still makes Jews frequent victims of stereotyping and antisemitism. Of late these feelings have been strengthened among those who disapprove of the American Jews' support of the state of Israel. The newly-rich Arab states have also added fuel to the fire by boycotting American firms with any ties to Israel, thus effectively discriminating against a number of American Jews. Jews are often described as clannish, seeking friendships only among their own kind. They are also characterized as being tight with their money and, in business dealings, exploitative of non-Jews. This so-called clannishness is actually the unity that has been the Jews' greatest strength, for in the struggle for survival, Jews have always helped one another. This characteristic as well as an attachment to their religious traditions, has enabled Jews to maintain their ethnic distinctiveness through the centuries after dispersal from their ancestral homeland.

In the United States, the Jews' rise in the stratification system was assisted by some aspects of their heritage. First, having been forbidden to own or cultivate land in the European countries from which they came, Jewish immigrants already had urban skills and were used to an urban way of life when they arrived in the United States. Second, they shared the dominant group's values regarding hard work, success, competition, and education. Third, Jews had a well-developed cultural tradition they cherished and passed on to their children. Finally, a family group that was tightly knit and therefore cooperative and stable, a strong feeling of community shared with other Jews both here and abroad, and a physical appearance not much different from that of the majority group have also helped Jews enter the mainstream of society.

[Spanish-Speaking Minorities]

Mexican-Americans, or Chicanos

In what ways do the Chicanos, as a minority, differ from the Jews? From the blacks?

Five million strong, Mexican-Americans make up the fourth largest minority in the United States. This minority group is not a unified community, nor does it possess a common culture. Rather, the group is fragmented because members came to this country at different times and from different places. Some Mexican-Americans settled in rural areas and others in urban centers. The only thing members really share is the Spanish language (at least in the first generation) and Spanish surnames, as well as the Catholic religion.

Most Mexican-Americans, or Chicanos as some prefer to be called, live in Arizona, California, Colorado, New Mexico, and Texas. Many are native-born Americans—descendants of the original Spaniards who occupied the Southwest before the colonization of the West Coast. Others arrived here in large migrations at the turn of the century. In spite of this, the Chicanos are one of the few ethnic groups for which there has been no increase in socioeconomic status between one generation and the next.[30] They have consistently remained in the ranks of unskilled and semiskilled blue-collar workers, and are at one of the lowest economic levels of the nonwhite minorities.

What suggestions would you make for a program designed to teach English to Chicanos as well as to encourage retention of the Chicano ethnic heritage? How should such a program be structured?

There are several reasons for the inferior economic and social status of native Chicanos. First, they are continually competing with cheap labor, because there is a steady influx of lower-class immigrants from Mexico without a corresponding departure of native Chicanos into higher social classes. Second, the nearness of Mexico permits frequent trips back to the native land. Close contact with Mexico and the inefficiency of the American school system in teaching English have resulted in most Chicanos' retaining Spanish as their principal language. This may be helpful in maintaining native culture, but it does little to enhance Chicanos' opportunity to get good jobs in the United States. Third, Chicanos are usually born into large families, and this makes upward mobility difficult. Fourth, the Chicano lacks visible models of achievement. His significant others are not helpful in socializing him to be upwardly mobile. Fifth, the Chicano's group loyalty, which is very strong, prevents him from departing too far from the norms of the group.[31] Chicano subcultural norms include such features as close ties to the land, a relatively slow sense of time, little stress on formal education, and a social structure founded on personal relationships.[32] Such norms do not encourage upward mobility in an urban, industrial society.

After World War II, more and more Chicanos moved to cities. This trend continues today. The Chicano, then, has exchanged his former status of underprivileged rural worker for that of unskilled, semiskilled, or blue-collar urban industrial worker. He thus shares the problems common to all members of the lower-class. Educational achievements have been almost as slow in cities as in rural areas. Urban life has also resulted in the breakdown of traditional Mexican family values, which, in turn, may be correlated to an increased rate

[30]Celia Heller, *Mexican-American Youth* (New York: Random House, 1966), p. 5.

[31]Fernando Penalosa, "The Changing Mexican-American in Southern California," in Yetman and Steele, *Majority and Minority*, p. 323.

[32]Penalosa, in Yetman and Steele, p. 325.

of juvenile delinquency. These problems are further complicated by discrimination in housing, which forces many Chicanos to remain in urban *barrios*, or slums.

Young Chicanos seem determined to strive for upward mobility and attainment of the rewards that this society has to offer. Chicanos are still faced, however, with the choice of becoming assimilated, adopting a pluralist existence, or clinging to biculturalism and bilingualism.[33]

Most Puerto Ricans in the United States live jammed together in the large cities of the East Coast.

[33]Penalosa, in Yetman and Steele, p. 331.

Puerto Ricans

Most of the 1.8 million Puerto Ricans live in the cities of the eastern seaboard, particularly New York, and in the large cities of the Midwest. The Puerto Ricans, like their Chicano counterparts, have one of the lowest standards of living in the country, higher only than that of the American Indians. Other features shared with Chicanos include the Spanish language, the Roman Catholic religion, the large families, low educational achievement (principally caused by the retention of Spanish), and a lack of skilled occupations. All these factors contribute to low social mobility. In addition, many Puerto Ricans encounter racial prejudice and discrimination because their skin color varies from light to very dark.

Problems encountered by Puerto Ricans are complicated by a lack of commitment to American institutions. Puerto Ricans come here primarily for economic reasons, and many return to their native land as soon as they can. Consequently, they have very little political power and cannot put pressure on the government to obtain benefits for themselves. (There are, however, indications that the young generation is moving increasingly toward political activism, and this should be an asset to the group.) Finally, Puerto Ricans are the latest group of immigrants to arrive in the United States, and traditionally, the latest arrivals have ended up at the bottom of the social scale.

Why does lack of commitment to our political institutions usually express itself as a lack of political activism?

Cubans

In marked contrast to other Spanish-speaking groups, Cuban immigrants who came here in the wake of Fidel Castro's takeover have fared very well. Reports indicate that Cubans, concentrated heavily in the Miami area, have attained a fairly high standard of living. More than half of the Cubans in Miami own their homes; one out of every three retail businesses in the city is owned by a Cuban; and Cubans control 30 percent of all new construction in Dade County. Cubans seem to have been accepted socially and are now enlarging their efforts in politics.

One reason for such spectacular success against linguistic, religious, and cultural odds is that most of the Cuban immigrants were members of the middle and upper classes in their society. They came here not out of need but because their superior status in their own country was destroyed by Castro. Instead of being unskilled blue-collar workers and rural laborers, they are professionals, businessmen, and craftsmen. As such, they have the same values and many of the same goals as the American majority.

How might the Cuban immigrants' commitment to American institutions have been affected by the stability of the Castro regime in Cuba?

[American Indians]

No minority has been more ignored than American Indians. Economically, Indians are truly the forgotten Americans, for they live in poverty and squalor unparalleled by other minorities. The only true natives of America, they have been stripped of their land, and decimated by the white man's diseases and by his guns. Their culture has been almost totally destroyed. The reservations allotted them are on land that no one else wants.

As a minority, the Indians have long been invisible to most other Americans, because after their land was taken, they were herded to barren rural areas, chiefly in the Southwest, where most of them live today. Small groups of Indians do, however, survive in rural sections of some urban states, such as Florida. Of the total number of Indians, some 500,000 live on or near reservations, and 200,000 have moved to cities and towns.

At various stages of American history, the dominant group has wanted to exterminate the Indians, to assimilate, or Americanize them, to segregate them, to protect them, and so on. The ravages created by these shifting policies have left a deep imprint on many Indians. Only now, with the growing activism of young Indians, are some members of the majority beginning to recognize the Indians' right to decide their own destiny.

In 1975, the Pine Ridge reservation was torn by battles between government representatives and the Indians. What economic conflicts may have aggravated the situation?

Even today, however, the attitude of the Bureau of Indian Affairs, which regulates the lives of reservation Indians, hardly encourages independent and mature action. Charles H. Anderson reports that on the Pine Ridge Reservation of South Dakota, the ratio of civil service bureaucrats to Indians is about one to one. If the budget for Pine Ridge were divided among the Indian families, they would have an average yearly income of $8,040, enough to give them a comfortable standard of living, instead of the $1,910 that they actually earn.[34]

Indian problems have been further complicated by tribalism. Many Indians think of themselves first and foremost as Navahos or Cherokees, for example, and only second as Indians. Thus, they have never had a unified culture to sustain them. Nor have they ever been able to exert political pressure as a united interest group. Even their present difficulties differ from tribe to tribe, so that it is difficult to generalize about them.

What has been the traditional response of the majority to a minority that did not want to be assimilated?

In addition, Indians have never been receptive to the European culture the settlers brought to the New World. They have successfully resisted numerous attempts at assimilation. The various tribal cultures have not fit into our urban industrial society. Thus, Indians have been relegated by the majority to a marginal existence.

Most Indians have had to adopt the outward appearances of the dominant group's way of life. Many Indians farm and raise cattle, and others work in industrial jobs. This is deceptive, however:

. . . modern studies of Indian communities show that adoption of the externals

[34]Anderson, p. 254.

American Indians have fewer life chances than any other minority in the United States.

of American life is not neatly correlated with accompanying changes in basic Indian attitudes, mind and personality. Studies . . . reveal the same inner Indian feelings about the world and man's place in nature, the same noncompetitive attitudes, the same disinterest in the American drive for progress and change.[35]

[35]Alexander Lesser, "Education and the Future of Tribalism in the United States: The Case of the American Indian," in Yetman and Steele, p. 336.

Belonging to a subculture that contradicts the surrounding society, many Indians have lost a sense of purpose, a will to live. A young Indian girl living in Pine Ridge Indian Reservation has commented in an interview: "Nobody ever asks a child here 'What do you want to be when you grow up?' because there's nothing to grow up to be."[36]

As with the other American minority groups, change seems to be in the offing for Indians. The change involves primarily the young generation, which seems determined to become educated, as increased college attendance shows. Young Indians are also becoming increasingly militant as recent confrontations, including that at Wounded Knee, illustrate. Change does not mean that Indians will choose to become assimilated and pursue the goals of the majority. It does mean, however, that whatever choice is made, is made by the Indians themselves.

[Asian Minorities]

The two largest Asian minorities living in the United States consist of the Chinese and the Japanese. These two groups are culturally different from one another, from the dominant majority, and from other, Western-oriented minorities.

Chinese immigration began in the middle of the nineteenth century following the news of a California gold rush. Later, Chinese men were also imported as cheap, "coolie" labor to work on the transcontinental railroads. A number of Chinese, taking advantage of the fact that there were few women in the pioneer West, became small businessmen in the areas of laundry work and cooking.

Each minority we have discussed has been in the position of being "Last hired, first fired." Why is competition for jobs such a crucial determinant of minority or majority status?

The rapid overpopulation of California, a state that was attracting vast numbers of people because of the tales of overnight rags to riches, soon overloaded the state's economy, putting many people out of work. Many whites were competing with Chinese for jobs, and losing, because the Chinese accepted such low wages. White workers were infuriated by the willingness of the Chinese to work for almost nothing. The last decades of the nineteenth century were marked by outright persecution and harassment of Chinese, including a riot during which eighteen Chinese were lynched. Consequently, many returned to China. Those who remained retreated to urban enclaves, or Chinatowns, where they could live in comparative safety according to their own cultural patterns. In 1882 legislation was passed ending Chinese immigration. Restrictions on immigration were not lifted until the passage of provisions in the immigration laws of 1952 and 1965. California also passed laws limiting Chinese opportunities in education, jobs, and choice of residence.

In spite of discrimination, the Chinese as a group have achieved

[36]Sally Batz, "Growing Up Is Difficult on Pine Ridge Reservation," *The Cleveland Plain Dealer*, February 2, 1972.

Embattled Chinese in a White District

Here is how one Chinese woman, the daughter of an herb store owner, described her experience of growing up in the 1940s in a white section of San Francisco:

When my parents would talk about the outside being a bad place, they would refer sort of generally to "the whites out there." . . . To me, of course, that meant the whites right around us. It meant the bar downstairs where . . . every night we'd hear this crashing, singing, people being thrown around down there, they would have brawls and they would pee on our doorstep. . . . But at the same time my parents kept reminding us that "the whites out there," the same people who would vomit and pee on our doorstep, were the people who had the power to take our home away from us. We had to do a little placating of them. Every Easter, every Christmas, every American holiday, I would be sent on a little tour of all the local businesses. I would go to the bakery across the street, the barbershop down the street, the realty company, and the bar. I would deliver a little cake to each one. We wanted to be known as that nice Chinese family upstairs or down the street, you know, whom you wouldn't ever want to hurt in any way. My family was very aware that they were embattled Chinese in a white district, that they had spent many years finding that place to live, and that at any moment they could be asked to leave. And somehow a quality I sensed out of all this, about being Chinese, was a vulnerability. At any moment you could be thrown out. So you had to watch your step and you had to be very clever, you had to placate, you had to maneuver. And no matter what happened you did not get openly angry, because if you did, you would have lost your dignity. No matter what they did you had to be stronger than they, you had to outlast them."

Quoted in: Victor G. and Brett de Bary Nee, *Longtime Californ': A Documentary Study of an American Chinatown* (New York: Pantheon Books, 1973), pp. 165–166.

much upward mobility, particularly through education. Many Chinese have excelled in mathematics and science. Because of their economic success, the Chinese are generally admired. Still, some prejudice and discrimination persist. The past decade has seen a renewed influx of Chinese from the mainland and from Taiwan. These new immigrants are young and unskilled, and have therefore had difficulty being accepted both by second- and third-generation Chinese and by the community at large.

The Japanese began arriving here at the beginning of the twentieth century. Like the Chinese they are heavily concentrated along the West Coast, especially in California. The white majority applied the same restrictions to the Japanese as they had to the Chinese. Prejudiced Americans considered the Japanese to be part of the "yellow peril" that was allegedly threatening to overrun the American way of life. In actuality, the Japanese held values in the best tradition of the Protestant ethic—they were hardworking, frugal, future-oriented, valued education for their children, and pursued family farming and business.

How does the course of international affairs affect the status of minorities within our own culture? Would the position of blacks here be improved if the United States had to deal with highly industrialized, powerful, black African nations? Why?

The real problems for the Japanese in the United States began with the advent of World War II. Labeled as security risks and potential traitors, Japanese-Americans were forced to sell or abandon their property, and were interned in concentration camps for the duration of the war. After the war, many families chose to remain in the area where they had been interned. The heavy concentration of Japanese in California was thus broken up. Since a few families in a neighborhood or in a town rarely seem as threatening as hundreds or thousands of families, the Japanese were readily accepted. Consequently, their assimilation into the mainstream of society may have been facilitated by their dispersal. In the process, however, Japanese culture and cohesion have suffered.

Like the Chinese, the Japanese value education for their children, who have proven to be very high achievers, especially in subjects that require the use of abstraction and conceptualization.[37] As a result of their educational achievements, many Japanese have taken a firm step into the middle class, both in terms of income and life-styles. Prejudice against them still occasionally surfaces, but Japan's industrialization is helping erase anti-Asian feelings, as well as the memory of World War II.

[Women]

What differentiates women from other types of minorities?

As we mentioned previously, the term *minority* applies not only to small groups, or ethnic or racial groups, but describes any group in a position of social inferiority. By this definition, that half of our population that is female constitutes a minority. Women are in a socially inferior position in our society. Men open doors and carry parcels for women, set women up as love objects and as inspiration for their art. But women are quite effectively kept out of decision-making positions in the government and in the economy. They are prevented from occupying high-prestige, high-income jobs in society, being favored instead for positions as housekeepers, cooks, child-raisers, teachers, nurses, and social workers. The implication is that women are not fit for social roles that require long and intellectually demanding training,

[37] S. S. Stodolsky and G. S. Lesser, "Learning Patterns in the Disadvantaged," *Harvard Education Review* 37 (Nov.): 546–593.

for the type of roles that gain males' position of high economic and political importance and high prestige.

Are women fit for specific roles because they are born with the temperament, or personality, or nature to which these roles correspond? Or are they fit for these roles because society molds them into beings who will occupy such roles without complaints? In other words, do little girls play with dolls because they are born with a predisposition toward such play, or because they are guided toward dolls? It is the old "nature vs. nurture" controversy. How significant is nature, and how significant is society's sex-typing of individuals from the cradle to the grave?

What, in your opinion, is the right role for a woman to occupy? Do you feel that there are any innate nonbiological differences between men and women? If so, what are these differences?

Inconsistency in Sexual Stereotypes

"Today," according to Barbara Deckard, "all jobs done mostly by men or mostly by women in one country are done by the other sex elsewhere." Nonetheless, employer rationales for sexual discrimination involve judgments about the innate abilities or "universal" character of all women that supposedly makes them especially fit or unfit for some jobs. The stereotypes different employers use show a high degree of inconsistency when juxtaposed, as in these cases compiled by Deckard:

—Women cannot be statesmen, captains of industry, or even auto mechanics because they are irrational, flighty, over-emotional, sentimental, and unmechanical. On the other hand, women cannot be great poets and painters because they are practical, unadventuresome, unspontaneous, and unimaginative.

—Men are not usually employed as phone operators because "they have less pleasant voices." But women are not usually employed as radio or television announcers because "they have less pleasant voices."

—Nursing is for women because it is a nurturing function, but doctoring is for men.

—There was a case in which a man was denied a job as an electronic circuit assembler "because women are better at this work," since women have more "finger dexterity." Yet some medical schools have said that women can't be brain surgeons because it "takes a steady hand."

—(Well-paid) accountants are mostly men "because women have no head for figures," but the (poorly paid) bookkeepers—who do much more arithmetic figuring—are mostly women.

Barbara Sinclair Deckard, *The Women's Movement: Political, Socioeconomic, and Psychological Issues* (New York: Harper & Row, 1975), pp. 5, 88–90.

The "Naturalness" of Women's Roles

There are many reasons why women find themselves in a subordinate position—a position reinforced and sanctioned by institutions and tradition in most societies. One argument concerns women's biological makeup. Since women bear children and have breasts with which to feed them, some people suggest that women were meant by nature to do these and related tasks. Today, of course, a child's survival no longer depends on being breast fed. Scientists are even working on reproducing babies in test tubes, so that women will no longer need to become pregnant and give birth in the old way. Yet many people insist that the woman's role must continue to involve only those child-bearing functions. This argument—about the "naturalness" of women's roles—probably derives from our basic fear of change. But if we follow it through, we see that it makes little sense. For we can also argue that since humans have no wings, it is not natural for them to fly, and since they have no wheels, it is not natural for them to ride. The fact that we have brains means that we do not depend solely on nature to make use of our bodies. Of course, we cannot discount biology entirely. Men and women do differ in physical and hormonal makeup. But they do not differ in such rigid terms.

As we shall see in later chapters on various social institutions, religion, politics, the economy, the family, and education all tend to reinforce sex roles in society. Which institution do you feel is the most responsible for this reinforcement? Why?

The belief that women must fulfill the role of housewives and mothers exclusively is not new, nor is it limited to our own society. The prevalence of the belief and the length of time it has persisted have created an ideology that assumes a woman's biological nature has decreed once and for all her role in society, and that she must be happy with that role.

Women Can Dig Ditches

To what extent do you feel that structural discrimination has affected women's performance in the professions? Why is performance in the professions such an important criterion of success in our society?

Women are proving that they can successfully fill roles that used to be reserved for men only. By 1965 in the Soviet Union, for instance, 75 percent of the doctors, 83 percent of the dentists, 36 percent of the lawyers, and 38 percent of the scientists were women. In the United States today, 6.5 percent of the doctors, 2.1 percent of the dentists, 3.5 percent of the lawyers, and 7.0 percent of the scientists are women. This is not to say that the Soviet Union is an egalitarian heaven—there are indications that the women doctors and lawyers come home and still do the cooking and laundry. In addition, these professional women are generally at the lower levels of their profession: they are the general practitioners and paraprofessionals rather than the skilled specialists. But the figures do show that where restrictions are removed, women perform as well as men.

Statistical data illustrate the unequal status of women in the United States. In the area of education, as many women as men complete a median of 12.1 years of school. Although more men than women drop out before completing high school, many more men than women continue on to attend college after high school. While there are quite a few more women high school graduates, there are quite a few more male college graduates. For males, college is considered a vital step toward a high occupational position. For females, it is considered less important, since women are encouraged to get married instead.

As a woman, have you ever been discriminated against? As a man, have you ever been discriminated against? How do you think such discrimination could be eliminated?

Only 42.2 percent of women over 16 years old are in the labor force, while 79.4 percent of males over 16 are in the labor force. Moreover, women are obviously underrepresented in the ranks of the higher occupations, but are numerous in jobs such as that of technician, nurse, dietician, nutritionist, teacher, bookkeeper, and librarian, and in assistant positions. Even though 70 percent of women college graduates are in the work force, almost 20 percent of them are employed in second-echelon administrative positions, or, more often, in clerical, sales, or factory jobs. Their average salaries are only 58 percent of the salaries of men with comparable educational backgrounds. The largest distribution of working women is found among those whose husbands earn between $5,000 and $10,000, indicating that they probably work out of necessity and not for the sense of accomplishment they may obtain. When we consider that over 10 percent of the families in the United States are headed by women who are their family's sole support, these facts and figures clearly show discrimination against women.

In the area of political representation, women fare even worse. From 1965 to 1969, out of 535 Congressional seats, women held 10 seats in the House of Representatives and one seat in the Senate.[38] In 1973, women constituted only 34.7 percent of all employees of state and local governments.[39] Women were not even allowed to vote until 1920. Since political power reflects social power, political representation is a good index of women's status.

Women's Liberation

The women's movement has for the past decade been producing various analyses of the position of women in society and of the historical development of sexism. One theory is that since women are biologically vulnerable, being smaller than men and subject to pregnancy, the men had to protect them, and consequently demanded a submissive stance from the women. Another theory is that a prehistoric pattern of matriarchy was overthrown when men became aware that pregnancy was not spontaneous; that men played a vital role in conception, hitherto unrecognized. The women's movement has also bor-

---

[38]*Statistical Abstract of the United States, 1974,* p. 433.

[39]U.S. Equal Opportunity Commission, *Minorities and Women in State and Local Government,* Vol. I (Washington, D.C.: Government Printing Office), p. *xx.*

Women have discovered they, too, are an oppressed minority, and have tried to take action to change their status and role.

Choose as a subject a woman who is currently a mother and housewife. Using standard wage scales for each function she performs, compute the wages she "earns" in a week and compare what she actually gets with the earnings she would receive if paid.

rowed from Marxist theory, in that many women view the family as an economic unit based on scarcity, in which the distribution of power favors the man and exploits the woman, especially in the area of unpaid housework. The women's movement is relatively new, of course, and therefore the various theories have not yet been incorporated into an umbrella theory of women's position in society. When such a theory is developed, as it may be in the next decade or so, it will have to take into account the growing awareness that if women achieve the goals of the women's movement, society as we know it could well be changed in ways we now have difficulty visualizing.

Not all women agree that their status in society is inferior. Many women have been so thoroughly socialized into traditional feminine roles that they are or seem to be perfectly satisfied in deriving their status and livelihood from their husbands. They maintain that if women were given more independence, if they pursued careers as men do, and left childcare and housekeeping to others, society would fall apart.

To what extent do men suffer from the continued subordination of women in society, in your opinion?

But other women have become increasingly interested in the social movements generally referred to as Women's Liberation. The immediate goals of the movement are to obtain equal treatment for women in education, jobs, working conditions, pay scales, and domestic responsibilities. This movement asserts that, with the exception of childbearing and tasks dependent to a great degree on muscular strength and speed, the capacities of men and women are interchangeable. To confine women to childcare and housecare roles is to neglect their intelligence and creativity—to the detriment of themselves and of society. And if women were not economically dependent on men, both sexes could achieve a greater amount of freedom and self-fulfillment as human beings. Moreover, if sexual roles were not so rigidly enforced, sexual stereotypes might eventually disappear.

Not all women are exploited to the same degree as other minorities. But women are treated less well than men in *any* given class or social group. No group has so consistently been kept in a position of second-class citizenship for as long as women and through as many political reforms. The roles that our society has traditionally assigned to women are limited and restrictive, tending to repress personal initiative and creativity in areas other than the home. And when women try to step out of those roles and succeed in what is generally a masculine world, they often do so at great personal costs. The movement can help minimize these costs by seeking better methods of institutional childcare and housekeeping. Not until the step out of the house has been taken will women be considered persons first, and wives and mothers second.

One slogan put forward by the women's movement is "The revolution begins at home." What do you think this slogan means? What does it imply about the goals of the women's movement?

[Summary]

Conflict seems to be an integral part of group life. It becomes especially sharp when it involves physical appearance or cultural traits. Appearance and cultural traits distinguish minority groups from the dominant group. Prejudice, discrimination, and institutions designed to economically exploit minorities have existed in all societies. The dominant group perceives minorities as inferior and forces them to occupy a powerless, subordinate socioeconomic position, despite the fact that they may in actual numbers make up a majority.

Racial minorities have been the victims of the ideology of racism, as well as of prejudice and discrimination. Racism is based on a faulty conception of the term *race,* in which the cultural traits and the behavior of a group are thought to be genetically inherited. Actually, scientists use the word *race* to make very broad distinctions among the physical traits of humans, who are all descended from the same stock and are all members of the same species. Physical differences are a consequence of the frequency with which certain genes appear in some population groups as a result of inbreeding. Aside from physical appearance, no substantial differences have been found to exist among races.

In contrast to race, *ethnicity* refers to a group's distinctive social factors such as language, religion, values, beliefs, food habits, and so on. Ethnic groups are subcultures within the larger society. Such groups are maintained by common national origin or history; by a strong in-group, "we" feeling; and by the belief in a shared destiny. Ethnocentrism—belief in the superiority of one's group—is a part of ethnic group loyalty. Ethnocentrism carried to excess may lead to racism, prejudice, and discrimination.

Prejudice is holding stereotyped, unproven beliefs about a minority group or individual. Discrimination is acting on such beliefs by denying members of a minority group equal access to the sources of wealth, power, and privilege. Of the different kinds of discrimination in existence, the institutional and structural are the most difficult to eliminate.

In the United States, the dominant group has tried various methods of dealing with its minorities. Ideologies of Anglo-conformity and of the melting pot have given way to cultural pluralism as an ideal to be aspired to. In a truly pluralistic society, various racial and ethnic minorities would each retain their culture but would coexist with the majority. All would enjoy equal access to the rewards of society. Before cultural pluralism can become a reality, the stratification system will have to be changed so that minorities will no longer be powerless in the political and economic areas of the society.

The United States, having long been a haven for immigrants from other nations, is particularly rich in minority groups. Some of these minorities have been absorbed into the mainstream of society. Others, however, remain distinct and are denied equal access to the rewards of our society, particularly status, privilege, and power. Among these groups are the blacks, the Spanish-speaking groups, and the American Indians. The Jews, Chinese, and Japanese are minorities that have achieved upward social mobility while retaining religious and cultural distinctiveness. Nonetheless, they are frequently still victims of prejudice and some types of discrimination.

Women represent a special minority. An analysis of the traditional roles that our society assigns women, and statistical data illustrating their limited participation in the economy and politics, clearly demonstrate their inferior status. Women are treated as second-class citizens in any class or group in which they are found. Because women are a majority of the population, if the women's movement succeeds in equalizing the status of women, society as we know it will be unrecognizably changed.

Terms to Remember

Anglo-conformity. A theory of minority absorption holding that the institutions, language and cultural patterns of England should be maintained.

Assimilation. A process whereby a minority group is absorbed into, or becomes, a part of the dominant group in a society.

Cultural pluralism. A theory stressing the importance and the desirability of maintaining the cultural distinctiveness of each ethnic and racial minority within the structure of allegiance to the total society.

Discrimination. Actions taken as a result of prejudicial feelings.

Ethnic minority. A group that differs culturally from the dominant group; that is, whose members speak a different language, have different customs, religion, food habits, child-rearing practices, values, and beliefs.

Ethnicity. A group's distinctive social, rather than biological, factors. Members of ethnic groups share common cultural traits such as language, religion, values, beliefs, food habits, tribe membership, and so on.

Ethnocentrism. Belief in the superiority of one's own group. Attitudinal discrimination. Negative behavior prompted by the personal prejudice of a member of the majority group. Further divided into individual and adaptive discrimination.

Institutional discrimination. Negative behavior prompted not by personal prejudice but the knowledge that such prejudice exists on a societal level. The individual (or group) discriminating against a minority individual (or group) is adhering to the norms of his society. Further divided into structural and cultural discrimination.

Melting-pot theory. A theory of minority absorption holding that it is possible and desirable to fuse biologically and culturally all the various racial and ethnic groups in society.

Minority groups. Any group in society that is kept from attaining a high status on the basis of culture, race, religion, or sex. A category of people that possesses imperfect access to positions of equal power and to the corollary categories of prestige and privilege in the society.

Prejudice. Prejudgment of an individual or group based not on fact or evidence but on stereotype and hearsay, and inability to change this judgment even when confronted with evidence.

Races. Subdivisions of the species *Homo Sapiens* based on differences in the frequency with which some genes occur among populations.

Racial minority. A group that differs biologically from the dominant group in such features as skin color, hair texture, eye color or slant, and head shape and dimensions.

Racism. The belief that racial groups display not only physical but also behavioral differences, and that both are inherited. Related to this belief is the idea that such differences are inferior or undesirable.

Structural discrimination. The system of inequalities at work within society. It prevents minorities from having equal access to sources of power, status, and privilege.

Sexism. Discrimination on the basis of sex.

Feminism. Social movement arising out of the desire to end inequality of status and sex discrimination against women.

Suggestions for Further Reading

Bahr, Howard M., Bruce A. Chadwick, and Robert C. Day. *Native Americans Today: Sociological Perspectives.* New York: Harper & Row, 1972. A collection of essays analyzing the various aspects of prejudice and discrimination against the American Indian, and his condition in relation to other minorities.

Brink, William, and Louis Harris. *Black and White.* New York: Simon and Schuster, 1969. In-depth interviews and opinion polls enrich this combined effort of a *Newsweek* editor and a national opinion pollster about the actual condition of race relations in the United States.

William H. Chafe. *The American Woman.* New York: Oxford University Press, 1972. A portrayal of the changing social, political, and economic roles of the American woman.

Clark, Kenneth. *Dark Ghetto.* New York: Harper & Row, 1965. A black sociologist probes several facets of lower-class culture.

Glazer, Nathan, and Daniel Moynihan. *Beyond the Melting Pot.* Cambridge, Mass.: M.I.T. Press, 1963. A well-documented and readable account of minorities becoming acculturated in New York.

Rose, Peter I. *They and We: Racial and Ethnic Relations in the United States.* New York: Random House, 1964. Minority group relations, especially the social processes of conflict and accommodation as they affect ethnic groups in America.

Tumin, Melvin M., ed. *Comparative Perspectives on Race Relations.* Boston: Little, Brown, 1969. Intergroup relations in a number of nations.

Yetman, Norman R., and C. Hoy Steele, eds. *Majority and Minority.* Boston: Allyn and Bacon, 1971. A collection of essays probing into the problems of ethnic and racial groups, their relations, and the discrimination they encounter on individual, institutional, and structural levels.

Social and cultural change in the modern era

WE HAVE BEEN emphasizing the group nature of human life, the importance of interaction through social processes, the creation of culture, and the divisions that exist within societies because of stratification systems as well as because of race and ethnicity. We have been discussing social structures, social organization, and social processes, from the standpoint of social statics. The term *social statics* refers to the study of social systems as they exist in any given historical period. But societies are not frozen in time. Pressures for new ways are continually being felt. Societies must either resist or accept change. The study of the sources of change is called *social dynamics.*

An ancient Greek philosopher observed that "There is nothing permanent except change." We ourselves change constantly: we gain or lose weight, we acquire gray hair and wrinkles, we get sick and then recover. Our attitudes, beliefs, and goals change: we may change religions and political parties, and occupations. Our physical environment changes: day shifts into night, summer becomes winter, meadows and fields give way to highways and cities.

Why might it be useful to develop both a static and a dynamic view of society?

Societies also change. They may grow, become wealthy, and acquire power. Or they may decline in size, wealth, and power. Societies may change their economic base—from hunting to agriculture or from agriculture to industry. Societies frequently change their system of government—from monarchy to oligarchy or to democracy. Culture is equally changeable. Since individuals, societies, and culture are so intimately related, changes in one invariably influence the other two. It is difficult to determine just where change does originate.

Sociologists do not, theoretically, view conflict as something to be avoided. However, sociologists are also human. How might their essential humanity affect their attitudes toward change?

Sociologists do not approach the phenomenon of change as anything abnormal, to be avoided or prevented. It simply exists, always and everywhere. Societies must constantly respond to challenges from outside and to contradictory forces from within. Moreover, the various segments of the social structure display their own built-in tensions. Such tensions and conflicts do not always or necessarily produce major social changes, but they do make it easier for social change to occur. Conflicts eventually led to legislation declaring segregation unconstitutional. Conflicts introduced the sexual revolution. And conflicts resulting from economic difficulties may still induce us to embrace a new economic system.

One of the criticisms of our modern way of life is that everything changes too rapidly. What do you suppose are some of the problems caused by change that occurs at too fast a rate?

Change is seldom accomplished overnight, and it generally occurs against a background of stability. Administrations come and go, but our basic governmental system, set up shortly after the American Revolution, is still in existence. The family has become small and nuclear, but we still get married, have children, and get together with our relatives on Thanksgiving. Religious dogma has undergone many changes, but many of our religions have survived for thousands of years.

For the last several hundred years, changes of a revolutionary nature have profoundly transformed our societies. The point of departure for these changes has been a speedup of technological progress, leading to the substitution of agrarian economies with industrial economies. The higher standard of living and the improved medical conditions resulting from an improved technology have led to population explosion. Population growth and industrialization have forced a change from rural to urban residence for most members of Western societies. Finally, increased population and urbanization of societies have required more efficient organization and formal associations with bureaucratic structure. In this chapter we will analyze some of the changes that mark the modern era. In the following chapter we will concern ourselves with how people have tended to react to change and instability in society.

[Social and Cultural Change]

Many explanations for change in the physical world have been offered by the exact scientists. They have told us how snow becomes water, how coal becomes electric power, or how a healthy organism becomes cancerous and dies. Social scientists are much less sure of what causes change in our social world.

Many social thinkers have attempted to construct theories of social and cultural change. Some have maintained that change is cyclical: that is, that societies, like living organisms, are born, mature, reach old age, stagnate, and finally die. Others have insisted that change is evolutionary, that is, that all things begin with a simple form and grow increasingly complex. Still others suggest that change is based on a number of important trends: societies change as they master their physical environment, as they become specialized, and as the individuals, groups, organizations, and other units in the social structure become increasingly interdependent. Some have speculated that when material culture changes more rapidly than nonmaterial culture, a cultural lag, marked by social problems, results. Finally theorists have asserted that change occurs because all cultures borrow some elements from one another, and that this borrowing naturally occurs as a result of the actions of individual men and women.

None of these theories has been really satisfactory in explaining change. Probably they all contain some elements of truth. But change is so complex that no single theory can explain it all.

Processes of Social and Cultural Change

Which of the theories of change that have been advanced appeals most to you? Does this theory describe the way you feel about your life?

[Processes of Social and Cultural Change]

While we can only guess at the cause of social and cultural change, we have been able to observe by what processes such change takes place. We can say generally that change in our society and culture comes from outside, through diffusion; or from within, through new technology or from the stresses and tensions of everyday interaction. For purposes of analysis we should distinguish between change that occurs in society, and change that occurs in culture. Society is a patterned system of interaction among individuals and groups. Social change, therefore, refers to change in these patterns of social interaction. As a result of change in these patterns, many members of society assume new statuses and play new roles. The abolition of slavery, for instance, was a social change because (theoretically, at least) it gave former slaves a new status—that of free people—in which they could fulfill new roles as equals of other citizens. Social change occurs through planning, reform, or revolution. Planning and reform are processes often initiated by governmental agencies. City governments are constantly planning projects that will change the city. They may plan a new airport hoping to attract air traffic and provide jobs. Or they may plan a housing project. A dramatic example of planning was displayed by the new Ethiopian government when it announced that it would change the ancient feudal political and economic system of the nation to a socialist system resembling that of modern China.

Reform and Revolution

Reform involves efforts by either citizens or governmental agencies to correct laws or institutions. During the Great Depression, laws were reformed to provide citizens with jobs, to provide them with the wherewithal to survive when they were unemployed, to help them with health care, and so on. In 1954, we reformed the law that allowed segregation. Recently we have reformed abortion and divorce laws.

To what extent does reform by government agencies rest on popular support? For example, how effective are the recent liberalized laws on abortion, in your opinion?

Revolution is change obtained through violent means by the people of a nation when their government ceases to be responsive to them. Revolution will be analyzed in the next chapter, when we take up the issue of social movements.

If you have ever read any science fiction, or seen any science-fiction movies, you have absorbed some of the projections of social change that are now being made. What are some of these projections for the future? On what existing conditions are these projections based?

Cultural Change

Culture, which includes norms, values and beliefs, is the product of social interaction. Cultural change takes place in the values, beliefs, and attitudes of society. Such changes generally occur as a result of scientific discoveries, technological inventions, new achievements in the arts, or changes in religious doctrines. During the history of Western civilization, cultural change of all types has occurred. The belief that slavery was justified has changed to the belief that it is morally reprehensible; the assumption that the earth is flat has changed to the knowledge that it is round. The invention of the automobile has been a cultural change of enormous importance. The automobile changed people's way of life; it has affected their sexual mores, their family traditions, and their conception of the world beyond their backyards.

Of course, society and culture cannot exist apart from each other. Changes in society cause changes in culture—and changes in culture cause changes in society. For example, the automobile—a cultural change—has had a tremendous impact on our society, which has become almost totally motorized. But although the effects of social and cultural change often overlap, the processes by which change occurs are different.

On a cultural level, change occurs through discovery, invention, and diffusion. Discovery and invention usually occur through the efforts of individuals. Diffusion often occurs without any conscious effort on the part of groups involved, but this is not always true.

Discovery

A discovery is new knowledge of an already existing fact or relationship. Principles of physics and chemistry existed before humans did, but it took centuries for people to perceive and understand them. The circulation of the blood, the presence of microbes, and the organization of the solar system are other examples of discoveries. Before a discovery can be put to use—and bring about cultural or social change—a society must be ready for it. A society must have other technological inventions to support it and it must value and have a need for the discovery. The principle of the steam engine was known some two thousand years ago. But it was not put into practice because the societies of the time did not have the necessary technology to build one. Parts that would make the engine workable did not yet exist. Similarly, Leonardo Da Vinci was making detailed plans for flying machines in the early sixteenth century. But only in this century did materials essential to the proper functioning of airplanes become available. Only recently, too, did people see a need for rapid transportation.

What is meant by the phrase "an idea whose time has come"? Can you give an example of something that is likely to be invented in the near future?

Invention

Invention is based on existing knowledge. Cultural ideas or objects already in existence are combined in a new way to produce something more important than the sum of their parts. The boat and the principle of the steam engine, for instance, existed as separate objects in many cultures. But when they were brought together to produce the steamboat, the new product became a more effective mode of transportation. When the steam engine was combined with a four-wheeled carriage, we had a train. And when the four-wheeled carriage was later combined with an internal combustion engine, we had the automobile.

In the same way, inventions can be made in nonmaterial culture. Old ideas are combined in new ways to yield new ideas. The United States Constitution may be thought of as a cultural invention resulting from the philosophical tradition of Western Europe and the experience of the colonists in the New World.

Diffusion

Diffusion is the spread of cultural traits from one society to another, and from one group within society to another. Diffusion is an important factor in the process of cultural change. For instance, while spaghetti and pizza were brought to America by Italian immigrants, today they are considered as American as apple pie. Even minimal contact between two cultures produces diffusion. Many anthropologists, in fact, maintain that most of the content of a complex culture is the product of diffusion.

Spaghetti is a form of pasta, which was brought to Italy from China in the Renaissance, just as tomatoes were brought from the Americas. Can you give further examples of diffusion?

Diffusion is always reciprocal. That is, each culture in contact with another gives something to the other, although not always in the same proportion. A simple culture, as a rule, borrows more elements from a more complex culture than the other way around. In the same society, many members of the lower social classes try to imitate some of the life-styles of the higher social classes.

A borrowing culture is generally selective. Only certain traits of a new culture are accepted. Japan readily accepted Western technology, but not the West's system of values. Americans borrowed the idea of representative government from England but did not give it a parliamentary form. Borrowing cultures also modify the traits they accept. American Indians smoked tobacco in pipes as part of ritual. When Europeans began using tobacco, however, they changed the form in which it was smoked from pipes to cigars and cigarettes. They also changed the practice from a ceremonial to a social one.

[Sociocultural Changes]

Sociocultural changes of enormous impact transformed, in the course of many centuries, the societies of the West from small, agrarian, rural, and traditional groups to large, industrial, urban, and associational groups. The events leading to these changes are all interdepen-

Cultural diffusion is one way in which cultures change. Here, diffusion is being furthered through advertising.

dent, so that it is difficult to tell what triggered the chain of events. Logic suggests that a speedup in the rate of technological progress led to industrialization, overpopulation, urbanization, and bureaucratic organization in a mass society. These changes, of course, have not been total. They have occurred against a backdrop of stability—we still live in families, believe in religions, celebrate major events in our lives, and so on. Nevertheless, change in our era has been very great.

Technology and the Industrial Revolution

Technology includes all the methods and devices that help humans manage and control their environment. For prehistoric humans, technology consisted of the use of sharpened sticks and stones. The discovery and use of fire and metals allowed prehistoric people to make more sophisticated tools and weapons.

Technology is cumulative: that is, all developments build on previous discoveries or inventions. Occasionally, however, some technological discovery or invention is so significant in terms of the sociocultural changes it produces that we may be justified in calling it a "technological revolution." One such revolution occurred during the Neolithic or New Stone Age between 5,000 and 3,000 B.C. In this period, for the first time in history, humans changed their condition from food gatherers to *food producers.* They domesticated some animals and put them to use; they invented the plow; they began using four-wheeled vehicles. Later they added the solar calendar, writing, numbers, and they began to use bronze. Still later, they added irrigation, sailboats, looms, the making of bricks, the process of glazing, and a great architectural invention, the arch.

Sociocultural Changes

The Incas, prehistoric peoples of South America, never invented the wheel. How do you suppose this noninvention affected the Inca culture, compared to that of other ancient cultures?

Results of the first technological revolution. What sociocultural changes followed this significant technological advance? First, tilling the soil and keeping flocks provided people with a fairly dependable food supply—even an occasional surplus. Since the rate of starvation was drastically reduced, populations boomed. No longer having to move in search of food, people could settle down permanently in one spot. A settled existence promoted the development of institutions. It allowed customs and traditions to solidify the family, religion, government, and the economy, and these important institutions all grew in complexity. Temporary settlements became permanent villages and towns. The labor that had to be done in the villages was divided for greater efficiency. Goods and services began to be exchanged between villages. New ways to control the environment accumulated.

For the next several thousand years, many sociocultural changes occurred in the societies of the world. Villages grew into towns and cities, and eventually became city-states and nation-states. Religions progressed from beliefs in magic to more sophisticated forms, including monotheism (belief in one god). The family also underwent a number of changes and took on different forms in different societies. Everything built on what had come before.

Why would a settled existence be likely to promote the development of institutions?

The Industrial Revolution

Not until the middle of the 18th century did a new technological revolution begin a new cycle of sociocultural change. Of course, 1750 is a somewhat arbitrary date to mark the beginning of such a revolution.

What is today called the Industrial Revolution of the mid-18th century actually has its roots in much earlier events.

Inventions and discoveries of the Industrial Revolution. The Industrial Revolution may be said to have begun with: (1) the invention of a small number of basic machines; (2) the invention and discovery of some new materials; and (3) the discovery of new sources of power. The wide-ranging effects of these discoveries and inventions were the mechanization of agriculture and manufacturing; the application of power to manufacturing; the development of a factory system; a tremendous increase in the speed of transportation and communication; and an increase in capitalistic control of almost all facets of the economy.

Among the most important machines invented during the first phase of the Industrial Revolution were the pendulum clock, the spinning wheel, the power loom, the blast furnace, and the steam engine. During the second phase, the most important invention was that of the combustion engine. The second phase of the revolution is thought to

Industrialization and automation have changed our culture drastically in the last two centuries.

have begun about 1860, and it is still going on. During this second phase, steel was substituted for iron as the basic material of industry; coal was replaced by gas and oil as principal sources of power, and we are currently attempting to harness atomic energy as a source of power. Electricity became a major form of industrial energy. Automatic machinery was developed, and labor became highly specialized. Light metals and alloys—aluminum and plastics—as well as the products of industrial chemistry have become common materials. The speed of transportation and communication has been radically increased by jets and satellite transmission. Economic organization has taken on new forms. Industrialization has spread all over the world. Now nearly all societies are either industrialized or aspiring to become industrialized.

Why would advances in the form of energy used tend to change the entire culture of a society?

Automation was developed somewhere around the 1930s. Automation is basically a process in which machines control other machines, as contrasted with mechanization, which is the substitution of machines for human and animal muscle power. We will discuss automation when we analyze the economic institution. For now, it is enough to mention that not all of the effects of automation have yet been measured. Some people have welcomed automation as simply a further development of basic mechanization, and foresee few problems in human adjustment to it. Others see automation as the beginning of another technological revolution. This period may be said to have begun after 1945 with the appearance of computers. Computers, in addition to creating their own spin-off, computer science, have been responsible for a knowledge explosion that has practically doubled our store of and access to knowledge in approximately twenty years. There is little question but that computers have ushered in a new era.

Industrialism. The system of production that came to be called "industry" represented a radical departure from previous methods of manufacturing goods. In the Middle Ages, artisans or craftsmen organized into guilds (types of unions) produced an entire article. That is, the individual craftsman, helped by an apprentice, bought the raw material, designed the article, and personally made or supervised the making of the article from beginning to end. Usually, he also sold the article directly to a buyer, though sometimes he sold it to a merchant.

Given what you know about how culture is transmitted and how individuals are socialized, what changes might come about as a result of the knowledge explosion?

As commerce expanded, those craftsmen who relied on merchants to dispose of their merchandise rather than waiting for customers to come to their shops to order made bigger profits. Eventually, craftsmen began to depend on merchants much as employees do today. Merchants, being in touch with the public, were much more aware of what the public wanted and in what quantities specific items should be produced. Soon the merchants took over the entire process of production, from supplying the raw material to selling the finished product. Needing more workers, merchants began employing entire fami-

Does the piece system still operate in our economy? In what parts of the economy?

lies who would produce a finished product from raw or unfinished material and who were paid by the piece. This system was alternately called the *piece, domestic,* or *putting-out* system. The piece system became the foundation of the English woolen industry. Farm families would supplement their small earnings from farming by spinning the yarn that merchants brought to their cottages (hence, the name "cottage industry").

Because of population growth in Europe and the expanding markets provided by the discovery of the New World, the piece system became increasingly specialized as more and more articles were produced. The production of an article was divided into several steps that different members of the family—or apprentices—could easily perform. Specialization and division of labor are especially efficient ways of organizing production.

With the invention and growing use of machinery in the manufacture of articles, it became more convenient to house both the workers and the bulky machinery under one roof. This step introduced the factory system as the basis of industrialism. The former merchants—now called *entrepreneurs* and *employers*—had much more control over their workers when all the stages of production were housed in one location. They could pace the work of their employees—decide how many pieces had to be finished per hour or per day. And they could use their capital much more effectively when everything needed for production was at their disposal.

Some social analysts have claimed that the Enclosure Acts were developed as a measure to provide labor for factories. Could a similar analysis be made of the abolition of slavery? Why or why not?

The factory system and industrialism in general originated as a result of a number of circumstances that came together at the right time and in the right place. In England, where the factory system was first established, rural residents were flocking to the towns because the Enclosure Acts had literally thrown them off the land.[1] Machines were becoming increasingly efficient and sources of power were becoming more dependable. Markets were expanding because of growing population in Europe and America and more investment capital was available. Technology was progressing at a rapid pace. Combined with a new economic ideology, which was to acquire the name of *capitalism,* the system of industrial production established itself as the foundation for the economies of Western societies for many centuries to come.

The Industrial Revolution crossed over into the United States from Britain in the early part of the nineteenth century. It spread to West-

[1]The Enclosure Acts were passed as a result of pressures from the large landowners of Britain who were seeking to increase the productivity of their land so they could take advantage of the new foreign markets. The Acts enabled them to gain control of several million acres of land that had formerly been common pasture land, woodland, and the farmland of individual small farmers. On this land, the landowners grazed sheep for the woolen industry. The Enclosure Acts had several important consequences. They forced the peasants into the city where they supplied the labor needed for industry. They made huge profits for the landowners, who invested in industry, contributing to its growth. And they swelled the ranks of a new social class, the bourgeoisie, or middle class.

Methodology: Demographic Analysis

The mid-nineteenth century was a period of great economic and social change throughout Europe. During the same period the suicide rates of most European countries rose significantly. Was there a connection? Emile Durkheim explored this question using demographic data in his now classic study, *Suicide* (1897), by a series of ingenious comparisons of the suicide rates among various countries and social groups. The patterns to be found in these rates of suicide, Durkheim believed, had a significance all their own, independent of the psychological factors that might precipitate individual suicides. He began his analysis by eliminating nonsocial factors such as insanity, heredity, and climate as explanations of suicide. He showed, for example, that variations in the distribution of mental illness did not match (or correlate with) variations in the distribution of suicides.

Durkheim then turned to possible social causes of suicide. He classified his findings into three types of suicide—egoistic, altruistic, and anomic—which, he said, corresponded to different effective causes. Egoistic suicide arises from a lack of group cohesion that leaves individuals to depend on themselves alone. This was why, he said, suicide rates were higher among Protestants than Catholics, and among those living alone than those living in families. Suicide rates decreased during national wars and political crises, he argued, because these events bound people together in a common cause and struggle. Altruistic suicide, on the other hand, which Durkheim found to be relatively rare, results when the collectivity takes on a greater reality than individuals, which sometimes leads them to die voluntarily for a communal cause.

In explaining anomic suicide, Durkheim noted that the institution of divorce and economic crises had aggravating effects on the suicide rate. This happened, he said, because in each case the social equilibrium was disrupted in such a way as to free the passions of individuals from their customary restraints. Uncontrolled desire leads to increased insecurity and disillusionment, he argued, and from there the leap is short to suicide.

The rate of suicide, Durkheim concluded, is an important barometer of the moral temper of a society. The rise in suicide rates in the nineteenth century, he said, was not the result of progress as such, but of the changes that, in uprooting traditional institutions, had put nothing in their place.

Emile Durkheim, *Suicide: A Study in Sociology,* trans. John A. Spaulding and George Simpson (New York: The Free Press, 1951).

ern Europe in the middle of that century, and to Japan at the end of the century. After the Russian revolution in 1917, that nation too began a serious effort at industrialization, and, in succession, so did China, India, and South America.

The Industrial Revolution is still going on; none of us can foresee where it will all end. But we can see what sociocultural changes the Industrial Revolution has already caused; tremendous increases in population; a move toward the city, or urbanization; and almost complete dependence on industry as the prime mover of our economy. In turn, these changes have produced social conditions that present us with many problems. These we must either attempt to solve or learn to live with.

[Population]

The biblical command to be fruitful and multiply reflected a time when the human species was small in numbers and at the mercy of the forces of nature. With an inadequate food supply, no knowledge of disease control, and no refuge from the ravages of ice and sun, humans did not live very long. A great many did not even survive infancy. Life expectancy was extremely low—an estimated 18 years during the Bronze Age.

The total world population of the hunting and gathering societies in existence eight to ten thousand years ago was only 20 million. By 1000 B.C., when many societies had reached the agricultural stage, population had increased to 100 million. So slowly did population growth occur, that by 1000 A.D., the total world population was only 300 million.

Why might the new technology have lowered the death rate but not affected the birth rate?

In the middle of the seventeenth century, however, population began to increase steadily. The improvements in agriculture and technology, as well as improvements in medicine and sanitation, were raising the general standard of living and radically lowering the death rate. The birth rate remained unaffected. The low death rate and steady birth rate created an imbalance—more people were being born than were dying. But in the seventeenth century, an increase in population could easily be accommodated.

Today, this imbalance is no longer tolerable. The present rate of world population growth is approximately 2 percent a year. By the year 2000 the current world population of 3.9 billion people will almost double. And it will keep on doubling approximately every 37 years.

Has your life-style been affected in any way by the scarcity of the world's resources?

What effects will overpopulation have on the world? In the industrial nations, overcrowding, or lack of space and privacy, is already an acute problem. Additional houses, highways, transportation systems, and sewage systems are continually built to accommodate the onslaught. Air and water pollution and inadequate police and fire protection—already serious problems—will become even more severe.

In the underdeveloped, or developing nations, the prospect is much more stark. Even today, in some areas of the world, an estimated 10,000 people die of starvation or malnutrition each day. Furthermore, the population growth of the underdeveloped nations is now twice that of the industrial nations. By 1980 it will increase to almost three times that of the industrial nations. By the year 2000, these nations will con-

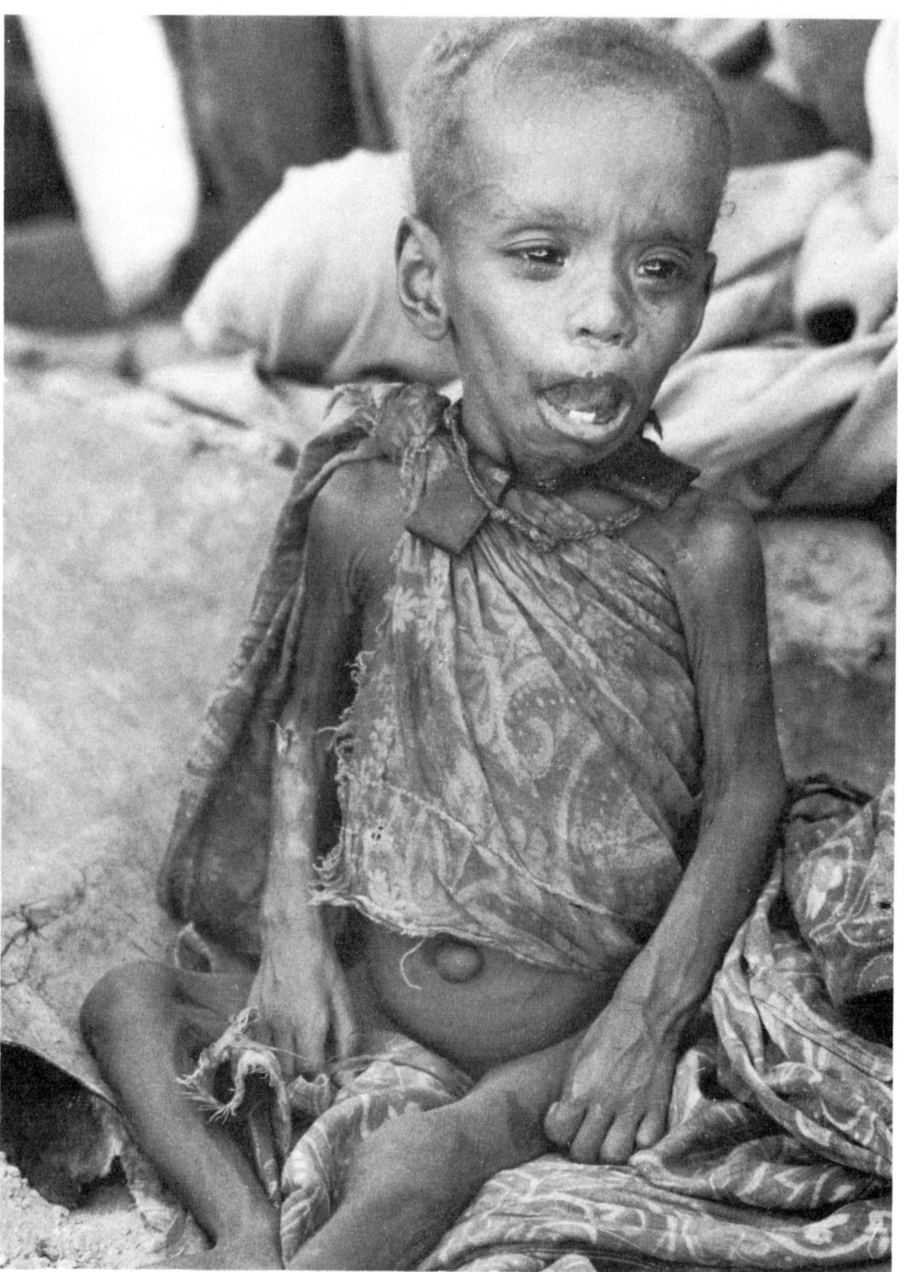

About 10,000 people die of starvation and malnutrition every day. This Ethiopian child is a casualty of drought and unequal distribution of the world's resources.

tain a combined population of 5 billion people, a number corresponding to 80 percent of the world's population. Such enormous growth presents not only problems of sufficient food, but also violence and social upheaval. The United Nations projects that half of the world's people will be residing in urban areas by the year 2000, whereas only 37 percent of them live in such areas today.

The world's birth rate is declining. But death rates are also decreasing rapidly because of medical advances that have prolonged life spans and reduced infant mortality. Life expectancy has been lengthened by twenty years during the last three decades. A world population of 12 billion is estimated for a century from now. It is doubtful whether our planet can physically support such a mass of people at that time.

Demography

Demography is the study of the growth or decrease of population, its distribution throughout the world, and its composition. The discipline concerns itself with the changes that occur over periods of time in rates of fertility, mortality, and migration, as well as with the effects of these changes on people and societies.

What factors might cause the birth rate to drop? The death rate?

Among the most useful concepts of demography are the terms *population growth rate, birth rate, death rate,* and *fertility rate.* Population growth rate is the rate, in annual percentages, by which a given population is either growing or declining. The world population growth rate is obtained by subtracting the number of deaths from the number of births and calculating what percentage of the total population the difference represents for that year. A stable population rate means that as many people die as are born; a growing population rate means that more people are born than die; and a declining population rate means that more people die than are born. A national or regional population growth rate must be adjusted to include immigration and emigration. For example, the population growth rate increased in the United States toward the end of the 19th and beginning of the 20th centuries because of immigration rather than an increase in births over deaths.

Birth rates and death rates are calculated on the basis of every 1,000 persons in a specific population for a specific year. A birth rate of 40 means that there have been an average of 40 births for every 1,000 persons in the total population. Death or mortality rates can, and usually are, calculated on the basis of other variables—sex, age, occupation, race, and so on.

The fertility rate represents the number of births in a population in relation to every 1,000 women of childbearing age (generally between the ages of 15 to 45). Fertility rates refer to actual births, whereas fecundity rates refer to the biological potential for producing offspring.

The Malthusian prophecy. One of the earliest demographers to warn

American Transience

Some demographic historians have attempted to measure population movements within the United States by calculating the percentage of people who remained in an area over a length of time. Comparing figures gleaned from 23 communities of varying size over a span of 150 years, Stephan Thernstrom has shown that in most cases only between 40 and 60 percent of the adult males could be found in the same location ten years later, whether in the early nineteenth century or the decade 1958–1968. In all but one of the deviant cases, even less than 40 percent of the population remained in the same community.

No long-term trends in the gross rates of persistence seem evident, although the class of men most likely to move shifted about 1920 from manual workers to white-collar workers like technicians and professionals. Perhaps most surprisingly, the percentage of people who stayed in a community was independent of its growth rate or its size. Farming communities in Massachusetts in the early 1800s and in Kansas in the first decades of the twentieth century fit the same pattern as large cities.

These figures suggest that the stable small town has been, in demographic terms, more a myth than a reality. The most visible segments of a community may have stayed, but transience was the norm among the majority. The volatility of America's populations may have been an important factor in our industrialization, suggests Thernstrom, as a mobile labor force is most responsive to changing economic conditions and new plant locations.

Stephan Thernstrom, *The Other Bostonians: Poverty and Progress in the American Metropolis, 1880–1970* (Cambridge: Harvard University Press, 1973), pp. 9–28, 220-232.

the world of the dangers of overpopulation was Thomas Robert Malthus. In 1798, this English clergyman, mathematician, and economist published an essay in which he claimed that under favorable circumstances populations would grow by geometric progression—by 2, 4, 8, 16, and so on. The food supply, on the other hand, would increase in arithmetic progression—1, 2, 3, 4, 5, and so on. Consequently, the food supply would eventually become exhausted, at which time the death rate would increase to reestablish a balance. Although he was quite pessimistic about the possibility of reversing this trend, Malthus suggested the use of preventive checks to control fertility. The checks he favored were late marriage and enforced celibacy—hardly successful

Why would late marriage and enforced celibacy probably be unsuccessful ways to control fertility?

alternatives.[2] Great advances in technology, agriculture, and methods of birth control have proven the Malthusian prophecy too gloomy as it concerns industrial nations. But it still has relevance for the developing nations where population growth exceeds food production.

The Demographic Transition

For most of human history, the rates of population growth were barely sufficient for people to replace themselves. A high fertility rate was necessary to compensate for the extremely high death rate. In addition, periods of famine, disease, and wars decimated many of the world's populations.

In the chapter on stratification it was suggested that inequality is related to scarcity of resources. How, then, might the population explosion extend and maintain inequality in the world?

The Industrial Revolution changed all that. But the suddenly exploding population growth failed to frighten people—despite Malthus's warning—because they thought that technology, particularly in the field of agriculture, would always ensure an adequate food supply. Population growth in the Western World was accompanied by an increase in the standard of living. This correlation was interpreted as meaning that rapid population growth was needed for economic expansion. After all, the more people there are, the more products are consumed, and the more people are needed in the work force to produce articles for consumption. Unfortunately, rapid population growth has the effect of erasing any gains derived from improvements in agricultural and industrial technology.

At any rate, the Western world has undergone, in the last two hundred years, what demographers call a "demographic transition." Western societies have gone from high mortality and fertility rates to low mortality and fertility rates. Population grew rapidly for a time, and death rates dropped before birth rates did. But soon birth rates too were falling and the population growth rate began to stabilize at a relatively low level.

In the belief that this transition represents a general pattern, demographers have pieced together a conceptual model of population growth. According to the demographic transition model, society passes through three basic stages of population growth. In the first stage, birth rates and death rates are both high, leading to a balance achieved through cycles of growth and decline. In the second stage, death rates decline but birth rates remain high, leading to unchecked population growth. In the third stage, there is evidence of a decline of birth rates, leading to a stabilization of population. The model allows for shifts in population growth following unusual events, such as wars and depressions.

According to the model, tropical Africa, tropical South America, and the eastern and middle sections of Asia are currently in the first stage. Parts of North Africa, the temperate part of South America,

[2]Thomas R. Malthus, *An Essay on the Principle of Population* (Homewood, Ill.: Irwin, 1963).

India, Communist China, and several other Third World nations are in the second stage. The United States, Australia, New Zealand, Japan, Canada, the United Kingdom, and northern and western Europe are all in the third stage.

Overpopulation in Developing Nations

There are no guarantees that the third stage of the demographic transition model will ever be reached by the developing nations. The problem is that industrialization is not proceeding spontaneously in those nations, as it did in the West. Industrialization is being imported wholesale from the West and superimposed on largely traditional societies. The social and cultural changes that have been made in Western countries in response to the improved living standards brought by industrialization—and that have resulted in a stabilization of population growth rates—simply have not occurred in the developing nations. While the importation of advanced technology has resulted in a drastic reduction of death rates, the people still have not changed their social and cultural customs and values sufficiently to permit a voluntary restriction of births.[3]

Population and Food

Americans are generally thought to eat too much for their own health. Can you devise a program that would let hungry people share in our wealth? What social changes might be required before such a program became feasible?

People need food for sheer survival and in order to be able to work and be productive. The more people there are in a society, the more food is required to feed them. On a world basis, food production has grown slightly faster than population in the last few decades (from about 1951 to 1971). But food production is not shared equally by the populations of the world. While more than half of the food produced was absorbed by the richest 30 percent of the world's people, the other half was unevenly distributed among the world's 70 percent of poor peoples, represented by the 2.6 billion of Asia, Africa, and Latin America.[4]

Since 1972 the world food production has decreased as a result of droughts, poor weather, and the rising consumption of beef in the developed nations. The increase in the price of petroleum has caused serious worldwide shortages of nitrogen fertilizers and has reduced the ability of some farmers in the developing nations to pump water for irrigation. The enormous American agricultural surplus that was so often a saving factor in preventing famines across the world has been completely depleted. The grain that would ordinarily be sold cheaply to feed the poor nations has become more expensive since it is used to feed the meat animals of the rich nations. Prices on the world food

---

[3]Paul R. Ehrlich and Anne H. Ehrlich, "Misconceptions," *New York Times Magazine* (June 16, 1974), pp. vi, 9.

[4]Roger Revelle, "Food and Population," *Scientific American* 230 (September 1974): 161.

If population continues to exhaust the food supply, the world will be faced with famine, at least. What kinds of social changes might accompany a world-wide famine?

market have also gone up to such an extent (mainly as a result of the USSR's tremendous importation of food in 1973 and again in 1975) that most poor nations, and most poor people in the rich nations, are faced with malnutrition if not outright starvation. Poor crops in the United States in the next few years could prove disastrous to the entire world.

In a debate discussing his book, *The Limits of Growth*, Dennis L. Meadows makes the following remarks on the necessity of reducing population and material growth:

> *First, we would point to the enormous political, biological and economic processes and forces which stimulate growth, and which are giving us an unprecedently high rate of population and material growth today. Second, we have come to identify a number of important limits to growth. We tended to focus on the physical limits; those dealing with the finite land area, the finite ability of the environment to absorb pollution and so forth, but we've recognized also some social and political limits as well. These limits suggest to us that material growth, as we currently know it, can't continue indefinitely, nor indeed can it continue very much longer. Certainly we'll begin to slow down within the lifetime of children born today. Third, we point to the very long delays in the response of society to these more fundamental problems—fifty, sixty, eighty years are involved in stabilizing a population, effecting a new change in social values, putting in place a new energy system. When you have a rapid rate of change and long delays, the system tends to be unstable like a drunken driver who is slow in responding to information about hazards. This instability causes overshooting collapse of the sort that we describe in our book.*[5]

The collapse that Meadows envisions if we continue to allow increases in population, draining of resources, and speeding up the rate of industrialization is not necessarily physical. Especially in the developed countries, such collapse might take the form of a reduction of personal freedom and in the quality of life. As preventive measures to avoid world collapse, Meadows and his group of researchers suggest we begin to practice both zero population growth and zero economic growth. As to the latter, it is doubtful that nations will willingly curtail their economic expansion. But the former has already been attained, at least in the United States and in other industrial societies of the West.

Zero Population Growth

What factors in our society may encourage zero population growth?

At the end of 1972, the Census Bureau issued new, extremely low projections of future population size. These projections were based on the decline of the fertility rate, which in that year had dropped below the replacement level (to 2.08 or 2.04) for the first time. (The replacement level is 2.11, 2 representing the rate if each person simply reproduces

[5]Dennis L. Meadows, "The Limits to Growth: A Debate," from *Speaking of Science*, a series of tape-recorded conversations among scientists produced by the American Association for the Advancement of Science.

himself or herself, and the 0.11 representing those people who remain childless.) The lower fertility rate can be best appreciated when we realize that as recently as 1961, the American rate was well over 3.6 children per family. Young women appear to want fewer children, and more are remaining single for longer periods of time. Still there is a potential for a rate increase as the children of the post-World War II baby boom reach childbearing age.

The United States, in attaining zero population growth, is following the lead set by other urban, industrial nations. Conditions in cities—where most people are concentrated in the industrial nations—do not lend themselves to large families. First, housing is scarce. Second, because industrial jobs are closed to children, a large family is not profitable. Finally, it is expensive to educate and provide health protection for many children.

Regardless of the dictates of religion and culture, then, urban families tend to voluntarily curb their fertility. For example, Ireland, France, and Italy are all Roman Catholic nations, and Roman Catholics oppose birth control. Yet the birth rate in these nations is among the lowest in the world and is actually declining in Ireland and France. Unplanned change has accomplished what extensive governmental planning and reform in other nations have not been able to do.

Although we have attained zero population growth, we should remain cautious. Our habits of conspicuous consumption still extract more ecological space and resources than do those of an Indonesian peasant. Even if we stop growing in numbers, our consumption rate will continue to be a burden on our environment. The United States is rapidly becoming as much a problem in its impact on the environment as India's tremendous overpopulation is.

[Urbanization]

Urbanization is the population trend in which cities and their suburbs grow at the expense of rural areas. Urbanization takes place in industrial nations because industry attracts labor to cities and labor attracts businesses.

Urbanization, however, does not account for all city growth. Because of an increased birth rate, a decreased death rate, or immigration from abroad, cities may grow without a parallel decrease in rural population. Or they may grow because of overall population growth in both rural and urban areas. In developing nations urban growth has not occurred at the expense of rural areas but because both cities and rural areas are increasing in population.

The shift from rural to urban living took its impetus from the Industrial Revolution in Great Britain. Factories located in cities attracted a large number of people who could no longer make a living on the land. Some of these people had been dispossessed by the Enclosure

Acts. Others came to the cities because science and technology had improved agricultural methods, and less manpower was needed on the land. New iron and steel plows, reapers, threshers, harvesters, and finally tractors and combines did much of the work once done by humans. Crop rotation, chemical fertilizers, irrigation, and insect and disease control increased yields per acre, without requiring much human labor.

How does efficiency in food production lead to further urbanization?

Agricultural methods have continued to improve. In the United States, the result has been a continuing decline in the rural population. In 1820, the average farm worker produced enough food to feed four people. By 1950, one worker produced enough to sustain 15½ people, and by 1969, enough for 47 people. Such superefficiency in food production has its drawbacks: the small farmer, whose yearly sales are low, is forced out of the market. This situation, in which only big farmers survive and profit, tends to move young people off the land. In 1969 the average age of farm proprietors was 51. By 1970, 25 percent of the national farm population was 55 and older.[6]

However, the new commercial agriculture, while displacing people from the land, creates a demand for agricultural machinery. Clearly, the next step is urbanization—the migration of people from rural to urban centers. The terms *urban* and *rural* are generally understood. But there is really little agreement as to their strict definition. Many localities are neither urban nor rural. We may think of urban and rural as extremes on a continuum distinguished chiefly by population density and size. Cities, or urban areas, are localities where a large number of people live and work. Rural areas are localities with a small number of people who, however, tend to be densely clustered. The United States Bureau of the Census considers the minimum population size for a city to be 2,500. Urban sociologists tend to use the term *ecological city,* which includes a central city (or the city proper), the suburbs that surround it, and satellite settlements that depend on the central city socially and economically.

To realize the extent of urbanization in the United States, we have only to look at a few figures. When the first census was taken in 1790, 95 percent of the American people lived in rural areas. Only 5 percent lived in cities. As of 1970, 73.5 percent of the population is urban, and only 26.5 is rural. In 1920 one in every three Americans was living on a farm. By 1971, it was only one out of every twenty-two. In the decade between 1960 and 1970 alone, approximately 80 percent of those who were changing residence moved from a rural to an urban setting. And an equal percentage of urban residents moved to the suburbs, which now house more Americans than rural areas and central cities put together.[7]

Some people are making a move back to the land, to small, self-sufficient farms. Do you think this trend will eventually offset urbanization? Why or why not?

[6]E. J. Kahn, Jr., "Who, What, Where, How Much, How Many?" *The New Yorker* 49 (October 15, 1973), pp. 137–157.

[7]Kahn, pp. 137–157.

The Urban Trend

Cities existed centuries before the word *industrialization* had been coined. Many had grown large, rich, and powerful. Cities had usually been built in fertile areas, and depended on the surrounding farms for their food supply. They often reverted to a rural status following wars and invasions.

The urban trend begun by the Industrial Revolution, however, was of a different nature. It brought together an astonishingly large number of people who had nowhere else to go to earn a living. Because the people were concentrated in a relatively small area, interaction between different groups—rich and poor, educated and illiterate, native and foreign-born—became unavoidable.

People of different backgrounds living in close quarters naturally gave rise to different life-styles and to new forms of social organization. Life in cities strengthened the importance of economic and political institutions, while religious and primary group ties were weakened. Class structure became more flexible because fortunes were made, not merely inherited. Social mobility began to characterize urban groups.

Urbanism

In contrast to urbanization, which is an ongoing process, urbanism is a condition, a set of attitudes, a quality, or a way of life distinct from the rural. The traditional rural values of predominantly agricultural societies are being replaced by urban values on a societal level. Mass communication is spreading urbanism in industrial nations. Because of television, radio, newspapers and magazines, people in urbanized industrial nations are beginning to look and think alike. In Third World nations, however, urban dwellers are retaining their previous rural values or at least are not replacing them with urban ones.

Traditional rural values. The traditional rural values that urbanism is destroying center mainly on life in the open spaces instead of in the cramped quarters of the city, and on the closeness and security of living in a large, extended family. Rural values involve intimacy with one's neighbors and friendships developed and maintained by attendance at the same school, the same church, and the same clubs.

Americans frequently hold an idealized stereotype of rural virtue. The citizens of Springdale, a real town of one thousand people in upstate New York with a mythical name were the subject of a classic study by sociologists Arthur Vidich and Joseph Bensman.[8] According to the study, Springdalers think of themselves as honest, trustworthy, neigh-

The word *urbane* describes someone who is sophisticated and cosmopolitan. Why might a word obviously derived from *urban* involve these qualities?

[8]Arthur J. Vidich and Joseph Bensman, *Small Town in Mass Society* (Princeton, N.J.: Princeton University Press, 1958).

Have you ever lived in the country? Did you feel that the people were better than people who lived in the city? Why or why not?

borly, helpful, sober, clean-living and all-around good folk. However, the researchers saw a slightly different picture. They found a corrupt governing body, elected by a political machine that chose candidates who were willing to keep taxes low and their voices down. What is more, the researchers discovered that the Springdalers depended greatly on the technology and culture of the city. In fact, even their view of themselves as virtuous rural people was chiefly derived from the mass media, which tends to idealize country life and people.

Political ramifications. The stereotype of the rural as good and the urban as bad has affected American politics. Proponents of popular democracy such as Thomas Jefferson, as well as early observers of the American scene such as Alexis de Tocqueville, had great faith in the rural citizens. They felt that the "simple folk," by their direct participation in the processes of democracy, would keep the system alive. This tradition led to the failure in many states to revise legislative and congressional districts in accordance with new population shifts toward the city. Such failure gave rural residents larger representation in state and federal legislature than their numbers warranted. The injustice was finally reversed by the *Baker v. Carr* Supreme Court decision. Yet even today the state of New York (densely populated) and Nevada (sparsely populated) are each represented by two senators, a situation that favors rural residents.

The Urban Transition

Because cities have grown so rapidly, very little planning has gone into their development. Much building has been haphazard and ugly. Because of the large concentration of people in cities, buildings are close together and tall. It is difficult to make cities look open, although planning by people concerned for the physical environment and for appearance does much to improve them.

Urban morals are of necessity varied. In the transition from rural to urban dweller, the individual has had to make adjustments that have had profound effects on personality and on social organization. First, he has had to limit his family to a nucleus: father, mother, and children. The grandparents, aunts, and uncles who lent both physical and psychological support have been dispersed. The friends and neighbors he knew and talked to every day have been replaced with strangers busy with their own concerns, who do not want to get involved outside of an occasional "Hello." In other words, the urban dweller has experienced the transition from primary groups and a Gemeinschaft (folk, traditional) society to secondary groups and a Gesellschaft (associational) society.

What effect has this transition had on the urban population? Above all, the release from the ties of the primary group has led to increased freedom of action. Freedom of action under circumstances of anonymity—when hardly anyone knows you or cares—often results in behavior that is frowned on by society. Freedom from the norms imposed by primary groups may also lead to normlessness. The individual no longer feels that he knows what is right or wrong. Finally, it may bring about a feeling of not belonging to any definite group, of not having anyone who cares.

Given this description of urban normlessness, what kinds of social change may be needed to bring about a decline in urban crime rates?

In some people, such feelings trigger the onset of mental illness. In others, they result in delinquent or criminal behavior. Still others become a part of the statistics of our high divorce rate, escapism through drugs and alcohol, and so on. Many people express such feelings by assuming a callous, indifferent, dehumanized mask, which they present to the world in self-defense.

The practical result of the decrease in informal controls by the primary group is an increase in formal controls. Without such formal controls, there would be little order. Laws are passed and police departments are formed to enforce them. More and more activities of the urban resident are controlled by codes and regulations. The urban resident pays the price of bureaucratization and impersonal life-styles for his freedom from primary-group interference.

Urban Life-Styles

The many groups and their subcultures coexisting in large cities have naturally produced a variety of life-styles. Urban sociologist Herbert Gans has distinguished five urban life-styles.

The first is that of the cosmopolitans. The latter are a highly educated, professional group with a very high income. They choose to live in the city because of its cultural facilities. The second life-style is that of single, or childless, groups. Single people choose to live in the city because there are various social activities and opportunities for meeting people. Single city dwellers tend to be upwardly mobile. They frequently move to the suburbs when they marry or have children. Another life-style is that of so-called ethnic villagers. These are immigrants who choose to live as they did in their homeland. Their only contact with outsiders occurs at work. Their interest is limited to their neighborhood, in which they live according to a more or less rural tradition. Still another life-style is that of the deprived, who are poor, nonwhite, and tend to live in fatherless households. The deprived live in the city not out of choice but because rents are cheaper, jobs are easier to find, and welfare payments tend to be higher than they are in other areas. The fifth, and last, life-style is that of the trapped. This group is made up of elderly pensioners who cannot afford to move out of the city and have to cling to their old neighborhood.[9]

If you have ever lived in a city, you have probably met people from each of the five types Gans describes. What category did you fall into? What neighborhoods did each of these types live in?

---

[9]Herbert J. Gans, "Urbanism and Suburbanism as Ways of Life: A Reevaluation of Definitions," in Arnold M. Rose, ed., *Human Behavior and Social Processes* (Boston: Houghton Mifflin, 1962), chapter 6.

An Urban Way of Life

Herbert Gans' understanding of "ethnic villagers" originated in his participant-observation study of second generation Italian-Americans in a Boston neighborhood. The West End had the external characteristics of a slum: high density, vacant lots, and decaying apartment buildings housing a predominantly working-class, low-income population from various ethnic backgrounds. Behind this facade Gans found a cohesive and vital social life among West Enders, unlike the culture of the middle-class and the "social disorganization" imagined by an earlier generation of urban theorists.

The focus of social life among West Enders was what Gans called "the peer group society," a combination of strong family and peer relationships, which, the evidence shows, is more a workingclass than an ethnic phenomenon. Although the second generation discarded many elements of Italian culture, they retained a social structure like that of their grandparents. This continuity in social structure over three generations was the result, Gans argued, of underlying similarities in the social place and condition of southern Italians and West Enders. Like their ancestors who lived in the crowded towns of southern Italy, West Enders turned to relatives as a source of group life and mutual aid in the face of poverty wages, low-status jobs, and community agencies run by more affluent and often hostile outsiders.

The West End Gans studied is no more. It was torn down in the late fifties as a slum, its residents dispersed, and their dwellings replaced by a luxury apartment house complex.

Herbert J. Gans, *The Urban Villagers: Group and Class in the Life of Italian-Americans* (New York: The Free Press of Glencoe, 1962).

Do you feel that cities are unfriendly? Why or why not? Why would the degree of social organization affect the success of solutions to urban problems?

The city is often used as a prime example of the way social disorganization expresses itself in a number of social problems. We are familiar with the cries of high crime rates, lack of involvement, absence of community feelings, the many suicides, and the unfriendly atmosphere that is alleged to predominate in cities. Such symptoms are usually signs that a social system does not function well. However, the fact that such a large variety of people, with such different life-styles live so closely together seems to deny the accusation of disorganization. Modern urban sociologists tend to agree that there is much more social *organization* in the city than we have been led to believe. If that is true, we can be much more optimistic about finding solutions for the city's problems.

The Ecology of the City

Cities are not simply a haphazard collection of residential, commercial, and industrial buildings. Buildings and people are distributed according to patterns within a geographic area. These patterns are interdependent. The study of distributive patterns and their interdependence is called urban ecology or *human ecology.*

What natural areas can you identify in your community?

Urban ecologists have found that in each city some natural areas come into existence spontaneously. These areas attract people of similar backgrounds, attitudes, and behavior. The people in them depend on one another, but do not actually interrelate with one another to a great extent. A central business district, a rooming-house district, and a dormitory district surrounding a university are all examples of natural areas.

Cities also consist of neighborhoods. These do not arise spontaneously, but usually result from planning. The residents of neighborhoods interrelate more closely with one another than do people in natural areas.

Natural areas and neighborhoods are constantly changing because of the ecological processes at work within them. One such process is

Three Conceptions of the Internal Structure of Cities

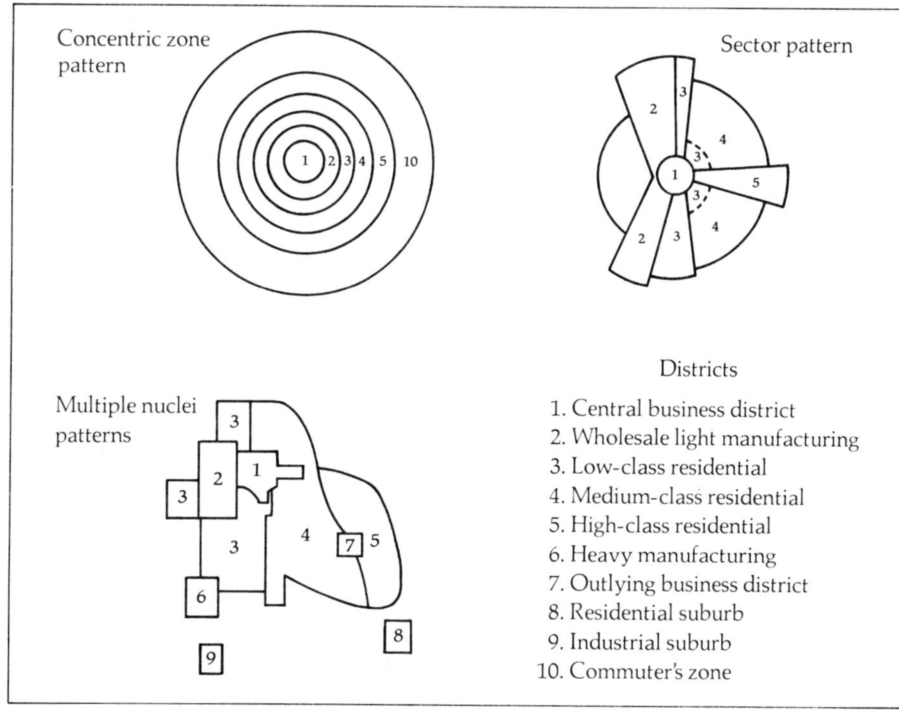

Source: C. D. Harris and E. L. Ullman, "The Nature of Cities," *Annuals of the American Academy of Political and Social Science* (November 1945): 12. Used by permission of the publisher.

concentration, or the gathering together of people in a specific area. Concentration is measured in terms of population density, or the number of people per square mile. Another ecological process is *dispersion,* the way in which people are scattered in different areas. Still another is *centralization,* or the tendency for business, industry, and financial and educational facilities to cluster in the central section of the city. *Decentralization,* on the other hand, is a relocation of such facilities in outlying areas when the central district becomes too congested. *Segregation* is the tendency for different areas of the city to specialize in specific activities or serve as the home of specific kinds of people. The Chinatowns of many cities are examples of segregation. Another example is Greenwich Village in New York City. *Invasion* is the ecological process by which a new group or institution takes over a formerly segregated area. For example, business and industry sometimes take over residential areas. One racial or ethnic group may take over a neighborhood previously inhabited by another racial or ethnic group. When invasion succeeds, the process is called *succession.*

Get a map of the community you live in, and, using the knowledge accumulated by various class members, identify and label the areas and processes that are shaping the community.

These processes produce consistent patterns in many American cities. Such patterns have been described by several urban development theories, the best known of which are the *concentric zone* theory, the *sector* theory, and the *multiple nuclei* theory. All three theories have several elements in common. According to all these theories, each city has (1) a central business district; (2) several transition zones housing slum dwellers and industry; (3) zones housing semiskilled, skilled, and clerical workers; and (4) suburban developments on the fringes or outside of the city proper.

Suburbanization and Metropolitanization

American cities are currently undergoing a period of profound crisis. The crisis is related to the trend toward suburbanization and metropolitanization, both movements out and away from the city. According to the 1970 census figures, more than three-fourths of the national population growth occurred in metropolitan, or urban, areas. But the growth was most significant in the suburbs—small communities on the outskirts of the central city and somewhat dependent on it. Residents of suburbs now outnumber residents of the central city.

The movement to the suburbs has occurred for several reasons. First, cities expanded so rapidly that industry and business have begun to take over residential areas. Many people have been forced to move further out. Second, a general increase in the standard of living has permitted people to build houses that are bigger and more comfortable than those in the city. And much of the dirt, crime, and noise of the city are avoided in the suburbs. Finally, improved methods of transportation, especially the automobile, have made it possible for people to commute to their jobs.

Changing City Ways

The patterns of urban social geography common today took shape in many American cities during the last half of the nineteenth century. Transport networks, shifting real estate values, and the flight of the middle classes from the inner city played significant roles in this process, transforming the city of mixed neighborhoods full of burgeoning industries, stores, and housing for all classes of people into the specialized and more segregated city of our time. Chicago was typical of this process. As the city's industries and population multiplied many times over in the decades following 1870, a combination of the sector and concentric zone patterns emerged.

Railroads, fanning out from the central city, were a major determinant of the sector pattern. Businesses whose space requirements could be satisfied vertically captured Chicago's center, while rising land values drove industries that needed more space along the rail lines. Residential areas sprouted in the wedges thus carved by factory and railroad.

While the wealthy grabbed the prime land north along Lake Michigan, the middle classes, aided by new developments in street transit, eagerly abandoned the factories and lower classes of the inner city for greener pastures. The demand for land at the center by industry and at the periphery by the middle classes increased its value, trapping the poor and working classes in the cheaper intermediate zones. By the turn of the century the outlines of the modern American city were complete, with urban areas segregated by class, by ethnic and racial strain, and by economic function.

Sam Bass Warner, Jr., *The Urban Wilderness: A History of the American City* (New York: Harper & Row, 1972), pp. 85–112.

Can you identify any bedroom communities in your area?

At first, the suburban movement was limited to the middle and upper classes. The suburbs were called "bedroom communities" because most heads of families simply slept there. But the working classes have increasingly joined the trend. Today, suburbs vary according to social class and income. There are upper and upper-middle-class suburbs in which almost every head of a household is a college-educated professional. There are suburbs in which residents are chiefly lower-middle-class people engaged in service occupations and sales. And there are suburbs containing the tract homes of predominantly working-class residents.

The suburbs, as the cities before them had done, have spawned their own life-style. This life-style revolves around the absence of the father for a long portion of the day; the necessity for a private vehicle and the chauffeuring of children; and the local shopping center, which has become a new focus of recreational activity for suburbanites.

What major physical changes would you suggest for your city? What developments are now being considered by the local city planning commission?

For a long time, suburbs depended entirely on the city for shopping and commercial, cultural and recreational activities. Later, city and suburbs became interdependent. The suburbs provided the labor force for city business and industry. Increasingly, however, the suburbs are becoming independent of the city. The huge shopping centers of suburbia have been followed by business, industry, and professionals. Both jobs and facilities are now locally available to the suburban resident. As of 1970, of the approximately 21½ million employed suburbanites, 75 percent worked in the county where they resided. Only a small minority were employed in a big city.

Suburbs, which developed in response to urban problems, now sprawl around all of our metropolitan areas.

Suburbs have mushroomed at the expense of the central city. When people, commerce, and industry moved away, the city lost an important tax base. Without incoming tax money, the city cannot provide important facilities, so even more people, commerce, and industry move out. The central city is left with a run-down transportation system, outmoded physical facilities, inadequate police protection, and poor schools. Those who have the means can use their own cars, send their children to private schools, and live in guarded apartment houses. Or they can move to the suburbs. Those without the means must remain in the city and cope as best they can.

The Metropolitan Area and the Megalopolis

Some suburbs have grown so large that they are now considered to be towns and cities. These small cities, regular suburbs, and the central city around which they are clustered make up the ecological city, the metropolitan area. The United States Bureau of Census uses metropolitan areas as the basis for measuring units of population. The Standard Metropolitan Statistical Area (SMSA) consists of one or more counties containing at least one city of over 50,000 or two cities totaling that number. In 1970, there were 243 such SMSAs in the United States, consisting of about two-thirds of the national population. Two years later, 21 additional SMSAs were reported, of which five were established in Florida alone.

The large number of metropolitan areas is leading to a new phenomenon in the United States. This phenomenon is *urban sprawl*, or the megalopolis, in which one metropolitan area is joined to another without interruption. One such complex is the Great Lakes chain, which begins in Buffalo and continues solidly to Milwaukee and further west. By the year 2000, an estimated 40 million people will be housed in this complex alone. The Boston–Washington complex will contain around 80 million people.

How would you reorganize local political divisions if you wanted to develop local government to cover a whole megalopolis?

Urban sprawl and the phenomenal growth of metropolitan areas means a tremendous concentration of people in comparatively small areas. All Americans seem to want to live where everybody else lives—in suburbs—and where the jobs are. Half of the inhabitants of this country are squeezed into only eight of its 50 states. These eight are California, Illinois, Michigan, New Jersey, New York, Ohio, Pennsylvania, and Texas. More than half of these people live just outside the big cities of these states, in the suburban areas. Thus we have the incongruous situation in which population density in New Jersey is 953.1 people per square mile, whereas in Alaska it is 0.5 people per square mile. Since 1900 the total population has been multiplied 2.6 times; metropolitan population four times; suburban population six times.

Megalopolis not only damages central cities, but also creates problems in local government. Each municipality, county, township, city, or village within the metropolitan area maintains its own government. This creates a bureaucratic maze in which agencies and officials of neighboring governments are often at odds with one another. The result is a waste of money and other valuable resources.

Urban specialists have long favored some form of metropolitan government. Some attempts to establish such a form of government have been made, but in a nation of individualists, the notion is not popular. Now, however, a federal study has concluded that urbanization in the United States is proceeding so rapidly that even metropolitan governments are no longer efficient, although broad regional governments may relieve the chaotic situation. The study further proposes that metropolitan complexes such as Boston to Washington and Chicago to Pittsburgh be joined into one metropolitan belt that would touch nineteen states.[10]

Devise a system of government that would divide the United States into districts based on population. What social problems might be solved and what new problems caused by such a division?

[10]Jack Rosenthal, "Regional Rule Called Vital as Urbanization Spreads," *The New York Times*, February 6, 1972, p. 1.

[Formal Organizations and Bureaucracy]

How many bureaucracies have you dealt with today?

One major sociocultural change has almost totally transformed traditional societies into modern ones. This change is the appearance of a new, dominant institution: bureaucracy. Bureaucracy is a form of organization that characterizes the large, complex, formal groups that perform functions formerly carried out by the family and kin groups. Today we are surrounded by these formal organizations and their bureaucracies. School bureaucracies include teachers, assistant principals, principals, office secretaries, nurses, counselors, janitors, and cafeteria employees, among others. These people all make sure that we enter the school by the right door, that we fill out all the right forms, in the right order, that we fulfill all the right requirements, and that we learn all the right subjects. Similarly bureaucracies guide us when we look for a job, get on an airplane, become politically active, or collect insurance. We spend most of our lives as members of or dealing with many large, complex organizations. The economy, the government, education, and religion are all increasingly characterized by bureaucratic structure. This major sociocultural change, like population explosion, industrialization, and urbanization, is also related to increases in the size of societies, as well as to shifts in ideology and values.

Changes in Size

Do you think the trend toward rule making can be reversed? How?

When populations began to grow, industry began to grow. The number and diversity of products manufactured became tremendous. Urbanization meant that large numbers of people congregated together. Cities became big centers, requiring the efficient production of goods and services and rapid transportation. The common denominator, then, is bigger size and greater complexity. Under such circumstances, in order to prevent chaos and promote efficiency, it has become necessary to organize activities according to rules.

When our ancestors lived in bands of several families, they had no need for a formal leader. Perhaps one of the older males, by virtue of his wisdom and experience, was listened to and followed more carefully than others. But most decisions could be reached simply by talking the issue over.

When a baby was born in such a group, there was no need to report this fact to any agency. Everybody knew about it personally. But what happened when the band became a tribe, or a collection of tribes, or much later, a nation? With thousands, and tens of thousands, and finally with millions in a society, individual members found it impossible to keep abreast of facts. Decisions concerning matters that would affect the group could no longer be reached by talking things over. Can you imagine thousands or millions of people talking things over? It is physically impossible.

So people had no choice but to organize their activities. They divided up the tasks of the society—the gathering of food, the sowing, the harvesting—so that no task would be neglected. With this division of labor and the establishment of lines of authority—some people telling others what to do and when to do it—the seeds of a bureaucratic form of organization were sown.

Changes in Ideology

Another sociocultural change resulting from the technological revolutions has been a shift toward rationalism. At one time, human thought was pervaded by mystery and magic. Scientific knowledge was scarce or nonexistent. People lived on faith. As a consequence, they directed their intellectual endeavors toward spiritual matters and the ultimate meaning of their existence.

Do you feel there are any trends today that promise to reverse our tendency to emphasize concrete, empirical matters?

With advances in science, however, many previously mysterious phenomena have been explained. Since we are now able to decipher many of nature's mysteries, our thinking has shifted from a preoccupation with symbolic meanings and spiritual values, to a concern for concrete, empirical matters. We are interested in scientifically establishing truths. As other historical eras were characterized by religious prophets and philosophers, so our era is characterized by scientists and engineers. Our world is becoming increasingly secular—concerned with material rather than spiritual values. And since most of us have to spend the majority of our time in the business of making a living we continually seek to perfect more efficient means of reaching objectives. Organization is one of the most efficient means to achieve a goal.[11]

[Formal Organizations]

Organization—in the sense of "order"—is not characteristic only of modern societies, or limited only to large groups. Without some degree of organization we could not communicate, for speech is organized sound. We could not have music without organizing tones. We could not have teams without organizing individual players. All human interaction acquires a degree of structure through repetition. When we are in a group of friends—which is a small, primary group—we all know how we are supposed to act. If we fail to act that way, our friends notice. In such informal groups, however, there are no written rules governing behavior, and no specific objective is sought. And here we must make an important distinction. In every society there are many small, primary groups: there are also statistical groups (high school graduates over thirty-five), societal groups (Italian-Americans),

We frequently place a high value on "being spontaneous." What limits are usually set on spontaneity in our lives? Why are such limits necessary?

---

[11]Peter M. Blau and Marshall W. Meyer, *Bureaucracy in Modern Society*, 2nd ed. (New York: Random House, 1971), pp. 5-6.

and social groups. They may have some structure, like the primary group, but in a sociological sense they remain unorganized. We are not concerned here with such groups.

Organization As Process

We are concerned with groups deliberately brought into existence through the formal process of organization. Groups formed through this process enable people who are not personally acquainted to carry on complicated relationships for the purpose of attaining specific goals. Through these groups we handle the activities necessary in large, complex, technological societies.

These groups, in the vocabulary of the social sciences, are called *formal organizations.* A nation's government is a network of formal organizations charged with the business of governing. A school is a formal organization designed to educate our children. An army is a formal organization that takes care of the business of war and defense. A corporation is a formal organization performing some function in a nation's economy.

There is a distinction between formal organizations and institutions. An institution is a procedure, an established way of doing things, a pattern of behavior, a custom. Institutions are not groups of people. You cannot join an institution: you can merely do things in an institutionalized way. When you marry, for instance, you carry out a human activity—establishing a paired relationship, propagating the species—in an institutionalized way. When you simply live with a mate, you carry out that activity in a noninstitutionalized way.

Formal organizations are groups of people. You may join such organizations, or have dealings with their members. When we speak of government, the institution, we mean the regular and established way in which political decisions are made, laws are enacted, and order is maintained in society. When we speak of *a* government, such as the government of the United States, we mean a formal organization composed of a number of highly organized groups of people who are elected and appointed, as well as the civil service employees in charge of carrying out the activities involved in governing.

A frequent subject of science fiction is the experience nearly all of us have had in trying to deal with a computer. Why are computers so closely associated with our experience of bureaucracy?

Formal organizations have created large and weighty bureaucracies. The term *bureaucracy* is frequently used in a negative and critical sense. It suggests red tape and inefficiency or, paradoxically, inhuman efficiency. Many people feel that our personal lives and our institutions are being swallowed by bureaucracy. The following discussion will look at what bureaucracy really is, what it attempts to do, and how well it functions. Examples of industry and labor will be used to show how the important activities of our society have been gradually taken over by formal organizations.

Although Americans are known as "joiners," in reality only a minority of people are active in voluntary associations. A large percentage of people report no membership in any associations, and only a very tiny minority reported over four memberships during the late sixties. Those who do join voluntary associations are generally urban residents in their middle years, married and with children, socially and economically upwardly mobile or already at a high socioeconomic level. These people tend to be residentially stable and well-educated. More whites than blacks are joiners, and more Jews and Protestants than Roman Catholics.[12]

[Bureaucracy]

Why would a chain of authority be necessary for efficient organization?

Large-scale organizations are administered according to the principles of bureaucracy. Bureaucracy is a hierarchal system for coordinating rationally the work of many individuals through a division of labor and a chain of authority. A bureaucracy, in other words, is a group of people organized in a pyramid fashion, who try to administer large-scale organizations in a rational (guided by reason) and efficient manner.

Although bureaucratic administration has been a part of society for centuries, it has only been since the advent of the Industrial Revolution that bureaucracy has assumed its present importance as a form of organization. In societies as large as the urban-industrial ones are, people could not manufacture goods or provide services, let alone govern themselves, without a bureaucratic form of organization.

Characteristics of "Pure" Bureaucracy

Max Weber held that the goal of bureaucracy is rational efficiency, that is, the employment of the best and shortest method in order to reach specific objectives. He systematically analyzed bureaucracy as an "ideal" or "pure" type. He tried to determine how bureaucracy should operate for maximum efficiency, in contrast to how it did operate in reality. An ideal bureaucracy, said Weber, should have the following characteristics:

Why is specialization, or division of labor, such an important factor in improving efficiency?

1. *Specialization, or division of labor.* Activities are assigned to individuals who are experts in doing them. These individuals then assume the responsibility—and are held responsible by their superiors—for the efficient performance of their task.
2. *A chain of command, or a hierarchy of authority.* Each official is responsible to the one above him, and each, in turn, is responsible for his subordinates. The scope and limits of each individual's authority and responsibility are clearly defined.

---

[12]Bernard Berelson and Gary A. Steiner, *Human Behavior: An Inventory of Scientific Findings* (New York: Harcourt Brace Jovanovich, 1964), p. 379.

3. *A body of rules.* The activities of large-scale bureaucratic organizations are governed by a body of rules that define the functions and roles of every person holding a position in the organization. These rules are abstract, applying not to a specific person, but to the position itself. The rules specify, for instance, what the functions of the chairman of the board are, and what the relationship of the chairman with other officials should be. These rules are binding regardless of who is filling the position, or even when the position is vacant. They are designed to guarantee the behavior of the individual who fills a position, and they facilitate the continuity of operation. Regardless of who fills a specific position, it will be filled in approximately the same way.
4. *Impersonality.* Each function in a bureaucracy must be performed impersonally. Each bureaucrat, or member of a bureaucracy, must remain impersonal in his relations with other persons within the organization or with those who have dealings with it. He cannot let personal considerations, such as liking or disliking someone, enter into such dealings. Impartiality and the equitable treatment of all concerned help guarantee efficiency. (Impersonality, however, is what makes the bureaucratic system so unpalatable to many.)
5. *Selection based on merit and job tenure.* Selection to a certain position is made strictly in accordance with the employee's merit, and not because of personal considerations. This type of selection insures the competence of employees. If the employee's performance is considered satisfactory by his superiors, he can expect his employment to continue (job tenure) and to be promoted to higher levels of the hierarchy. He may expect to make a career out of his work for a particular large-scale organization.

Why would merit hiring and job tenure help to guarantee organizational efficiency? Do you think these rules always guarantee efficiency? Why or why not?

In Weber's view, then, bureaucratic organization is one in which specific goals can be attained rapidly and efficiently, and with a minimum amount of conflict between people. Each individual's duties and responsibilities are clearly defined to avoid misinterpretation. Tasks are highly specialized to assure maximum efficiency. The personality of individuals filling positions matters little to the organization, because each position consists of specific activities regardless of who fills it. This formality gives the organization stability, predictability, and continuity. Relations among people are kept impersonal and formal because bureaucratic efficiency is increased in direct proportion as relationships are kept free of emotional involvement. This method of organization works equally well for private and public associations.

This type of organization is in principle applicable with equal facility to a wide variety of different fields. It may be applied in profit-making business or in charitable organizations, or in any number of other types of private enterprises serving ideal or material ends. It is equally applicable to political and to reli-

gious organizations. With varying degrees of approximation to a pure type, its historical existence can be demonstrated in all these fields.[13]

Theoretically, bureaucracies are forms of organization designed to serve people. In the private sector of the economy, a consumer expects a corporation to produce a good product at a reasonable price, and to offer repair services cheaply and conveniently. In the public sector, a citizen expects to receive services from governmental agencies—protection by the police, or financial support from the unemployment office. In both cases, the bureaucratic organization of the economic and governmental units greatly facilitates the goals of consumer and citizen.

Characteristics of Formal Organizations

A formal organization comes into being when a number of individuals join together for the purpose of reaching certain objectives or improving certain conditions. General Motors came into being when a number of businessmen decided to organize for the purpose of making a profit by manufacturing automobiles. All their subsequent activities revolved around these objectives. They needed a policy to guide them, and a force of executives, administrators, and laborers to carry them out.

Formal organizations display certain definite characteristics. First, formal organizations have a *formal structure.* Their goals and programs for carrying them out are formally stated in policy guidelines, constitutions, and other bylaws. Formal organizations also include a body of officers whose relations with one another and with other members of the organization are specified in writing.

Second, formal organizations are *relatively permanent.* Some of them—especially those established for profit-making—may prove to be temporary if no profits are made. The expectation, however, is that a large-scale organization will last as long as it performs its original tasks.

What problems might be created by a too-rigid adherence to written rules?

Third, authority is organized in a *hierarchal order.* The leadership of the organization is assumed by a number of individuals who are ranked from high to low. The high-ranking individuals give the orders, the low-ranking individuals obey. In industry the highest level of authority is the board of directors, who select officers and elect an executive committee. The board, at the recommendation of the executive committee, determines policy. An administrative executive carries out this policy, helped by an assistant, who in turn has a staff to assist him.

Fourth, formal organizations have a *formal program* of which all members are aware, by which to attain their goals. Relationships among members are systematic and complex. People relate to others whose authority and functions differ from their own—people of higher or lower rank—according to guidelines specified in the program.

---

[13]Max Weber, *Theory of Social and Economic Organization,* Trans. A. L. Henderson and Talcott Parsons (New York: Free Press, 1957), p. 334. First published in 1925.

How do voluntary associations compare to other formal organizations? Would you expect the differences to affect efficiency in voluntary associations? In what ways might they do so?

Voluntary Associations

People join some formal organizations out of necessity. For example, they may have to get a job in a large corporation in order to make a living. They join other formal organizations by choice. These organizations are called *voluntary associations.* Most of their members are spare-time volunteers, although there may be a core of full-time, paid, professional employees who carry out day-to-day business. Examples of voluntary associations are church organizations, professional groups like the American Medical Association, and recreational associations like the American Contract Bridge League.

Voluntary associations bring together people whose particular interests are not shared by the whole society. For instance, planned parenthood is not the goal of everyone. It is, however, the goal of a good number of people in the society. Coming together in a voluntary association enables those who share this goal to pursue it effectively, and perhaps to convince an indifferent or hostile majority of its value. Voluntary associations may become a testing ground for a number of social programs that are still too controversial to be handled by the institutional organizations. Many welfare programs now administered by the federal government originated first with voluntary associations. They also provide a channel through which the private citizen can share in the decision-making process of society. This is particularly true of interest groups, political parties, and social movements.

Bureaucracy as It Really Is

Life, however, is not lived in theory, but in reality. And in reality, bureaucracy does not always function to serve people. For one thing, it tends to resist change, whether from within its own ranks or from outside the organization. Perhaps as a result of the rigidity of rules, change is viewed with suspicion, while traditional ways of doing things are encouraged.

What kinds of experiences have you had with bureaucracy? How have you handled red tape in the school bureaucracy?

Another effect of the rigidity of rules is that in bureaucracy many members may begin to believe that the rules are ends in themselves, rather than means to an end. A rule that a certain form has to be filled out in triplicate because copies have to go to three different departments, might continue to be obeyed even after two of the departments are closed. The reason: "It's always been made out in triplicate."

But rules are established to fit into or forestall certain anticipated situations. In unanticipated situations, it may actually be to the organization's benefit to ignore the rules. Obeying rules, regardless of circumstances, can result in inefficiency. The familiar phenomenon of "red tape" is frequently the result of following obsolete rules.

Blind loyalty to rules may also effectively stifle personal initiative. When an unexpected cold wave hit a certain southern city plunging

The Self-Made Bureaucracy?

Who decides the policies public bureaucracies execute? In theory it is the public, through periodic elections and politicians who hold hearings and pass legislation. The bureaucracies of the welfare state, however, have become active forces in their own behalf. Indirectly determining the very policies they are supposed only to execute, assert Richard Cloward and Frances Fox Piven. Basing their argument on the proposition that "public bureaucracies strive chiefly to maintain the conditions necessary for their stability and expansion," Cloward and Piven describe three ways in which public bureaucracies, in pursuing their organizational goals, become active political agents.

First, public bureaucracies such as those involved in welfare and public housing attempt to expand their jurisdictions by using their previously acknowledged expertise to lobby for more specialized personnel and new "comprehensive" programs. Second, bureaucracies and influential politicians often form mutually beneficial liaisons. The bureaucracies increase their influence in the process, while political leaders, by leaning on the testimony of bureaucratic "experts," are able to disguise politically sensitive welfare issues as more palatable technical problems. Finally, public bureaucracies attempt to control their low-income clients through investigations, surveillance of client behavior, and by using their considerable bureaucratic discretion to decide client eligibility on the basis of conformity to organizational goals.

The active role welfare bureaucracies now play, Cloward and Piven argue, has meant increasing regulation for poor people. The welfare bureaucracies, afraid of losing their middle-class support and unwilling to disturb their own equilibrium or cede the power that genuine reforms would imply, present a solid wall of opposition to the reform efforts of low-income groups.

Richard A. Cloward and Frances Fox Piven, *The Politics of Turmoil: Essays on Poverty, Race, and the Urban Crisis* (New York: Pantheon, 1974), pp. 7–27.

the temperature below freezing, the city's street department blithely continued to clean the streets by sprinkling them with water. This usual procedure resulted, of course, in the water freezing and the icy streets creating traffic jams and general bedlam. No one in the department had had the common sense or initiative to stop the sprinkling on a day when the temperature was below freezing.

Related to lack of initiative is a tendency to want to "pass the buck" by shifting the responsibility for decision making to someone higher up in the hierarchy. If the decision turns out to be wrong, there is always someone else who can be blamed for it. A private citizen, when trying to get something done by an agency of a large-scale organization often feels that he is getting the "runaround." He is sent from office to office in an effort to find some official willing to make a decision in his case.

Bureaucracies have a tendency to become devoted to their own welfare rather than to the ends for which they were created. Many governmental agencies established for specific purposes continue to demand funds and to exist long after the problem they were meant to alleviate has disappeared. Similarly, an executive in an industrial complex will try to reinforce the stability of his job by seeing to it that his department puts out not the best product, but the cheapest.

One of the difficulties that multinational corporations have met in establishing branches in foreign countries is the difficulty of adapting bureaucratic rules to another culture. If you were a manager sent overseas to establish such a branch, how would you deal with such difficulties?

Using the bureaucratic structure of organization as a point of departure, two authors have come up with an explanation of why things go wrong in sophisticated societies. Why are cities built on the flood plains of large rivers where they are sure to be periodically inundated? Why are indoor baseball stadiums so constructed that fielders cannot see fly balls on bright days because of the glare of skylight? Why do appliance manufacturers always expect that their products will break down during the period of warranty, and so on? The explanation, humorously named the Peter Principle, is that in a hierarchal arrangement, each employee is promoted until his or her level of incompetence is reached. There the employee remains, creating all this wasteful, inefficient chaos![14]

The negative aspects of bureaucracy are side effects of a system originally designed for efficiency, rationality, and equality. Rarely are such negative aspects intentional. A government employee, for instance, is basically an employee of the people. But in his capacity as government official he may be called on to make unpleasant decisions against some people. A clerk in the Health, Education and Welfare Department may have to tell an unwed mother that she is not eligible for Aid to Dependent Children because she has not met certain requirements. Although the clerk is there to serve her, this mother may perceive the clerk as her oppressor. The clerk may take refuge in the rules and procedures of his department, which he has followed to the letter. If situations like this continue, the rules and procedures might become more important to the bureaucrat than the end, which is service to the people. However, if the clerk makes an exception to the rules for this specific mother, he may be opening the door to favoritism and the eventual possibility of corruption. To remain absolutely

How would you handle the situation described if you were the clerk? If you were the client?

[14]Laurence J. Peter and Raymond Hull, *The Peter Principle* (New York: William Morrow, 1969).

fair, he must follow the same rules, regulations, and procedures for everyone, in every case, even though such objectivity may sometimes result in gross injustices for individual citizens.

The dynamism of bureaucracy. Some social scientists have pointed out that bureaucracy has a dynamic quality that enables it to respond to changing conditions in society. Peter M. Blau and Marshall W. Meyer note that bureaucracies change for a number of reasons. First, workers are more prosperous in the more technologically developed nations, and are not as dependent on their superiors. Second, the willingness of people in general to accept authority has been sharply declining. Coercive authority—authority by reason of force or threat of force—is being questioned. Uninformed and illogical uses of power are no longer meekly accepted. The credibility gap in the Vietnam war and the scandal of Watergate aroused skepticism in many private citizens. Finally, technological advances have given great importance to technical specialists, such as scientists and technicians. These specialists have taken much of the real power in the bureaucratic hierarchy away from the managers, whose lack of technical knowledge puts them at a disadvantage.[15]

Scan a national newspaper for reports that suggest public skepticism about governmental bureaucracy. What attitudes held by the public are implied or expressed, concerning bureaucracy?

Bureaucracies may also be instrumental in promoting innovation in a society. Blau and Meyer suggest that the ideas of scientists alone could not lead to the inventions that in turn trigger social change. In today's complex societies, bureaucratic machinery is needed to translate the ideas of scientists into products and to furnish scientists with laboratories and an environment where they can collaborate on new developments. The authors conclude that while not all social change is instituted through the medium of bureaucracy, still ". . . deliberate introduction of a social innovation on a large scale, whether it involves the production of a new weapon or the enforcement of a new law, depends on bureaucratic methods of administration.[16]

Informality in Bureaucracy

The bureaucracy of large organizations also has an informal side. Networks of personal relationships build up among employees. Sometimes things get done through the influence of individuals, rather than through the regular channels of authority. A group of clerks from the accounting department who have lunch together regularly, or who play poker together on Friday nights have personal relationships. The company Christmas party or annual picnic at which various hierarchical levels mix also involve personal relationships. These relationships are governed by an informal structure with almost as many rules and prescriptions for behavior as the formal bureaucratic structure. But these

Have you ever tried to get around bureaucratic rules by using the informal structure of an organization? What issues were at stake? How did you solve the problem?

[15]Blau and Meyer, pp. 139–143.
[16]Blau and Meyer, p. 105.

rules and patterns of behavior tend to be nonverbal and are not visibly acknowledged.

The informal structure is designed to get around the rules of the formal structure. For example, suppose that a secretary in a large organization wants to take the afternoon off to go shopping. The official rule states that he can leave early only if he can prove he is ill and has the written permission of his office manager. The office manager, a typical bureaucrat loyal to the company, can see very well that the secretary is not ill, and if asked she would deny him permission to leave. The wise secretary, then, instead of asking permission through this regular channel, asks one of the executives who has been particularly friendly to him on several occasions. And he gets the afternoon off. Or, if the secretary is a good actor, he can also feign a terrific headache, and get the afternoon off that way. Lying is often rewarded in a bureaucratic structure whereas the truth is sometimes punished.

Have you ever disregarded bureaucratic structure in order to do something? What was the reaction to your behavior?

These informal systems defy the purpose of the formal bureaucratic organization, which is specifically organized to prevent any form of favoritism and corruption from occurring. However, in the long run they may help to reach the original goals of the official bureaucracy. We have all seen war movies in which the hero disregards the orders of his commanding officer, and in so doing saves his entire battalion, or turns the tide of the battle. Similar situations occur in real life quite frequently. The informal structure of organizations is very important to the survival of the formal organization. The informal structure also boosts morale by making the organization more personal.

Bureaucracy and Oligarchy

The democratic system of organization is comparatively new and still not entirely successful. Most systems of organization have always assumed that a few men, drawn from the upper classes and therefore better educated than the masses, were the only ones in a position to lead. Democratic ideas proclaimed that leadership belonged to the people, and the will of the people was made manifest through its representatives. A number of organizations emerged in which control was supposedly in the hands of the people, the rank-and-file membership. Eventually, however, it was noticed that effective control had drifted into the hands of a few leaders of the organization. At first, people blamed leaders for being power hungry and distorting the principles of democracy. Others said that perhaps the rank and file was still too uneducated and apathetic to effectively keep control and lead itself.

A European social scientist, Robert Michels, set out to discover the source of these authoritarian tendencies, which appeared in even the most democratic of associations. Michels finally came to the conclusion that it was neither lust for power nor the immaturity of the members that caused the control of an organization to fall into the hands

Melting Down the Iron Law of Oligarchy

China, the country with the oldest tradition of bureaucracy, is the first country to attempt to subvert the "iron law of oligarchy" on a mass scale. This effort to prevent the growth of a bureaucratic class reached its greatest intensity during the 1966 Cultural Revolution. During this period, grass-roots "revolutionary committees" sprang up all over China to criticize, and in some cases, supplant the party bureaucracies. Criticism focused on tendencies among bureaucrats to become divorced from the common people in whose interests they were supposed to be serving. Bureaucrats were criticized for developing a distinct and privileged life-style and acting as though they were superior to manual workers and manual labor. "The 700 million Chinese are all critics," was one slogan of the Cultural Revolution and it points to a major thrust of the movement: to encourage the great masses of people to participate more actively in problem solving and political criticism.

What the ultimate success of the goals of the Cultural Revolution will be is of course impossible to say. Mao however never looked upon it as a one-time event. "Two or three cultural revolutions should be carried out every hundred years," he said.

David Milton, Nancy Milton, and Franz Schurmann, eds., *People's China: Social Experimentation, Politics, Entry onto the World Scene, 1966 through 1972.* The China Reader, vol. 4 (New York: Random House, Vintage Books, 1974).

of a few leaders. Rather, this situation was the result of inevitable patterns that emerge in every organization. He called the emergence of such patterns the "iron law of oligarchy."[17] Oligarchy, or rule by the few, develops in all sorts of organizations, of any size, and with any goal. An oligarchy depends on patterns of participation. The rank-and-file member of any organization generally attends meetings infrequently and consequently is poorly informed about what goes on in the organization. A few interested individuals who do become knowledgeable and who are willing to invest their time in the organization, take the opportunity to assume control. They may not deliberately set out to assume control; they assume it simply because no one else wants to be bothered.

Have you ever seen the "iron law of oligarchy" operate? What advantages might there be to oligarchic structure in an organization?

Large, formal organizations with their complex bureaucracies are

[17]Robert Michels, *Political Parties: A Sociological Study of the Oligarchical Tendencies in Modern Democracy* (Glencoe, Ill.: Free Press, 1949), p. 342.

particularly well suited for the development of oligarchies. Once an oligarchy is installed, it may be very difficult to replace. Oligarchs, members of the oligarchy, have considerable means at their disposal to maneuver events in their favor, and they do so very effectively. The tendency toward oligarchy can be broken only by an active and interested membership, interacting on a primary level within strong local units of the large organization.

[Summary]

The modern era has been marked by several technological revolutions that have brought countless sociocultural changes. Change is an integral part of nature and of humans. The structures that humans build—societies and their systems, and cultures—are likewise subject to change. Stability is equally a characteristic of individuals, societies, and cultures. No one theory to explain change is completely adequate, but all provide some insights into the causes of change.

The mechanisms of sociocultural change are easier to determine than its causes. The principal processes of cultural change are discovery, invention, and diffusion. Change in the structure of society, on the other hand, occurs through planning, reform, and revolution. Both cultural and social change are also subject to drift.

Modern sociocultural change has been mainly triggered by technological progress. Technology includes all the methods and devices that help humans manage and control their environment. The first real technological breakthrough was the invention of agriculture, which brought many sociocultural changes with it. A second technological breakthrough was the advent of the machine era, or the Industrial Revolution. Although this movement accelerated in the middle of the eighteenth century in Great Britain, its roots go back several centuries. Its effects are still being felt by the world today. The most significant sociocultural changes brought about by the Industrial Revolution are: a surge in the growth of population, industrialization, or the dependence of the economy on industry, and urbanization, or the growth of cities at the expense of rural life.

The Industrial Revolution has led to the problem of overpopulation. There are too many people for the resources of the earth. The industrial nations, which are also those most highly urbanized, have stabilized their growth. But the industrially-emerging nations will have to implement birth-control programs if the problem is to be solved.

The mechanization of agriculture and the factory system has led many people to move from the land to the city, where the jobs are. Life in the cities has given rise to new life-styles and traditions which, spread through the mass media, are becoming dominant in our national culture, and have strengthened economic, educational, and political institutions, at the expense of religion and the family.

Summary

A current development of urbanization is the trend toward suburbanization and metropolitanization. To escape from urban problems, people began to move to the suburbs. Today more people live in suburban areas than in inner cities and rural areas. The inner cities have suffered, and the problems of the cities have been inherited by the suburbs. Suburbs have grown at such phenomenal rates that cities surrounded by a number of large suburbs are considered metropolitan areas. These areas have given rise to megalopolises which create unique problems, including the need for an expanded governmental bureaucracy.

While there is a certain amount of organization and structure in all human activities, organization on a large scale and the consequent bureaucratization are characteristic of contemporary societies. Organization creates groups in which people who are not personally acquainted with one another, are able to carry on complicated relationships for purposes of attaining specific goals. Most of the activities of modern societies are performed in these groups.

These groups are called *associations* or *formal organizations.* They are usually large and highly organized in a pattern called a *bureaucracy.* Formal organizations are characterized by a formal structure, a degree of permanence, hierarchical order of authority, and fixed relationships among members.

People join some formal organizations by choice. These organizations are called *voluntary associations* and bring together people with similar interests. Although Americans are known as joiners, in reality only a minority of the people belong to voluntary associations.

Bureaucracy is a hierarchical arrangement based on division of labor and a chain of authority for the purpose of coordinating rationally the work of many individuals. Bureaucratic organization in its ideal, or pure, form seldom corresponds to bureaucracy as it really functions. Bureaucratic organization tends to resist change; rigidifies rules to the point where ends and means become confused; stifles personal initiative; and makes employees indecisive. At the same time, some social scientists claim that bureaucracy is dynamic enough to respond to changes and promote innovation within society.

Although the bureaucracy of large organizations encourages attitudes of impersonality and formality, informal organization develops within this framework. This informal organization, although it defies the purposes of the formal organization, may in the long run be beneficial to the organization. Some even claim that the informal structure is vital to the survival of formal organizations.

Oligarchy is another form that large organizations may take. Even in the most democratically-organized associations leadership eventually falls into the hands of a few leaders. The "iron law of oligarchy" suggests that oligarchy is inevitable because rank-and-file members of groups are generally apathetic regarding the interests of the group, so the few individuals who are interested naturally assume leadership.

Terms to Remember

Bureaucracy. A type of hierarchical arrangement based on division of labor and a chain of authority for the purpose of coordinating rationally the activities of many individuals. Personnel organized in a pyramid fashion administering large-scale organizations in a rational and efficient manner.

Cultural change. Change in values and beliefs, which may be brought about by scientific discoveries, technological inventions, new achievements in the arts, or shifts in religious doctrine.

Social change. Change in the patterns of social interaction, in which a substantial number of society's members assume new statuses and play new roles.

Megalopolis, or urban sprawl. The condition in which one metropolitan area follows another without interruption.

Demography. The study of the growth or decrease of population, its distribution throughout the world, and its composition.

Diffusion. A process of cultural change in which cultural traits are spread from one society to another and from one group within society to another.

Discovery. A process of cultural change in which an already existing fact or relationship is newly perceived.

Invention. A process of cultural change in which old cultural ideas or existing objects are combined in a new way, thus producing something more important than the sum of its parts.

Factory system. The current system of industrial production in which all the machinery and the workers are housed in one building or a complex of buildings where all, or most, of the processes of production take place.

Organization. A formal process deliberately bringing into existence a group of people for the performance of a specific activity. It is through this process that associations are formed in which people not acquainted with one another can carry on complex relationships for the attainment of common goals.

Formal organizations. Associations of people in which most of the activities of contemporary societies are handled. Large-scale, highly organized groups, with a formal structure, a body of officers, the expectation of permanence, and a hierarchical organization of authority.

Iron law of oligarchy. Sociologist Robert Michels' formulation that even in the most democratic organization, leadership eventually is controlled by a few interested individuals willing to work for the organization.

Metropolitan area. Small cities, suburbs, and the city around which they are clustered.

Sociocultural drift. The unplanned changes occurring in society.

Standard Metropolitan Statistical Area. Term used by the United States Bureau of the Census to designate units of population consisting of a county or counties that include a city of 50,000 or more.

Suburbs. Small communities on the outskirts of the central city and somewhat dependent on it.

Technology. All the methods and devices that help humans manage and control their environment.

Urbanism. A condition, a set of attitudes, a quality, or a way of life distinct from the rural.

Urbanization. A population trend in which cities grow at the expense of rural areas.

Voluntary associations. Formal organizations joined by choice rather than out of necessity.

Suggestions for Further Reading

Allen, Francis R. *Socio-Cultural Dynamics: An Introduction to Social Change.* New York: Macmillan, 1971. Theories of social and cultural change exhaustively analyzed.

Blau, Peter M., and Marshall W. Meyer. *Bureaucracy in Modern Society.* 2d ed. New York: Random House, 1971. A lucid discussion of bureaucracy and all it involves.

Faunce, William A. *Problems of an Industrial Society.* New York: McGraw-Hill, 1968. Industrial society is seen as the inevitable cause of alienated, ambivalent, and ambiguous behavior.

Mack, Raymond W. *Transforming America: Patterns of Social Change.* New York: Random House, 1967. Changes at work in our society viewed in a straightforward and easy-to-follow style.

Martindale, Don. *Social Life and Cultural Change.* Princeton, N.J.: Van Nostrand, 1962. Social and cultural change in a historical perspective.

Redfield, Robert. *The Primitive World and Its Transformations.* Ithica, N.Y.: Cornell University Press, 1953. An analysis of the effects of modernization on nontechnological societies and cultures.

Wirth, Louis W. "Urbanism as a Way of Life." *American Journal of Sociology* 44 (July 1938): 1–25. A classic work defining the urban personality and life-style.

Collective behavior

Have you ever found yourself in the middle of a frantic crowd? What kinds of behavior did you observe? Did you yourself do anything unusual?

SUPPOSE YOU ARE shopping in a crowded department store—it is the week before Christmas—and all of a sudden you notice a man running down the aisle, yelling "Fire! Fire!" Would you finish your transaction, then wait patiently to have your package wrapped, and leave in your usual manner? Such a reaction would be very unlikely. It is much more likely that both you and the salesperson—not to mention all the other customers within earshot—would drop whatever you and they were doing, and would start running for the nearest exit. Probably, too, while everyone was running, they would begin to scream hysterically, and trample and shove aside whomever and whatever was in the way.

The reason for behaving this way, following no societal norms or guidelines, intent only on the idea of getting out, is that a fire in a department store is an unusual event. You may never have witnessed the outbreak of a fire before. You may have no previous experience of how to act in a situation involving fire. In such circumstances, you are likely to act spontaneously, perhaps illogically and irrationally, influenced by the actions of others who happen to be near you at the time.

Why is it so difficult to plan how you would act in a crisis? What kinds of crisis behavior are highly valued in our society?

The type of behavior that is apt to occur when someone yells "Fire!" in a crowded place also occurs in riots, lynchings, religious revival meetings, crowds, and mobs. A similar type of behavior also takes place when people follow fashions, fads, and crazes; when they are a part of a public or an audience; when they act on public opinion, propaganda, and rumors; and when they act on the goals of certain social movements. Sociologists call the type of behavior that occurs in these circumstances *collective behavior.*

Collective behavior does not only happen in groups. Rather, the term refers to behavior that, unlike most of our behavior, is relatively unpatterned and unstructured. People involved in some situations, in other words, really do not know how to act. They do not know what to expect of others or what others expect of them. As a result, they tend to improvise and follow each other's example. Since the usual cultural norms that regulate people's behavior do not apply in these situations, behavior tends to be unpredictable and contains a great deal of emotional charge.

Collective Behavior

What term would a sociologist use to describe a crowd in a department store? Why is it not a group?

We have said that collective behavior is relatively unpatterned and unstructured. Rarely is there a complete lack of structure in the behavior of any group of people. Only in situations when an individual's life is threatened is he likely to act with a complete lack of awareness of others. In most situations where collective behavior prevails, such behavior is partly structured and partly unstructured. A crowd in a department store is not a social group in the sociological sense. Nevertheless, there is a great deal of awareness of others, a certain amount of interaction does take place, and the crowd behaves in accordance with general norms. If the norms are too obviously flaunted—if a customer gets up on a counter and starts to undress—negative sanctions are rapidly applied. The customer will probably be thrown out. But because a department store crowd is not a cohesive group, its behavior can, without too much difficulty, become disorganized and unpredictable. That is why the cry of "Fire!" in such a crowd can easily precipitate a panic in which the people become a mindless, destructive mob. In a more cohesive group—say, in a classroom—people would be much more likely to line up in front of a fire escape and listen to directions from someone in charge.

Some situations of collective behavior start out being fairly structured and end up being completely disorganized. An audience at a rock concert may surge forward, jump on the stage, and destroy the musical instruments. Others start out by being disorganized and end by being structured. Many social movements—the labor movement, for one—begin by being nothing more than disorganized protests at first. Later they develop definite goals, they apply ranked roles to their members, and they evolve norms and techniques for social control such as characterize any organized group.

Why, in your opinion, is there a tendency for people to develop organizations that are less spontaneous than collective behavior?

Because of its unpredictability, collective behavior has become a subject of great fascination for sociologists. This type of behavior is frequent in periods of rapid social change, when cultural norms are in transition or are poorly defined. Sociocultural change and/or new values and norms are often triggered by the spontaneous, unstructured, and unpatterned behavior of groups of people. Many social movements, a large number of religious denominations, and many governments have originated in some form of collective behavior. The labor movement in the early decades of this country eventually led to the unionization of a great number of workers, for example. The Reforma-

Crowds provide the individual with support for unusual behavior.

tion resulted in the establishment of Protestantism, which later splintered into a variety of denominations and sects. Finally, our own government and nation developed when a large number of American settlers became dissatisfied with British rule. Sociologist Ralph Turner, who has specialized in the study of collective behavior, describes sociologists' interest in such behavior:

If you saw a mindless mob about to do something you disapproved of, how might you go about opposing the crowd or changing the direction of its behavior?

> *It is the unusual character of mob behavior, of social movements in which otherwise meek individuals dare to threaten the established powers, of rumor process in which normally critical people seem to accept the improbable without a second thought, of dancing and revelrous behavior in which modest and sedate people make public spectacles of themselves, and of panic in which usually considerate people trample others to death, which leads investigators to single out a special field of study.*[1]

As fascinating as the field may be, it is also one of the most difficult to study with the methods of science. While participant observation seems to be the most logical technique of research, a member of a mob in flight from a fire is unlikely to stop to answer any investigator's questions. Because of the high content of emotion in collective behavior, this area of sociology is closely related to the discipline of psychology. In fact, it is generally considered to be an area of social psychology.

---

[1]Ralph H. Turner, "Collective Behavior," in Robert E. L. Faris, ed., *Handbook of Modern Sociology* (Chicago: Rand McNally, 1964), p. 382.

The sociologist is interested in collective behavior first because it is in the realm of social experience, and second because many collective phenomena differ so from the everyday norms, values, and institutions. At the same time that they differ, they also in many cases announce and predict the shape of the world to come.

Sociologists have been accused of preferring to analyze stable, structured, and institutionalized types of behavior, such as the behavior found in cohesive social groups. And, naturally, stable phenomena are much easier to study and theorize about. Yet, as sociologist Lewis Coser says:

> *. . . collective behavior arising spontaneously, and not based on pre-established norms and traditions, should be studied closely if only because such behavior may enlighten us as to how an old order dies and a new social order emerges. Mob or crowd behavior arising amidst the decay of previously established systems of social control is the very opposite of institutionalized behavior; it may be considered 'abnormal' if a stable social system is taken as a point of reference. But just as, on the individual level, study of the abnormal may furnish important clues to an understanding of the normal, so on the social level the study of disorganized, unorganized, and irrational crowd behavior may illuminate the very basis of social order.*[2]

As our Western movies show, collective behavior in the form of lynch mobs was a frequent occurrence in the old West. What social conditions might have allowed these situations to arise?

As unorganized, disorganized, and spontaneous as collective behavior is, it can still be measured and predicted to an extent. The sociologist addresses himself to the same questions as in other areas of social life: Why does collective behavior occur? How does it occur? When does it occur? Where, and under which conditions does it occur?

[Determinants, Mechanisms, and Theories of Collective Behavior]

Collective behavior occurs in all societies. Certain religious ceremonies, for instance, create a common mood that prompts behavior totally different from everyday behavior. And panics, lynchings, and punitive mobs are also universal.

Have you ever participated in a religious ceremony that prompted collective or mutual behavior? What function might such ceremonies serve in our society?

However, collective behavior is more frequent in urban, industrial, complex, mass societies that are undergoing a great deal of rapid social and cultural change. Sociologist Neil J. Smelser has listed six features or conditions of modern societies he feels lead to, or determine collective behavior.[3] These conditions apply primarily to social movements and social change, rather than phenomena such as fashions and fads.

---

[2]Lewis Coser, *Sociology Through Literature* (Englewood Cliffs, N.J.: Prentice-Hall, 1963), p. 328.

[3]Neil J. Smelser, *Theory of Collective Behavior* (New York: Free Press of Glencoe, 1963), pp. 15–17.

Conditions That Lead to Collective Behavior

The first condition Smelser refers to as *structural conduciveness.* Smelser says that phenomena of collective behavior are much more likely to occur within the framework of a mass society. A mass society is characterized by a great deal of anonymity and the relative psychological isolation of the individual. Relationships among people in a mass society are comparatively impersonal. This type of society develops because of (1) industrial and commercial revolutions; (2) the growth of population and shifts of population from rural to urban areas; (3) the extensive use of the mass communication media; and (4) the consequent decline of traditional patterns of behavior.

What kinds of generalized beliefs may have underlain the so-called "witch-hunts" of the McCarthy era of anti-communism (in the 1950s)?

The second condition under which collective behavior appears is one of *structural strain.* By this term Smelser means that conflicts and real or imagined deprivation encourage collective behavior. Poor people, minority groups who feel oppressed, religious groups who believe they have been dealt with unjustly, and privileged groups who perceive a threat to their status are especially open to expressions of collective behavior.

The third condition is the *growth and spread of a generalized belief.* Before any kind of collective behavior takes place, a belief pinpointing the source of the problem and how it may be solved has to emerge among the participants. For example, race riots depend on the generalized belief that a social group is at fault for problems.

The fourth determinant of collective behavior is the existence of *precipitating factors.* The stage for some kind of collective behavior is set by some previous action or event—an arrest, the cry of "police brutality," an exchange of insults, or a fight. Such an event signals a normless situation.

The fifth predisposing factor is *mobilization for action.* When people complain vocally about a specific perceived wrong, leaders begin to express the people's discontent. A state of readiness for action emerges. Tension may build up for months or even years before exploding.

The period of the Russian Revolution was preceded (and followed) by nearly a decade of "general strikes." Why would one expect a general strike to develop from situations of collective behavior?

The sixth and last determinant of collective behavior is the *ineffectiveness of traditional social controls.* Effective leadership on the part of the police, the government, the media, and the community could theoretically prevent the onset of collective behavior at any stage of the cycle. Collective behavior indicates that all these sources of social control have been ineffective or have begun to break down.

One of the most important determinants of collective behavior is rapid social change. The results of collective behavior become in turn vehicles for further social change. The purpose of revolutions and even of less violent social movements, for instance, is to change the political and social order. Even minor riots and demonstrations often bring changes in the social, economic, or political order.

The Age of Crowds

Many contemporary ideas about crowds, including the contagion theory and the emphasis on the irrationality of crowds date back to the conservative French social psychologist Gustave Le Bon. Under certain circumstances, Le Bon said in his most famous work *The Crowd* (1895), an aggregate of individuals is transformed into a single psychological entity, a "collective mind," which is different from the sum of individuals of which it is composed. The qualities of such a crowd, Le Bon believed, stemmed from the unconscious life shared by the majority of its members—a kind of lowest common denominator of a people, which, to Le Bon, meant that in crowds impulsiveness, mediocrity, stupidity, and extreme emotions reign supreme. The irrationality and unpredictability that Le Bon saw in crowds he likened to similar tendencies in those "inferior forms of evolution . . . women, savages, and children." As if hypnotized, people in crowds temporarily lose their power of reasoning and become highly susceptible to suggestion, sometimes acting contrary to the way each would act in isolation. History's leaders, he believed, had an intuitive grasp of crowd psychology that gave the leaders great power.

Crowds also had a much broader significance to Le Bon. "The age we are about to enter," he wrote, "will in truth be the ERA OF CROWDS." He was referring to what he felt was the growing influence of the common people in the shaping of modern societies, a trend whose result he thought would be the downfall of civilization: "The populace is sovereign, and the tide of barbarism mounts." Le Bon believed the study of crowd psychology had a practical use: it would allow a nation's rulers to better control their subjects and perhaps hold back this tide.

Gustave Le Bon, *The Crowd: A Study of the Popular Mind* (New York, Viking Press, 1960).

Mechanisms of Collective Behavior

Smelser has given us an indication about the kinds of conditions that prevail in a society ready for a potential outbreak of collective behavior. But how does collective behavior actually originate and spread? Turner proposes certain additional theories that attempt to answer these questions.[4]

Contagion theory. According to the contagion theory, collective behav-

[4]Turner, in Faris, pp. 382–392.

ior must be viewed as a process. In this process, moods, attitudes, and behavior are rapidly communicated to a *collectivity*—an aggregation of persons who do not interact on a regular basis. These moods, attitudes, and behavior are uncritically accepted by the collectivity by a further process called *circular reaction,* or *emotional contagion.* For example, someone in a crowd yells, "I see the devil!" Another says, "I see him, too!" Support reassures the first person, who proclaims his vision even louder. Soon, everyone in the crowd is yelling, "I see the devil!" The same process occurs when an emotion such as anger is displayed. This process is also called *social contagion* and is incited by milling and rhythm. In milling, the crowd surges back and forth and individuals move with it. In rhythm, the crowd spontaneously erupts in hand-clapping, foot stomping, or shouting. These processes eventually involve even the "coolest" spectators, those who intended to remain only onlookers.

Have you ever tried to remain detached in a crowd that is clapping or dancing? How did you feel about yourself under the circumstances?

Other factors involved in contagion are suggestion, imitation, identification, anonymity, and loss of individuality. In suggestion and imitation, clues for behavior are readily accepted from others and are imitated. In identification, each person feels a common bond with every other person and with the leader of the event. Anonymity and loss of individuality make individuals susceptible to a breakdown of inhibitions.

During the later Middle Ages, well over 100,000 witches were burned at the stake by mobs and by the Inquisition. What social conditions may have prompted these outbursts?

Convergence theory. Whereas the contagion theory emphasizes the temporary effect of the group on the individual, the convergence theory stresses that collective behavior merely brings out into the open feelings already present in the individual members of the collectivity. In short, the collective situation simply brings together people with similar tendencies. When such people are together, they are likely to engage in some form of collective behavior especially if outsiders are present, if individuals not committed to the dominant mores of the society are present, or if a target becomes available and no other outlet for frustrations is present.

Emergent norm theory. In the emergent norm theory, collective behavior is viewed as behavior that is still governed by norms. Although norms do emerge in collective situations, they may be different than the norms in existence in regular group situations. The new norms that emerge in instances of collective behavior often indicate that those norms governing regular group behavior are no longer valid.

[Crowds]

A crowd is a temporary collection of people gathered in the same place at the same time. The crowd may be casual: a line of people waiting to buy subway tickets or a number of people stopped at a red light. Or the crowd may be organized or conventional: people attending a football game or a rock concert.

At any rate, the assembled people do not become a crowd until they respond to a common stimulus. Even the casual crowd may evolve into a panic crowd, a mob, or a riot if the stimulus demands it—if someone yells "Fire!" or "They're shooting us!" The organized crowd is much more receptive to mob behavior than is the casual crowd, because people have come together in anticipation of some emotional experience.

Crowds may be expressive, that is, they gather for the purpose of expressing feelings. Religious revival meetings are an example of expressive crowds. Crowds may also be acting, in which case they gather to act out feelings, generally of a hostile nature. Mobs, riots, and some protests are acting crowds.

What aspects of rock music might be conducive to collective behavior?

People in crowds tend to develop a common mood, probably because they are in close physical contact with one another and because they are concentrating on the same source of attention. Emotions reach a higher pitch in such a mood—it becomes easier to love or hate. A common conception of what constitutes proper behavior at the moment emerges.[5] For example, rock stars must frequently be protected from their audiences, which get carried away by complex love-hate emotions. At such concerts, the band may be pelted with cans, bottles, and firecrackers. Political leaders may also be singled out for similar collective reactions.

Crowds may engage in unpredictable behavior because they are temporary, and individual members can remain anonymous. A crowd usually lacks definite norms, although it is still under the influence of the cultural norms of the larger society. Furthermore, a crowd is removed from the social control exerted both by primary groups and by social agents. Under such circumstances, the individual member of a crowd exchanges his individual feelings for group feelings. He ceases to act as a single individual and acts solely as a member of the group. It is easy, then, for him to perform antisocial acts, shifting his guilt feelings about the violations of norms onto the group. He is able to say, in effect: "I did not do it. The crowd did it." It is as though the collectivity of people expressed feelings and acted as an individual.[6] The individual, in this situation, is relieved of any moral responsibility for his actions.

Why might groups more easily throw off norms and social control than an individual could?

Relationships among members of a crowd, and particularly among members of two opposing crowds, are impersonal. Usually, a soldier can kill an enemy soldier comfortably only if he does not think of him as a person, but as "the enemy." In a competitive sport, members of opposing teams must forget personal friendships and think only of victory for "their own" team. In other words, if people begin to in-

---

[5]Ralph H. Turner and Lewis M. Killian, *Collective Behavior* (Englewood Cliffs, N.J.: Prentice-Hall, 1957), p. 83.

[6]Kurt Lang and Gladys E. Lang, *Collective Dynamics* (New York: Crowell, 1961), pp. 118–121.

Here, Japanese police are battling a crowd of militant demonstrators, who have come prepared with helmets and long flagpoles that serve as lances.

Our police forces are increasingly being trained in methods of crowd control. What methods of crowd control are you familiar with? What may the situation suggest about social conditions in our society?

teract on a personal level, they cease to act as a collectivity.

Crowds are generally unstructured, they lack definite behavior patterns, and responsibility has been shifted from the individual to the group. Crowds also tend to lack designated leaders. Consequently, members of a crowd are particularly open to suggestions. Anyone suggesting an action to a crowd in a decisive and authoritative manner is likely to be obeyed.[7] In addition, crowds are subject to social contagion—a condition in which members stimulate one another and respond to the reciprocal stimulation by an increased emotional involvement—as the contagion theory we mentioned previously suggests.

Many crowds that are typical in our society are happy crowds, not intent on doing damage. All sports events or concerts attract such crowds. But any crowd, or even any collectivity that becomes a crowd when specific stimuli are introduced, is potentially dangerous. A crowd's behavior may get out of control for a number of reasons. A peaceful audience may become a panic crowd if a bomb is exploded in its midst and everyone attempts to flee at the same time. It may become a mob if people are aroused to a high emotional pitch and an available target is suddenly found to act as a scapegoat for long-harbored discontent. A mob may become a riot if the discontent is centered around problems of race, religion, ethnicity, or deprivation.

---

[7]Lang and Lang, pp. 221–225.

Crowd Behavior Is Self-Limiting

We have all heard accounts of atrocities committed by crowds. Some regions in our society have a long history of lynchings, for instance, in which victims, in addition to being killed, were often horribly tortured, mutilated, and dismembered. Much destruction of property as well as wounding and killing took place during the riots of the sixties. Massacres were committed by our soldiers in Vietnam. But while the crowd becomes more than the sum of its parts—individual members—still, crowds *are* collectivities of individual members. Even though unrestrained, irrational, and subject to emotional contagion, crowd behavior is still limited by several factors: (1) the emotional needs and self-concept of individual members; (2) the norms of the society and the internalized norms of individual members; (3) the leadership of the crowd; and (4) the external controls that are exerted over the crowd.

These limiting factors on crowd behavior ensure that a crowd seldom does anything that individual members do not want to do, and that is not somehow justified in the light of the society's norms. A crowd that kills, or loots, or burns, or destroys, does not do so at random. Rather, such behavior is directed against a group or a person that crowd members perceive as unjust and oppressive, or somehow "bad." And even a destructive crowd soon spends its fury after committing acts that are strongly prohibited by societal norms.

We have all seen movies in which a single person opposes a lynch mob. What techniques does such a person use to gain his ends?

[Other Forms of Collective Behavior]

We have already mentioned that collective behavior has a particularly fertile soil in mass societies. We defined the mass society as one that is marked by contractual, secondary-group, and functional relationships. Mass society is the farthest removed from the traditional Gemeinschaft society, and its members are largely anonymous, mobile, specialized, and unwilling or unable to obey traditional values and norms.

In a mass society, people often take part in certain forms of collective behavior that differ in degree of intensity from those we already mentioned. Such behavior is characterized by a rapid diffusion throughout the society. It is also unstructured, unorganized, and uncoordinated. But whereas crowd behavior is temporary and people behave as a group, mass behavior is more permanent and is acted out by many people individually. Masses are not collectivities of people, as crowds are. They are generally scattered or isolated, and individuals do not interact with one another. Rumors, fashions, fads, crazes, and mass hysteria are instances of mass behavior.

Rumors

Rumors often begin riots, panics, or mobs. A *rumor* is an unsupported report of an event or a projected event. The report is not backed up by facts but continues to spread by word of mouth or through the mass media. In situations of stress, accurate information is not readily available. By accepting a rumor, people tend to hear what they want to hear. A rumor may help them rationalize their participation in some form of collective behavior, or it may seem to clarify a confused situation.

Try an experiment with rumor formation. Have one person in the class whisper a "secret" to the next person, and so on. In what form does the information arrive at the last person in the class? What has happened to the information?

Social scientists have been particularly interested in the rumor as a social process because the exchange and spread of information by this medium so often precedes the development of more active forms of collective behavior. Experiments on the transmission of rumors, reported in a study by Gordon Allport and Leo Postman, suggest that basically three things happen in the process of rumor transmission.

1. *Leveling.* The farther a rumor travels, the shorter it tends to become. People repeat only its bare outline, so that it is easier for the next person to understand. Fewer and fewer words and details are used to describe it.
2. *Sharpening.* During a rumor's diffusion, a limited number of details is selected for perception, retention, and reporting. One or two facts remain in the rumor and become its dominant theme. Others are dropped.
3. *Assimilation.* Certain items in the rumor are invariably changed. They are influenced and molded by the customs, values, attitudes, cultural themes, and feelings of those who hear the rumor and repeat it. Rumors are distorted so that they fit in with the norms of the group in which they circulate.[8]

How does the phrase "Where there's smoke, there's fire" apply to rumor formation?

Allport maintains that no riot or lynching ever occurs without the help of rumor.[9] The building up of hostility that precedes a violent outbreak is encouraged by stories of the alleged evil perpetrated by the hated group. New rumors may serve as a call to action—to riot or to lynch. Hostility that has been brewing for a long time can be brought to the surface by rumors. The Detroit riots of the forties were sparked by the rumor that carloads of armed blacks were heading for Detroit from Chicago. More recently, the Watts riot began with the story that a white policeman had beaten a pregnant black women. Finally, during the heat of violence, rumor sustains the excitement of the moment, and allows it to continue.

A rumor, regardless of its truth or falsity, is functional during a period of stress or tension in that it fulfills the need of people for some sort of answer or explanation of what is going on. Sociologist Tamotsu Shibutani has termed rumor a form of collective problem

---

[8]Gordon W. Allport and Leo Postman, *The Psychology of Rumor* (New York: Russell & Russell, 1965), pp. 75–115. First edition published by Henry Holt in 1947.

[9]Gordon W. Allport, *The Nature of Prejudice* (Reading, Mass.: Addison-Wesley, 1954), pp. 63–67.

solving. Shibutani points out the importance of the roles of messenger, interpreter, and skeptic. The messenger is the person who brings a piece of relevant information to a group. The interpreter is the person who puts this news in proper perspective, evaluates it in the light of past events, and speculates on its future implications. But the skeptic is doubtful about the authenticity of the rumor. He demands proof concerning its truth, and urges caution about the course of action.[10]

Other Forms of Collective Behavior

What personal gain does the messenger receive for delivering a rumor message? How do you feel about gossip?

Fashions, Fads, and Crazes

Fashions, fads, and crazes differ from the kinds of collective behavior already discussed in that they are not quite as temporary or as action-directed. *Fashions* refer to manners in dress, architecture, or house decor. They tend to reflect the interests, values, and motives of a given society or group within it. *Fads* and *crazes* are minor fashions that are much more irrational and shorter-lived than fashions. Crazes have an even more obsessive character than fads. The famous flagpole-sitting and goldfish-swallowing contests of the 1950s are considered crazes.

Fashions may serve to express the values of a society or subgroup of society.

What fads, crazes, and fashions are currently popular? How many can you identify as being partially spread by the mass media?

Mass hysteria is similar to fads and crazes in that it is compulsive and irrational. It may exist among a large number of people, such as the screaming fans of a popular singer or group. Or it may express it-

[10]Tamotsu Shibutani, *Improvised News: A Sociological Study of Rumor* (Indianapolis: Bobbs-Merrill, 1966, p. 15.

self in scattered instances—when, for example, a particularly colorful criminal act is followed by a rash of similar incidents. Airplane hyjacking is one recent example.

Fashions, fads, and crazes begin as a departure from tradition—a bit of nonconformity in a conforming society. But they soon establish a new tradition from which new fashions, fads, and crazes depart. The bearded, long-haired college student at first represented a radical departure from his Joe College counterpart of the 1950s. By now he has been imitated to such an extent that he will have to shave to baldness if he wants to stand out.

Several groups in the counterculture have, in fact, begun to shave their heads. Can you identify these groups and the reasons they give for such self-expression?

Collective behavior that expresses itself in some of the actions we have just described continues to baffle social scientists. They know that the actions emerge out of frustrations or discontent, or as vehicles for releasing built-up tensions and wish-fulfillment. Sociologists can predict—and therefore help control—some situations in which collective behavior is likely to arise. But the unpredictability of the human personality keeps us from knowing exactly at all times what crowd situation will produce which effects.

[Publics and Public Opinion]

Collective behavior does not occur only in crowds and masses, but also in publics. A *public* is defined as a scattered collection of people who share a common interest or a concern about an issue, or are affected by a common occurrence. The readers of the Sunday edition of the *New York Times,* university students, moviegoers, voters, members of a fan club, all these are examples of publics. The bond that holds a crowd together is emotion, whereas the bond that holds a public together is intellect. A crowd is gathered at one place. But a public is dispersed, and each member of a public is able to communicate directly with only a small number of other members of the public. The mass media help to create and hold publics together.

What publics do you belong to? In each case, what is the common bond of intellectual interest?

Publics tend to be temporary and their composition changes quickly. For instance, all those watching a television program at 7:30 on Saturday night constitute a public. But at 8:00 the same night, some members of the former public will go out to a restaurant, others will read a book, still others will visit some friends. They will no longer be the same public they were half an hour earlier. A public is an unstructured collectivity in which some members are constantly losing interest in the event that made them members of a public, and constantly being replaced by others.

Publics are more characteristic of complex societies than of simple ones. Complex societies are heterogeneous and members have innumerable and varying interests. Members are constantly confronted with a large number of issues, of both a local and a national nature. These issues may be at odds with one another. One group may want to preserve our national forests, while another may want to be able to hunt game or to log the timber in them. One group may want to build a new addition to the local high school; another group opposes this move as wasteful and unnecessary. One group considers abortion an issue for each woman to decide individually; another group considers abortion as the murder of innocents. In a less complex society, such issues are not likely to arise: norms and values are accepted by all to a much greater extent, and very few question the traditional way of doing things.

Public Opinion

What issues of public opinion are currently being probed by pollsters and explored in the mass media?

The large number of publics, each concerned with its own issue or activity, attitude and opinion, give rise to public opinion. *Public opinion* is the attitude or judgment of a large number of people on a specific issue. Public opinion may be thought of as being the dominant opinion on that issue among a specific population. It may also be viewed as the position taken by a large public on a particular issue.

Public opinion has meaning only in a mass society—and is diffused through the mass media—because only in these societies does it matter what people think. In traditional societies, conflicting issues do not normally arise. In such societies, governments, as well as other institutions, tend to be run according to tradition, and the leaders do not care to as great an extent as in democratic societies what societal members think about specific issues.

How Is Public Opinion Formed?

It would seem logical that public opinion reflects the values and attitudes of a society. But values and attitudes internalized in childhood remain fairly continuous throughout an individual's lifetime, whereas public opinion fluctuates, sometimes very rapidly. Although there may be consensus in the society about the value of peace, public opinion may be divided at any given time about a particular war or military action in which the nation happens to be involved, as was the case with the war in Vietnam.

Social background and group membership are more likely to influence the formation of public opinion. People belonging to certain groups—religious or ethnic, racial or social class—hold similar opinions on specific issues. Of course, all of us belong to more than one group. Which group is most influential in the formation of individual opinion depends both on the kind of group and on our allegiance to it. If we are Catholics, our opinion on a woman's right to abortion may be influenced by the Church but our opinion of a candidate for state governor is less apt to be influenced by the Church. On this issue, our opinion is most likely to be influenced by our reference group, which is a group to which we either belong or aspire to belong. Our most important reference groups tend to reflect our occupational or social class status.

Opinion can also be influenced by individuals who are important in the community. There are several such opinion leaders in each community. Their influence is most intense in specific areas of concern—consumerism, political affairs, religion, and so on. Finally, public opinion is formed through interaction with others. An individual, unsure of how to react in regard to a particular event, debates, discusses, and exchanges information with others on the issue.

The mass media of communication strongly influence the formation of opinion. Some people even feel that the mass media create public opinion. Newspapers sometimes prompt public action by exposés of corruption in city government or some other local social problem. On the other hand, newspapers often vainly support certain issues, or the election of specific candidates. For example, the media supported Dewey to the point of announcing his winning the presidency, when in fact Truman had won. All we can be sure of is that newspapers are able to enhance or alter opinions that already exist.

Motion pictures and especially television have often been accused of creating public opinion. Again, there is little question that they do indeed influence the public in many ways. Movies and situation comedies show how different classes of people, in different social settings, behave. Television has done the same, and has also attempted to influence the consumption habits of the viewing public. This attempt is not only limited to the consumption of *products,* but in recent years has been expanded to include people. Political candidates for office, including those for the highest office in the land, have apparently been "bought" by the television viewing public as if they had been toothpaste. The selling techniques of the mass media strongly influence public opinion, reinforcing the influences of primary, reference, occupational, and status groups.

Measuring Public Opinion

To what uses are public opinion polls put?

In a democratic society, political leaders must be apprised, in theory at least, of the opinion of the mass of people. The measurement of public opinion has therefore been a part of our society for at least fifty years. Measurement is generally undertaken by the public opinion poll. A number of commercial enterprises have developed that regularly present their findings to the public through the mass media. The best known of these enterprises are George Gallup's American Institute of Public Opinion, the National Opinion Research Center, and Louis Harris and Associates. These polling organizations have expert research staffs, and they have been remarkably accurate in some of their predictions, particularly in the matter of national elections. Still, the business of opinion polling is beset by problems.

Sampling. First, since obviously not every person in the population can be personally questioned, pollsters operate on the basis of samples. Pollsters select a small number of people who represent all the variations that are present in the total population. If the surveyors are sampling voters, they break down a certain quota or proportion of voters according to region, political party, sex, age, race, and so on.

Another widely used polling technique is random, or probability sampling. The concept of probability ensures that each population unit has an equal chance of being selected for inclusion in a sample. For instance, in the draft lottery, the birthdates of all prospective draftees were written down, placed in capsules, and shaken in a drum. Then the first, second, and third birthdate capsules were drawn out one at a time. Each capsule had an equal chance of being drawn first, second, and third.

The sampling technique is only the first step in public opinion polling. The next step, and a very difficult one, is the way the questions are worded and the manner in which answers are interpreted. The questions must be worded clearly and without any possibility of being misinterpreted. They must not offend any respondent, nor can they include any hint of bias or be emotionally loaded. The interviewer must develop a good rapport with the respondents so that they answer questions willingly and truthfully. A final problem is that people have a tendency to give their opinions even on questions they know nothing about.

Develop a questionnaire on an area of social concern, and test the questions on your classmates. Did the questions elicit the kind of answers you wanted? What unexpected responses were given? Would the sample represent the entire school? Why or why not?

Interpretation. Interpretation of findings is also difficult. The views of a public sometimes shift very rapidly. If the issues are not close or important to the respondents, their answers will not be stable enough to count. Sometimes the events of a campaign result in shifts of opinion. All in all, however, the pollsters have been remarkably accurate in their predictions for the last twenty years.

Public opinion polls are criticized by people who maintain that, especially in predicting the results of national elections, people tend to vote for the predicted winner. There is no way to know whether, and to what extent, this may be true. Certainly there are people who, not being deeply committed to any issue or candidate, would just as soon be on the side of the winner. On the other hand, public opinion polls do help determine the will of a large, inarticulate, and unorganized citizenry.

How might opinion-interpretation be related to labeling theory in sociological analysis?

Public Opinion, Propaganda, and Censorship

The manipulation of public opinion is of great benefit to many groups in society. Car producers want the public to buy their cars. The manufacturers of a specific brand of cereal want everyone to eat their product. Political candidates want to be elected. Teachers want to have their salaries increased. The administration in office wants to be supported. Parents want their children to accept their moral values. The nation wants its citizens to maintain a patriotic tradition. How do all these groups attempt to influence public opinion? Two ways of exerting such influence are through propaganda and censorship.

Write several slogans to sell yourself as a candidate for the Presidency. What emotional issues are you stressing to make your point?

Propaganda is a deliberate attempt to persuade the individual to accept a particular belief uncritically or to make a certain choice. All kinds of advertising, sales promotions, public relations, political campaigns, fundraising drives, billboards, and even Sunday school lessons use propaganda. Propaganda is a deliberate attempt at persuasion and is a manipulative device. We therefore distinguish it from education, which attempts to develop in the individual the ability to make his or her own judgments on issues. Propaganda, on the other hand, seeks to persuade the individual to accept wholesale the ideas, beliefs, or judgments of others. However, some propaganda seeps into all teaching. A teacher, as a subjective human being, can hardly keep his or her ideas totally hidden, especially in subjects where interpretation is called for.

Propaganda is a deliberate attempt to influence an individual's beliefs or choices.

Successful propaganda depends on an emotional appeal, often on the fears and anxieties of people. That is why advertisements for cosmetics, deodorants, and toothpastes are so successful in our society. They promise to make us attractive and young, and attractive and young people in our society attain success. Propaganda also relies on the "good old values" of the past ("Apple pie like momma used to make") and assures people that whatever it is the propagandist is selling, it is very popular ("Everyone's doing it").

Propaganda is most successful when it does not attempt to change the opinion of people too drastically. If the issue of the propagandist is one in which members of the public have little interest and are not

How to Become a Folk Hero

During the summer of 1974, in offices and factories across the land people talked of the "Event of the Century," as it was billed: Evel Knievel's upcoming attempt to jump the Snake River Canyon in a "Skycycle." People were attracted by the claims of America's latest folk hero and by the nature of the event. It was a relief from daily routines; it was daring; like Knievel himself, it was "macho." For months Knievel traveled the country, giving speeches, appearing on television, advertising himself.

Intimidation, fraud, and the manipulation of the public and the press were the hallmarks of this propaganda campaign, according to one reporter. Early in 1974 Knievel publicly received a $6 million advance—actually, it was $250,000. Two test failures were advertised to heighten suspense—both were deliberate. Knievel's promised million-dollar party became a free round of beers in the bars of Butte, Montana. Knievel publicly prohibited TV coverage of the event—actually, he had made a deal with ABC (American Broadcasting Corporation) to have it broadcast the following weekend, and ABC put on two shows the preceding week to promote the stunt. "He'd say these things that were lies so emphatically," one Knievel worker said, "that he just about made you believe them—even though you knew they were lies. . . . It seems to me he scares the press and they wind up eating out of his hand because he strikes some bully cord in them. . . . They just let themselves be run over."

One photographer who refused to smile when Knievel ordered was put in the hospital for his pains—Knievel had beaten him with his diamond-studded cane and pushed the photographer's camera into his face. "It's selective intimidation," another reporter said, "just like Nixon, and it works!"

Joe Eszterhas, "King of the Goons: Deliver Us from Evel," *Rolling Stone*, November 7, 1974, pp. 40–72.

Why might "overkill" propaganda defeat it's original purpose? What conditions may have been necessary for the success of Hitler's propaganda?

personally involved, propaganda is likely to effect opinion change. If the opposite is true, however, a "boomerang" effect could emerge, in which situation the public rejects the propaganda completely and renews its loyalty to its original opinion. For example, George Lincoln Rockwell's Nazi propaganda was too vehement, and was thus rejected even by those segments of our society that hold racist views.

Propaganda has other limitations, too. For one thing, propagandists, particularly in democratic societies, have a lot of competition. They must also establish their credibility before the public will accept their propaganda. Many propagandists establish credibility by giving their organizations official-sounding or patriotic names. The education and sophistication of the public further limits the effectiveness of propaganda. If the individual member of the public holds intense beliefs and values, he will also be a less likely prey to the propagandist. Finally, cultural drifts and strong social trends cannot ultimately be affected by propaganda, although they may be retarded or thwarted by it.

What types of censorship do you support, if any?

Censorship. Propaganda gives a one-sided interpretation to an issue or shows only the good side of a product—and so distorts the information available to the public. Censorship, on the other hand, deletes all or parts of the information. Many of our institutions use censorship. The government and the military censor some information in the name of national security and defense. Families and religious organizations tend to censor information regarding sex. Political candidates tell us only what they want us to know about themselves and their intentions once in office. Manufacturers choose not to tell us that the car or the refrigerator they are selling us is built so that it must be replaced every few years. The mass media censor information given to the public.

Neither propaganda nor censorship are "bad" in and of themselves. It is the use to which they are put that makes them either of benefit to people or detrimental to them. Both techniques raise moral questions that should be answered individually. In a democratic society, there should theoretically be enough conflicting propaganda and public investigation that neither technique will control opinion. As Abraham Lincoln said, you can fool some of the people all of the time, and all of the people some of the time. But you cannot fool all of the people all of the time.

The Function of Public Opinion in Society

Why is freedom of the press such an important element in democracy?

Public opinion performs several functions in society. First, public opinion clarifies and crystallizes situations and issues that are new or ambiguous. Public opinion thus serves to institutionalize new cultural norms.

Public opinion also helps maintain social control over the leaders and the population at large. If leaders in a democracy behave in a way

Methodology: Content Analysis

In content analysis the researcher analyzes the content of human expressions in order to discover patterns that reflect something about a people's or an institution's attitudes, values, styles, and so on. The idea behind quantitative content analysis is to count the number of times a particular act, attitude, personal characteristic, and so on, appears in a given context. In itself, content analysis tells us nothing about the effects of a content. Violence on TV, for example, may not influence the behavior of television watchers.

A current popular subject for content analysis is the mass media. One study that makes extensive use of this method is Robert Cirino's study of the biases and distortions of the news media. On the assumption that the news media have a powerful influence on what we consider important issues, Cirino investigated the scale of priorities in the news. He watched the NBC and CBS nightly national news broadcasts for a period of two months in the summer of 1969, recording the number of times a particular issue was mentioned and the time devoted to that issue. During this period he found that NBC never mentioned hunger, while CBS "had a few items on hunger included in its coverage of space. In contrast to this neglect, both newscasts together had 82 items, using 18:57 minutes, on the stock market; 36 items, using 71:07 minutes, on trivia; 22 items, using 54:54 minutes, on sports; and 134 items, using 269:34 minutes, on space." In another sample, Cirino found that out of over 4,800 items appearing on two major national news TV broadcasts, two hourly radio broadcasts, and the front pages of three major newspapers during various months in 1969, only 10 were devoted to prison conditions. Similarly, between 1962 and 1969 only 7 of the cover photographs of the major news weeklies (*Time, Newsweek,* and so on) were devoted to pollution, population, or hunger, while 182 covers were devoted to entertainers.

Cirino used a similar method to catalog the biases of three major newspapers in their reporting of the Vietnam War. Here, he coded headlines, articles, pictures, and captions as favorable or unfavorable to Saigon and the Pentagon. In 1968 he found a significant bias towards Saigon and the Pentagon's side. Cirino concluded that the mass media manipulate public opinion in favor of the establishment and thereby are eroding true democracy. Only by allowing all political views to have equal access to the major media forms could this be halted, he said.

Robert Cirino, *Don't Blame the People* (New York: Random House, Vintage Books, 1972).

that is perceived as inappropriate by the majority of the people, negative public opinion will eventually oust the leaders. The potential of such a situation keeps many leaders from behaving in a norm-deviating way, as happened following the Watergate scandals.

Finally, public opinion can serve as a binding element in society. In today's heterogeneous societies public opinion is seldom unified. Still, there are occasions, particularly in times of great crisis, that demand a collective effort. Such an effort is greatly aided if public opinion is unified. On such occasions, as in times of war or during the recent oil shortages, propaganda and censorship are generally employed and accepted.

[Social Movements]

Do you identify with any social movements today? What are the goals of the movement?

Another manifestation of collective behavior is the kind of collective action that sociologists call a "social movement." *Social movements* have been defined as "collective enterprises to establish a new order of life,"[11] and as collective efforts to either change the sociocultural order, or to resist such change.[12] This type of collective action represents the personal involvement of individuals and their intervention in directing, redirecting, furthering, or resisting change.

All forms of collective behavior not only reflect societal change, but also create change in the guise of altering perspectives. Collective behavior introduces new lines of action and establishes new institutions. Historically, sociocultural change has occurred whenever group identity changes—when group loyalty shifts from a religious base to a national base, for instance. Sociocultural change has also occurred when certain conceptions of reality were modified. People from Europe could not travel to the Americas before changing their ideas about what the world was like.

Changes in perspective take time and involve a tense period during which people are looking for some systematic way of interpreting the emerging perspectives. During such periods, people are very receptive to ideologies. Ideologies are systems of beliefs, or doctrines, that provide a basis for collective action.[13] Ideologies tend to develop around a central value, such as equality or racial purity. Ideologues also claim to speak for major social groups in society. Marxist socialists insist they speak for the working class; women's liberationists, for women. Some ideologies defend or rationalize the status quo. Others criticize it and want to change it. All ideologies maintain that only they give the true picture of what the world is really like. Changing perspectives and ideologies are very important factors in social movements.

---

[11]Herbert Blumer, "Social Movements," in A. M. Lee, ed., College Outline Series: *Principles of Sociology* (New York: Barnes and Noble, 1951), p. 200.

[12]Lewis M. Killian, "Social Movements," in Faris, p. 430.

[13]Karl Mannheim, *Ideology and Utopia* (New York: Harcourt Brace Jovanovich, 1936).

Any collective action, in fact, can be considered a social movement when the following factors are present: (1) when it has a specific perspective and ideology; (2) when it has a strong sense of idealism and solidarity, evolving dedication and loyalty in members; and (3) when there exists an orientation toward action, that is, when people feel that they ought to do something about the situation they want to change.

Social movements are rooted in the same kind of discontent that

The Formation of Social Movements: a Different View

One recent major piece of historical research conducted by Charles, Richard, and Louise Tilly challenges the view that social movements flourish during periods of rapid social change and social disorganization. The Tillys gathered representative material on collective violence in France, Italy, and Germany. Using both quantitative methods and qualitative analysis, they traced the patterns of collective violence in these countries over a century's time, from 1830 to 1930. The pace and levels of collective violence, they found, did not match the pace of industrialization or urbanization in the areas where collective violence occurred or among the groups who engaged in it. Sometimes, the levels of collective violence actually decreased during periods of rapid industrialization. The groups that engaged in collective violence were not primarily migrants or marginal people; rather, they were for the most part people in established communities and organizations who were "defending rights which had long enjoyed public recognition and even legal protection."

Patterns and differences in collective violence in the three countries, they said, were best explained by "the organization of contenders for power, the character of repression, the extent and form of political participation [and] rights in conflict." Although they used collective violence as a way of organizing their research, the Tillys came to see it as a "by-product" of more general collective action in the struggle for power. In this, they find support for the "solidarity" thesis proposed by Marx, which emphasizes collective organization and group solidarity as necessary preconditions for collective action, and which sees collective action primarily as a struggle for power between competing groups.

Charles Tilly, Louise Tilly, and Richard Tilly, *The Rebellious Century, 1830–1930* (Cambridge: Harvard University Press, 1975).

gives rise to many of the short-lived forms of collective behavior. However, members of social movements are interested in long-range solutions. Because of this, they develop and depend on an ideology that supports their actions. Members of social movements, though separated by continents, are united by a common commitment, by dedication to a cause, and by the idealistic belief in their cause.

Although some social movements are almost entirely unorganized, most are pursued in voluntary groups, or associations. These are secondary groups organized for the attainment of a definite goal. Both social movements and voluntary groups are characteristic of urban industrial societies that are experiencing rapid social change. In some nations, such social movements develop into political parties, attempting to pursue their goals by attaining political power. Marxism is an ideology that has prompted social movements in a number of societies. In some societies, for example in the United States, Marxist goals are pursued in voluntary associations. In other societies—most recently, Portugal—Marxism has attained the position of a political party. Finally, in societies such as China, the movement has become the party in power. In Chile, Marxism came to power, but was subsequently overthrown by a military coup.

The Purpose of Social Movements

Why might a period of apathy and anomie have set in after the Civil War in this country?

Social movements are sometimes called "institutions in the making" because their ultimate aim is to effect change to the extent that it becomes institutionalized. And they often succeed in this. Political parties, international ideologies (socialism, for instance), women's suffrage, and even nations have come into existence as a result of social movements.

The soil of social movements. Social movements promote social change. At the same time, rapid social change in a society produces an atmosphere in which social movements flourish. When a society is in a period of transition from an agricultural to an industrial economy, disorganization occurs. Formerly accepted norms and values are questioned and people become subject to feelings of anomie and alienation. As we have already noted earlier, anomie is a feeling of normlessness, or not knowing which behavioral guidelines to follow in a society in which several sets of norms prevail at the same time. Alienation is a feeling of separateness from society, of powerlessness, normlessness, and isolation that convinces individuals that they are helpless to influence their fate.

Social movements in addition to attracting those who are dissatisfied on ideological, intellectual, and moral grounds, also attract people who are restless and confused, and who need some focus in their lives. Therefore, a society characterized by anomie and alienation will also be characterized by many social movements.

Social movements also flourish when there is a general dissatisfaction with the status quo in a society. One source of dissatisfaction is relative deprivation. Relative deprivation is the feeling people get when they compare themselves with others and believe themselves to suffer in the comparison. The Bedouin desert-dweller who possesses only a tent, some cooking utensils, and the clothes on his back, and who accepts his station in life and the values of his society, does not consider himself deprived. But once he begins to question these values, and compares himself with the sheikh who has many possessions, he begins to feel deprived. Many of the poor in our society, when compared with the poor of other societies, might be considered well off. Compared to the wealthy in our society, however, they are indeed deprived, and many of them feel relative deprivation strongly. The mass media, by displaying and valuing wealth, contribute to this social phenomenon.

Do you feel disadvantaged in comparison to the characters you see on television? In what ways?

Related to the dissatisfaction based on relative deprivation is the failure of rising expectations. Rising expectations are experienced when the standard of living—and expectations of a better life—begins to rise in a society. These expectations are frustrated if the standard of living declines for some reason or does not rise fast enough. Expectations are also frustrated if a group is denied access to the higher standard of living enjoyed by others in the society.

Third World peoples, and the underprivileged of our own society are, for the most part, victims of the feeling of relative deprivation and the failure of rising expectations. They also see themselves as victims of social injustice. The perception of social injustice, however, is not limited to the underprivileged classes. A wealthy person who suddenly finds himself relieved of his fortune may also feel that an injustice has been done him. In any case, the significant factor is not the actual presence or absence of social injustice. It is people's *perception* that they are victims of social injustice that makes them apt to respond to social movements.

Why People Join Social Movements

People subject to status inconsistency are likely to become involved in social movements. Status inconsistency, you recall, occurs when not all of a person's statuses are ranked on an equal level. For example, in our society, a black doctor tends to be ranked as a black first and then as a doctor. The status of black is considered before the status of doctor. Thus, the black doctor's potential for acquiring the high status of doctor is diminished. Naturally, he or she feels discontent.

Another factor that encourages people to join social movements is geographic mobility. Geographic mobility, a characteristic of urban industrial societies, promotes feelings of rootlessness. Mobility partly explains why all kinds of social movements flourish in California, a state

Who Participated in the 1967 Ghetto Rebellions?

From eyewitness accounts, interview surveys, arrest records, and a study of Detroit arrestees, the Kerner Commission compiled this profile of the typical participant in the 1967 ghetto rebellions:

The typical rioter in the summer of 1967 was a Negro, unmarried male between the ages of 15 and 24. He was in many ways very different from the stereotype. He was not a migrant. He was born in the state and was a lifelong resident of the city in which the riot took place. Economically his position was about the same as his Negro neighbors who did not actively participate in the riot.

Although he had not, usually, graduated from high school, he was somewhat better educated than the average inner-city Negro, having at least attended high school for a time.

Nevertheless, he was more likely to be working in a menial or low status job as an unskilled laborer. If he was employed, he was not working full time and his employment was frequently interrupted by periods of unemployment.

He feels strongly that he deserves a better job and that he is barred from achieving it, not because of lack of training, ability, or ambition, but because of discrimination by employers.

He rejects the white bigot's stereotype of the Negro as ignorant and shiftless. He takes great pride in his race and believes that in some respects Negroes are superior to whites. He is extremely hostile to whites, but his hostility is more apt to be a product of social and economic class than of race; he is almost equally hostile toward middle class Negroes.

He is substantially better informed about politics than Negroes who were not involved in the riots. He is more likely to be actively engaged in civil rights efforts, but is extremely distrustful of the political system and of political leaders.

Report of the National Advisory Commission on Civil Disorders (New York: Bantam Books, 1968), pp. 128–129.

Germany was undergoing a severe economic crisis during Hitler's rise to power. How might such a crisis have contributed to his success?

to which large numbers of people continually migrate.

Social mobility also makes people receptive to social movements. This is especially true of people who belong to a downwardly mobile class or who fear becoming downwardly mobile. Upward mobility, however, also tends to unsettle people.[14]

[14]James A. Geschwender, "Explorations in the Theory of Social Movements," *Social Forces* 47 (December 1968): 127–135.

Social movements attract people who have weak or nonexistent family ties. The cliché that when you have a mortgage to pay off you can't afford to be involved with hotheads seems to be true. In fact, most members of radical social movements either have no families or have broken all family ties. The campus radicals of the late 1960s, for instance, according to one psychiatrist, seem to have been reared in homes in which their parents denied them emotional reassurance and guidance. When family ties are strong, a person feels less need to join social movements. This is one reason why most revolutionary movements discourage family life and family authority.[15]

Isolated and marginal people may likewise feel the need to belong to some group. Isolated people set themselves apart from the rest of society, either voluntarily or because of their occupations. Marginal people are not quite accepted and integrated into society or relevant groups in it.[16] Still, the need to belong exists, and social movements help fill this need.

Given what you know about industrial societies and primary groups, would you expect more or fewer social movements to arise in the United States than, say, in Nepal? Why?

Although social movements prosper in certain conditions more than in others, we must stress that these conditions are *not* causes of social movements. Their conditions merely predispose people to join such movements. In many of these conditions cause and effect are confused. Geographic mobility causes rootlessness in people. People who feel rootless do not readily accept the norms of the community in which they temporarily live. They are more inclined to join social movements than are old-time residents of the community. But which came first, the rootlessness or the mobility? It is, of course, possible that mobility is merely a reaction to an already existing rootlessness. The same may be said for lack of family ties as a factor that predisposes people to join social movements. Are family ties already severed, so that the individual feels a need to belong somewhere, perhaps to a social movement? Or do ties become severed as a result of the time and effort the social movement takes away from the family?

Some Kinds of Social Movements

There are many kinds of social movements. In some, like migratory movements, discontent is eliminated when members leave one geographic location for another. The waves of immigrants who came to this country were members of such movements. In expressive movements, members' reactions to their environment are changed, because the environment itself cannot be changed. Many religious movements, including the contemporary fundamentalist expressions, are expressive movements. In utopian movements, an attempt is made to establish

[15]Herbert Hendin, "A Psychoanalyst Looks at Student Revolutionaries," *New York Times Magazine* (January 17, 1971), pp. 16 ff.

[16]William Korhauser, *The Politics of Mass Society* (New York: Free Press of Glencoe, 1959), chapter 12.

new societies with new standards and values. The rash of communes formed by young people in the late 1960s were utopian in nature. Finally, in change-resistant movements, people attempt to stem the tide of change because they fear change is proceeding too rapidly. Many organizations of the right and the radical right are change-resistant movements.

Reform Movements

In the past several centuries, the two social movements that have had the most influence on societies and their governments have been revo-

Radical Lesbians

Radical Lesbians represent one of the more radical factions in the Women's Liberation movement. Women, they say, have traditionally been defined and defined themselves as those who are acceptable to men. They seek to replace this self-conception with one that does not derive from male culture and that will allow themselves to be considered as persons rather than deviants. This new sense of self that "only women can give to each other," they term the "woman-identified woman." Like many other revolutionary groups, they emphasize the potential for group solidarity and individual transformations of consciousness in the process of struggle, as the following selection from their manifesto illustrates:

[The woman-identified woman] is the primacy of women relating to women, of women creating a new consciousness of and with each other which is at the heart of women's liberation, and the basis for the cultural revolution. Together we must find, reinforce and validate our authentic selves. As we do this, we confirm in each other that struggling incipient sense of pride and strength, the divisive barriers begin to melt, we feel this governing solidarity with our sisters. We see ourselves as prime, find our centers inside of ourselves. We find receding the sense of alienation, of being cut off, of being behind a locked window, of being unable to get out what we know is inside. We feel a real-ness, feel at last we are coinciding with ourselves. With that real self, with that consciousness, we begin a revolution to end the imposition of all coercive identifications, and to achieve maximum autonomy in human expression.

Ellen Bedoz, Rita Mae Brown, Barbara XX, Lois Hart, Cynthia Funk, March Hoffman, "The Woman-Identified Woman," in Wendy Martin, ed., *The American Sisterhood: Writings of the Feminist Movement from Colonial Times to the Present* (New York: Harper & Row, 1972), p. 338.

lutionary and reform movements. Reform movements represent an attempt to change some feature of an existing social order without changing the entire order. Such movements are most successful in democratic societies. In such societies, there is relative freedom to criticize institutions, and there are channels through which reforms can be put into effect.

What major reform movements of this country have affected your life today? In what ways have they done so?

Our own society offers many examples of reform movements. The most prominent examples are the civil rights movement, which has splintered into revolutionary and moderate factions; the movement for equality and liberation of women; and the movement for removing the social stigma attached to homosexuality.

It is sometimes difficult to distinguish between a reform and a revolutionary movement, because many generalized movements produce a wide range of action-oriented groups. For example, the Women's Liberation movement includes such organizations as the National Organization of Women (NOW), the aims of which are conservatively reformist, as well as such groups as Radical Women, Women's Liberation Front, and Women's International Terrorist Conspiracy from Hell (WITCH). The program and actions of a group, rather than its name, determine whether it is reformist or revolutionary.

Sometimes the program of a group differs widely from its actions. Can you give an example?

Revolutionary Movements

The distinguishing feature of revolutionary movements is that their members do not merely seek to correct some aspect of the present social order. They consider the social order so inadequate, corrupt, unjust, and beyond salvation, that they seek its complete removal and substitution with an entirely new order. In effecting such absolute change, revolutionary movements must often resort to violence.

Revolutionary movements are principally of two types. In *nationalistic revolutionary movements,* a predominantly foreign government is overthrown and replaced with a native one. *Class revolutionary movements* substitute one ruling class for another in the same society. The American revolution was nationalistic, whereas the French, Russian, Chinese, and Cuban were all class revolutions.

Revolutionary movements should not be confused with revolts, or *coups d'etat.* In revolts, individual members of the ruling class are replaced with other individuals, but the structure of the major social institutions remains the same.

Why might you expect revolutionary movements to be more characteristic of totalitarian governments than of democratic governments?

Factors encouraging revolutionary movements. The same factors predispose people to join revolutionary situations that predispose them to become members of other social movements. These conditions may, however, be extreme or may be perceived as being extreme. Revolutionary movements are more characteristic of totalitarian societies than they are of democratic ones. In democracies, public opinion and reform movements exert pressure, which generally leads to the changes desired by the people. In totalitarian regimes, public opinion is often ignored, and social movements are not tolerated. The only way people can make changes, then, is by overthrowing the government.

The most important condition for revolution is the widespread realization that the legitimate government has failed and that it is necessary to bring about change at any cost. This condition is called a *crisis of legitimacy.* When a crisis of legitimacy takes place, it is a sign that the government has been ineffective and has not eliminated discontent by making changes.

Find out how many people died in the Cuban Revolution, compared to how many died in a five-year period preceding that, under Batista.

Revolution is also aided by a breakdown of discipline and efficiency in the ruling body. Some members of this body, especially the intellectuals, become disillusioned and may even join the revolutionary movement. Others abandon the role of rulers. Therefore, in many cases, very little violence is actually needed to wrest the government from the hands of the rulers. Revolutions are relatively bloodless compared to wars and wholesale genocidal programs such as were carried out in Hitler's Germany.

Results of revolution. The results of revolutions are seldom as drastic or as ideal as they promise to be. Customs and institutions, though certainly subject to change, are difficult to uproot. Sometimes precisely the unpleasant features of the old social order survive the revolution. Nonetheless, many revolutions—the American, the Russian, and the Chinese, to use the most obvious examples—have brought about changes of tremendous importance for the people of their societies.

In what ways does the idea of permanent revolution correspond to the idea that change is the only constant in our world? Would permanent revolution tend to create a stable or an unstable government?

The characteristic pattern of development and the effects of the revolutions mentioned above apply more closely to the "classic" revolutions—the French, American, and Russian—than they do to the more recent ones. For example, the Chinese Revolution, although basically a class revolution, did not follow the same kind of development as older revolutions. First of all, it was fought in guerilla style, over a long period of years. Its charismatic leader, Mao Tse Tung, had won the wholehearted support of China's millions of peasants. After the initial revolution, the government did not settle into a familiar rut. On the contrary, the idea of a permanent state of revolution permeates current Chinese thought. As soon as there are indications of any kind of "system" developing, the party leaders launch another "cultural revolution" complete with theoretical and physical purges.

We should also point out that we have been using the term *revolution* here in a very narrow sense. Today, however, this word is often used more broadly to refer to any profound change. The broader term is also used today in reference to the aspirations of Third World peoples and groups in our society. This is the area in which the broad and narrow usages overlap. The many small but fanatical revolutionary movements that surface from time to time address themselves to these same aspirations. They feel that "the people"—meaning the dispossessed masses—must gain control of economic resources and their political futures. In short, they must organize and carry out a revolution.

Change-Resistant Movements

Revolutionary movements get a great deal of notoriety because they reflect the discontent of people who believe that change is occurring too slowly. Other movements reflect the belief of other people that change occurs too rapidly. These movements are called *change-resistant movements.* Their purpose is to stop or eradicate change in society. The Ku Klux Klan is the best-known American change-resistant movement, but there are many others. Any new situation that threatens the status quo brings into existence scores of change-resistant movements. Increased immigration, the policies of the New Deal, and civil-rights legislation all caused change-resistant movements to flourish. The reaction to immigration in the middle decades of the 19th century prompted the founding of the Native American Party (not to be confused with American Indians) and the Know-Nothing movement. The reaction against the New Deal established movements that combined propaganda with antisemitism, isolationism, and antiforeign sentiments. The White Citizens' Councils effectively delayed school integration in the South for a number of years. Today, the most influential change-resistant movement is the John Birch Society, whose chief outward concern seems to be the denouncement of persons involved in our political system as agents of a communist conspiracy to take over the country. The John Birch society tends to oppose any kind of social reform.

Change-resistant movements frequently attract members from both the upper and the lower classes. What issues might unite these two different groups in this country?

The Stages of Development in a Social Movement

Each social movement is unique in its goals and in its eventual fate. Still, there are certain stages in the life cycle of social movements that all such movements share. These stages have been described by sociologists Dawson and Gettys as unrest, excitement, formalization, institutionalization, and dissolution.[17] The unrest stage is characterized by the restlessness of the people who develop a sense of social injustice and frustration because their established way of life has been disrupted. Such a stage can last for several generations and is always a part of social change and disorganization. Certainly the civil rights movement experienced such a stage when blacks expressed their frustration at their position on the bottom of the stratification system.

The excitement stage begins when vague dissatisfactions find a focus. Causes are pinpointed and action is proposed by various movements. Many of these movements are short-lived because of inefficient

What stage(s) has the women's movement already passed through in this country?

[17]Carl Dawson and W. E. Gettys, *Introduction to Sociology* (New York: The Ronald Press, 1934, 1948), pp. 708–709.

The Ku Klux Klan is one of the most widely known change-resistant groups in the United States.

leadership and inability to organize. This stage tends to be short—people are either ready to take action, or to forget about the issue. The peaceful resistance period of the civil rights movement, with its sit-ins in Southern coffee shops, its rallies in response to Martin Luther King, its refusal to sit in the back of buses, is an illustration of this stage.

The formalization stage occurs in those movements that attempt to change or reform some facet of society. Formalization involves the establishment of a bureaucratic structure with a chain of command, an apparatus for fund raising, and a clear ideology. What was formerly an undisciplined mass of excited people with an ambiguous cause becomes a disciplined organization with officers and a practical program for achieving its goals. Militant black organizations such as CORE and SNCC were examples of the formalization stage.

Finally, the institutionalization stage was characterized by the stricter enforcement of the antisegregation law and by federal programs such as affirmative action. Federal injunctions that a certain proportion of minority members must be hired by both private and public enterprises, represented the institutionalization stage of the civil rights movement.

If a movement survives long enough, it eventually becomes institutionalized, acquiring a pattern, a tradition to uphold and pass on, and sometimes vested interests to defend. Many religious movements make the transition to full-fledged denominations that are accepted as part and parcel of our society's religious institution.

At what point did the antiwar movement in this country lose momentum?

Finally, the dissolution stage occurs when a movement has achieved its objectives. When the movement for women's suffrage ended in women obtaining the vote, the movement dissolved. Not all members of movements agree to dissolution. Sometimes a movement is reduced to a small core of faithful intent on pursuing goals that may very well be unattainable.

Recently, sociologists have updated their description of the life cycle of social movements, but although their terminology is slightly different—one calls the stages "preliminary, popular, formal, and institutional"—the essence of the stages is the same.[18] The important thing to remember is that even if a social movement is not totally successful —that is, if it does not become institutionalized—it still exerts some sort of pressure on the society. And since social movements originate in social unrest and discontent, it is wise for those in charge of administering the nation's affairs to be sensitive to social movements.

[Summary]

Collective behavior occurs in situations that are highly charged with emotion and in which the norms we use in ordinary interaction are useless. Such situations include behavior in crowds—riots, mobs, panics —in fashions, fads, and crazes, in publics and audiences, in public opinion and propaganda, in rumors, and in social movements.

Collective behavior is relatively unpatterned and unstructured, and is characteristic of societies undergoing rapid social change. Instances of collective behavior are more frequent and dramatic in a mass soci-

---

[18]Rex D. Hopper, "Revolutionary Process: A Frame of Reference for the Study of Revolutionary Movements," *Social Forces* 28 (March 1950), pp. 207–279.

ety. They occur most frequently (1) where people perceive conflict and deprivation; (2) where they are able to pinpoint the cause of such conflict and deprivation; (3) where precipitating factors predispose the people to mobilize for action; and (4) where traditional social controls are no longer effective. The mechanisms of collective behavior are described by the contagion theory (which posits a process in which moods, attitudes, and behavior are communicated to the collectivity); by the convergence theory (which stresses that collective behavior brings out into the open feelings already present in the members of the collectivity); and by the emergent norm theory (which views collective behavior as governed by new and different norms).

One type of collective behavior occurs in crowds that are collections of people who respond to a common stimulus. Crowds may be casual or organized, expressive or acting. People in them develop a common mood and a shared concept of how to behave at the moment. Crowds are temporary and their members remain anonymous and impersonal. Therefore crowds can commit atrocities without their members feeling guilty.

Among the other types of collective behavior, rumor is particularly fascinating to social scientists. The exchange and spread of information by rumor often precedes more active forms of collective behavior. Rumors are characterized by distorted simplifications that serve to clarify and encourage other forms of collective behavior.

A form of collective behavior also occurs in publics. A public is a scattered collection of people who share a common interest or concern about an issue, or are affected by a common occurrence. Publics are temporary and changing, and are more characteristic of complex societies than of simple ones.

The large number of publics in contemporary societies gives rise to the formation of public opinion. Public opinion is the attitude or judgment of a large number of people on a specific issue, or the dominant opinion on that issue among a specific population. Public opinion has meaning only in a mass society. It is diffused through the mass media of communication. Public opinion is influenced by social background and group membership, by individuals important in the community, and by interaction with others. The mass media greatly influence, though they do not form, public opinion. The measurement and interpretation of public opinion have become extremely sophisticated in our society.

Public opinion is manipulated by some segments of our society through propaganda and censorship. Propaganda is a deliberate attempt to persuade the individual to accept uncritically a particular belief or to make a certain choice. Censorship distorts information by suppressing it or by deleting parts of it. Both propaganda and censorship attempt to influence public opinion.

Another form of collective behavior is represented by social movements. Social movements are collective attempts to establish a new order of life, to either change the sociocultural order, or to resist change. Important factors in social movements are changing perspectives and ideologies. A collective action of any kind is a social movement when: (1) it has a specific perspective and ideology; (2) it has a strong sense of idealism and solidarity; and (3) there is an orientation toward action.

Social movements are rooted in discontent—as are the shorter-lived instances of collective behavior—but their goal is a long-range solution. Their ultimate aim is to effect change to such an extent that it becomes institutionalized. Social movements promote social change and vice versa. In particular, social movements originate when a society is characterized by anomie, alienation, relative deprivation, and rising expectations. Their growth is encouraged (1) when many people are subject to status inconsistency; (2) when there is a great geographical and social mobility; (3) when family ties are weak; and (4) when many marginal and isolated people exist within a society.

Types of social movements include migratory, expressive, utopian, and change-resistant movements. In recent times, reform and revolutionary social movements have been most influential in contemporary societies. Reform movements represent an attempt to change some feature of an existing social order without changing the entire order. Revolutionary movements seek the complete removal of the existing order and its substitution by a new order. Revolutionary movements may be nationalistic—with the goal of overthrowing a predominantly foreign government. Or they may be class movements—with the goal of substituting one ruling class for another in the same society. The most important condition for revolution is a crisis of legitimacy. Although we seem to have experienced such a crisis in the late 1960s, the New Left movement in our society did not succeed. Movements to resist change—with the goal of stopping or eradicating change in society—appear whenever new social reforms are enacted.

Social movements follow a common life cycle that includes the following stages: unrest, excitement, formalization, institutionalization, and dissolution. Some movements pass through all these stages, while others fail at one or another stage.

Terms to Remember

Collective behavior. Type of behavior that occurs in crowds, mobs, fashions, fads, crazes, rumors, panics, and also in publics, public opinion, and social movements. This type of behavior is characteristic of a collectivity of people who are responding to a common stimulus under conditions that are generally temporary, unstable, and unstructured.

Contagion theory. A theory in which collective behavior is viewed as a process during which moods, attitudes, and behavior are rapidly communicated to a collectivity, and uncritically accepted by it by emotional contagion. Additional factors involved in contagion are suggestion and imitation, identification and anonymity, and loss of individuality.

Convergence theory. A theory of collective behavior stressing that collective behavior merely brings out into the open feelings already present in the individual members of the collectivity.

Emergent norm theory. A theory of collective behavior in which such behavior is viewed as being governed by norms that emerge in collective situations, although distinct from the norms existing in normal group situations.

Crowd. An aggregate of people gathered in the same place, at the same time, either casually or for a predetermined reason, and responding to a common stimulus. Crowds are divided into expressive and acting. An acting crowd may develop into a panic, mob, or riot.

Fashions. A minor kind of collective behavior concerning manners in dress, architecture, or house decor.

Fads and crazes. Minor fashions, short-lived and irrational.

Rumor. An unsupported report of an event or a projected event. Important in bringing about manifestations of more active types of collective behavior.

Mass hysteria. Compulsive and irrational behavior of a temporary or scattered nature.

Public. Persons who are geographically dispersed but who share a common interest, who express that interest, and who know that others are aware of this interest.

Public opinion. The attitudes and judgments of publics.

Propaganda. A deliberate attempt to persuade the individual to uncritically accept a particular belief or to make a certain choice.

Censorship. A device used to limit the information available to the public.

Social movement. A collective attempt either to change the sociocultural order or to resist change.

Relative deprivation. A source of dissatisfaction with the status quo conducive to the rise of social movements. The individual, though not deprived in comparison to people in other societies, perceives himself as deprived in comparison to others in his society.

Failure of rising expectations. The feeling experienced by members of a society when the standard of living has begun to rise, but has then suffered a reversal, or is not proceeding fast enough.

Migratory movement. A social movement in which discontent is eliminated when members leave one geographic location for another.

Expressive movement. A social movement in which the members' reactions to their environment is changed.

Utopian movement. A social movement in which members try to establish new societies with new standards and values.

Change-resistant movements. A social movement reflecting the discontent of people who believe that change is occurring too rapidly and who want to stop or eradicate change.

Reform movement. A social movement in which members attempt to change some feature of an existing social order without changing the entire order.

Revolutionary movement. A social movement in which members seek the complete removal of the present social order and substitution of it with an entirely new order.

Nationalistic revolutionary movement. A revolutionary movement in which a predominantly foreign government is overthrown and replaced with a native one.

Class revolutionary movements. A revolutionary movement in which one ruling class is replaced with another in the same society.

Suggestions for Further Reading

Berelson, Bernard and Morris Janowitz, eds. *Reader in Public Opinion and Communication.* New York: Free Press, 1966. Influences and diffusion of public opinion and propaganda are discussed and dissected.

Cameron, William Bruce. *Modern Social Movements: A Sociological Outline.* New York: Random House, 1966. Many examples illustrate this brief survey of social movements.

Cantril, Hadley. *The Psychology of Social Movements.* New York: John Wiley, 1963. Chapter 4 gives an especially memorable description of two lynchings, as seen through the eyes of the lynchers.

Gusfield, Joseph R., ed. *Protest, Reform, and Revolt: A Reader in Social Movements.* New York: Wiley, 1970. A fairly comprehensive collection of essays on social movements.

Lang, Kurt and Gladys Engle. *Collective Dynamics.* New York: Crowell, 1961. A basic text, but one with interesting chapters on crowds, rumors, panics, fashions, and other forms of collective behavior.

Lincoln, E. Eric. *The Black Muslims in America.* Boston: Beacon Press, 1961. A black sociologist uses the method of participant observation to describe a social movement.

Morgan, Robin, ed. *Sisterhood Is Powerful: An Anthology of Writings from the Women's Liberation Movement.* New York: Random House, 1970. The ideology of the Women's Liberation Movement stated by a number of the movement's supporters.

Smelser, Neil J. *Theory of Collective Behavior.* New York: Free Press, 1963. A contemporary sociologist attempts to develop and apply a theory that can be used to analyze collective behavior.

Turner, Ralph H., and Lewis M. Killian. *Collective Behavior.* Englewood Cliffs, N.J.: Prentice-Hall, 1957. A text in which most issues of collective behavior are exhaustively covered.

Van Leeuwen, Arend Theodor. *Development Through Revolution.* New York: Charles Scribner and Sons, 1970. Revolution analyzed as social change.

Pivotal Institutions

Family, Religion, Education

WE HAVE LOOKED at the human being as an individual—a separate personality—as well as in the role of member of various groups. We have seen that humans live in societies and that as a consequence of their interaction with one another in these societies, they develop an abstraction we call *culture.* We are aware that values and norms are important parts of the culture that a society evolves. They guide and direct human behavior, making it unnecessary for each person who is born into the society to learn through his or her own personal experience what to do and how to do it to survive, or what not to do because it is harmful.

We have also seen that the group way of life, though necessary and comforting in many respects, results in conflicts. Some of the conflicts center around the unequal distribution of the goods and services produced by each society. Unequal distribution gives rise to the universal problem of social injustice. Other conflicts revolve around the heterogeneous nature of most modern industrial societies. Because such societies are made up of many racial and ethnic groups and because people tend to harbor hostile feelings against strangers, prejudice and discrimination arise.

Furthermore, we have established that society and culture, as well as people, are continually changing. Change does not always occur at an even pace. Sometimes it is rapid; at other times it is slow. Sometimes only particular groups accept change. At other times segments of culture change before groups are ready for it. These differences create stresses and strains in social organization.

In this and the following chapter we are going to look at the patterns of behavior that our culture has established for us. Patterns of behavior are the habits, or traditional ways of doing things, that have accumulated around an important human function. Sociologists refer to such patterns, or habits, as *institutions.* As is true with most terms, sociologists use this term quite differently from the way other people do. For instance, in everyday conversation we hear people speak of *mental institutions,* of *penal institutions,* and of such buildings as orphanages and schools as *institutions.* But these are not institutions in the sociological sense. They are only isolated, physical representations of the abstract concept of institution.

[Pivotal Institutions]

Certain human functions are essential to the survival of the individual and the group. One essential function is control of the process of reproduction. A society must ensure a continuous supply of societal members and must provide these new members with a nurturing environment. Other essential functions of society include the provision of a livelihood for each member; they guarantee that members contribute to the group, rather than harm it, and the maintenance of order, at least to the extent that people are prevented from killing one another over every disagreement. Then there is the function of passing on important knowledge to each new generation. And finally, a society must find ways of answering questions such as: What is the meaning of life? What happens after death? Where do we come from before birth?

All human societies have had to perform these functions. All have risen to the challenge and have met it to the best of their ability, though in different ways. To make sure that reproduction proceeds in an orderly fashion and that infants are well taken care of until they are able to be independent, every society has some kind of family institution. To make sure that every member can support himself, every society has some kind of economic institution. To ensure a minimal degree of order, every society has some kind of political institution. To make sure that the young of each generation are taught what is important in their society, every society makes provision for supplying an education through the educational institution. Finally, to explain that which cannot be explained if people rely only on their senses, every society provides for some kind of religious experience through its religious institution.

These, in skeleton form, are the basic, or pivotal, institutions of human societies. Around each institution there have developed a number of folkways, mores, and laws, which all members of society are expected to follow to make their life in society easier. These folkways, mores, and laws, of course, vary from society to society because institutional forms themselves are different. In our society, the family institution determines that we marry one husband or one wife at a time; that we live with out mate alone; and that either one or, ideally, both spouses are heads of households and not subservient to elders. In the same way in our society we go to the polls to elect our president, while elsewhere people choose leaders from among several young men who prove their ability by walking across burning coals. The same pattern of variation in the framework of a basic institution is true of all the other functions we have mentioned.

Characteristics of Institutions

Because the members of each generation face the same basic problems, and because they maintain ties with both the past and the future through their parents and their children, the organized habits that we call *institutions* are durable. At the same time, people are not totally conforming but act as individuals. Societal members both follow institutional patterns, and continually create new patterns. The forms of these enduring institutions are therefore constantly changing.

Besides helping individuals satisfy some of their basic needs, institutions also provide the cement that holds societies together. If each individual lived in his own way and did only his "own thing," we would soon face utter chaos. Without some means of steady support, parents might abandon their infants or let them die, for we cannot be sure that parental love is an instinct and is not rather a responsibility taught by the family institution. If there were no organized ways of obtaining a livelihood, competition and conflicts would be so fierce that many people could not survive. The law of the jungle would prevail if there were no institution that maintained order. In other words, institutions enable societies to keep functioning. Institutions are the foundations, or pillars, of society.

Institutions are also interdependent. Usually, the child first learns about the value of making a good living, about the necessity for order, about religious principles, and about educational goals in the family setting. The family institution supports the other institutions, and is in turn supported by them. The condition of the economy in your society determines whether you can obtain a good job and establish your own family. The government may decide whether you finish college or go into the armed services instead. Your religion may teach that birth control is wrong. If you and others are faithful to the teachings of this institution, the results may affect all other institutions.

Institutions display tension between stability and change. Workable ways of doing things, repeated over and over, tend to become rigid forms. This is why mere habits become institutions. Looked at from this point of view, institutions tend to maintain stability and the status quo. But as new ways of doing things appear and are found workable, they challenge stability and impel institutions toward change.

Finally, it is important to remember that institutions are simply abstract concepts of organized habits and standardized ways of doing things. We cannot see institutions. What we can see are families, schools, banks, federal buildings, churches, and yes, jails and mental hospitals. But these would be nothing but empty symbols without one vital ingredient: individuals. The behavior of individuals gives institutions their form. And institutions give form to individual behavior.

[The Family]

British psychologist R. D. Laing levels this harsh accusation at the institution of the family:

The family's function is to repress Eros; to induce a false consciousness of security; to deny death by avoiding life; to cut off transcendence; to believe in God, not to experience the Void; to create, in short, one-dimensional man; to promote respect, conformity, obedience; to con children out of play; to induce a fear of failure; to promote a respect for work; to promote a respect for "respectability."[1]

Eros was the Greek god of sexual energy. Why might Laing therefore accuse the family of repressing Eros?

Can Laing be talking about the same family institution that is basic to all other institutions and to the origin of the individual? Is he referring to that same family that is praised by church and state, that nurtures society's infants to survival, that prepares its members to assume constructive roles, and that offers a haven from the bruises of life—that is, to paraphrase Robert Frost, the place where they have to take you in when you have nowhere else to go?

Other analysts deplore the decline of the family's influence. The disintegration of the family will, the prophets of doom declare, lead to the collapse of society and civilization. Whom are we to believe? Is the family too much with us, or not enough? Are we paying too high a price for the initial care, security, and affection that the family offers? Does the family actually perform essential functions, or is it simply a tool society uses to stamp and mold us as it sees fit?

There are many besides Laing who claim that the family has outgrown its usefulness. These critics note that most of the family's original functions have been taken over by other institutions. Alternative institutions could also perform its remaining functions, control of reproduction and the care and socialization of the young. Modern contraceptives can solve the problem of unwanted children. And reproduction need not remain a function only a family can perform, since test-tube babies have already been produced from only the sperm of a living male and the ovum of a living female.

A survey of the literature written about the Israeli experiments suggests that there is very little difference between children reared in kibbutzim and those reared in the traditional way.[2] In general, however, communally reared children have much lower rates of emotional disturbance and more positive relations with their parents than do children growing up within traditional families. The reason for this appears to be that the communally reared children think of the entire kibbutz as their family. In fact, they marry entirely outside of the group in which they were reared, explaining that they could never marry one of their own

---

[1]R. D. Laing, *The Politics of Experience* (London: Penguin Books, 1967), p. 35.

[2]Larry D. Barnett, "The Kibbutz as a Child-Rearing System: A Review of the Literature," in Jeffrey K. Hadden and Marie L. Borgatta, eds., *Marriage and the Family* (Itasca, Ill.: Peacock, 1969), pp. 405–407.

The Growth of the Sentimental Family

Modern attitudes towards the family and patterns of family life are a comparatively recent development in Western society, according to the French social historian Philippe Ariès. The portraits Ariès paints of family life in the medieval towns and cities of France differ strikingly from the images of family life to which we have grown accustomed today.

In medieval times, says Ariès, a person's life was lived in public; the focus of social life was not the family but the crowded streets, the great houses, the workplace. From about the age of seven, children were seen as miniature adults who often were apprenticed to others or lived with relatives. Children learned not in their own homes or with their peers in organized schools, but through participation in the adult world, working, playing, mingling with people of all ages. Far from being thought of as a pillar of society, the family was relegated to a relatively unimportant place in social life.

The extension of school education in the fifteenth century gradually began to alter the relationships of children to their families and of families to society. Families, like the schools, came to assume a moral and spiritual function that they formerly did not possess. As the family grew in importance, public social life declined. By the eighteenth century, middle-class families began to isolate themselves from the world, partly to protect their children from what they saw as the harmful and promiscuous effects of contact with adults of lower social classes. In the view of Ariès, modern child-centered families are a development of this desire to secede from the diverse and unpredictable social life of crowds. Families became more private, regulating who came and when, and attempted to replace the old sociability with the intense relations of nuclear family life.

Ariès, Philippe, *Centuries of Childhood: A Social History of Family Life,* trans. Robert Baldick (New York: Alfred A. Knopf, 1962).

brothers or sisters.[3] It seems, then, that in the kibbutzim the family has not actually been dispensed with but has simply been extended.

Another interesting result of these Israeli experiments is that communal rearing has been very successful in preparing individuals to fit into the life of the kibbutz. It has not, however, prepared individuals for life

[3]Melford Spiro, "The Israeli Kibbitz," in Arlene S. Skolnick and Jerome H. Skolnick, eds., *Family in Transition,* pp. 501–508.

Time Out for the Kids

Long hours spent commuting and on the job, numerous commentators on modern American families have noted, prevent many fathers from actively participating in child-rearing. Working hours of course often coincide with the hours children are awake, but these facts alone would hardly seem to account for some surprising statistics compiled by some sociologists. Two recent studies attempt to document the time fathers actually spend with their small children. In one investigation, middle-class fathers told interviewers that they played with their one-year-old infants an average of fifteen to twenty minutes a day. In another study, researchers, not relying on what fathers told them, placed microphones on the infants to record the interactions. Between father and infant, "the mean number of interactions per day was 2.7, and the average number of seconds per day was 37.7," the researchers found. They summed up their conclusions with what appears to be a classic understatement: "fathers spend relatively little time interacting with their infants."

Bronfenbrenner, Urie. "The Origins of Alienation." *Scientific American* 231 (August 1974): 53–59.

in an urban industrial society with its stress on individualism and competitiveness. In such a society, kibbutz-reared individuals are maladjusted and cannot develop to their full potential.[4] As a result, socialization within the nuclear family is again the prevailing mode in Israel.

What problems might a communally-reared child encounter in a competitive society? Do you think communes should be abolished, or society changed?

It is doubtful that any human being can isolate himself completely from a primary group, whether he calls it his family or his kibbutz, in order to enjoy total freedom. Humans are contradictory creatures; although we want to be free, we also want to belong; and although we want to be part of some group, we also want to be individuals. Perhaps some family form of the future will give us what we are looking for.

The mass media continually bombard us with information about the family. Numerous articles appear about the crisis of the family and the decline of the good old family virtues. What, in fact, is taking place? Very simply, the family is being transformed by cultural and societal complexity and by the rapid pace of sociocultural change.

[4] Stanley Diamond, "Collective Child-Rearing: The Kibbutz," *Social Problems* 5 (Fall 1957): 71–79.

[Basic Patterns of Family Organization]

The origins of the family institution have been long forgotten, but it is generally accepted that the family began the cycle of institution building. In the course of human history, in all known societies, it was the family that provided the individual with an identity, with a social status, and with economic well-being. The other institutions have only slowly emerged from the family, and have for a long time been dependent on the family. Even today, when our institutions are all in some disarray, the family remains a pervasive force in our lives, the most relevant of primary groups, and the most important element in the socialization process.

It has been widely accepted that the family is a universal institution. Anthropologist George Murock studied 250 societies and found evidence of a nuclear family (consisting of father, mother, and their children) in all of them.[5] Murdock explained the universality of the family by postulating that such an institution is functionally necessary because it performs the four functions fundamental to social life: the sexual, the economic, the reproductive, and the educational. These functions are vital to society, because if sex and reproduction were not provided for, society would die out; if survival were not ensured, then life would come to an end; and if education were not provided for, then culture would cease to exist.[6]

Why might Marx and Engels have advocated the destruction of the family institution as it now exists?

This functional interpretation, although it seems to make very good sense, has been challenged on several grounds. First, as is true with all functional theories, we must ask the question for whom is the family functional? (Since societies are made up of a number of groups, it usually turns out that phenomena are functional—or work to the advantage of—one or several of such groups.) And second, we should be aware that some of those functions may be provided by agencies other than the family.

Functions that seem to be more universal than those suggested by Murdock are really side effects of the family arrangement. These functions are the social placement of individuals in the social system and the regulation of social alliances between family units.[7] In essence, the family is responsible for replenishing the society and for placing people in the system of statuses and roles.

Family and Kin

Although we use the terms *family* and *kin* or *kinship group* interchangeably, the two ideas are distinct. Kin is a network of relatives, some of whom may live in a common residence, and others not. The kinship

---

[5]George Peter Murdock, *Social Structure* (New York: Macmillan, 1949).

[6]Murdock, p. 2.

[7]Rose Laub Coser, ed., *The Family: Its Structure and Functions* (New York: St. Martin's, 1964), p. *xiv*.

group is usually related to the individual through the process of reproduction, but a biological basis is not the only determinant of kinship. The concept of kin is also—perhaps principally—a social way of specifying who is related to whom. In some societies, only those descended from the father's ancestors are counted as kin; in others, everyone biologically related in considered kin. The basis of kinship is the the family, a cooperative unit of blood relatives that comes into existence through marriage and biological reproduction.

Forms of Marriage

Obviously, the forms of marriage are different in different societies. But the purpose of marriage is the same: a man and a woman, or various combinations of men and women, live together in a sexual union for the purpose of reproducing and establishing a family. This definition is the traditional one; today it needs to be amended, as increasingly often men and women marry to obtain affection and companionship, and choose to remain childless. Their relationship is defined and sanctioned—that is, permitted and encouraged—by tradition or law. The definition of their relationship includes not only guidelines for behavior in matters of sex but also the particulars of their obligations to their offspring, the way labor is to be divided, and other duties and privileges of marital life.

The two broad subdivisions in forms of marriage are monogamy and polygamy. *Monogamy* is the union of one man with one woman. *Polygamy* is plural marriage, which can be subdivided into *polyandry,* the union of one woman with several men; *polygyny,* the union of one man with more than one woman; and *group marriage,* involving several men with several women.

Bigamy, or double marriage, is illegal in our society. What norms does bigamy violate? Can you suggest any advantages to bigamy?

Historically, monogamy has been the most common form of marriage. Polygyny, the most frequent form of polygamy is practiced today in a number of Muslim nations, primarily in parts of Africa. Polygynous relationships, however, create physical inconveniences; because many children are produced, large houses and a good income are necessary. Therefore, polygyny does not fit into urban industrial societies and will, in all probability, disappear with the spread of industrialization.

Polyandry is an uncommon form of marriage, practiced chiefly in areas where physical existence is difficult and seminomadic. Group marriage, though it exists, has never been practiced consistently in any known society at a society-wide level, although experiments have been intermittently tried.

In many officially monogamous societies an unofficial form of polygamy is practiced. What forms does this polygamy take?

Limitations on Marriage

Every society regulates its members' choice of mates by specifying whom they may marry and whom they may not. All societies, for instance, require that marriage occur outside a particular group, whether it be family, clan, tribe, or village. In our own society, people must not marry close blood relatives such as parents, sisters, brothers, and in some states, first cousins. This procedure is called *exogamy,* or marriage outside the group.

Societies also require that people marry within other specified groups. In simple societies, members must choose their mates from among members of their clan, tribe, or village. In our society, people are encouraged to marry within their own race, religion, and social class. This process is called *endogamy,* or marriage within the group.

Can you think of any reason why the Ptolemaic dynasty of ancient Egypt might have consistently married within the family (brothers to sisters?)

Another limitation on marriage—as well as the primary example of exogamy—is the universal *incest taboo:* prohibition of sexual relations between mother and son, father and daughter, and sister and brother. This taboo has been broken by particular members of past societies—the ancient Egyptians, the Hawaiians, the pre-Columbian Peruvians—and continues to be broken in every society on occasion. Every known society, however, has had clear prohibitions against incest.

Forms of Family

The family may be defined as a social group that has the following features: (1) it originates in marriage; (2) it consists of husband and wife, and children born of the union; (3) in some forms of the family, other relatives are included; (4) the people making up the family are joined by legal bonds, as well as by economic and religious bonds, and by other duties and privileges; (5) family members are also bound by a network of sexual privileges and prohibitions, as well as by varying degrees of emotions such as love, respect, affection, and so on.[8]

The family has existed in two main forms. One is the *extended,* or *consanguine,* family. *Consanguine* refers to blood relationships. The extended family includes a large or small number of blood relatives who live together with their marriage partners and children. The extended family is typical of traditional, agricultural societies, for in these societies, it is advantageous to cooperate in obtaining a secure livelihood. An extended family provides individual members with many psychological advantages, too. Child rearing becomes the responsibility of many members. One person is not saddled with the entire task. Because the child can form affectionate relationships with persons other than his parents, the emotional content of the parent-child relationship is eased. Physical neglect or mistreatment within the confines of the extended family is almost unheard of. But individuality does tend to be stifled because the good of the family unit is always considered before the welfare of the individual. In addition, extended families usually have a well-defined hierarchy of authority, and the individual is subservient to that authority. For instance, extended families are often *patrilocal* (all married sons reside with father) and daughters-in-law are lowest in status and subjected to mistreatment until they produce sons.

The other form of family is the *nuclear,* also called the *conjugal,* form.

---

[8]Levi-Strauss, in Skolnick and Skolnick, p. 56.

A nuclear family consists of the nucleus of father, mother, and their children. For the children, such a family is *consanguine* because they are related to their parents by blood ties. For the parents, such a family is one of *procreation,* because their relationship does not depend on blood ties but on having produced children.

The nuclear family is usually the product of urban industrial societies, in which there is significant geographical mobility. This kind of mobility promotes situations in which relatives are left behind in rural areas while new families are established in urban centers. In an industrial economy, opportunities for social mobility are also greater. An upwardly mobile individual tends to break the ties binding him to an extended family, especially if that family is of a low social class.

Leaving the nuclear family is often encouraged as a step toward maturity in our society. What social values are involved in the encouragement of such a break?

Another reason why the nuclear family is typical of industrial societies is that functions originally performed by primary groups have been transferred to secondary groups. A large family group is not essential. Many functions of the family institution—protection, education, health care, money lending and so on—have also been taken over by separate institutions. Finally, in an industrial society, achieved status is more important than is ascribed status. What a person does through his own effort is usually considered more important than his family's social position. These, at least, are some of the conclusions of sociologist William Goode, who analyzed extensively the many changes in family structure that followed industrialization in the United States, Europe, Japan, India, China, Arab Islam, and sub-Saharan Africa.[9]

In China, collective farms and communes have sprung up since the revolution. How might these groups be related to the family?

In the United States, the nuclear family has become the norm following industrialization and urbanization. The nuclear family is compatible with the values of industrial societies and their more open stratification system. Almost all developing nations are trying to industrialize, of course, and the values of industrial societies are spreading throughout the world.

Family Organization

In different societies, families are organized in different ways. Differing patterns have evolved regarding such matters as who holds authority, with whom a newly formed family resides, how transfer of property is accomplished, and what obligations parents and their children have to one another. Families in which authority is vested in the oldest living male are called *patriarchal.* This has been the traditional pattern in both Muslim and Western societies, although in the latter patriarchy is being increasingly challenged. In patriarchal families the father holds great power over wife and children.

Less common are *matriarchal* families, in which the source of authority is the mother. Today, a variation of this form, referred to as *matrifocal* families, is found among the lowest socioeconomic classes of many

[9]William J. Goode, *World Revolution and Family Patterns* (New York: Free Press, 1963).

societies. These families are without a male head of household because the man has left the family or was unable to provide a living. In very few instances have females had authority in both familial and social structures as a normal pattern of behavior.

Today's average American family is in transition from the heavily patriarchal form. Although the mother frequently dominates in the absence of the father, whose occupation keeps him away from home, in reality it is the father whose income and profession largely determine the family's status. The word *egalitarian* is sometimes used to denote the contemporary American family. However, families in which the husband and wife have equal authority seem to be more a future goal than a present reality.

Historically, families have also differed in the way in which they trace descent for the purpose of passing along the family name and determining inheritance. In a *patrilineal* arrangement, family name, inheritance, and other obligations are passed through the male line, or the father's ancestors. In a *matrilineal* arrangement, the opposite is true, and descent is traced through the mother's ancestors. In a *bilateral* arrangement, both parent's lines determine descent and inheritance patterns.

The residence of a newly married couple also varies according to family organization. In the *patrilocal* kind of organization, the couple takes up residence with the husband's parents. In the *matrilocal* kind, the couple resides with the wife's parents. The current trend is toward *neolocal* arrangements, in which the married couple lives away from both sets of parents. Neolocal residence and bilateral descent and inheritance are characteristic of the American family system.

What characteristics of industrial society would lead one to predict a neolocal family arrangement in the United States?

Family Functions: Old and New

Since the family is one of the earliest human institutions, it is probable that at one time it performed almost all of the functions that facilitated survival. Today, family functions are much reduced. The family in traditional, nonindustrial societies is the fundamental economic unit—it both produces and consumes goods and services needed for the survival of members. In urban, industrial societies, however, the family has become strictly a consuming unit. In the past, religion and education were the responsibility of the family; today other institutions have taken over these tasks. Recreation, protection of members, health care, and care of the aged are other family functions that have largely been replaced by other institutions.

Which functions have been retained by the family, then? The family theoretically still attends to the regulation of sex; that is, it sees to it that sexual relations take place between persons who have legitimate access to each other—access sanctioned by society, rather than dependent on chance encounters. Of course, in our society sexual norms are in such a state of transition that sex within the family only is an ideal, and does not reflect reality.

Ensuring the reproduction of the species is another universal function of the family. This function has endured to the present, although in vastly changed circumstances in many countries. These changes represent dramatic decreases in the number of children born to each family, including the decision by some couples to forego parenthood altogether. Pressures stemming from world overpopulation, the women's movement, a preoccupation with individual fulfillment, and improved methods of birth control have all played a part in the decrease.

The family's most important function remains the socialization of its young. Parents play a crucial role in this process, but schools and peer groups have taken over a large part of the transmission of information and attitudes. The family seems to be particularly influential in the selection of mates for dating and marriage, and in determining political behavior.

The provision of affection and companionship is yet another important function retained by the family. The needs for affection and companionship seem to be fundamental human needs. Without affection and companionship, a person may experience emotional and mental problems, and sometimes outright death. Whereas companionship may be found in other groups, it is principally the nuclear family which is responsible for providing affection. This responsibility is sometimes too heavy a burden on families which are unable to sustain an affectionate relationship, particularly in nuclear families where this responsibility falls on a few members.

Finally, one last function which has remained practically unchanged has been the family's provision of status for each new individual. In other words, each newborn baby acquires the ascribed statuses of sex, age, and order of birth, as well as the social, racial, religious, and economic statuses of the parents.

Characteristics of the Contemporary American Family The family institution in the United States acquired its basic forms from the Puritan immigrants who brought with them a monogamous form of marriage, a patriarchal family organization, and a Judeo-Christian religious ideology, in addition to the austere ideas of the Protestant Reformation. However, because our society is so heterogeneous, there is no uniformity in family norms. In addition, many of the past norms are in a state of transition today.

The Liberalization of Sexual Norms In the past decade, sexual norms have been greatly liberalized. Change has taken place, for instance, in the formality of the relationship between two people having intercourse, as shown by a study based on the decade 1958–1968. In 1958, 10 percent of the girls in the sample had intercourse while dating, 15 percent while going steady, and 31 percent while engaged. In 1968, 23 percent had premarital relations while dating, 28 percent while going steady, 39 percent while engaged.[10] More recent research yields much more radical

What norms do you feel should be applied to premarital sex, if any?

[10]Robert R. Bell and Jay B. Chaskes, "Premarital Sexual Experience Among Coeds, 1958 and 1968," *Journal of Marriage and the Family* 32 (February 1970): 81–85.

conclusions, indicating that people are having premarital relations at a younger age than they did in the past.

Such statistics indicate a significant change in premarital sexual behavior patterns. They show the increasing gap between the conventional ideals of the adult world and the actual behavior of both adults and young people. It may be that we are not witnessing the advent of a new morality but honesty about the old morality.

What changes might occur in the family if extramarital sex continues to increase?

Division of Labor and Changing Sex Roles

A common feature of every society has been a division of labor between males and females. Definitions of what is man's work and what is woman's work vary from society to society, but the division itself is visible everywhere. In some societies, sex roles are clearly defined and rigidly enforced. In others, they are generalized and casual.

Women's roles. The definitions of sex roles in different societies are not based on strictly biological differences. The tasks assigned to women revolve around child care, are of a type that can be performed close to home, and are such that they can withstand the frequent interruptions demanded by child care. The tasks assigned to men are generally performed away from home and involve much more adventure and risk taking. The interpretation of sex roles has been a distorted one. Both men and women have believed that men's tasks are superior, more important, and more meaningful than are women's tasks.

Changes in women's roles. Sex roles have also been influenced by economic conditions. For example, the rigid pattern of home-based female sex roles in the United States broke down with the Industrial Revolution and the shift from the home to the factory. Resultantly, today working women make up almost 48 percent of all women in the nation. Of these, 23.3 percent are single, 19 percent are widowed, divorced or separated, 26 percent have husbands who earn below $10,000, and 31.7 percent have husbands earning over $10,000.[11]

What relationship might there be between increased education and an increase in working women?

The new norm seems to be for women to work outside the home for several years prior to marriage, stay at home while children are small, and then return to work until retirement age.

Working wives create several changes in a nuclear family. They want a new method of division of labor, one that is not based on the traditional male and female sex roles. Then there is the problem of child care. In a nuclear family, there are no relatives to care for children. Some couples have experimented by working in six-month shifts so each parent assumes both roles of provider and housekeeper. Day-care centers seem to offer an ideal solution .

Egalitarianism in sex roles is a definite trend, especially among the young. However, in the majority of today's families, there is still an

---

[11]"Women at Work," *Newsweek* (December 6, 1976) pp. 68–69.

important separation of sex-linked roles. Society still defines the mother's role as expressive—as nurturing, comforting, and holding the family together. The father's role is still defined as the instrumental one. It is he who is presumed to provide the major links to the outside world through his occupation, and he who is the provider.[12] If equality of the sexes is to be achieved, these patterns of socialization will have to be broken. The expressive and the instrumental roles will have to be shared equally by both parents.

Minority Status and the Family

Much has been made of the allegedly disorganized condition of the family among minorities, especially blacks, and the poor in general—the high divorce and abandonment rates, the illegitimacy, the mother-headed households, the neglected children, and so on.

Anthropologist Oscar Lewis maintained that capitalist societies encourage the development of a "culture of poverty," in which the poor perpetuate the self-defeating conditions of poverty. The culture of poverty, Lewis believed, was an adaptation and a reaction to the general structure of society in which the poor are forced to live only with hopelessness and despair. There is very little chance that they will achieve success of the sort the society values. Being hopeless and desperate, the poor do not postpone the pleasure of the moment for the sake of some future benefit. As a consequence, the circle of poverty is repeated: they fail to acquire enough education, they fail to obtain well-paying jobs. They find themselves unemployed, in need, and hopeless. The typical family living in a culture of poverty was described by Lewis as possessing the following traits: (1) absence of childhood as a special stage of the life cycle; (2) early experimentation with sex; (3) a high incidence of censensual, or "free," matings; (4) a high proportion of abandonment of wives and children; (5) a tendency toward female or mother-centered households; (6) a strong leaning toward authoritarianism; (7) an attempt at family solidarity that usually fails because of rivalry among members; and (8) much competition for maternal affection and scarce goods.

What do you think is meant by "absence of childhood as a special stage of the life cycle"? What might happen to a person deprived of childhood?

Other sociologists subscribe to a *situational* approach in analyzing the poor family. These sociologists claim that even though the behavior of poor families may not be the same as that of middle-class families, their cultural values are essentially the same. It is just that, being economically and politically deprived, the poor are thwarted in obtaining the same results as the middle-class families. Their actual behavior, then, is simply an adaptation to the conditions of poverty in which they are forced to live. The fact that many generations tend to remain poor is not necessarily a function of cultural transmission. Rather, the reality is that a child is likely to experience, on his or her own, the same failures, for

---

[12] William J. Goode, "Industrialization and Family Structure," in Norman W. Bell and Ezra F. Vogel, eds., *The Family* (New York: Free Press, 1968), p. 71.

the same reasons, as the parents. [13] The poor do not reject the dominant cultural values of their society, but only stretch them to fit their own conditions. They develop an alternative set of values that helps them survive in deprived conditions.[14]

Family Crisis and Reorganization

Families do not always remain together as units. *Family disorganization* is the sociological term for a breakup of the family unit.[15] Sociologists suggest that there are six basic causes for family disorganization or family breakup: (1) illegitimacy; (2) annulment, separation, divorce, or desertion; (3) male-female, parent-child conflicts resulting from changes in the definition of cultural roles; (4) living in an empty-shell family, in which members fail to communicate and give emotional support to one another; (5) external events, such as death, imprisonment, natural catastrophes; and (6) internal events, such as mental and emotional illness, and chronic physical illness.[16] The term *disorganization* is expressive of a value judgment: from whose point of view is a family disorganized? Consequently, we prefer to use a more value-free terminology.

Do you consider your family disorganized or organized? What is your definition and value judgment of disorganization?

Divorce. Family breakup involving divorce is becoming the most common form of family dissolution. It is commonly viewed as a danger to the future of the family. This view is based on religious attitudes, whereby marriage is considered a holy union sanctioned by God and therefore not dissolvable by mortals. Also, our romantic notion that marriage is based on everlasting love makes it difficult to accept the fact that some marriages are temporary.

Any situation in which two individuals, with differing needs and desires and possibly with different values and backgrounds, live together for long periods of time produces some tension and conflict. These tensions frequently destroy marriages, especially if expectations have been too high. In some societies, particularly those in which mate selection is a family affair, the expectations of what the partners are to find in marriage are not great. Members of such societies value the kinship network over the husband-wife relationship. They consider some irritations and conflicts in marriages as unavoidable. Because of the romantic ideas that surround mate selection in our society, expectations of marital happiness are very high. A spouse is expected to fulfill all of our needs for affection, security, companionship, and so on. It is a small wonder that many marriage partners fail to live up to such expectations.

What expectations do you, or would you, have of a marriage partner?

Divorce American style. The high rates of divorce in urban industrial

[13]Elliot Liebow, *Tally's Corner* (Boston: Little, Brown, 1967)

[14]Hyman Rodman, "The Lower-Class Value Stretch," *Social Forces* 42 (December 1963): 205–215.

[15]William J. Goode, "Family Disorganization," in Robert K. Merton and Robert Nisbet, eds., *Contemporary Social Problems* (New York: Harcourt Brace Jovanovich, 1971), p. 468.

[16]Goode, in Merton and Nisbet, p. 469.

Marriage and Divorce Rates per 1,000 Population

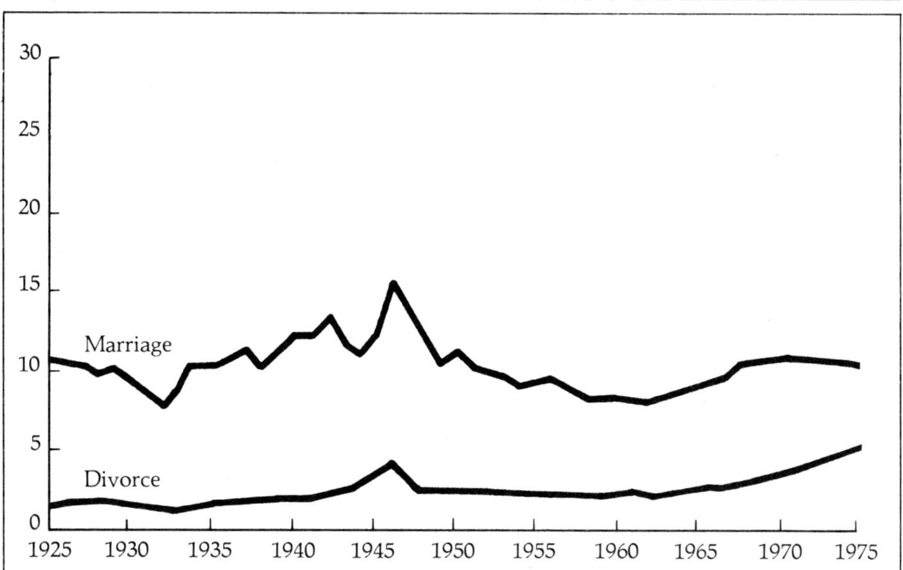

SOURCE: Adopted from U.S. Bureau of Census, *Statisical Abstract of the United States: 1974*, 95th edition, (Washington, D.C., 1974) p. 52.

societies reflect (1) the separation of marriage from religion; (2) the emancipation of women; and (3) the change in values to a new emphasis on individuality and personal happiness. Among Western nations, the United States has one of the highest divorce rates (one out of every four marriages ends in divorce). The majority of divorces are granted to young people (20 to 35 years old), who have been married a short time and who were married when the wife was a teen-ager. Some 6 percent of married couples have been married three or more times. In 80 percent of the cases both partners will remarry, indicating that divorce occurs more frequently among couples who remarry. At the same time, the fact that couples do remarry indicates that it is not the institution of marriage that is spurned, but the individual partner. Marriage itself is a highly prized status. The frequency of divorce and remarriage has led analysts of the family to call the institution "serial marriage" or "throwaway marriage." Such terms reflect the nature of our society with its habits of indiscriminate consumption and indifference to the environment.

Do you feel you would ever get divorced? For what reasons would you divorce a husband or wife?

According to one sociologist, divorce occurs most often among people in particular situations and with particular backgrounds: (1) they live in urban areas; (2) they married at sixteen to nineteen years of age; (3) they married after a short period of acquaintance or after a short engagement; (4) they grew up with a poor model of marriage presented by their parents; (5) they are nonchurchgoers or of different faiths; (6) their marriage evoked disapproval from their family and friends; (7)

Do you feel divorce is an admission of failure? Why or why not?

their backgrounds are dissimilar; and (8) they have differing definitions of their role obligations.[17] Research data also indicate that marriage instability is inversely proportional to socioeconomic status. In other words, those at the low end of the stratification system, as measured by income and status of profession, have the highest rate of divorce. The reasons for this are not entirely clear. It is possible, however, that husband and wife are dissatisfied with both the quality of the husband's job and its economic rewards. This dissatisfaction leads to severe tension in the marriage.[18]

The legal grounds on which divorces are obtained range from cruelty, which has come to mean incompatibility (60 percent of all divorces), to desertion (17 percent), adultery, drunkenness, and failure to provide a living. The real causes for divorce are difficult to determine because the reasons given by marriage partners are frequently superficial. There are often underlying causes of which they may or may not be aware. Women tend to give such reasons as nonsupport, adultery, gambling, drunkenness, and desertion. Men tend to complain about unsatisfactory sexual relations, or frigidity in their wives. And both tend to use lack of affection as justification for divorce.

Do you feel that people should get divorced if they have children? Explain your answer.

One effect divorce has on the family, besides the breakup of a partnership, is that children are being increasingly raised in single-parent homes, or have multiple parents. Children are no longer the deterrent to divorce that they were in the past. Statistics indicate that in the decade from 1953 to 1963, the number of children of divorced parents increased by 77 percent. Today, more than 10 million children are living with only one parent, (one of seven lives without a father) and 2 out of 3 of them are products of divorced or separated parents.

The American Family: Change or Decay?

Any discussion of the institution of the family provokes controversy. Some people believe that it stifles individuality. Others think that society cannot exist without it. Many deplore the high divorce rate, sexual permissiveness, the stress on youth, glamour, and the pleasures of the senses, and the declining birth rate. Others have interpreted the changes in family structure as functional—appropriate to today's urban industrial society. Some, though admitting that the family is in a state of disorganization, believe that this condition is only a prelude to change.

Where does all this leave us? Whose theory are we to accept? Will the American family withstand the onslaught of change, or will it collapse and drag the whole society down with it? There are no pat answers. A great deal depends on individual values. People who value a stable, well-disciplined society, in which there is emphasis on the welfare of the group, must be appalled at the changes taking place in the

[17]Goode, in Merton and Nisbet, pp. 500–501.
[18]William J. Goode, *Women in Divorce* (New York: Free Press, 1965), chapters 4 and 5.

family. People whose chief goal is personal fulfillment think the family is changing in the right direction.

In trying to predict the shape and form of the future family, social scientists have engaged in fascinating speculations. If current trends reach their logical conclusion, the family in 1990 may have these characteristics:

1. Parenthood will no longer be considered "fun" and every couple's duty or right; rather, procreation will be subject to communal control, a fact that will automatically wipe out illegitimacy.
2. The roles of husbands and wives will be finally and inevitably equalized among the majority of people, although there may remain a minority of traditionalists who prefer the old arrangement. New forms of marriage will come into existence, particularly forms that individuals themselves contract for. Trial marriages for three or five years will be an additional option, as will permanently childless marriage.

In what ways would you like to see the family change?

[Religion]

Some form of religion is found in every society that we know about. Religion is universal because human beings do not live by bread alone, as the saying goes. People have consistently refused to believe that they might be a sheer accident of fate whose lives and deaths matter to no one except a small circle of people. This refusal has led people to conceive of themselves as part of a system that includes them, but that also transcends them. In this system, or cosmos, there is harmony, justice, and purpose. Central to this system is the promise that in the end everything will turn out all right. Historically, religion has provided people with a framework for expressing their intuition of the cosmic experience.

Religion: A Response to the Human Condition

The first characteristic of the human condition is that we live in perpetual uncertainty. We do not know how or when our safety and welfare may be jeopardized. Death and catastrophe are always at our side. The human condition, then, is distinguished by its uncertainty, its contingency.

What relation may religion have to the characteristics of the human condition described here?

Another characteristic of the human condition is that our ability to control our environment is limited. At some point, our condition becomes one of powerlessness.

A third characteristic of the human condition is that because most societies still have economies of *scarcity*, we face relative deprivation and thus frustration. There is never enough to go around. People need some way to adjust to scarcity and to unfulfilled needs.

In the functionalist view, religion acts as a mechanism through which people adjust to the inevitable facts of human existence. Contingency, powerlessness and scarcity, frustration and deprivation, not to mention death, suffering, and coercion, largely direct human lives. But the regular norms of society provide no comfort during these experiences and no guide for correct behavior to circumstances that seem neither just nor meaningful. In short, according to the functionalists, areas in the social structure that fail to provide adequate explanations and guides for behavior under stressful circumstances are breaking points. At these breaking points in the social structure, people reach out beyond their ordinary experience. Through religion they establish a link with the sacred. Additional functions of religion include the following:

Establishment of identity. Through its ritual of worship, religion offers human access to the beyond. In this transcendental relationship, the individual's doubts about his security (What will happen to me?) and his identity (Who am I?) are reassured. Religion contributes to an individual's recognition of his identity not only in relation to the universe but also in a more limited sense, within his own society. Membership in a religious organization, in which people share in the same ritual, helps the individual to define for himself who and what he is. This function is particularly important in times of rapid social change, in which problems of identity are critical. A sociological study of religion in America cautions that an important way in which members of our society establish their identity is by recognizing themselves as Protestants, Catholics, or Jews.[19]

Support of societal norms and values Because socialization is never perfect, deviance from societal norms is frequent. Religion supports the norms and values of established society by making them divine laws. Religion is thus an adjunct of the process of socialization.

What methods of relieving guilt are available in the religions you have experienced?

Relief of guilt. Religion also provides a means of relieving the deviant's guilt, as well as a way for him to become reestablished in society as a law-abiding member. Most religious organizations provide some kind of ritual for the forgiveness of sins, whether through the sacrifice of an animal or through confession. This function is important because the existence of a large number of deviants who cannot reenter society and are forced to live outside it presents a definite threat to a society.

Legitimization of power. The supportive function of religion is vital to social control and to the maintenance of the status quo. Every society is faced with the necessity of distributing power, for which purpose political institutions emerge. In legitimizing these institutions, the society has to justify the use of physical violence, which underlies power. Religion mystifies the human institution by giving it extrahuman qualities. The phrase "The King wills it" soon bears the same weight as "Thus sayeth the Lord."[20]

---

[19]Will H. Herberg, *Protestant, Catholic, Jew* (Garden City, N.Y.: Doubleday Anchor Books, 1960).

[20]Peter L. Berger, *The Sacred Canopy: Elements of a Sociological Theory of Religion* (Garden City, N.Y.: Doubleday, 1967), pp. 1–92.

Subversion of the status quo. Religion may, conversely, subvert rather than support the status quo. The prophetic function of religion causes the beliefs and values of society to be considered inferior to the laws of God. Because of its subversive function, religion often leads to protest movements and to eventual social change. The prophets of biblical times had such an effect on their society. In modern times, the abolition of slavery and the passage of humanitarian laws for the disadvantaged were caused, in part, by the influence of religion.

Aid in the critical stages of life. Another function of religion is the help it offers the individual in critical stages of his growth and maturation. Psychologists suggest that humans develop through progressive stages. At each stage, the individual is faced with new problems. Religion seems to help people to accept the new roles forced on them. It does this through *rites of passage,* the rituals that have been established around critical times, such as birth, puberty, marriage, and death.

Feeling of power. A final function of religion may be the feeling of power that members of a religious group derive from their special relationship with a superior being. The survival of the Jews as a religious and ethnic group, in the face of severe and repeated persecution, was largely a result of their feeling of being a chosen people.

Not all of these functions are performed by religion in all societies, or at all times, or for all people. Sometimes one function may be more significant than another. In societies that lack scientific knowledge, religion's most important function may be that of explaining the physical and supernatural environment.

What functions has religion performed for you?

Common Features of Religion

Although religious expressions vary greatly from society to society, in their institutionalized form religions have some elements in common.

Beliefs. In almost all known societies there exist religious beliefs, often spelled out in doctrines, or articles of faith. Christian and Jewish beliefs are contained in the Bible, Muslim beliefs in the Koran. Beliefs probably appear after other aspects of religion have become established. Their function is to explain and justify the sacred and the ritual attaching to it. Within religions today, the role of religious beliefs has grown stronger. The role of ritual and the worship of sacred objects has become weaker. In addition, beliefs have been refined and altered not only to make them consistent with scientific evidence but to give them relevance to behavior outside the religious sphere.

Ritual. Ritualized behavior is an important mechanism for maintaining sacredness. Any kind of behavior may become ritualized: dancing, gathering in a specific spot, drinking from a specific container, or eating a particular food. Once something becomes ritualized, the behavior and the objects involved are set apart and considered sacred in their own right. Ritual becomes a very important practice because it is considered to be the correct form of behavior toward the sacred. It eases some of

What types of rituals have you participated in? What did you feel was accomplished by these rituals?

the dread connected with the sacred. By behaving in the prescribed way toward the sacred, people think that they are protecting themselves against supernatural wrath.

Organization

The institutionalization of any societal function requires that it become organized. If religion is to remain effective, leaders must be recruited to make sure that there is always a place available for worship, that ritual is conducted in the proper manner, and that followers treat the sacred with the proper respect. In nontechnological societies, institutions are not highly differentiated, so the family or the political institution (as represented by a chieftain) usually performs these functions. Modern societies have developed a hierarchy of personnel that has the specific responsibility of running religious affairs. The Roman Catholic hierarchy includes priests, bishops, archbishops, cardinals, and the pope, as well as various orders of monks and nuns.

Given what you know of bureaucracy, why do you suppose modern religion has developed such extensive hierarchies?

Structural Organization of Religion

Western societies exhibit a large number of religious groups. Christianity, which is the predominant faith of the West, contains an immeasurable variety of religious expressions. It is useful, therefore, to divide religious organizations into categories. The most frequent classification of religious organizations is into church, sect, and cult.

Churches. In its sociological definition, a *church* is an association that is thoroughly institutionalized and well integrated into the social and economic orders. It seeks out its members according to residence and family. Participation in it is routine. The highly institutional nature of the church includes a hierarchically arranged official body of administrators, an official doctrine or ideology intended to meet most of the problems encountered by members, and a traditional ritual. The church is integrated into the social and economic orders because it retains close ties with the family, the school, the state, and the economy, all of which reflect its teachings.

If the church has a monopoly on religious belief, it is called *universal.* For example, the Catholic Church of Medieval Europe was a universal church. When a substantial majority of, but not the entire, population, profess to be members of a church, that church is called an *ecclesia.* In a society that has an ecclesia, the beliefs and values of the secular, or worldly, social system and those of the religious one are closely related. The Anglican Church in England and the Catholic Church in modern Latin America have great influence in nonreligious areas of life.

In a society that accepts a number of religious organizations on an equal basis, the organizations are known as *denominations.* Denominations are divisions of a faith, such as Protestantism or Catholicism, and have autonomous organizations and differeing practices and doctrines. This kind of religious organization is most familiar to Americans and is particularly characteristic of pluralistic societies. Denominations—Episcopalian, Presbyterian, and Methodist, among others in the Protestant Church, and Orthodox, Conservative, and Reformist in Judaism—coexist in comfort when there is separation of church and state. They are tolerant of other denominations; their membership is hereditary (although, of course, voluntary); and they do not make great demands on their members for religious commitment, but are content with occasional church attendance and financial support.

Sects. A sect differs from a church in several important ways. A *sect* may be formed by a group that breaks away from either the church or from a denomination of the church. Such a group is a revolutionary movement that rebels at the conservatism of the established religious organizations. The sect rejects an official priesthood, preferring to divide religious responsibilities among its lay members. Often, however, a sect has a charismatic leader who makes up for his lack of professional training with his emotional commitment. Commitment and participation by the members is high, and valued. Sects emphasize religious emotions and expression to a far greater degree than do churches. They are also less concerned with the formal and traditional aspects of religion. Church and sect are frequently in conflict. The sect stresses the need for the purity of religious thought and uncompromising faithfulness to the spirit of religion. The church emphasizes the necessity of maintaining a stable institution and faithfulness to the letter of religion.

Cults. The least conventional and institutionalized form of religious organizations—some would deny that it even belongs to that category—is the *cult.* Cults are usually temporary groups of followers clustered around a leader whose teachings differ substantially from the doctrines of the church or denomination, or even from those of the sect. Followers of Father Divine in the past, or those of Maharaj Ji today are followers of cults. Persistent cults often develop into sects. A belief in the supernatural or in a relationship between humans and the sacred are not necessarily part of these organizations. Because membership in cults tends to be drawn from the alienated of society, cults are so small that they do not usually influence the course of society.

Have you ever joined a cult? What kinds of experiences did the cult offer?

Characteristics of Religion in America

Religion in the United States had a peculiar character even before industrialization took place—in fact, from the very beginning of the nation. Except at the start of the colonial period, the United States has never had a state, or national, religion. Instead, numerous religious expressions have coexisted.

One effect of the existence of numerous denominations in the United States is that, like wordly organizations, religious organizations must compete for the attention of the buyer, or prospective member. As a result, religious expression in this country is characterized by much

Cargo Cults

Religious movements that promise collective salvation in this world through a coming reign of peace, prosperity, and justice are known as *millenarian*. The word derives from *millenium*, which originally referred to the thousand-year period during which Christ would rule on earth, as foretold in the Bible's Book of Revelations. Some of the most famous examples of millenarian movements are the "cargo cults" that sprang up among the peoples of Melanesia in response to the impact of an alien (that is, Western) culture. The "cargo" consisted of the strange manufactured items that the white colonizers unloaded from their ships, and later, planes. Unaware of the processes of industrial production, the natives interpreted these items as the long-awaited gifts of their ancestors risen from the grave.

With the establishment of European colonial rule, these cults assumed diverse forms, and like other millenarian movements, flourished among the poor and oppressed as an expression of their desire for liberation. In one section of New Guinea, for example, between 1937 and 1938 a prophet persuaded the natives that their ancestors living in a volcano had manufactured and sent the goods for their benefit, but that the whites had intercepted them for their own use. However, retaliation was imminent, he said, because the ancestors were bringing a new shipment themselves that would expose the whites and end their domination. Many cargo cults contained an implicit, and sometimes explicit, attack on the white plantation system and the practices of the Christian missionaries, according to many anthropologists. The natives wanted the material fruits of the white people, but without their domination.

Vittorio Lanternari, *The Religions of the Oppressed: A Study of Modern Messianic Cults*, trans. Lisa Sergio (New York, Alfred A. Knopf, 1963), pp. 161–190.

more optimism and much less emphasis on self-sacrifice and punishment than it is in other countries. The prosepctive member is more likely to choose a religion that promises him peace of mind and the freedom to enjoy the fruits of his labor than he is to choose a religion that promises him eternal damnation and the need to repress his desire for pleasure. The extent to which religion is sold as a panacea for whatever ails humanity is made apparent by the numerous radio and television shows that "sell" religion in the same breath that they sell pamphlets and other articles that promise to bring salvation. The Gospel as preached by the radio preachers represents an extremely sectarian and marginal religious expression. But it has an audience of hundreds of thousands, as canned and packaged as it is. There is no doubt that whatever is being sold has a market.

Other methods that religion has borrowed from the marketplace include secondary inducement. Church buildings are now used for recreational purposes—people can play cards, and bingo, discuss books and political issues and candidates, and form interest-related clubs. To keep up with the times, churches concentrate on nonreligious activities that are principally family- and child-centered.[21] Today abortion information and drug counseling can be obtained through church-sponsored agencies.

Finally, there is a new ecumenical or unification movement within American Protestantism. This movement has been described in business terms as cartelization, or as mergers of several denominations for the purpose of cornering the religious market.[22] There are even indications that Catholicism and Protestantism may eventually merge. A joint theological commission recently reported that it had reached substantial agreement on the Eucharist, a doctrine flatly rejected by the Anglican Church after its sixteenth-century split from Roman Catholicism. Ecumenicism is designed to minimize religious differences that have been traditionally conflict-producing. It therefore contribues to the standardization of religious expression.

Are you prejudiced against any of the major religions in the United States today? Why or why not?

Religion and Dimensions of Stratification

It is said Christ declared that it is easier for a camel to pass through the eye of a needle than for a rich man to enter the kingdom of God. Ironically, however, Christianity has both initiated and helped to maintain systems of stratification. When the Catholic Church became institutionalized and reached the height of its power in Medieval Europe, it continued to emphasize the basic equality of all men in the eyes of God while retaining the idea that poverty was a virtue. But Catholicism found no contradiction between these ideas and the stratification system in which many lived in dire misery and a few, including the upper echelon of Catholicism's hierarchy, lived in majestic splendor. Relying on the dictum that "The poor will always be with us" and will obtain their reward in an afterlife, the Catholic Church helped maintain a rigid system of stratification that permitted almost no social mobility.

The Protestant Reformation, spurred primarily by the new merchant middle classes, challenged the established views of Catholicism. Protestants believed that God favored those who accumulated wealth through hard work, a belief that, according to Max Weber, gave added force to the emergence of capitalism. The reverse side of this belief is that those who do not accumulate wealth are obviously not in God's grace. Lower-

What social function may have been served by placing a high religious value on poverty?

[21] Berger, in Smelser, pp. 376–375.

[22] Robert K. Merton, Leonard Broom, and Leonard S. Cottrell, eds., *Sociology Today: Problems and Prospects* (New York: Harper & Row, 1959), p. 161.

class characteristics became associated with sin: God did not favor the poor because they were lazy, they drank too much, and had no self-control and no self-discipline. At the same time, middle-class values became established as virtues. Poverty became a condition not to be pitied ana remedied, but to be reprimanded and censured. Protestantism, then, also helped to maintain a system of stratification. But Protestants did leave the door open to social mobility by encouraging the poor to embrace middle-class virtues and rise in the system.

Religious Affiliation and Social Class

In the United States, the relationship between religion and stratification can be seen most clearly in the religious affiliation of different social classes. Americans of highest status—as measured by income, prestige, power, and education—have consistently been Protestant, particularly Episcopalian (Anglican), and Jewish. Those of lowest status have usually been Catholics and members of fundamentalist sects—Baptists, for instance—that broke away from denominational Protestantism.

What roots in the social stratification system do each of the major religions have today?

Although significant class differences among the members of different denominations continue to exist, caution should be used in interpreting the data. In a very general way, Roman Catholicism has been the faith of the urban industrial masses. Protestantism, on the other hand, draws its members from the business and professional communities. Of the Protestant denominations, the Presbyterian and Episcopalian churches attract the educated elite, whereas the Lutheran, Methodist, and Baptist churches attract the urban middle-classes and rural farmers. Small Protestant denominations, such as the Quakers, Congregationalists, Unitarians, and Christian Scientists, tend to attract middle-class and upper-class members on a local basis. Working-class Protestants tend to be attracted by the colorful rituals of radical sects.[23]

[Contemporary Trends]

We have seen that religion has adopted many mechanisms of the marketplace to win and keep supporters. But even though it has employed such methods, the influence of the established, institutional religions is progressively waning. At present, religious influence is felt most strongly within the family institution—in other words, on an individual, rather than on a social level.[24] As a unifying force in society, religion is being displaced by ideologies like nationalism, communism, and democracy.

A large portion of our cultural beliefs, values, and goals are becoming gradually secularized, or separated from religious, or spiritual, influence. Nowhere is this more apparent than in religious festivals,

---

[23] E. Digby Baltzell, "Religion and the Class Structure," in Seymour Martin Lipset and Richard Hofstadter, eds., *Sociology and History: Methods* (New York: Basic Books, 1968), p. 313.

[24] Berger, in Smelser, p. 373.

Methodology: Causal Explanation

When Gerhard Lenski did the research for *The Religious Factor,* his famous study of religion in the Detroit area, he wanted to know whether religious commitment plays a significant role in shaping the everyday lives of contemporary urban Americans. Results from the extensive sample survey Lenski conducted allowed him to find many patterns of association between religious affiliation and depth of religious commitment on the one hand, and secular characteristics of the population on the other. He found, for example, that white Protestant males tended to move higher up in the class structure than did Catholics. Correlations like those between religious affiliation and social mobility, however, do not explain anything; they only show that two phenomena are associated, or matched. In itself, the correlation does not tell us whether religious affiliation has any influence on social mobility. It might be the case that social mobility influences a person's religious affiliation rather than the other way around, or the association might be the result of a third factor, with neither a person's religious affiliation or social mobility having any influence on each other.

To find out whether religion was a significant influence on secular institutions, Lenski had to go one step further in his analyses. He had to establish a probable causal connection rather than just an association between religious affiliation and secular behavior. First, he manipulated his data to exclude other possible causes as explanations of the relationships he found. Next, he attempted to show "a temporal sequence in which religious differences existed *before* differences in secular behavior appear." Finally, Lenski made comparisons of secular behavior within a religious group. If those most involved in their group were more likely than those less committed to act in a way characteristic of the religious group as a whole, this added further weight to his argument. In these steps Lenski could not *prove* a cause-and-effect relationship; what he could do was assemble enough evidence to demonstrate probable cause.

Religion, Lenski concluded on the basis of this analysis, not only influenced the behavior of individuals in a myriad of ways, but it had a significant influence through these individuals on many secular institutions as well. Religious institutions were certainly not the only influence on secular institutions, he said, but they often are "a *necessary* cause of certain patterns observed in secular institutions."

Gerhard Lenski, *The Religious Factor: A Sociological Study of Religion's Impact on Politics, Economics, and Family Life* (Garden City: Doubleday, 1963), pp. 1–34, 319–366.

Do you observe any major religious holidays? Is your observance primarily secular or religious?

which have become nothing but social occasions. The Christian holidays of Christmas and Easter, and the Jewish holidays of Hanukkah and Passover, are increasingly secular. They are occasions for exchanging gifts and eating traditional foods but, for most people, they are almost completely devoid of spiritual meaning. What is more, the norms that were previously invested with religious sanctions have also lost much of their effectiveness. Witness, for example, the nonchalance with which divorces are obtained and sexual activities pursued. Finally, religious beliefs are becoming almost universally a matter of personal choice rather than of social necessity.

Bureaucratization

The denominations most highly institutionalized have met the fate of most other large associations in urban industrial societies. They have become bureaucratized, specialized, and efficient in their administrative functions, particularly in financial matters. Today, denominations have headquarters in downtown skyscrapers and branches in the suburbs. They are, in the words of Harvard professor Harvey Cox, "a perverted form of Christianity, deodorized and afraid of smell."[25] Dehumanized and despiritualized forms of religious expression may help to explain why sectarian religion is flourishing and denominational religion is languishing.

In modern society religious organizations resemble other voluntary associations, offering practical help, and promoting such values as mental health, peace of mind, family togetherness, and even patriotism. Therefore, although religious activity is rather high—as measured by membership in churches—the supernatural, or sacred, facet of religious life is definitely declining.

In spite of the general trends of secularization and bureaucratization discernible in institutionalized religion, some counter trends are equally apparent. A return to more fundamentalist forms of religion, such as that expressed by the Jesus movement, may indicate a need for more emotionalism in religion. The popularity of the human potential movement and of transcendental meditation similarly point to the aridity of institutional religion, and to a desire to put more feeling back into human relationships with the divine.

[Education]

After "Mommy," "Daddy," and "God," the person and place that become most important in an American child's life are "teacher" and "school." In more simple times only a very few felt the need to acquire knowledge formally. Most learned all there was to know, or all they

[25]"Religion in the Age of Aquarius: A Conversation with Harvey Cox and T. George Harris," *Change: Readings in Society and Human Behavior* (Del Mar, Calif.: CRM Books, 1972), p. 211.

needed to know, from their families and other adults with experience in specific matters. But for all of us who have been born in industrial societies, school was as inevitable as the proverbial death and taxes.

The educational institution in the United States is tremendously large and complex, involving not only masses of people (close to 60 million students, about 2 million teachers) but operational expenditures that run in the billions of dollars yearly. Moreover, the institution appears to have been very successful when measured in terms of the literacy of the population and the number of people graduating from high school and, increasingly, from college. Ours is an open, universal educational system that is in sharp contrast to the elitist systems still largely prevalent in other societies. The goal of a universal system is to provide more or less equal educational opportunities to all children in a society, regardless of social class or any other considerations. The aim of an elitist system, on the other hand, is to separate the wheat from the chaff—that is, to educate the more talented or privileged for positions of leadership in which they will obtain more of the resources the society has to offer.

Why do you suppose formal, mass education is characteristic of industrial societies?

Education today, no less than the family and religion, finds itself at a crossroads. Criticism of the institution is pouring in from all sides. There are those who accuse the institution of failing in its most basic function, instilling knowledge in the young. Others point their finger at the limits to knowledge set by short-sighted schools that teach basic skills but fail to teach critical thinking. Some maintain that the schools perpetuate the stratitication system of society by effectively preparing upper-class students for leadership roles and lower-class students for the less desirable roles society offers. Some say schools try to homogenize the students, erasing differences that could enrich individual lives. Others maintain that rather than preparing students from minority and disadvantaged backgrounds to enter the mainstream of society, schools help them retain characteristics that work against upward mobility. Very few seem satisfied with the schools as they are, and almost everyone agrees that change would be of benefit. The dissatisfaction so many feel with this institution stems from the fact that as a society we have demanded too much of it.

Has your experience of education been primarily positive, or negative? What criticisms would you make of the educational institution in our country?

Goals and Functions of Education

What we call education today is the institution—those patterns of behavior, values, and norms—that, fundamentally, functions to transmit the accumulated culture of a society from one generation to the next. The primary vehicle through which this function is accomplished is learning: the new generation must learn from the old. Learning is a process that has several components.

The first component is change. Something must happen to the student as a result of the learning experience. The student should be a different person after the learning experience than he or she was before.

The second component is interaction between the learner and the instructor. The instructor may be a teacher, or another student, or even a teaching device. In any case, the learning experience takes place in a social setting, or within a social system in which people play roles according to the expectations accompanying their statuses. Successful learning therefore depends on a satisfactory social system.

Do you feel that your education has given you an adequate preparation in skills and an adequate amount of information? Explain.

The third component is substance. People learn—or do not learn—"something." This something may be categorized as: (1) information, and (2) skills, such as reading or using tools. An additional category, the capacity to think clearly or to act upon a rational analysis of a problem, should be viewed as a combination of the other two categories, or as the ability to use skills on information, and the other way around.[26]

Learning takes place throughout our lives, in every circumstance. We even learn how to become human. Education in today's society, however, is considered to be formal learning that takes place in schools, or other specialized organizations. Within this formalized learning structure, however, there is no agreement on what to teach. Still, there is general consensus on the following categories of goals for education:

1. Cognitive goals—the schools must teach, and students must learn, basic information and skills.
2. Moral or value goals—the schools should teach, and the students learn, how to be good citizens who hold the proper values for living and participating in a democracy.
3. Socialization goals—the school should make of its students well-adjusted individuals who function well in interpersonal relations.
4. Social mobility goals—the school should act as a potential vehicle for upward social mobility, compensating for the disadvantages of poverty, minority status, or unsatisfactory family background in those instances where the individuals were willing to work hard toward that goal.[27]

What major values do you think education should provide?

Though there may be a consensus on these goals of education, not everyone agrees that the goals are important to the same degree. To some, the cognitive goals are the only ones worth instilling. To others, the socialization goals are of uppermost importance. Still others quarrel about what moral or value goals really are, suggesting that they are ways of maintaining an unacceptable status quo of society.

Manifest and Latent Functions of Education

These generalized goals represent the good intentions of a majority of society. The institution apparently does not achieve most of these goals, since it has been estimated that only about one-third of American students have a successful learning experience. Nonetheless the educational institution performs a number of functions—both intended and

How would you evaluate what constitutes a "successful learning experience"?

---

[26] Sarane S. Boocock, *An Introduction to the Sociology of Learning* (Boston: Houghton Mifflin, 1972), pp. 4–5.

[27] Boocock, p. 6.

unintended—for the society. Among the intended or manifest functions, are:

Transmission of culture. Schools teach a majority of people how to read and write and compute, who founded this country, how the government works, how people live in other countries, what makes the rain fall, and why the sun rises in the east and sets in the west every day. By exposing students to the history and literature of their society—and of Western civilization—the schools help preserve the cultural heritage of the nation. They also point out to students the values, beliefs, and attitudes of the society.

Recruitment and preparation for roles. Schools function to help select, guide, and prepare students for the social and occupational roles they will eventually hold in society. The learning of social roles includes socialization that results in the shaping of the kind of personalities needed for our society. In short, we learn to be competitive, to value success, to work hard, to be conforming. We also learn what we might grow up to *do* in our society. This process is an important function in industrial societies in which occupations are highly specialized and diversified and must be increasingly learned in schools. Schools first familiarize students with the large number of occupations they can choose from and then offer courses to train students for certain occupations as early as the secondary level. Universities and colleges offer such preparation in their professional schools.

Cultural integration. In our society, schools have traditionally reinforced the values and norms of the majority. During the influx of large masses of immigrants, the idea was that children from different backgrounds could learn to become Americans by reciting the pledge of allegiance, by learning to play baseball, by finding out why we celebrate Thanksgiving, and so on. The purpose of such experiences was to give students a common ground, to foster in them a sense of unity, solidarity, and nationhood. Critics of the schools have decried this function in recent years. They maintain that what the schools are actually doing is forcing white, middle-class values and norms on all students. This practice is considered unfair to those students who have been socialized into a different set of norms and values that they consider equally valid. Some representatives of ethnic groups have also criticized attempts to Americanize students, on the basis that these attempts rob children of a rich ethnic heritage.

Innovation. In addition to preserving and disseminating past and present cultural knowledge, schools also function to generate new knowledge. This function consists of searching for new ideas and new methods of research, for innovative techniques, and for inventions designed to solve problems or facilitate life. The mysteries of genes and atoms, as well as many unknown factors of human behavior, are unraveled in university laboratories.

Learning Your Place

Some sociologists and social critics believe the central function of contemporary American schooling is teaching students work discipline, respect for authority, and acceptance of their future places in the class structure. "Contrary to the educational myths propounded by the early school reformers and promoted in our own time," writes one such critic, Stanley Aronowitz, "schools are instruments not of social advancement, but of social stasis. . . . Indeed, the child learns in school. But the content of the curriculum is far less important than the structure of the school itself." Aronowitz sees the school as a kind of microcosm of the class and authority relations of the larger society. As in the general stratification system, authority in the school is hierarchically arranged, with promotion as the reward for what the authorities define as good behavior and performance. Critics like Aronowitz see schools as a sorting process that, beginning at an early age, allocates students through tests, grades, and tracking to future placement in the occupational hierarchy. As Aronowitz puts it, schools are the "traffic police for the prevailing social division of labor."

The primary ideological function schools perform, he believes, is to impress upon the students that their placement and their failure to rise is their own fault, the result of their own lack of effort or intelligence, rather than the fault of the school system. The labels of ability and worth that are assigned to students, and the differential treatment they receive as a consequence, are so pervasive, Aronowitz believes, that most students eventually come to internalize the labels as accurate reflections of themselves.

Stanley Aronowitz, *False Promises: The Shaping of American Working Class Consciousness* (New York: McGraw-Hill, 1973), pp. 69–91.

In addition to these obvious functions of schools, there are other, the so-called "latent functions," which are unintended consequences of the process of education. For example, schools seem to reinforce the stratification system of society. Students are sorted into different categories, theoretically according to ability, and are then channeled into courses that prepare them for different job opportunities. In most cases middle-class students are assigned to academic, college preparatory programs of study, whereas lower-class, black, and other minority students, are assigned to general and vocational study programs. Of course, education can be and often is, used to an individual's advantage. Lower-class and minority students can, with hard work, succeed academically and use their skills to rise in the social class system.

Schools also perform custodial functions. They act as babysitters, keeping children off the streets and away from home for the best part of the day. They also ensure that those under 16 will not enter the job market in competition with adults. This function of schools is also referred to as the "cooling-off" role of schools.

Why is it advantageous to keep teen-agers off the job market? What social conditions does this advantage suggest?

The fact that students are brought together for long periods of time for a minimum of ten to twelve years also contributes to the formation of youth subcultures. Some of these subcultures become deviant, or countercultural. All are very influential on the young and contribute to generational conflicts. At the same time, such constant and continuous interaction between young males and females facilitates the initiation of romantic or sexual relationships that often lead to marriage.

Finally, eduation affects attitudes. Studies indicate that high school graduates are more tolerant of political and social nonconformity than those who did not complete high school. College graduates are more tolerant than high school graduates.[28]

Why might high school students be less tolerant than college students, aside from the possibility that the latter are more educated?

Students in the Classroom

What affects the performance of students in a classroom? Is performance strictly a matter of intellectual ability, or are there other factors that enter into consideration?

The most important determinant of scholastic success seems to be the family. The family is the source of ascribed status: socioeconomic condition, race, and religion. Second, the values, attitudes, and behavior of members of a family have a direct relationship to future academic success.

Socioeconomic status. The best predictor of school performance is socioeconomic status. The higher the socioeconomic status of the family, the higher the achievement of the student. This fact has been established through numerous research projects, and seems to hold true even in the face of such variables as ability and past performance.[29]

The relationship between socioeconomic status and school achievement is tied to other characteristics of the family. For example, families in lower socioeconomic levels tend to be larger. Both parents and older siblings are likely to be at work most of the day. And the verbal skill of the parents is probably limited. The lower-class child consequently faces

---

[28]Burton R. Clark, *Educating the Expert Society* (San Francisco, Chandler, 1962), pp. 27–30. See also Gertrude Jaeger Selznick and Stephen Steinbert, *Tenacity of Prejudice* (New York: Harper & Row, 1969).

[29]See Patricia Sexton, *Education and Income* (New York: Compass Books, 1964), pp. 25–30; Robert Havighurst et al., *Growing up in River City* (New York: John Wiley & Sons, 1962); and J. S. Davie, "Social Class Factors and School Attendance," *Harvard Educational Review* 23 (1953): 175–185.

What attitudes toward education have been instilled in you by your family?

What institutions in our society are most responsible for inequality, in your opinion?

school with a verbal skill disadvantage right away.

Middle-class families communicate to their children a view of life that encourages occupational success. Such success is thought to be possible only through educational success and children in such families tend to work harder in school. Lower-class families, aware of their lack of opportunities, value education less as an avenue for upward mobility.

Middle-income families place more stress on self-direction. Children are expected to control their behavior and to explore the world around them, finding out how things work. Lower-class parents want their children to conform and obey the rules of various authorities, and to appear "good"—be well-groomed, well-mannered, and obedient. Lower-class parents also punish their children more frequently for disobeying rules, whereas middle-class parents punish what they perceive as a loss of self-control by the child.[30] These different expectations of parents produce different results in how their children learn.

Some have challenged the relationship between socioeconomic status and scholastic achievement on the basis that America is becoming a middle-class society, and that middle-class values permeate the entire society as a result of the mass media. Differences in income persist, however. A lower-class family with middle-class aspirations still lacks the funds to enter a middle-class way of life. In a number of studies on school dropouts, the prevalent reason given for quitting school was the need to get a job. Although scholarships and educational grants have been increased after the urban disturbances of the sixties, congressional investigations brought to light the correlation between poverty and high mortality rates, nutritional deficiencies, disease and mental retardation, and the probability of suffering rat bites. It seems unrealistic to expect high scholastic achievement when one has to battle such obstacles first.

Race and ethnicity. The other characteristic of ascribed status that the family confers on its children and that is related to school performance is race and ethnicity. This variable is highly correlated to socioeconomic status. In our society, most members of racial minority groups are also located at the lower extremity of the stratification system. We will not concern ourselves here with the interracial differences in ability and intelligence, a subject which has raised much controversy but little conclusive evidence. We will concentrate on the effect of belonging to a racial or ethnic minority group on the goal of "making it" in school.

The most exhaustive research study on the relationship between race or ethnicity and school performance was that initiated by Coleman and his associates. Actually, the Coleman report attempted to pinpoint the differences between schools attended by whites and those attended by racial or ethnic minorities. The report analyzed data involving more than 600,000 children and 60,000 teachers in 4,000 schools. The report concluded that the differences between schools attended by white and those

[30]M. L. Kohn, "Social Class and the Exercise of Parental Authority," *American Sociological Review* 24 (1959): 352–366.

attended by minority students were quite few in terms of physical facilities, curricula, and quality and quantity of teachers. In fact, there was more variation in achievement within the same school than between schools, and this variation was accounted for primarily by family background. Incidentally, the findings of this study showed substantial differences between the achievements of racial groups.

Having established the existence of interracial differences, Coleman and his associates proceeded to conduct further research to find out the reason for the differences. Their findings may be summarized in the following terms:

1. Even if minority children (particularly blacks and Puerto Ricans) value education and achievement they are less likely to be successful students.
2. A sense of control of their own environment is less characteristic of minority group children.
3. Successful students tend to have a high sense of control over their environment.

In short, minority group children believe it is not in their power to make it . . . and consequently they seldom do make it.

Do you feel your ethnic background has affected your attitude toward education? In what ways?

Most studies attempting to relate race or ethnicity to school performance conclude that socioeconomic status, rather than race and ethnicity, is the determining factor in school performance. One carefully designed study, however, points otherwise. The research design of this study calls for breaking down test performance into several areas, on the hypothesis that social class and ethnic influences encourage or discourage different intellectual skills in different environments. The authors of the test concluded—after replicating the experiment in another city, with another sample—that while social class and ethnic-racial group membership affect the level of performance, it is ethnicity that encourages the development of certain ability patterns. These mental patterns persist in spite of the socioeconomic status of the respondent, the only difference being that the higher that status, the better the performance. The researchers believe that specific subcultural groups in society foster special potentials and skills in their members. We should not expect, therefore, that uniform modes of education have uniform results for all.[31]

The vicious circle. If family background, and especially socioeconomic status, determine student achievement, what good is equal opportunity in education? Of what value are the numerous federal programs designed to improve the quality of the schools with the ultimate aim of bettering the educational experience of students so they can achieve academically and eventually rise in the social system? Of very little value, concluded Harvard sociologist Christopher Jencks and seven of his colleagues, in their book *Inequality.* [32] The basic point the authors make is that even if all students could achieve academically equally well, in equally good schools, they could not go on and obtain equally good jobs. Consequently, social inequality would still not be erased. Economic success, argue the authors, is not a result of the kind of schooling a person receives. Rather, much of it is due to luck and to other subtle differences in personality that are difficult, if not impossible, to measure. The authors make such definite statements as: ". . . the evidence suggests that equalizing educational opportunity would do very little to make adults more equal"; ". . . the character of a school's output depends largely on a single input, namely the characteristics of the entering children"; and ". . . everything else—the school budget, its policies, the characteristics of the teachers—is either secondary or completely irrelevant."[33]

This work has been the subject of much controversy and criticism, principally because it has been interpreted by political conservatives as indicating that we might as well stop trying to make our schools as effective as they possibly can be. Income equalization is of course not the primary function of schools, nor their goal. Still, even Jencks has to admit that college graduates earn at least twice as much as those who do not attend high school, so that there is *some* relationship between education and income, whatever the origin of the differences. And James Coleman, the author of the original research that concluded that the

---

[31]S. S. Stodolsky and G. S. Lesser, "Learning Patterns in the Disadvantaged," *Harvard Educational Review* 37 (Fall 1967): 546–593.

[32]Christopher Jencks, et al., *Inequality: A Reassessment of Family and Schooling in America* (New York: Basic Books, 1972).

[33]Jencks et al., pp. 255, 256.

quality of schools had little to do with academic success, still maintains that:

For those children whose family and neighborhood are educationally disadvantaged, it is important to replace this family environment as much as possible with an educational environment—by starting school at an earlier age, and by having a school which begins very early in the day and ends very late. . . . This implies new kinds of educational institutions with a vast increase in expenditures for education—not merely for the disadvantaged, but for all children.[34]

Trends

American education has had a phenomenal rate of growth during this century. There is no reason to believe that this trend will reverse itself. But while more and more people go through the educational system, fewer and fewer of them seem to be learning even the most basic of skills. A 1970 Harris Poll showed that 18.5 million Americans 16 years or older could not fill out basic forms such as an application for a Social Security number, application for a driver's license, application for a personal bank account, and application for medical aid. Another poll initiated by the National Assessment of Educational Progress found that 17 percent of the nine-year-olds it tested could not understand a short passage made up of the simplest words. Twenty-nine percent of 13-year-olds could not make out the simplest road map. Fourteen percent of young adults aged 26 to 35 could not read a recipe for making muffins. In the Los Angeles area, a county grand jury found that only one in five of the graduates from four inner city high schools can read at an acceptable level, while more than half of the graduates are almost totally illiterate. The educational institution seems to be failing its function of transmitting basic skills to a significant proportion of the population.

Why are the three R's—reading, writing, and arithmetic—such important skills in a highly technological society?

A variety of reforms have been suggested. Some people have proposed that we "deschool" society, that is, remove the compulsory aspect of education and let only those who want to go to school. As appealing as that idea sounds, it is probably impractical. We cannot unmake our society and return to the era of the horse and buggy. We live in a complex industrial society in which we need to know how to read and write and simple mathematical concepts just to survive. Innovative and experimental programs in traditional schools, as well as open classrooms and free schools have also been tried in almost every school district. These have helped some students. However, the institution of education in America is being affected by the same social revolutions as is the rest of society. These revolutions are proceeding at such a pace that no one can extrapolate from today what tomorrow will bring.

Have you ever participated in an experimental educational program? What were its goals and methods? Did you feel it was successful?

[34]James S. Coleman, "Equal Schools or Equal Students?" *The Public Interest* 4 (Summer 1966), p. 70.

[Summary]

The term "institution" in sociological language refers to traditional patterns of behavior that surround important human functions. Pivotal institutions include the family, religion, education, the economy, and government. Institutions are durable, although they change and fluctuate; they are interdependent; they are in continuous tension between stability and change; and they represent abstract concepts of organized habits and standardized ways of doing things.

The institution of the family is in a state of transition, and is torn between critics who accuse it of having outlived its usefulness and those who maintain that it needs to return to a former, traditional form.

The family appears to be a universal institution although its form has varied from time to time and from society to society. Most societies accept the concept of kinship—a social way of specifying who is related to whom. The basis of kinship is the family—a cooperative unit of blood relatives that comes into existence through marriage and reproduction. Monogamy—marriage of one man and one woman—has been the most common form of marriage. Polygamy—plural marriage—and especially polygyny—union of one man with more than one woman—has also been an accepted form of marriage in some societies. Societies regulate their members' choice of mates by specifying whom they may or may not marry.

The family is defined as a social group that originates in marriage. It consists of husband, wife, and their children, and sometimes includes additional relatives. The members of a family are joined by legal, economic, and religious bonds as well as by a network of sexual privileges and prohibitions, and such emotions as love, respect, affection, and so on.

The two primary forms of the family are the extended or consanguine—which includes a number of blood relatives who live together with their marriage partners and children, and the nuclear or conjugal—which consists of father, mother, and their children alone. Industrial societies have typically adopted the nuclear form of the family.

Families are also organized into patriarchal form, in which the father holds a great deal of authority; matriarchal form, in which the mother holds most of the power; and egalitarian form, in which power and authority are shared between the marriage partners. The patriarchal form has been traditional in Western societies, although the trend today is toward the egalitarian form.

At one time the family performed all the functions necessary for the survival of the individual, but presently the functions of the family have been greatly reduced. The family still retains the functions of regulating sex, ensuring reproduction, socializing the new generations, providing affection and companionship, and establishing the individual's status in society.

The American family was originally molded in the image of our austere Puritan ancestors. Today, because we are a heterogeneous society, there is little uniformity in family norms which are in a period of transition. In the last few decades, we have witnessed the liberalization of sex norms, changing sex roles with increasing numbers of women working outside the home and, consequently, a trend toward a new division of labor. However, these new norms have still not stabilized.

Many American families appear to be disorganized in the sense that they do not remain ideal, nuclear units. Poor and minority families are particularly subject to breakup by divorce or abandonment. Such problems are not attributable to a different value system from that of middle-class America, but rather from a response and adaptation to economic and political deprivation.

Family crises occur because of illegitimacy, annulment, separation, divorce or desertion, or from various forms of conflict and external events. The most common form of family dissolution is currently divorce, a fact which is disturbing to many who feel that it portends the fall of the family institution. The high divorce rate in industrial societies has been attributed to the fact that marriage is no longer viewed in religious terms, to the increasing emancipation of women, and to the change in values to include a new emphasis on individuality and personal happiness. Most divorces occur among the young who have been married a short time, among those who grew up with poor models of marriage, and among those who have dissimilar backgrounds and definitions of roles. In addition, the highest rates of divorce appear at the lowest end of the stratification system as measured by income, status, and profession. However, marriage is a prized status and most divorced couples remarry.

Whatever one's feelings toward the family institution, most agree that it is in a state of transition. The family of the future may bear little resemblance to the family of today.

Religion in some form has been a characteristic of every society. The human need for religion has existed through the ages because the human condition has always been distinguished by contingency, powerlessness, and scarcity. Since the regular norms of society provide no adequate explanation or comfort against these negative aspects of the human condition, religion acts as a mechanism through which people can cope. It does so by allowing people to reach out beyond their ordinary experience to establish a link with the sacred.

In addition to this basic function, the religious institution also aids in the establishment of an identity, in the support of societal norms and values, in relieving guilt, in subverting the status quo, in offering support at the critical stages of life, and in helping to attain feelings of power for the members. The common features of religions everywhere include beliefs, ritual, and organization. In Western societies, religious groups are organized into churches, sects, or cults.

In the United States, numerous denominations coexist side by side. Religion in our society tends to be stratified. This is exemplified by the fact that those of highest status tend to be Protestants, especially Episcopalians, while those belonging to lower social classes tend to be Catholics and members of fundamentalist Protestant sects. However, these are only generalizations which may change with other future trends of religious institutions. Such trends include a progressively waning influence of the established, institutional religions while there is a revival of interest in the more personal, fundamentalist forms of religion. Today, a heavy bureaucratization renders many churches indistinguishable from other voluntary organizations with secular goals.

Education is the institution in charge of transmitting the knowledge of the past and present generations to the new generations. In the past this function too was performed by the family, but today there is too much knowledge of a specialized nature for families to transmit. The educational institution in the United States involves tremendous numbers of people since its goal to provide equal educational opportunities to all the children in the society. This goal has not been realized, and the criticism regarding the functioning of the educational institution is getting increasingly louder.

The mechanism of education is learning which consists of change, interaction, and substance. Most people would agree that the young should acquire cognitive facts and skills, moral ideals, socialization abilities, and should use education as a vehicle toward upward social mobility.

These goals are not always achieved, but education does perform other manifest functions, such as transmitting culture, recruiting and preparing the young for occupational roles in the society, integrating children of various cultural backgrounds into living according to the "American way," and acting as an innovator in the society through the generation of new knowledge gathered through research.

Education also performs functions that are latent. These functions are not intended, but accidental. For instance, schools seem to reinforce the stratification system of society by dividing students into different tracks which prepare them for different roles; schools also perform custodial functions by keeping children off the streets and ensuring that they will not enter the job market; schools aid in the creation of youth subcultures and bring young men and women together for sex and marriage; finally, schools affect people's attitudes—as those with more education appear to be more tolerant and liberal than those with fewer years of schooling.

Who succeeds in our schools? It seems that the family is the most important determinant of scholastic success, and specifically, the higher the socioeconomic status of the family, the higher the achievement of the student. This relationship has been proven by many studies and has withstood a number of challenges. Since socioeconomic status is correlated to race and ethnicity in our society, it follows that minority students do not fare as well in our educational system as do white students, especially middle-class whites. Busing to achieve racial integration and other head-start-type programs of recent years have been an attempt to remedy the obstacles of race, class, and culture. Their success, however, has not been overwhelming.

The educational institution has grown at a rapid rate in size and specialization in the last several decades, and this trend shows no sign of abating. Nonetheless, it seems certain that the institution will have to undergo several transformations in tune with the social changes affecting the rest of society in order to once again be effective.

Terms to Remember

Institutions. Patterns of behavior, or habits in the form of mores, folkways, and laws that have clustered around particular human functions. Members of society are expected to follow them to simplify their lives.

Monogamy. A form of marriage consisting in the union of one man with one woman.

Polygamy. Plural marriage.

Exogamy. Marriage outside the group.

Endogamy. Marriage within the group.

Incest taboo. Prohibition of sexual relations between mother and son, father and daughter, and sister and brother.

Extended family. A form of family common in traditional societies. It includes a number of blood relatives together with their marriage partners and children.

Consanguine. The extended family; the nuclear family as it appears to children who are tied to their parents by blood ties.

Nuclear, or conjugal family. A form of family consisting of father, mother and their children.

Patriarchal. A family organization in which authority is vested in the oldest living male.

Matriarchal. A family organization in which authority is vested in the mother.

Egalitarian. A future goal of family organization in which authority will be vested equally in the mother and the father.

Family disorganization. A breakup of the family unit as a result of the failure of one or more members to perform his role adequately.

Religion. A system of beliefs and rituals dealing with the sacred.

Contingency. A characteristic of the human condition, whereby people live in perpetual uncertainty.

Powerlessness. Another characteristic of the human condition, whereby people's ability to act is limited.

Scarcity. A third characteristic of the human condition, which results in frustration.

Rites of passage. Rituals established around critical times of growth and maturation: birth, puberty, marriage, and death.

Ritual. Behavior that follows the creation of sacredness and provides a mechanism for maintaining the sacred.

Church. A religious association that is institutionalized, well-integrated into social and economic life, and in which participation is routine.

Denomination. A subdivision of the church, considered equally as valid as the church.

Sect. A revolutionary movement that breaks away from the church or from one of its denominations. It stresses the spirit, rather than the letter, of religion.

Cult. The least conventional and least institutionalized of the religious organizations. It consists of groups of followers clustered around a leader whose teachings differ substantially from the doctrines of the church or denomination.

Education. The formal aspect of socialization in which a specific body of knowledge and skills is deliberately transmitted by a corps of specialists.

Transmission of culture. The chief function of education.

Dissemination, innovation and preservation. The functions of education that foment social change at the same time that they conserve the traditional cultural heritage.

Recruitment and preparation for social and occupational roles. The functions of education through which schools both prepare students for occupational roles in terms of actual training and select them for specific roles more or less according to ability.

Integration. A function of education in which subcultures are integrated into the mainstream of society and given a shared cultural identity and purpose.

Suggestions for Further Reading

Bell, Robert R. *Marriage and Family Interaction.* Homewood, Ill.: The Dorsey Press, 1971. The latest edition of a text that examines exhaustively, yet in a readable manner, the subject matter of marriage and the family.

Benson, Leonard. *The Family Bond.* New York: Random House, 1971. Another basic text, with a particularly fine last section on the past and future of the family institution.

Gordon, Michael. *The Nuclear Family in Crisis.* New York: Harper & Row, 1972. A collection of essays exploring the communal alternatives to the nuclear family.

Lemasters, E. E. *Parents in Modern America.* Homewood, Ill.: Dorsey, 1970. The parental role analyzed from a sociological point of view.

Roszak, Betty and Theodore Roszak. *Masculine-Feminine: Readings in Sexual Mythology and the Liberation of Women.* New York: Harper & Row, 1970. A collection of readings on the feminist movement.

Scanzoni, John. *Sexual Bargaining.* Englewood Cliffs, N.J.: Prentice-Hall, 1972. A readable paperback in which the author contends that modern marriage is neither collapsing nor passé.

Skolnick, Arlene S. and Jerome H. Skolnick, eds. *Family in Transition.* Boston: Little, Brown, 1971. An excellent collection of essays on all aspects of the family.

Suggestions for Further Reading

Berger, Peter L. *A Rumor of Angels: Modern Society and the Rediscovery of the Supernatural.* New York: Doubleday, 1969. A famous sociologist theorizes that religion is of great importance even in this age of science and rationalism, because many human experiences can be understood only in terms of a belief in the supernatural.

Comstock, W. Richard, ed. *Religion and Man: An Introduction.* New York: Harper & Row, 1971. An overview of religious phenomena as social and historic facts appearing in human cultures.

Cox, Harvey. *The Feast of Fools.* New York: Harper & Row, 1969. The need for festivity, fantasy, and mysticism in human life and in religion.

Glock, Charles Y., and Rodney Stark. *Religion and Society in Tension.* Chicago: Rand McNally, 1965. Much survey research analyzed to show the strain between today's culture and religious values.

Herberg, Will. *Protestant, Catholic, Jew.* New York: Doubleday, 1960. A comparative historical account of our three major religions, showing that religion is particularly important to Americans as a means of establishing their identity.

Lenski, Gerhard. *The Religious Factor.* New York: Doubleday, 1963. An important sociological work showing the relationship of religious participation and membership to class, politics, and life styles.

Lessa, William A., and Evon Z. Vogt. *Reader in Comparative Religion.* New York: Harper & Row, 1972. A comprehensive collection of readings on the general subject of religion from anthropological and sociological perspectives.

Becker, Ernest. *Beyond Alienation: A Philosophy of Education for the Crisis of Democracy.* New York: Braziller, 1969. The past and present of education is examined, and an alternative for the future is offered by the author.

Boocock, Sarane S. *An Introduction to the Sociology of Learning.* New York: Houghton Mifflin, 1972. An exhaustive, but readable, compendium of the latest research in the sociology of education.

Caplow, Theodore, and Reece McGee. *The Academic Marketplace.* New York: Doubleday Anchor Books, 1965. A view of the institutions of higher learning, detailing the "publish or perish" syndrome and other particulars of making it at the university level.

Jencks, Christopher, et al. *Inequality.* New York: Basic Books, 1972. A controversial book that argues that the power of education to cause upward mobility is limited.

Koerner, James. *Who Controls American Education?* Boston: Beacon, 1969. The takeover of education by small administrative groups furthering their own interests rather than the students'.

Litcher, S., et al. *The Dropouts.* New York: Free Press, 1968. High-school students who become the victims of our educational jungle.

Sexton, Patricia Cayo. *The American School: A Sociological Analysis.* Englewood Cliffs, N.J.: Prentice-Hall, 1967. The major issues in American education presented with a wealth of relevant details from research done by the author and others.

Pivotal Institutions

Economics and Government

THE ECONOMY IS one of the five pivotal institutions of human societies. It is a pattern of behavior, a customary way of doing things to satisfy universal human needs. The human needs, in this case, are those essential for survival: the need for food, shelter, and clothing. Food, shelter, and clothing are resources that are not abundantly found in most human societies. They are scarce resources that people must gather, or collect, or hunt, or make. The habits that evolve around the gathering, collecting, hunting, or making of resources necessary for survival are the economy.

The economic institution functions to tell each new generation how to produce, distribute, and consume the scarce and finite resources of the society so that they can be used most efficiently by the members. It is a system of behavior through which individuals in society make decisions and choices aimed at satisfying their needs and combating the problem of scarcity.

[The Sociology of Economics]

The study of the structure, functions, and general working of the economy is a task of economics, a social science. Why, then, are we concerned with the economy here? Simply because the term *the economy* is only an abstract concept that in reality represents specific relationships among people and groups of people. The relationships of people in the orbit of the economy span such interactions as those between employer and employee, store owner and customer, producer, wholesaler, and retailer, labor unions and industry, the Internal Revenue Service and the individual taxpayer, and so on. Anytime we deal with relationships among people, we find ourselves in the realm of sociology.

In addition to the structure of relationships that revolve around economic activities, there is another structure of relationships in society that revolves around the need to make authoritative decisions for the society. This is the structure that exists in the political order. Relationships in the political order are those between a ruler and his subjects, a candidate and the voters, government agencies and the industries they regulate, or the Internal Revenue Service and the individual taxpayer. Some relationships are the same in both the economic and the political orders. The two affect each other and frequently overlap. Sometimes, or in some societies, they are one and the same institution. In most traditional societies and in communist nations, the economic order depends totally on the political order. Political authorities make economic decisions in these societies. In most modern industrial societies, the two orders are closely interrelated, the political order regulating and supplementing the actions of the economic order.

Economic Decision Making

Using current magazines and newspapers, develop a list of leaders who have both economic and political power.

In a modern industrial society economic and political power are often interchangeable. The individual who has a powerful position in the political order can make decisions that affect and perhaps determine the course of the economy of that nation. At the same time, managers of giant corporations, holders of powerful positions in the economic order, are responsible for decisions concerning what will be produced, how much of it will be produced, and at what price it will be sold. Labor leaders are in the same category, since they can call strikes that paralyze industries and sections of the country and that can help change the distribution of wealth in our society.

[Economic Decision Making]

The fundamental economic problem of every society is that all human needs cannot be easily satisfied because of the problem of scarcity of resources. Today, and even in the technologically advanced societies of the world, although the basic needs for food and shelter have been fulfilled more or less well for everyone, there are other needs of a social nature, that have not. These social needs seem to be never-ending—at least, no economic system thus far has been devised that is capable of satisfying all human demands. In the face of this perpetual problem of scarcity, each society is confronted with the following problems:

1. What commodities should we produce, and in what quantities?
2. How should we produce these commodities with greatest efficiency?
3. For whom should we produce these commodities?

Of what commodities would you like to see more produced? Of what commodities would you like to see less produced?

In solving the first problem, people in a society have to decide whether it is more important to produce food or clothing, and in what proportions. In solving the second problem, people in a society must decide which resources to use to produce the commodities needed by the members. The third problem concerns distribution. In most societies, this becomes a function of the stratification system. Some social classes obtain more of the commodities produced because they wield more power and have more status than others. Just how this process works, and the inequality, poverty, and other problems it produces has been discussed in the chapter dealing with stratification.

Some economic crises are caused by overproduction. How might such a situation come about? What might the result of overproduction be?

People in different societies solve these economic problems in several different ways. Some societies solve all their problems by relying only on custom and tradition. Other societies allow these decisions to be made by command. Either an arbitrary ruler or an elected body of representatives makes the decisions basing them on tradition, on what they think will benefit the people, on personal aggrandizement, or on other considerations. Finally, in some societies these decisions are made as a result of the functioning of a market dependent on supply and demand, on prices, profits, and losses. Such societies are said to follow a free-market, private-enterprise economic system.

Very few economies today are based entirely on only one of the systems we have just described. Most are a mixture of two or even all three of them. In our economy both private and public (governmental) organizations exercise economic control.

[Economic Systems of Industrial Societies]

Contemporary societies are still adjusting to the dramatic process of modernization. One of the most significant changes has been the transformation of basically agrarian societies into industrial ones. Today, the most powerful and wealthy societies of the world have almost completed this transformation and are said to be entering a post-industrial stage. All others are desperately trying to catch up. The reason is that the industrial mode of production creates much more wealth for many more members of society than does the agricultural mode.

Given what you know about industrialization, what characteristics might a postindustrial society have?

The transformation from agrarian to industrial society is marked by conflict. Fundamental changes occur in the class structure and in the values and beliefs of a society. In agrarian societies, for example, wealth, power, and status belong to those who own most of the land. In feudal Europe, this class was the aristocracy. In the pre-Civil War South, it was the plantation owners.

When industry becomes the chief mode of production, the status and power shift to those who are in control of industrial and financial capital. Historically, industrialization rapidly followed the creation of a middle class (bourgeoisie) in England whose values and beliefs facilitated the accumulation of capital and its continued reinvestment in business ventures. In our society, much power is vested in the hands of corporate conglomerates in the fields of manufacturing, trade, and finance.

The second major change that occurs in the transformation of societies from agrarian to industrial is the shift in values and beliefs of a majority of societal members. In preindustrial societies, such values tend to be communal and spiritual. Before industrialization on a grand scale can take place, these beliefs and values have to give way to other, more individualistic ones. The individual person has to want personal fulfillment in terms of a better social status, wealth, and prestige. This can be done through working and accumulating money. The profit motive is thereby introduced, and work is infused with positive social value.

Do you feel you value work as highly as your parents' generation? Why or why not?

The Protestant ethic. The transformation of work to a means of accumulating capital was assisted by certain religious ideas that were circulating in Europe at the time when industrialism was experiencing its own birth pangs.[1] The ideas of the German monk Martin Luther and the Swiss theologian John Calvin were especially influential in changing attitudes toward work. These leaders of the Protestant Reformation claimed that all people had a calling to serve God, and that God's service was best accomplished through work. Work, they argued, was a useful and dignified way to decrease each individual's anxiety concerning his salvation. According to the doctrine of the elect, wealth was a

Do you think the Reformation or the emergence of capitalism developed first? What sociological thinkers would agree with your position?

[1]The relationship between the new religious ideas and the emergence of capitalism was analyzed by the eminent sociologist Max Weber in his classic work *The Protestant Ethic and the Spirit of Capitalism* (New York: Scribner and Sons, 1930).

sign of God's favor. One idea suggested by this doctrine was that since hard work and diligence accumulated wealth, work was good. This value has come to be known as the Protestant Work Ethic. The value shift supported hard work and the struggle to be successful, even though the goal was spiritual salvation. The Protestant Reformation was thus instrumental in shifting the interpretation of work from the sacred to the secular.

[Three Economic Systems]

Economic institutions are both cultural and social systems. They are social systems because people hold specific statuses and play the roles corresponding to these statuses. They are cultural systems because patterns of behavior, values, and expectations emerge around a system of production. These patterns are then made legitimate by a philosophy or ideology that the people accept as valid. In the modern industrial societies of the world three economic patterns of behavior and their legitimizing ideologies prevail.

Capitalism

Of what obligation did the idea of private property free the upper classes?

The economic system that came into being in Western Europe on the heels of the Industrial Revolution was Capitalism. In this system of economic production, wealth came to be considered chiefly as the private property of individuals or families, rather than as the property of the state or of a society as a whole. The principle of capitalism was that an individual invested his property with the expectation of accumulating more property through his own work and enterprise.

Capitalism, as the system was described in its early years, was supposed to function according to a mechanism called *the invisible hand.* This term was coined by a Scottish professor of philosophy, Adam Smith, in his book, *The Wealth of Nations* (1776). Smith sought to define and rationalize the system of capitalism. The invisible hand was really a mechanism that derived from each individual's greed and self-interest, which Smith thought were "natural" human sentiments. Pursuing their own self-interest, individuals in the long run were acting for the good of the whole society. Smith believed that competition, without any intervention or control would lead to the greatest good for the greatest number. In attempting to become wealthy, investors would find better and less expensive methods of production. Consumers would buy the best products at the cheapest prices, so that inefficient methods of production, or consumer products that were not wanted, would automatically be discontinued. Competition and supply and demand without any formal regulation would make, according to Smith, for a free and open market, the best system for economic progress. The noninterventionism advocated by Smith has come to be known as *laissez-faire* policy.

That the free market ever functioned as perfectly as Smith assumed is doubtful. Today, Smith's conception of the free market has long been discarded. The huge size of today's corporate structures and labor unions enables them to withstand many of the pressures of competition. They can concentrate on long-range profits and benefits rather than on immediate ones. The government has been playing an increasing role in the market, so that the market is less and less "free." The basic principles of self-interest and competition survive as ideals, not realities, of economic behavior in capitalist societies.

What government agencies and private interest groups now seek to ensure competition in the economy?

Rise of the corporation. The end of the 19th century saw the development of the corporation. A corporation is officially a public institution. Shares of a given enterprise are sold to the public instead of belonging to one individual or a family. The owners of the enterprise become those persons who buy stock in it. The managers are hired by those who represent the owners, that is, the board of directors. The foremost advantage of the public corporation is its ability to accumulate vast amounts of capital in a short period of time.

The economic system we call *industrial* or *Modified Capitalism* is the result of extensive reforms to the laissez-faire market of the preceding century. Monopolies and price fixing have been made illegal. Privately owned industry has largely been replaced by public stock companies. Owners have been replaced by managers. The government regulates the activities of corporations, presumably protecting the public from misrepresentation and the manufacturing of harmful products. Unions have taken on the responsibility of protecting the rights and welfare of workers through collective bargaining. And the government has recognized its role as a protector of the people, aiding in the support of fatherless children and of adults unable to work, providing unemployment insurance, some forms of health care, and social security benefits.

Can you identify some near-monopolistic corporations in our country? Find out what interconnections they may have with government.

Corporate power. But although some of the gross inequities of the capitalistic heyday have been regulated, our economic system is far from perfect. Many corporations that are virtual monopolies are allowed to exist because their managers are powerful enough to influence government officials and agencies. It is estimated that the 500 largest industrial corporations represented, in 1974, 66 percent of the sales of all United States industries.[2] This concentration of economic power enables a handful of corporations to determine the course of action for any industry, immune from the pressures of competition.

The transition from family to industrial capitalism has necessitated the emergence of a class of managers who have the expertise to manage the large resources of capitalist enterprises. This transition has been called the *managerial revolution*[3] and has given rise to a number of new professions.

---

[2]Bro Uttal, "The *Fortune* Directory of the 500 Largest Corporations," *Fortune* 91 (May 1975): 209.

[3]James Burnham, *Managerial Revolution* (Bloomington, Ind.: University of Indiana Press, 1960). First published 1940.

Industrial capitalism has won for our society a high standard of living and the highest per capita income in the world. The large number of consumer goods of every conceivable variety are our reward for the highly mechanized production techniques, mass production and distribution systems, and a complex sales system that includes advertising campaigns in the mass media. Nevertheless, the system creates as many new problems in the area of the quality of life as it solves.

Socialism

Some societies have developed economic systems whose premises differ radically from the premises of capitalism. Socialism is one such system. The basic premise of socialism is a preoccupation with the welfare of the collectivity, with the whole of society, rather than with the individual. All individuals are believed to be entitled to the necessities of life. They are not left to compete for survival, as under capitalism. Accordingly, in a socialist society, the government levies high income taxes that help redistribute the society's wealth more equitably. Individuals may own property, but only if the ownership does not deprive other members of society in any way. Essential industries are owned and operated by the government in the name of all the people, and the government controls and directs the economy in general.

Do you feel that major industries in this country should be nationalized? Why or why not?

For example, in Great Britain, which has a partially socialist economic system, the government owns and operates the coal industry, banks, transportation facilities, utilities, and television. The managers of nationalized industries are appointed by the government, and their profits are returned to the state. Both Great Britain and Sweden have extensive systems of social welfare designed to care for the individual from the cradle to the grave, and to promote his health, welfare, and standard of living. In Sweden, the system seems to be extremely successful. The substantial majority of people are middle class and comfortable, while extremes of wealth and poverty do not exist. In Great Britain, class divisions have a long history and the cleavages between the upper classes and the lower classes are more difficult to heal.

The long-range plans of socialist economies include the coordinated planning of all sectors of the economy through government regulation of industry, agriculture, commerce, and the professions. Production in such an economy is not undertaken for profit but because of the needs of the people. Workers and professional people are not expected to be guided by the profit motive either, but by a desire to serve society and express themselves through their work. The ultimate objective is a total redistribution of income.

Communism

These last two goals of socialism—total government control and total income redistribution—are also goals of communist nations. Such nations are theoretically determined to stamp out the profit motive entirely,

How Commercialization Leads to Bad Blood

Capitalist competition, it has often been said, promotes productivity, quality, efficiency, and an equilibrium of supply and demand. In England, blood for transfusion is freely given and centrally organized and controlled. In the United States, there is a market in human blood; it is highly competitive, without central organization, and, for some, highly profitable. Here, almost all blood for transfusion is bought and sold directly or contracted on a credit-debit basis. Compared to the British system, says Richard Titmuss in a comparative study of blood collection and distribution systems, the commercialized blood market in the United States is inefficient, bureaucratic, and characterized by chronic shortages and waste. Blood in the United States is many times more expensive and much more likely to be contaminated than in Britain. Titmuss summarizes the other social effects of the private market in blood in the United States in this way:

> *. . . the commercialization of blood and donor relationships represses the expression of altruism, erodes the sense of community, lower scientific standards, limits both personal and professional freedoms, sanctions the making of profits in hospitals and clinical laboratories, legalizes hostility between doctor and patient, subjects critical areas of medicine to the laws of the marketplace, places immense social costs on those least able to bear them—the poor, the sick and the inept—increases the danger of unethical behavior in various sectors of medical science and practice, and results in situations in which proportionately more and more blood is supplied by the poor, the unskilled, the unemployed, Negroes and other low income groups and categories of exploited human populations of high blood yielders. Redistribution in terms of blood and blood products from the poor to the rich appears to be one of the dominant effects of the American blood banking system.*

Richard M. Titmuss, *The Gift Relationship: From Human Blood to Social Policy* (New York: Random House, 1972), pp. 245–246.

as well as economic individualism of any sort. Individuals are encouraged to think and labor for the collectivity and work toward the even distribution of society's resources, so that eventually a classless society may be attained. The major difference between socialist and communist economies is that in the latter the state is the sole producer and distributor, and consequently the sole employer. Private ownership of business

Why might communism appeal to people who have a very low standard of living?

is discouraged and sometimes forbidden. Communist economies are thoroughly planned in the upper echelons of government, and the government assumes almost total responsibility for the people, providing nurseries and day-care facilities for working mothers, as well as exhaustive social services.

All three economic systems lie at different points on an ideal continuum. What differentiates them is the extent to which the government intervenes in the economy. In modified capitalism, government interferes least, although intervention is increasing. In socialism government interferes in the essential industries. In communism the government determines all economic action. The economies of modern societies are matters of degree, rather than kind.

[Social Problems and the Economy]

We may be, as a society, enjoying one of the highest per capita incomes, as well as one of the highest standards of living. But our high rates of crime, drug dependence, alcoholism, mental illness, and family instability do not seem to indicate an idyllic life situation. Much unhappiness or discontent has been interpreted as a failure of the economic system. Our environment, the communities we live in, and our work are all shaped and directed by the idea of maximum profit and highest productivity, all for the private gain of selected individuals. Meanwhile, our public gains as societal members are relatively small. The existence of poverty is one instance of the uneven rewards of the economic system. Another is the relationship of people to work.

Job satisfaction. We are an employee society, in which only a very small number of workers are their own bosses (around 8 percent of the work force). The remainder of the work force is composed of employees paid by wage and salary. Work, then, is organized for people, and the majority have little to say about how and when it is going to get done.

The fact that work is organized is related to income inequality, although much income inequality derives from great differences in inherited wealth. Most of us work for either a governmental or private corporate hierarchy in which salaries and wages are differentiated according to the division of labor. Lines of authority—and consequently compensation—dwindle downward from the managerial top, through the intermediate supervisory levels, down to the base of the hierarchy composed of masses of clerical, white-collar workers and skilled and semiskilled blue-collar workers.

Have you ever worked on an assembly line? What was your reaction to the experience?

Job satisfaction, in addition, is frequently lacking. Some workers are overqualified for the jobs they perform. Specialization restricts the individual's ability to learn or perform a wide range of skills. Assembly-line division of labor creates bored, angry workers. The dissatisfaction manifests itself in high rates of absenteeism, high job turnover, industrial sabotage, and disinterest or sheer negligence in job performance. Dramatic improvements in job benefits and security for workers in the past

Why "Women's" Jobs Pay Less

Discrimination by employers in their hiring practices and the belief of many women that they are fit only for certain types of jobs (a consequence of their socialization) have resulted in a high degree of occupational segregation by sex, says Barbara Deckard in a review of the literature on women workers. Most women work in occupations that are more than 70 percent female, while most male workers are in occupations that are more than 70 percent male. In clerical and service occupations, where women predominate, wages for both men and women are lower than the median wage for all males, even though the women's educational level may be far above the median educational level of all males. Within these occupations, as in most other occupations, women are paid far less than their male counterparts, regardless of educational levels.

The industries in which women are primarily segregated, research has shown, tend to be smaller and more competitive than the larger, predominantly male industries where monopoly conditions often prevail and where wage increases can be passed along to the consumer. Competition among these smaller industries, Deckard argues, encourages them to pay lower wages in order to survive. Women's resistance to these low wages is undercut by several factors. First, the many women looking for work in these sectors (partly because they are denied access to higher-paying, higher-status "male" occupations) increases competition for scarce jobs, which depresses wages. Second, many women, Deckard says, will work for lower wages than men will. Third, smaller industries are more difficult to organize than large plants, while the prejudices and discrimination of union leaders makes organizing these industries a low priority. (One of four male workers is a union member, while only one of seven women workers is organized). Finally, sexist prejudice among male coworkers acts as a further obstacle to unionization.

Barbara Sinclair Deckard, *The Women's Movement: Political, Socioeconomic, and Psychological Issues* (New York: Harper & Row, 1975), pp. 75–112.

decade seem not to have compensated for diminishing job satisfaction.

Unemployment and automation. A very real source of dissatisfaction associated with work is the chronic unemployment experienced by a portion of the potential work force. That portion is made up mainly of lower-class blacks, of older workers, of undereducated young people, and of

Have you ever experienced unemployment? How did you react to that status? How did other people rank you?

workers whose skills have become obsolete as a result of automation or other types of "progress." Unemployment rates among these categories of people remain high even in times of economic affluence, assuming tragic proportions during times when the economy is experiencing a downtrend.

Unemployment has social as well as economic consequences. The unemployed do not suffer only because they get no paycheck at the end of every week. Work is an important part of our belief system, and to a great extent it gives people their identity, sense of worth, and their place in the social system. A man in our society—and, increasingly, a woman—is supposed to work, and not only support his family on what he earns from his job, but also know who he is from what he does.

Conversely, those who do not work, especially the chronically unemployed, suffer a loss of self-esteem and feelings of worthlessness. They react by accepting their unsatisfactory self-image and passively give in to the loss of status that often accompanies unemployment. They may also react by rebeling against the system by joining a social movement with militant overtones. Another, and in many respects the most problematic, reaction is the establishment of a subcultural way of life in which living on welfare checks or engaging in petty crime come to be seen as legitimate alternatives to regular employment.[4] Other more individual reactions include leaving home and the responsibility for taking care of the family. This reaction is encouraged by our welfare system, which is more generous with families that lack a male head.

Workers in an industrial society are also confronted by the specter of automation. Although automation represents progress in that it speeds up labor productivity, it can and does displace workers from their jobs. Economists insist that technological advancement has not, in the long run, cost workers their jobs. Still, in particular industries and regions of the country, such changes in technology have proven disastrous to local workers.

If automation increases, how will our economy provide for displaced workers? What social changes may be necessary in the institution of government?

Most workers displaced by machines are able to find work at the same level or higher, sometimes even in the same organizations. Nevertheless, there is an element of hostility displayed by workers against the job-displacing machines. The hostility is understandable, since workers are not equitably displaced. Manual workers, especially those in farming and related industries, have been displaced at a much higher rate than white-collar workers. In the decade between 1950 and 1960, close to 9 million rural Americans left the country to look for work in the city. Often the plight of the displaced urban worker is even more dramatic, as such workers tend to be in their middle or older years. For an older worker, moving to a better job becomes a difficult or impossible prospect.

---

[4]Michael Schwartz and George Henderson, "The Culture of Unemployment: Some Notes on Negro Children," in *Blue-Collar World: Studies of the American Worker,* Arthur B. Shostak and William Gomberg, eds. (Englewood Cliffs, N.J.: Prentice-Hall, 1964), pp. 458–468.

The U.S. Unemployment Problem

SOURCE: Bureau of Labor Statistics.

The end of working life. Even the end of the individual's working life is fraught with problems in industrial society. Work is a master role (the major role) in our lives. Since it defines what we are, as well as enables us to survive, losing this role creates confusion and frustration for many retirees.

The most problematic aspect of retirement—which in some companies is mandatory and is most customary at age 65—is the sudden cut in income. Retirees become dependent on social security and other pension plans. Other problems revolve around the psychological stresses of losing one's occupational role and realizing that one is approaching the end of productivity as an individual.

[Is the Work Ethic Dying?]

For many centuries now, work has been considered a "good" thing to do. The person who refused to work or could not work was looked down upon as somehow morally tainted. There are indications now that this so-called "work ethic" is losing its grip on many people. The older generations still espouse it, but among younger people, especially those

Do you support the work ethic? Why or why not?

from middle-class comfortable homes, the work ethic seems to be losing much of its appeal.

Why is work being devalued? It is possible that this is simply an expression of a social trend that has a sound economic reason. We have increasingly become a service economy. Because of automation and technology advancements, many jobs once done by people are now done by machines. Machines, however, must be serviced. Continued industrial expansion also demands specific kinds of services: banking and insurance, employment agencies, computer services, advertising, and so on. More than 50 percent of the labor force today is occupied in such service occupations. These service occupations are still "work." But they do not require the same physical exertion as industrial work.

If we can eventually make enough to live on with a four-day week, and a four-hour day, what will we do with ourselves?

Another indication that work may be losing its central role in contemporary society is a trend that began to evidence itself as long ago as in the late forties. At that time, people began preferring to have more leisure in which to spend their money than to have more working time in which to make money.[5]

The growing distaste for the old ideas of success, for the employment conditions of industrial society, and for other traditional work values expressed by many members of the counterculture in the late 1960s and early 1970s, as well as by the many young people in general, may be interpreted as a further development of this same trend. Whether this trend portends a civilization of leisure and a much changed attitude toward work remains to be seen. The next several years will be especially telling. Will we be glad to work at anything as long as it allows us to eat? Will we force our government to take care of our basic needs according to socialist, rather than capitalist, principles? Will we ever achieve a garden of Eden where work and play are one and the same?

What status definitions may change if unemployment affects more than half the population?

Government. The words "politics," the "political system," or "the so-and-so government," become familiar to most of us at a very early age. Somehow we soon get the idea that whoever represents "politics" or "government," has power and authority over us, and even over those people whom we consider our superiors. As we grow older, we begin to have first-hand experiences with the political system. We may be drafted into military service by an act of the federal government. Before we can drive a car, we have to pass a test and be licensed by an agency of the state government. And, many times thereafter, we may be ticketed for our inadequate driving skills by an agent of a local, municipal government.

The institution we are experiencing in all these various ways is government. Politics is the process of acquiring and using power, and government is the ultimate source of legitimate power in society. The

---

[5]David Riesman, "Work and Leisure in Post-Industrial Society," in Eric Larrabee and Rolf Meyersohn, eds., *Mass Leisure* (Glencoe, Ill.: Free Press, 1958), p. 363. Also, David Riesman, *Abundance for What? And Other Essays (Garden City, N.Y.: Doubleday, 1964). pp. 147–184.*

political institution includes a system of norms, values, laws, and general patterns of behavior that legitimize the acquisition and exercise of power. The institution also defines the relationship between government and members of society.

[Purpose and Functions of Government]

Why do societies need government? Why do they give to someone or to some governmental body the power to make decisions binding on all? The answer lies in the group nature of human life. Since we live in societies, we need a certain degree of social order. There are certain things we must do, and others we must refrain from doing, not necessarily for our individual benefit, but for the benefit of the entire group. Perhaps, on an individual level, it would benefit some of us to kill some member of our group. But if everyone were free to kill for personal reasons, the whole society would fall apart. So instead we create norms and values that define killing as wrong and immoral. We punish those who kill in defiance of these prohibitions.

Who is to make sure that important norms are upheld by laws? Who is to make sure that murderers are in fact punished? Who is to settle any of thousands of disputes that come up whenever people live together? Who is to determine who gets what in terms of social rewards? Who is to exert enough control to ensure social order, in brief?

When societies are small and simple, the family institution is probably strong enough to perform all these functions. The family exerts sufficient social control on its members to assure the relatively peaceful survival of the society. When societies grow in size and complexity, the family can no longer perform all such functions alone. Other institutions—education, religion and government—take over the functions of maintaining social order. The general pattern in our society is that the family begins to socialize the individual. The school continues this process. Religion teaches ethical principles that reinforce the family and school. When these forms of socialization and informal means of control fail, government takes over, ensuring, with violent means if needed, that the norms of the society are indeed upheld.

Because the freedom of one individual invariably intrudes on the freedom of others, absolute freedom is impossible for humans living in groups. Thus, as a society, we find it convenient to have some body with the authority to make and enforce rules and regulations that help maintain order and protect everyone's freedom. Social order is a by-product of group life and is implemented through various means of social control. Social control is the process by which the group—society or smaller groups within it—induces or forces the individual to behave in a designated way. When social control becomes institutionalized—when it becomes sufficiently surrounded with customs and traditions to set a pattern—it is called *government.* Government is the ultimate source of social control.

Functions of Government

The military institution in this government is often criticized for being larger than necessary. What dangers in this development are perceived by the critics?

The most important function of government is to implement social control. In addition to maintaining order, settling disputes, and coordinating the activities of members of society, government also protects its citizens from external threats. It does this by creating and maintaining armies, by manufacturing or providing such armies with armaments, and by securing strategic military installations. In some societies, the military institution itself acts as the government. In most, however, civilians are in charge of the government, and the military is subordinate to it although the government may spend a large proportion of its budget on military activities.

The government is in charge of planning and maintaining those facilities and activities that involve large portions of the population. Government tries to regulate the economy. Government also builds highways, is in charge of traffic regulation, funds schools, maintains national parks and museums, helps run hospitals and provides some health care, and so on. Government, finally, subsidizes activities that are valued by the society in theory more than in practice—the arts for instance.

Government like other institutions also has latent functions: it produces results that are neither desired nor intended. One latent function of American political institutions, for example, is the creation of party machines that were so prominent several decades ago and that still operate in some regions. Even though such machines run counter to the democratic ideology and are often corrupt, they have resisted numerous reform attempts because they apparently fill a need that the legitimate political system does not.

Another latent function of government is the creation of power elites and the maintenance of social classes. Even in communist nations, where a classless society is the goal, administrative and managerial elites have come into existence. Later in the chapter we will examine power elites and the relationship between political power and socioeconomic status.

Government and state. Government is also a process that includes the group of people who exercise political power. The state, on the other hand, is the abstract embodiment of the political institution. The state is an institution that incorporates the institution of government.

Can people advocate the overthrow of the government without advocating the overthrow of the state? Why or why not?

To put it another way, whereas government provides social control through its political processes, through the laws it establishes and implements, and through the work of its agencies, the *state* is the formal structure of government. The state is the institution whose functions are carried out by the government. Government is the working, active arm of the state. Although individuals and groups that make up the government—and their laws and procedures—change with time and with administrations, the state goes on. The government and the state are not, however, completely separate entities. Only for purposes of analysis is any attempt made to distinguish between them. State and government are closely related aspects of the weblike institutional setting of society. The institution of government in complex societies becomes merely an aspect of the institution of the state, as well as an agency of it.

Government and nation. The same processes that were responsible for institutionalizing social control in the state (with its agency, the government) have also been responsible for the creation of nations. The continuous growth in size and complexity of societies led people to seek political organization first in clans based on kinship, later in tribes that were collections of clans, and, finally, in city-states. In the fifteenth century, city-states gradually emerged as nation-states. Whereas the state represents a politically organized society that functions through a government, the *nation* is a culture group residing within the territory of the political state. What makes a group of people a nation is the spirit of nationhood.

Nation-states are a relatively modern phenomenon—in fact, they appear about the time that industrialization begins. Why might these two developments appear simultaneously?

The factors that help unify a people into a nation are (1) geographic boundaries—separation of an area by mountains, rivers, or the sea; (2) the development of commercial ties throughout this geographic area; (3) a common language, or if there are different linguistic groups, the knowledge of a common language. With the establishment of a central government, these factors become even more significant, and additional factors appear: an attempt to subordinate older loyalties to the new political order, and the development of a common literature, a common history, and a sense of a common future. Eventually, the people making up a nation come to have a "we," as against "they," feeling toward those who are not part of the nation. This sense of unity is so strong that, in spite of deep cleavages among the people of the nation—including a lack of total cultural uniformity—they consider themselves as separate from all others, whom they designate as foreigners.

Nationalism

Nationalism, which is the ideology behind the nation-state, has played an important part in modern history. It has been essential to the creation of modern societies, for it has destroyed the narrow provincialism of loyalties to family, kin, and community typical of preindustrial societies. *Nationalism* is a complex social phenomenon. In brief, it may be defined as a set of beliefs about the superiority and differentness of one's own nation, and a defense of its interests about all others. It implies the individual's identification with the nation, its culture, its interests, and its goals. It is ethnocentrism that cuts across all other loyalties to stress loyalty to the national group. In this ideology, the nation—whether it is already in existence, or whether its people are hoping or fighting for its independence—is the ultimate goal of the social, political, and economic efforts of the people.

[Political Power: Legitimacy and Authority]

Power is central to the political process because whoever exerts social control on a society must have power to do so. Power is an elusive concept, very difficult to define. Weber defined power as ". . . the probability that one actor within a social relationship will be in a position to carry out his own will despite resistance.[6] Power plays a significant part in all kinds of social interaction. A parent has power over his or her children, a professor has power over students, an employer has power over employees, and so on. People have greater or lesser amounts of power according to the statuses they fulfill in society and the roles they play. What is important is that all power involves the ability to affect decision making.

How much power in or against the government do you feel you have?

Power can be asserted in several ways. One way of getting someone to do what you want him to do is to promise something the person wants in return for compliance. Another way to assert power is through the opposite tactic—coercion by threatening punishment if the person does not comply. Finally, one can assert power through influence by being able to manipulate information or have an effect on values, attitudes, and feelings.

---

[6]Max Weber, *The Theory of Social and Economic Organization* (New York: The Free Press, 1957), p. 152.

Not all individuals, obviously, are equally successful in exerting pressures and consequently in wielding power. Much depends on the individual's wealth, prestige, knowledge, and ability to persuade.

Legitimacy

Political power is the kind of power exercised by the state. The state, as we will see, is the abstract representation of the political system of a society. The state has the authority to employ force or violence to implement social control. In fact, the state has a monopoly on the legitimate use of physical force in the enforcement of order. People accept the authority of the state and this acceptance or consent justifies the state's actions.

When power is held by an individual or group not acceptable to the members of society, the power is illegal and illegitimate. A man holding a gun to your head while he takes your wallet has power over you. His power is backed by force, or the threat of force. But it is illegitimate power. When the man holding a gun is a policeman trying to arrest you, however, he has the authority to exert power over you. *Authority* is the legitimate possession of power. Power becomes legitimate authority when members of society accept its use as right and proper.

Can a government exercise illegitimate power? In what ways?

What do we mean by "legitimate possession of power?" "Legitimacy," writes political sociologist Seymour Lipset, "involves the capacity of the system to engender and maintain the belief that the existing political institutions are the most appropriate ones for the society.[7] Before the authority of a political system is accepted, that system must convince a substantial majority of societal members that the power it holds is justified, or legitimate. A political system is generally considered legitimate if its goals and values coincide with the goals and values of a majority of people. No political system, not even one born of violence and functioning through force, can survive for very long without legitimacy.

When a government has legitimacy, its laws are followed and its officials respected by a majority of people in the society, regardless of their feelings toward both the laws and the enforcers. If a majority of people does not believe that the government is legitimate, they disregard the laws and lack respect for law enforcers. Such a situation is called a *crisis of legitimacy.* No government undergoing a crisis of legitimacy can last for very long. Such situations tend to occur during periods of rapid social change. These crises are especially severe if major institutions are threatened or if major groups in society have no access to the political system.[8]

Has the United States ever suffered a crisis of legitimacy? Explain.

---

[7] Seymour Martin Lipset, *Political Man* (Garden City, N.Y.: Doubleday, 1963), p. 64.
[8] Lipset, *Political Man,* p. 65.

Authority

We have said that the state has the ultimate power—the legitimate use of force, including the right to take a citizen's life in certain situations. But this power does not rest primarily on force, or on the threat of force, as we have seen. It rests on the state's legitimacy in the eyes of its citizens. When power is legitimate, it is *authority.* Authority refers to power over, or control of, individuals that is socially accepted as right and proper. For instance, everyone expects to pay a certain amount of his or her income to the government in the form of taxes. We may complain about it, but we rarely question the government's authority to collect taxes. But if someone other than the government were to demand that we pay a yearly sum under pain of bodily harm, we would protest and have the person arrested for blackmail.

Types of Authority

How do certain people or groups or governments acquire authority? How does power become legitimized? Weber formulated a now-classic thesis about the sources of authority. These sources, Weber says, are traditional, legal-rational and charismatic.[9]

Traditional. Authority that depends on tradition is the oldest form of power that people know. In this type of authority, legitimization derives from the past. Authority is accepted because "it has always been so."

Why would heterogeneity lead to legal-rational forms of authority?

Legal-rational. This type of authority rests on rules that are arrived at in a rational manner. Political and other systems based on legal-rational authority are organized in a bureaucratic fashion. The bureaucratic pattern of social organization limits the exercise of power because in a bureaucracy power resides in a social position and role rather than in a specific individual. In addition, this pattern of organization defines and specifies the exact amount of power that each role entails. Authority is based on obedience to the "rule of law" rather than on loyalty to any given individual.

As may be expected, this type of authority appears in complex, multigroup societies. In such societies, members are heterogeneous, belonging to many subcultures. These societies usually experience rapid social change, resulting in a lack of uniformity in values, attitudes, and beliefs. The United States is a society with a legal-rational base of authority.

Have you ever experienced charismatic authority? Who was exercising it?

Charismatic. In both types of societies—those with a traditional base of authority and those with a legal-rational one—charismatic authority may appear in the person of an exceptional leader. To their followers, charismatic leaders seem to possess special characteristics that are magnetic, fascinating, and extraordinary. The authority such leaders hold does not

[9] Weber, pp. 324–369.

rest on tradition, reason, or law. It rests on their outstanding qualities as leaders and as unusual human beings.

[Political Ideology]

In his book on government, Robert MacIver asserts that it is not force but the *myth complex* of society that makes governors acceptable to the governed. This myth complex lends government a justification without which no prince or parliament, no tyrant or dictator, could ever rule.[10] We have already stated that a government needs legitimate authority. But we have not explained how authority is legitimized.

The underlying fabric of authority is ideology. An *ideology* is a system of values, ideas, beliefs, and attitudes that a society, or groups within it, share and accept as fact. An ideology contains a set of attitudes toward the various institutions and processes of society. These attitudes furnish the believer with an image of the world both as it is and as it should be. Some ideologies organize the complexities of the world into fairly simple and understandable images. Others are complex, sometimes forcing the believer into accepting more than one ideology or even into holding conflicting beliefs. An ideology is a set of interrelated beliefs that provide a picture of the world as a whole.

Given this definition of political ideology, to what ideology do you subscribe?

Political ideology is a system of beliefs that explains, interprets, and rationalizes why a particular kind of political order is best for the society. The political order may already exist, or it may be planned. Political ideology also offers a definite strategy for the attainment or maintenance of the preferred political order, including processes, institutional arrangements, and other programs. Therefore, political ideology is like a blueprint for the good society, complete with practical instructions about how to reach it and keep it.

Ideologies are not monolithic, but contain differences within them. Democracy, for example, can be divided into democratic capitalism and democratic socialism. The followers of each maintain their belief in democracy, yet they differ both in what they believe to be the ends of democracy, and the means of achieving these ends. The same is true of communism. There are disagreements between the Soviet Union and China, and disagreements with both by the Eastern European nations, about the interpretation of communist ideology.[11]

By examining political ideologies, then, we can uncover some interesting facts about the people who formulate them and believe in them. We may see, for instance, how the people of a particular society see themselves in relation to their environment; what their goals are, how and why they expect to attain those goals; and what the final consequences of their views and beliefs are.

---

[10]Robert M. MacIver, *The Web of Government* (New York: Macmillan, 1947), p. 17.

[11]T. Sargent, *Contemporary Political Ideologies* (Homewood, Ill.: Dorsey, 1972), pp. 1–8.

Democracy

Democracy has many meanings and has been applied to the political systems of many different nations. *Democracy* is an ideology, a philosophy, a theory, and a political system. In each democratic nation, people have borrowed some elements of the ideology and rejected others, adapting democracy to their own particular circumstances. In addition, democracy was not created by one person at a definite period of time. It emerged in ancient Greece, but it did not gain wide acceptance until this century. Even now, it has as many detractors as it has followers.

Assumptions and principles of democracy. One of the basic assumptions of democracy is that the individual is valuable. In most political systems, the individual is considered only as part of a larger social mass. But in democratic political systems, the human being is considered the primary unit of society. From this basic assumption it follows that, in the democratic frame of reference, the ultimate purpose of the state is to ensure the self-fulfillment of every individual.

The ideology of democracy is founded on specific beliefs about the nature of humans. Followers of democracy believe that individuals are free, rational, moral, equal, and possess certain rights. Equality does not imply that each individual has the same qualities as every other individual. It refers to each person's possession of particular moral and rational faculties, by virtue of which he is entitled to the same freedoms and rights as any other person. Democracy recognizes and respects the uniqueness of each individual.

Do you feel that every person possesses "particular moral and rational faculties"? Should anyone be excluded from the democratic process? If so, who?

Democratic ideology is based on the principle of popular sovereignty. Popular sovereignty is the idea that ultimate power resides in the people. The assumption is that a person is not subject to any authority but his own and is capable of directing his own behavior. This is a basic article of democratic faith, for if the individual is free and self-governing, he must be in control of political power. Finally, an important principle of democracy is the belief that each person is entited to certain freedoms and to the opportunity to pursue his goals.

Autocracy

Autocracy is the ideology most directly opposed to democracy because it holds that government should be in the hands of one individual or group who has supreme power over the people. Autocratic government has taken many forms throughout the ages: primitive kingships, despotism, tyranny, and absolutist monarchies of the type that existed in Europe as late as the early twentieth century (Czarist Russia, for instance). Military dictatorships and other forms of temporary or emergency rule may also be considered autocratic. The distinguishing feature of autocratic regimes is that the ruler does not have to account to anyone for his actions. He makes all decisions and reaps the consequences of them. He is not subject to any law but, in effect, *is* the law.

In modern times, traditional autocracy has been replaced by

ideologies of the right and the left that we call *totalitarian.* Totalitarian regimes differ in major ways from the autocracies of the past. They are kinds of autocracies based on modern technology and mass legitimation.[12]

There are also types of autocracies in existence today that can be best described as authoritarian in their ideology. In these regimes, power is held by either an absolute monarch or dictator, or by a small elite. Power is limited to the political sphere, and the ruler makes no attempt to invade other spheres of human life. Such regimes are more or less like the totalitarian model. With time, they may become more totalitarian or less so.

This brief examination of the ideologies underlying the political systems of modern societies indicates once again that the behavior of humans is dependent on their normative system. Norms direct our behavior in all aspects of life. Our political behavior is no exception. It is shaped by the values of the prevailing political ideology of our society. This ideology molds not only the institutions we establish to carry on the political process but also the way we respond to those institutions. Of course, because of our individual and group differences, we do not always interpret the ideology in the same manner. Our political institutions and our political behavior therefore do not always necessarily reflect our ideology exactly.

The Distribution of Political Power in the United States

To govern is to have the power to make decisions binding on the entire society. Who has this power in the United States? The people, as the democratic ideology would seem to dictate? Or some people, as reality would seem to indicate?

Pluralism. There are two opposing schools of thought on how power is distributed in our society. One is the school of political pluralism or *broker rule* (rule by compromise). According to this view, power is diffused among numerous interest groups rather than being concentrated in any single place. Although interest groups continually compete with one another, they unite in coalitions when it is to their benefit to do so. They attempt to reach compromise solutions to the problems of decision making.

Political scientists maintain that a model of political pluralism includes the following assumptions and arguments. First, the basis of politics is the struggle for power. The parties to this struggle are organized interest groups. Second, the stability of the political system is promoted by the great number and diversity of these organized interest groups. Stability is ensured by an underlying consensus (agreement on basic issues) that acts to restrain group conflicts. Stability is further

Does this definition of pluralist politics fit your impression of American politics? Explain.

[12]Carl J. Friedrich and Zbigniew Brzezinski, *Totalitarian Dictatorship and Autocracy* (New York: Praeger, 1966), p. 4.

enhanced by the role of politicians as brokers; by overlapping memberships in interest groups; and by the possibility of the continuous formation of new interest groups. Change, as well as stability, is provided through the emergence of new groups. Although group bargaining is performed by elites—small groups with the power to make significant decisions—elites are responsive and accountable to the people through elections.[13]

Those who agree with political scientist Robert A. Dahl that power in our society is distributed according to a pluralistic model believe that neither a majority nor a minority is responsible for governmental decision making. Rather, such decision-making results from "steady appeasement of relatively small groups."[14] And the process through which appeasement occurs is continual bargaining, or broker rule.

Elitism. Directly opposed to the pluralist view is the elitist view. C. Wright Mills was a prominent exponent of this view in this century. Elitism is a school of thought that maintains that power in a society belongs to a limited number of individuals or groups. Elitists do not believe that this ought to be so, or that it is advantageous to the society to have power so concentrated. They simply state the facts as they see them, and reserve any value judgments. Mills believed that the most significant decisions including those concerning war and peace, are made by a handful of men who represent the corporate rich, the military upper echelons, and the political directorate. According to Mills, the consensus that supposedly exists in this nation is, in reality, brought into existence by elites, who manipulate the masses through mass communication. Pluralist competition occurs only when issues are minor. Elitists do not deny the existence of innumerable interest groups, but they question whether their interaction results in a diffusion of power. Another sociologist, William Domhoff, maintains that power wielded by the power elite is in effect monolithic, because the elite resemble one another in social background and have developed a community of interests and values. Consequently, they tend to act in liaison.[15]

In what ways is the pluralist theory opposed to the elitist theory of politics?

Who has the power? Which is the reality of the American situation? Can we determine who really has the power? Political scientists Thomas R. Dye and L. Harmon Ziegler suggest that power may fall somewhere between the conceptions of the ruling elite and the plural elite.[16] In neither view is the power thought to be in the hands of the people. Both views agree, in fact, that people are too apathetic, ill-informed, and self-interested to participate in the kind of system that democratic ideology prescribes. The pluralists, however, maintain that those who exercise power are responsive to the people, as uninterested as the people may

[13] John C. Livingston and Robert G. Thompson, *The Consent of the Governed* (New York: Macmillan, 1971), p. 107.

[14] Robert A. Dahl, *A Preface to Democratic Theory* (Chicago: University of Chicago Press, 1956), p. 146.

[15] William G. Domhoff, *Who Rules America* (Englewood Cliffs, N.J.: Prentice-Hall, 1967).

[16] Thomas R. Dye and L. Harmon Ziegler, *The Irony of Democracy*, 2nd ed. (North Scituate, Mass.: Duxbury, 1972), p. 60.

be. Ultimately, there is government by elites—or professionals—but they are approved by the people. They remain accountable to the people because they attain their elite position through people's votes. The people don't make the decisions, but they choose the persons who do.[17] The debate as to whether we are governed by ruling or pluralist elites will no doubt be rekindled by the events of Watergate. Did Americans really approve of an administration that spied on and attempted to harm its political opponents?

Conflict and consensus. Whether one tends to interpret the location of political power according to the pluralist or the elitist theory also depends on how one views the interplay of conflict and consensus in society. Both conflict and consensus (agreement on basic ideology) exist in society. Because politics revolves around the question of who will have power, conflict among individuals and groups is unavoidable in the political process. At the same time, if there were not at least a general consensus on the way conflict is to be mediated—in other words, on the rules of the game—the political system could become chaotic.

But although everyone agrees that both conflict and consensus exist, there is disagreement about which element predominates in American society. Pluralists are associated with the consensus school of thought. Consensus theorists, though not denying that conflict exists, insist that it takes place within a general framework of consensus.

Elitists are usually identified with the conflict school of thought. They believe that force holds society together. Yet force is seldom displayed by the elite. Instead, it is disguised as an ideology supporting the status quo. This ideology, forced on the masses by a manipulative elite, becomes an apparent—though not real—consensus. If this line of reasoning sounds familiar, it is because you have heard it before. Karl Marx was the forerunner of the conflict theorists. He maintained that much social change is prompted by the self-interest of the ruling class.

[Political Behavior in the Mass Society]

Since humans live in groups, it has long been recognized that they are political creatures. Never before, however, have the groups been quite as large, and never before have humans felt quite so alone, despite their large numbers. Life in a mass society is disconcerting and confusing, and political behavior reflects this confusion.

How might mass society contribute to mediocrity in political candidates?

We have discussed various aspects of a mass society at other points in the book. The term refers to a society consisting generally of a large population that is characterized (1) by the anonymity of its members; (2) by their continual social and geographic mobility; (3) by secondary relationships and by a lack of traditional values and goals; (4) by a

[17] Livingston and Thompson, pp. 114–115.

Only Your Journalist Knows . . .

The mass media presents packaged presidential candidates. We see only the finished product. The journalist, however, is in a position to catch glimpses behind the public relations facade as candidates change their position on controversial issues, depending on what audience they are with. Here is how Hunter Thompson, a journalist for *Rolling Stone* who followed the 1972 presidential candidates along their campaign trails, described his personal view of one candidate:

> *There is no way to grasp what a shallow, contemptible, and hopelessly dishonest old hack Hubert Humphrey really is until you've followed him around for a while on the campaign trail. The double-standard realities of campaign journalism, however, make it difficult for even the best of the "straight/objective" reporters to write what they actually think and feel about a candidate.*
>
> *Hubert Humphrey, for one, would go crazy with rage and attempt to strangle his press secretary if he ever saw in print what most reporters say about him during midnight conversations around barroom tables in all those Hiltons and Sheratons where the candidates make their headquarters when they swoop into places like Cleveland, Pittsburgh, and Indianapolis.*
>
> *And some of these reporters are stepping out of the closet and beginning to describe Humphrey in print as the bag of PR gimmicks that he is. The other day one of the Washington Post Regulars nailed him:*
>
> *"Humphrey has used the campaign slogans of John Kennedy ("Let's get this country moving again") and of Wallace ("Stand up for America") and some of his literature proclaims that 1972 is 'the year of the people,' a title used by Eugene McCarthy for a book about his 1968 campaign."*

Hunter Thompson, *Fear and Loathing: On the Campaign Trail '72* (New York: Popular Library, 1973), pp. 209–210.

specialization of roles and statuses; and (5) by a desire to conform to popular standards of behavior. In such a society a mass culture develops, and everything from ideas and art forms, to kitchen gadgets is marketed to the population through the mass media. These cultural items obtain immediate and widespread popularity. And since they must appeal to the widest possible public without offending any segment, their most significant attribute tends to be mediocrity.

The dissemination of this culture is largely accomplished through the mass communication media, which include the radio, television, newspapers, and mass circulation magazines. The mass media are characterized chiefly by their impersonality. They simply present their message. The audience generally accepts it, having no opportunity to reply, challenge, or express its opinion. And, as with the rest of mass society, the message must appeal to the largest possible number, without offending anybody.

The mass media have created—and are now supported by—the key institution of the mass society: advertising. From its origins as a source of information about new products, advertising has evolved into a device for stimulating both the desire for and the actual consumption of goods. It has done this so successfully that it has become an instrument of social control.[18] It has been as successful in selling mouthwashes as cures for loneliness as it has in selling candidates as cures for social conditions. And the title of a bestselling book, *The Selling of the President,* suggests just how far up the ladder of social control advertising has reached. The American public is presented with a presidential candidate in the same way it is presented with new soaps and deodorants. As we buy soaps and deodorants to make us successful and happy, so we buy a president to save our country from various menaces.

The vague feelings of frustration and helplessness experienced by people in mass society have been engendered by the gigantic size of social institutions, the seeming unsolvability of certain problems, the impersonality of huge bureaucratic structures, and the covert but very real threat of extinction through nuclear holocaust. In the sphere of politics, these feelings tend to produce two reactions: activism in extreme political movements, or apathy. In our own society, we are increasingly polarized between the "silent majority" of those satisfied with the governmental system—or not actively opposing it—and the minority of those actively dissatisfied with the system. The latter are the radical, more or less militant, activists of the left and of the right. Most political parties are actively engaged in this tug-of-war, the battle for the vote of the silent majority.

Scan the newspapers for political advertisements. In what ways, if any, are these advertisements geared to the average audience?

Can you suggest any alternatives to the current use of the mass media to publicize political candidates?

[Interest Groups: Purpose and Functions]

As we have pointed out, people in all societies belong to many different groups for many reasons. When a distinct organizational structure is added to a group, to help it promote a particular shared interest, such groups become organized interest groups.

The existence of a large number of interest groups is a distinctive—though not unique—feature of the American political system. *Interest groups* are coalitions of individuals with similar attitudes and interests

[18]David M. Potter, *People of Plenty* (Chicago: University of Chicago Press, 1954), p. 176.

who attempt to influence *public policy.* Public policy is that which government does or does not do. In attempting to influence public policy, interest groups resemble the political parties. They differ from them, however, in the manner in which they pursue their goals. Interest groups do not run candidates to officially represent their interests and they do not aim for a complete control of government.

What interest groups represent you? Do you support the way they are dealing with issues that affect you? Why or why not?

Almost 64 percent of Americans belong to some kind of interest group. Those who are not officially members of such organizations are probably nevertheless represented by at least one interest group. The great number of interest groups results from democratic ideology, which recognizes that people differ in what they consider to be the public interest. No individual or group can know what the public interest is, even if there is such a thing as "the" public interest, since social and economic interests vary from group to group.

Interest groups provide group representation based on something other than geographical region, which is how we are represented in Congress. Today's interests are generally more closely related to occupation than to geography. Another function is to clarify opinions and stimulate discussions of political issues. This function includes sifting, studying, and debating various aspects of a particular issue so that the issue is made clear.

What are some of the dangers that interest groups present to democratic functioning?

Some interest groups "lobby," or seek to influence the enactment or defeat of specific legislation, since congressmen can hardly know every shade of opinion and every problem of their constituents. Interest groups act as channels of communication between their members and public officials. Specific interest groups are the best informed sources on the issue they are trying to further.

Interest groups also function as checks on other interest groups, and on individual public officials. If the activities of one interest group become unreasonable or improper, another interest group brings this to public attention. Similarly, if public officials become lax in the performance of their duties, their irresponsibility is also frequently exposed by interest groups.

Organized interest groups—also called *pressure groups* (although this term has a more negative connotation)—abound in almost all democratic societies. In such societies the chief purpose of interest groups is to turn the interests of specific groups into government policy.

[Political Parties: Purpose and Functions]

Although some form of opposition to a government in power has existed in most preindustrial republics, political parties as we know them developed less than a hundred years ago. Political parties represent the third base of democracy, the other two being a system of representation, and the right to participate in the government by voting. This third element is the right to organize an opposition for the purpose of gaining access to power in the process of decision making.

Political Parties: Purpose and Functions

Many political observers have said that modern democracy would be unthinkable without political parties.[19] This is because the unanimity and one-party system of authoritarian politics is often forced on the people and therefore is in opposition to democratic principles. The only unanimity required by a democratic system is on the issue of the desirability of the democratic system itself. In all other areas, democratic theorists recognize that conflict is inevitable, and they propose to mediate such conflict through the institution of a government of temporary coalitions.[20] The job of placing a particular coalition in power is left to political parties.

The fundamental purpose of political parties is to gain control of government and to take on the responsibility for conducting its affairs: to seize and exercise political power by legal means. The job of political parties in a democracy is to win elections. This is done in the name of the electorate, whose interests the parties loosely represent.

One of the most vital functions of political parties is to determine and define the ideals of the people and to clarify them as issues and ideologies. These issues are then organized into a *platform,* and presented to the electorate, which either approves them or disapproves them. The party with the most issues approved wins the election and attempts to carry out the policiesof its platform by making them the policies of the government.

A second function of the political parties is to provide the personnel to run the government. This is done by nominating, electing, and recruiting public officials. A political party can also act as the critic of the party in power, its "loyal opposition," by stopping the implementation of unpopular policies and presenting viable policy alternatives. Political parties also perform the educational function of helping to socialize the individual in political matters. For many individuals, the party becomes a point of reference from which to make judgments on a confusing array of candidates and issues.

Why do you suppose American politics are dominated by only two parties?

American political parties should be viewed as uniting forces, rather than divisive ones. Since there are only two major parties, a broad spectrum of interests must be encompassed by each. To win the support of the largest number of voters possible, the parties cannot afford to embrace extremist positions. Consequently, they adopt rather moderate, middle-of-the road positions and are able to draw together a very heterogeneous group.

Differences between parties are not based on differing ideologies. But while both parties agree on certain premises and goals—the value and continuation of the democratic system, the Consitution, and our social and economic institutions—they disagree in emphasis and priorities on how to achieve these goals. The aims are the same, but the means are different.

---

[19] E. E. Schattschneider, *Party Government* (New York: Farrar and Rinehart, 1942), p. 1.
[20] William H. Riker, *Democracy in the United States* (New York: Macmillan, 1965), p. 88.

Political Socialization

People acquire political attitudes and opinions through their interaction with others, through the process of socialization. Political socialization is one aspect of general socialization. By far the most important agents of socialization are the people with whom we are in intimate contact: our family, our close friends, and our work associates. More impersonal groups also have influence—political parties or labor unions, for instance—but in a conflict of opinion, the small primary groups are apt to be more influential.

Beyond the family and the peer group, the formation of political attitudes and opinions is influenced by the individual's social class, place of residence, education, income, race, and religion.

[Citizen Participation in the Political Process]

In an ideal democracy, the political system is based on an informed, politically active body of citizens who agree on essential democratic values, but who may disagree on matters of policy. Differences are solved by these wise, well-informed citizens in a tolerant, rational manner through orderly discussion of the issues involved. Reality is quite different. Social scientists, who in the recent past have been studying voter behavior and the climate of American public opinion, have uncovered some disillusioning tendencies among the electorate.

First, the researchers found that there is a rather cynical lack of faith in democratic processes, and in the right of some people to self-government. Second, democratic principles and values evoke a wide consensus when referred to in general terms. But when these principles are applied to specific issues, consensus is displaced by some form of conflict. And finally, there is a greater commitment to democratic principles among the leaders, the politically active, well-educated elites, than there is among the masses of people.

Voter Participation

What kinds of political activity have you participated in?

Although the United States was one of the first nations in the world to extend universal adult suffrage, only about 60 percent of its citizens vote in presidential elections. Local elections sometimes draw out only 10 percent of the electorate, despite the efforts of volunteers and interest groups. Elections during off years (nonpresidential elections), when all of the United States Representatives, one-third of the Senators, and almost half of the governors are chosen, produce a turnout of about 50 percent of all registered voters, and less in some years.

Yet voting is universally considered an important channel of political participation. In theory, voting leads to the popular control of government and to the control of leaders by the citizenry. Why the poor record then? Various reasons are offered by social scientists. The most frequently mentioned are apathy on the part of some, and political

alienation on the part of others. Apathetic voters may feel that there is so little difference on the issues between the two parties that it really does not matter whether a Democratic or a Republican candidate wins.[21] The feeling among the politically alienated is that conventional political participation is meaningless. This segment of the population believes that nothing the individual does will alter the course of political events. Such a feeling is especially prevalent among persons in the lower social and economic classes.

The reverse tends to be true of the college-eduated, professional-managerial, and white-collar citizens. These tend to be urban or suburban dwellers, belong to many voluntary organizations, and are over twenty-five. They have the highest voter-turnout record and are also active in other forms of political participation.[22]

Traditionally, the under-twenty-five voter has been uninterested in politics. This disinterest may be merely a consequence of stringent residential and registration requirements that have acted as dampers on highly mobile young voters. The extension of the vote to eighteen-year-olds, and the seemingly increased political motivation of the young during the sixties have not brought a reversal of this disinterest.

The information gap. Research indicates that the level of political information among the masses of the electorate is very low. Gaps in

---

[21] Robert E. Lane, "The Politics of Consensus in an Age of Affluence," *American Political Science Review* 50 (December 1965): 874.

[22] Fred J. Greenstein, *The American Party System and the American People* (Englewood Cliffs, N.J.: Prentice-Hall, 1963).

Methodology: Analyzing the Vote

The analysis of America's elections has mushroomed in recent decades among sociologists and political scientists. In vote analysis researchers usually combine actual election results with information gathered from opinion polls in which respondents are asked their views on various issues, together with how they plan to vote or how they voted in the past. One controversy among vote analysts revolves around whether people are "rational" in their voting behavior; that is, whether the electorate votes on the basis of current issues or on the basis of other criteria like party affiliation or personal whim. One study that bears on this issue is V. O. Key's *The Responsible Electorate.* The significance of Key's study is that in it he tried to show that many voters did indeed vote on the issues, at a time when most prevalent theories of voting behavior emphasized the social determinants of voter choice and the psychological effects of manipulative propaganda. "The perverse and unorthodox argument of this little book." Key wrote, "is that voters are not fools."[1]

To demonstrate this, Key examined data gathered by the Gallup poll and other survey research organizations for the presidential elections between 1936 and 1960. Key was particularly interested in those who had not voted in the previous election and "switchers"—that 13 to 21 percent of the electorate who voted for one

information lead to contradictory opinions and eventually to irrational voting. People often vote to cut taxes and expand governmental services at the same time. Issues and candidates are almost never examined in the light of an ideology, but rather are judged by whether they are "for" a certain group or "for" a certain policy, or on the basis of personality or party affiliation.

In a critically acclaimed examination of the American electorate, political scientists Richard Scammon and Ben Wattenberg describe the American voter of the 1970's as typically unyoung, unpoor, unblack. In fact, the typical voter may be represented by a forty-seven-year-old wife of a machinist living in suburban Dayton, Ohio.[23] The likely brand of politics that this voter supports will not result in progress for those for whom the political system has not worked well. The problem remains of how to turn the young, the poor, and the black into as ardent voters as is the housewife from Dayton, Ohio.

Devise a uniformly adequate system for providing political information to the public. What difficulties do you encounter in designing such a program?

[23]Richard M. Scammon and Ben J. Wattenberg, *The Real Majority* (New York: Coward, McCann and Geoghegan, 1970), p. 46.

party's candidate in one election and the other party's candidate in the next—as a measure of voter rationality. Voters, he found, "in their movements to and fro across party lines and from an inactive to an active voting status behaved as persons who made choices congruent with their policy preferences." In general, he said, voters acted more in response to past presidential policies than they did to new programs proposed by opposition candidates. Key only demonstrated that there was a parallel between voters' policy positions and their choice of candidate; he did not prove there was a connection.

According to one recent review of the voting literature, issue-orientation has not been as important a factor in voter choice, especially in the 1960s and 1970s, as Key presumed it would be. This does not mean that the choices of voters are not rational, only that the rationality has not been uncovered by the questions pollsters tend to ask. One reason for the many contradictory findings in voting surveys may be that candidates do not offer a rational choice in the first place. As Key put it: "even the most discriminating popular judgment can reflect only ambiguity, uncertainty, or even foolishness if those are the qualities of the input [candidates] into the echo chamber [electorate]."[2]

[1]V. O. Key, VC, *The Responsible Electorate: Rationality in Presidential Voting, 1936N 1960* (Cambridge: Harvard University Press, 1966).

[2]Michael Margolis, "From Confusion to Confusion—Issues and the American Voter (1956–1972)," *American Political Science Review*, in press.

[Summary]

The economy is an abstract concept representing relationships among people and groups of people that center around the satisfaction of basic human needs for food and shelter. The basic function of the economy is to make choices as to the production, distribution, and consumption of goods and services in the face of constant scarcity.

In preindustrial societies, economic organization was usually based on either custom or tradition. In other cases, organization was based on the command of a central, authoritarian ruler who made sure that tasks were performed. A third pattern of organization emerged with the development of a market economy. In this type of economy, each individual, motivated by the possibility of personal gain, performs the tasks necessary for survival without the intervention of either tradition or authority. The theories explaining and rationalizing the market economy came together in the ideology of capitalism.

The mode of production of modern economies is industrialism. Industrial organization consists of a complex machine technology and a bureaucratic corporate structure, including executives, middle management, and a white- and blue-collar labor force. In our society, corporations have grown so large that they wield great power on both a national and an international level. Their power has robbed the consumer of his ability to choose how much will be produced, what will be produced, and at what price it will be sold.

Among the earliest victims of industrialism were workers. Today, industrial workers are effectively unionized and even suffer some of the same ills of bureaucratic organization that corporations do. Unionization has not, however, as yet solved the two major problems workers face today: the fear of automation and alienation in relation to their work.

Other modern industrial societies have developed slightly different economic systems. One such system is socialism. Its premise is the preoccupation with the welfare of the collectivity, the society as a whole, rather than with the individual. Under socialism, the government owns and operates essential industries and runs an extensive social services system that cares for the individual from cradle to grave. Private ownership is allowed where it does not harm the public good. Income is redistributed through high taxes.

Total government control of the economy as well as total income redistribution are goals of communism, another economic (and political) system developed by some contemporary societies. In communist societies, private ownership is discouraged and the profit motive abhorred. Economies in communist nations are completely planned at high government levels. The government is also responsible for all the needs of the individual.

All three economic systems are at different points of an ideal continuum. What differentiates them is the extent to which the government interferes in the economy.

Work is a master role in industrial societies. It tends to define our identity and our self-esteem. The fact that it is so important also creates many problems—alienation, inequality, unemployment, and displacement as a result of automation. Although the work ethic has held sway over us for many centuries now, it appears that the younger generations are moving away from it. We may be developing a postindustrial, leisure civilization, in which work will be a sometime thing.

Societies need government, or a political order, because of the group nature of human life. Living in groups, we cannot enjoy total freedom of action, but must submit to a certain amount of control. Government provides the ultimate source of social control.

Whereas the chief function of government is to maintain order by implementing social control, other functions of government are neither intended nor desired. The establishment of party machines and power elites are two such functions that run counter to the democratic ideology underlying our political system.

The state is the formal, abstract structure representing government. The state's chief aim is to impose organized political control over its citizens. It can impose such control because it has a monopoly over the legitimate use of force within its territory.

The organization of society into nation-states is comparatively recent. The creation of a central government to oversee a particular territory in which people usually have similar characteristics develops a sense of unity among those people. Nationalism, which is the ideology behind the nation-state, is also a comparatively recent social phenomenon. It may be defined as a set of beliefs about the superiority of one's own nation and a defense of its interests above all others. Nationalism stresses loyalty to the national group as its foremost goal.

The political process centers basically around the question of who will have the power to make decisions for the society. Power is defined by Weber as the ability of one individual in a social relationship to get his way despite resistance. How much power anyone has in society depends on his or her status in the society.

Power that is legitimately held and is acceptable to members of society is called *authority.* Authority is institutionalized power, legitimately possessed, and accepted by a majority as right and proper. Authority may have its basis in tradition, in reason and law, or in the charisma of a leader. Both authority and power are derived from force or the threat of force.

The power of government must be legitimate to be accepted. A substantial number of citizens, in other words, must believe that the power of government is justified because it reflects their own beliefs and values. Some governments begin in violence and earn legitimate power. Others begin legitimately but undergo a crisis of legitimacy when they engage in actions contrary to the central beliefs of a society.

An important reason why the governed accept the authority of the governors is that they accept the ideology of the governors. An ideology is a system of values, ideas, beliefs, and attitudes that a society, or groups within it, shares and accepts as fact. Political ideology is a system of beliefs that explains interprets, and rationalizes the political order. The United States subscribes principally to the ideology of democracy. This ideology assumes above all that the individual is valuable, and that the ultimate purpose of the state is the self-fulfillment of the individual. Autocracy is the ideology most directly in opposition to democracy. It assumes the importance of the society over the single individual and holds that government should be in the hands of one or several individuals possessing power over the people. In today's world, societies with a tradition of autocratic ideology are generally totalitarian in nature.

To govern is to have the power to make decisions binding on the entire society. Who has this power in our society? According to the democratic ideology, individuals participate in the decisions of government. But since total participation is almost impossible, the function of governing has been taken over by competing interest groups, or by an elite, depending on which theory one accepts. According to the school of pluralism, power is diffused among many interest groups. According to the elitist view, the most significant decisions in our nation are made by a handful of persons. In reality, political power probably falls somewhere in between these two opposing views.

All societies display both conflict and consensus. People agree on some issues, and disagree on others. According to the pluralists, a basic consensus exists in the United States. Elitists, on the other hand, believe that ultimately it is force that holds society together. Force is not openly displayed; it is concealed in the form of an ideology that the masses are forced to accept. This ideology becomes an apparent, but not a real, consensus.

Because humans have always lived in groups, there has always been some conflict as to who will have the power of making decisions. This problem has been multiplied a thousandfold in contemporary societies, especially in heterogeneous mass societies. In such societies, people are confronted daily with countless choices in all areas of life, including the political area. The political process in such societies is somewhat simplified by political parties, by interest groups, and by individual participation.

Political parties have the principal function of placing particular groups in power. The purpose of political parties is to gain control of government and take on the responsibility for conducting its affairs. They also define and clarify issues that are organized into a platform; provide personnel to run the government; act as the source of opposition and political socialization; and unify forces in the society.

Participation in the decision-making process is also sought through membership in interest groups. Interest groups are coalitions of individuals with similar attitudes and interests, who attempt to influence public policy—that is, what the government does or does not do. Interest groups resemble political parties, but do not present candidates for election or aim for the complete control of government. There is a large number of interest groups in the United States.

The ordinary citizen participates in decision making principally by voting. The well-educated, high-income minority of the population most consistently engages in political activity, including voting. The large mass of less-educated, low-income people are usully either too apathetic or too ill-informed to vote, or they feel that their vote will have no impact on the way things are.

Terms to Remember

The economy, or the economic order. Those relationships among humans in society that exist as a result of the necessity to produce, distribute, and consume goods and services.

Corporation. A product of capitalism. A form of enterprise organized for large-scale production that includes an all-encompassing bureaucracy.

Automation. A process in which machines, rather than humans, control and run other machines.

Mixed Economy, or Regulated Capitalism. The contemporary condition of the American economy which retains elements of the free enterprise system, but depends upon governmental intervention to maintain economic growth and prosperity.

Protestant Ethic. A religious ideology that stressed the value of work and the accumulation of wealth, developed simultantously with the new economic system of capitalism.

Capitalism. An economic system in which wealth is in the hands of private individuals, production is engaged in with the expectation of profits, and supply and demand, as well as competition, regulate prices, wages, and profits. Modern capitalism is a much more regulated system than the free market system envisioned by its early supporters.

Socialism. An economic (and political) system whose premise is a preoccupation with the welfare of the collectivity, rather than with the welfare of the individual. In this system, essential industries are owned and operated by the government in the name of all the people, and high taxes are levied for the purpose of redistributing wealth more equitably.

Communism. An economic (and political) system whose goals are total government control of the economy and total income redistribution with the eventual creation of a classless society. The state is the sole producer and distributor, and consequently the sole employer as well as the planner of the economy. The state assumes almost total responsibility for the survival of the individual in the society.

Alienation. A term coined by Karl Marx to describe the feelings of helplessness and powerlessness displayed by industrial workers.

Authoritarianism. A type of autocracy in which power is held by an absolute monarch, a dictator, or small elite. Power, however, is limited to the political sphere.

Autocracy. An ideology directly opposed to democracy, in which government rests in the hands of one individual or group who holds supreme power over the people.

Charismatic authority. According to Max Weber, a type of authority based on the leadership of a person with charisma. A charismatic leader is thought to possess special gifts of a magnetic, fascinating, and extraordinary nature.

Democracy. An ideology, philosophy, theory, and political system assuming the basic value of the individual, his rationality, morality, equality, and possession of certain rights.

Government. An institution arising out of the need for social order; it developed within the family, and it lends support to the other institutions of society.

Ideology. A system of values, ideas, beliefs, and attitudes that a society of groups within it share and accept as true.

Legitimate authority. Authority that a substantial portion of members of society consider justifiable. A government is considered legitimate if its goals and values coincide with the goals and values of a majority of the citizens.

Nation. A culture group residing within the territory of a political state.

Nationalism. The ideology behind the nation-state. A set of beliefs about the superiority of one's own nation and a defense of its interest above all others.

Power. The probability that one individual in a social relationship will carry out his own will despite resistance. The ability of one person or group to direct the behavior of another person or group in a desired direction, under the ultimate, though not always obvious, threat of force.

Legal-rational authority. According to Weber, a type of authority accepted by members of society because it is based on rational methods and laws and is exerted for their benefit.

State. The formal counterpart of government, which develops when the activities involved in the process of government become numerous and complex, necessitating special persons to carry them out, as well as a body of laws to define and maintain certain societal values and mores.

Totalitarianism. A kind of autocracy, of the left or of the right, characterized by a totalist ideology, a single party, a secret government-controlled police, and a monopoly over mass communications, weapons, and the economy by the ruling elite.

Traditional authority. According to Weber, authority that is based on reverence for tradition—particular actions are right because they have always been done in that way.

Democratic pluralism. An interpretation of American political institutions under which plural elites operate. This interpretation assumes that there are multiple centers of power, creating a situation in which political power is fragmented and diffused.

Politics. The forces that make up and direct the government of the state, its policies and its actions. Also, the institution that makes the decisions as to "who gets what, when, how" in society.

Political party. An organization that brings together diverse elements of the general population into a coalition whose primary purpose is to seize political power—through legal means—and to exercise it.

Ruling elite. A group composed of representatives of corporate, financial, military, and governmental interests who—according to theories of some social scientists—make all the relevant decisions in the nation, irrespective of the wishes of the population at large.

Interest groups. Coalitions of individuals with similar interests who compete with each other for their share of political power, attempting to influence legislation in their favor.

Lobbying. The principal activity of pressure groups, consists of an attempt to influence public officials into passing legislation beneficial to the pressure groups.

Suggestions for Further Reading

Edwards, Richard C., Michael Reich, and Thomas E. Weisskopf. *The Capitalist System.* Englewood Cliffs, New Jersey: Prentice-Hall, 1972. The structure, functioning, problems, and alternatives to American capitalism, from a radical viewpoint.

Galbraith, John Kenneth. *The New Industrial State.* Boston: Houghton Mifflin, 1967. The role of the economy in industrial society discussed by one of America's best-known economists.

Heilbroner, Robert L. *The Worldly Philosophers,* rev. ed. New York: Simon and Schuster, 1961. The thinkers who shaped our economic fate, described in an extremely well-written and interesting account.

Heyne, Paul T. *Private Keepers of the Public Interest.* New York: McGraw-Hill, 1968. Corporate organization's lack of social responsibility is critically evaluated.

Kerr, Clark, et al. *Industrialism and Industrial Man.* New York: Oxford University Press, 1964. An examination of the cultural conflicts that arise in the wake of industrialization.

Roman, Richard and Melvin Leiman, *Views on Capitalism.* Beverly Hills, Calif.: Glencoe Press, 1970. Conservative, liberal, and radical views of capitalism.

Christenson, Reo M., et al. *Ideologies and Modern Politics.* New York: Dodd, Mead, 1971. An up-to-date, readable, and complete account of current ideologies.

Dye, Thomas R., and L. Harmon Ziegler. *The Irony of Democracy,* 2nd ed. North Scituate, Mass.: Duxbury Press, 1972. A refutation of pluralism, which is the prevailing ideology in the literature of political science. The authors attempt an explanation of American political life on the basis of an elitist theory of democracy.

Gillam, Richard, ed. *Power in Postwar America.* Boston: Little, Brown, 1971. A collection of essays by well-known social scientists dealing with the distribution of power on different levels of American society.

Hoffer, Eric. *The True Believer.* New York: Harper & Row, 1951. A longshoreman turned intellectual speculates on the reasons for joining radical causes and mass movements such as nationalism.

Key, V. O. *Politics, Parties and Pressure Groups.* 5th ed. New York: Crowell, 1964. A classic and authoritative analysis of the subjects mentioned in the title.

Lane, Robert E. *Political Ideology.* New York: The Free Press, 1962. The impact of ideology on political behavior analyzed through psychological concepts.

Lipset, Seymour Martin, *Political Man: The Social Bases of Politics.* Garden City, N.Y.: Doubleday, 1963. A classic of political sociology, the first part of which deals with the underlying motives for the creation of democracy in modern societies.

Michels, Robert E. *Political Parties.* New York: The Free Press, 1962. A classic sociological study of the oligarchical tendencies in modern democratic institutions. An excellent introduction by Seymour Martin Lipset.

Mills, C. Wright. *Power, Politics and People.* New York: Ballantine, 1963. A number of essays by the well-known polemic sociologist, covering such subjects as elites and political power in the United States and the nature of public opinion.

Index

Abkhasians, 82–83, 84
Abnormality. *See* Normality
Accomodation, 44, 56
Achieved status, 46–49, 57
Adorno, T. W., 173–174
Advertising, 349
Aggregates, 29, 56
Agrarian society, 63
Alienation, 353, 359
Allport, Gordon W. and Leo Postman, 256
American Indians, 187–190
Anderson, Charles H., 188
Anglo-conformity, 177, 199
Anomie theory, 117–119, 125
Aries, Philippe, 286
Aronowitz, Stanley, 312
Ascribed status, 46–49, 57
Asian minorities, 190–192
Assimilation, 44, 56
Assimilationist minorities, 162, 198
Associational societies, 38, 56
Associations. *See* Formal organizations; Voluntary associations
Australians, 68
Authoritarian personality, 173–174
Authoritarianism, 345, 359
Authority, 11, 24, 142, 156
  charismatic, 342–343, 359
  in families, 291–292
  hierarchy of, 233
  legal-rational, 342, 360
  legitimate, 341, 342, 357, 359
  traditional, 342, 360
Autocracy, 344–345, 359
Automation, 209, 359
  unemployment and, 333–334

Beauvois, Simone de, 47
Becker, Howard S., 119–120
Beliefs, 301
Belong, desire to, 77
Belong, struggle to, 177–179
Berger, Peter L., 2, 80
Bierstedt, Robert, 5, 163
Biology
  effects on culture of, 69
  socialization and, 97–99
Black Americans, 179–182
Black-white relations, 182, 183
Blau, Peter M. and Marshall W. Meyer, 239
Blauner, Robert, 141, 168
Blood for transfusion, 331
Body contact, 97–98
Broker rule, 345–346
Bronowski, J., 16
Bureaucracy, 37, 56, 94, 230, 232, 234–242, 243, 244
  dynamism of, 239
  informality in, 239–240
  and oligarchy, 240–241
  pure, 233–235
  rules in, 234, 237–239
Bureaucratization of religion, 308

Calvin, John, 327
Canadians, 60
Capitalism, 328–330, 359
Cargo cults, 304
Case study, 18–19, 24
Caste system, 49, 148–149, 156
Category, 29, 56
Causal explanation, 307
Censorship, 264, 280
Centralization process, 226
Chain of command, 233
Change, 201–202
  education as, 309–310
  See also Social and cultural change
Change-resistant movements, 275, 280
Charismatic authority, 342–343, 359
Chicanos, 184–186
Children, socialization of, 97–99, 287, 293
  See also Education; Family
Chinese-Americans, 190–191
Chinese people, 128, 291
Christianity, 305–306
Churches, 302–303, 322
Circular reaction, 252
Cirino, Robert, 265
Cities
  internal structure of, 225–226, 227
  See also Urban life styles; Urbanism
Citizen participation in political process, 352–355
Clark, Kenneth B., 179–180
Class. *See* Social classes; Stratification
Class revolutionary movements, 273, 281
Class system, 150–151, 156
Closed society, 148–149, 156
Cognitive goals, 310
Coleman, James S., 314–315, 317
Collective behavior, 246–281
  crowds, 251, 252–255, 280
  defined, 246–247, 279
  determinants of, 249, 250
  fashions, fads, and crazes, 257–258
  mechanisms of, 251–252
  rumors, 255–257, 280

Collective representations, 107
Colonialism, 167–168
Common sense, 11, 24
Communism, 330–332, 359
Competition, 40–42, 56
 capitalist, 328–329, 331
Competitiveness, 118
Computers, 209, 232
Comte, August, 8
Concentration process, 226
Concentric zone theory, 225, 226
Concepts, 15–16, 23, 24
Conflict, 42–44, 56
Conflict
 and consensus, 347, 358
 majority and minorities, 158–200
Conflict model, 9–10, 24
Conflict theory, 132–133, 156
Conformity, 118–119
Conjugal family, 290–291, 321
Consanguine family, 290, 321
Consensus, conflict and, 347, 358
Contagion theory, 251–252, 280
Content analysis, 265
Contingency, 299–300, 321
Convergence theory, 252, 280
Cooley, Charles Horton, 32, 102
Cooling-off role of schools, 313
Cooperation, 40, 56
Corporate power, 329–330
Corporations, 329, 358
Coser, Lewis, 249
Countercultures, 88–90, 92
Coups d'etat, 273
Covert culture, 85–86
Crazes, 257, 280
Craziness, 115
Crime and delinquency, 120–122
Crisis of legitimacy, 274, 341
Crowds, 251, 252–255, 278, 280
Cubans, 187
Cults, 303, 304, 322
Cultural change, 204, 244
Cultural content, 69–78
Cultural determinism, 95, 107–112, 124
Cultural differences, 80–83
Cultural discrimination, 176
Cultural integration, 311, 322
Cultural pluralism, 178–179, 199
Cultural relativity, 82–83, 92
Cultural uniformities, 83–85
Cultural universals, 85, 91, 92
Culture, 65–69, 91
 complex, 78, 92
 ideal vs. real, 85–86
 institutions in, 78–80, 92
 of poverty, 295–296
 as structure, 78–80
 trait, 78, 92
 transmission of, 311, 322

Dahl, Robert A., 346
Dahrendorf, Ralf, 10, 133
Darwin, Charles, 130, 167
Data collection and analysis, 13
Davis, Kingsley, 131*n*
Dawson, Carl and W. E. Gettys, 275
Decentralization process, 226
Decision making, economic, 325–326, 358
Deckard, Barbara Sinclair, 193, 333
Delinquency and crime, 120–122
Democracy, 343, 344, 359
Democratic pluralism, 345–346, 360
Demographic method, 21–22, 211
Demographic transition, 216–217
Demography, 214–216, 244
Developing nations overpopulation, 217
Deviance, 85, 110–111, 112, 114–120, 122, 124, 125
 limits of, 116
 respectable, 118
 roots of, 116–117
 theories of, 117–120
Diffusion, 205, 244
Direct observation, 14
Discoveries, 204, 244
 Industrial Revolution, 208–209
Discrimination, 174–177, 199
Dispersion process, 226
Division of labor, 233, 294–295, 332
Divorce, 296–298
Domhoff, William G., 129, 346
Double standards, 110
Downward mobility, 153
Durkheim, E., 21–22, 107, 211
Dye, Thomas R. and L. Harmon Ziegler, 346–347

Ecological city, 220
Economic systems, 326–332, 356
 capitalism, 328–330
 communism, 330–332, 359
 socialism, 330, 359
Economy, the, 324–361
 social problems and, 332–335
Education, 308–317, 320–321, 322
 goals and functions of, 309–310
 manifest and latent functions of, 310–313
 student success in, 313–317
 trends in, 317
Egalitarian family, 292, 294–295, 321
Elites, power, 339, 346–347
Elites, ruling, 346, 360
Emergent norm theory, 252, 280
Emotional contagion, 252
Employment. *See* Jobs; Work
Enclosure Acts, 210*n*
Endogamy, 290, 321
Engelhardt, Tom, 172
Equality, 126–128
Equilibrium theory, 131
Eskimos, 61
Estate system, 149–150, 157
Estates, 48–49, 149

Index

Ethical neutrality, 12, 24
Ethics of sociological investigation, 7
Ethnic minorities, 161, 199
Ethnic villages, in cities, 223, 224
Ethnicity, 170–171, 197, 199
  scholastic success and, 314–317
Ethnocentrism, 80–82, 92, 171, 197–198, 199
Evolutionary model of sociology, 8, 24
Exogamy, 290, 321
Experiments, 20–22, 24
  field, 113
  laboratory, 79
Expressive movements, 271, 280
Extended family, 290, 321

Factory system, 210, 244
Fads, 257, 280
Failure of rising expectations, 269, 280
Family
  basic patterns of organization, 288–299
  Black American, 180
  disorganization, 296, 321
  forms of, 290–291
  functions, 292–294
  future of, 298–299
  as institution, 285–287, 318–319
  kindship and, 288–289
  organization, 291–292
  power of, as institution, 142
  sentimental, 286
  as socialization agent, 100, 338
Fashions, 257, 280
Fathers, 287
Feminism, 195–197, 200
Feral children, 98
Fogel, Robert William and Stanley Engerman, 181–182
Folk heros, 263
Folkways, 71, 72–73, 91
Food and population, 215–216, 217–218
Field experiments, 113
Formal organizations, 231–233, 235, 244
French children, 110
Functional model, 10, 24
Functionalist theory, 131–132, 156

Galbraith, John Kenneth, 144
Gallup's American Institute of Public Opinion, 260
Gans, Herbert J., 223, 224
Geimeinschaft and Gesellschaft societies, 38–39, 55, 56, 64–65, 222
General roles, 109
Generalization, 13
Generalized belief, 250
Generalized other, 104
Goffman, E., 14, 27
Gouldner, Alvin, 21
Government, 336–337, 356–357, 359
  and nation, 339–340, 359
  purpose and functions of, 337–340
  and state, 339, 360

Greene, Felix, 128
Griffin, John H., 19
Group level, 45
Group marriage, 289
Groups, 26–58
  classifications of, 31–36, 54–55
  concept of, 16, 26–27
  life lived in, 27–29
  majority and minority, 158–200
  nature of, 29–39
  size of, 36–38
  sociological definition of, 29–31, 56

Hawthorne effect, 113
History, 126
Horizontal mobility, 151, 153
Horticultural society, 63
Human ecology, 225
Humphreys, Laud, 7
Hunter, Floyd, 143
Hunting and gathering society, 62–63
Hypothesis, 13

Ideal continuum, 32
Ideal vs. real culture, 85–86
Ideology, 343, 359
Immigrants. *See* Minority groups
Impersonality in bureaucratic system, 234
Incest taboo, 290, 321
Industrial capitalism, 329–330
Industrial Revolution, 207–212, 221, 242
Industrial societies, 63–64
  economic systems of, 326–328, 355–356
Industrialism, 209–212
Inequality, 126–128, 130–134
In-groups, 34
Innovation, 119, 311, 322
Insane vs. sane, 115
Instincts and human creativity, 97
Institutional discrimination, 176–177, 199
Institutional racism, 168
Institutions, 282–283, 318, 321
  characteristics of, 284
  culture complexes as, 78–80
  organizations compared with, 232
  pivotal, 283–284
  See also Economy; Education; Family; Religion
Integration, cultural, 311, 322
Interaction. *See* Social interaction
Interest groups, 349–350, 360
Intergroup level, 45
Interpersonal levels, 45
Interview method, 143
Intuition, 11, 24
Invasion process, 226
Inventions, 204–205, 244
  Industrial Revolution, 208–209
Involuntary groups, 36
Iron law of oligarchy, 240, 244
Israeli kibbutzim, 285–287

Japanese-Americans, 191–192
Jencks, Christopher, 316
Jews, 182, 184
Job discrimination, 333
Job satisfaction, 332–333
Job tenure, 234
John Birch society, 275

Kallen, Horace, 178
Kennedy, Ruby Jo Reeves, 178
Kerner Commission, 270
Key, V. O., 354–355
Kibbutzim, 285–287
Kinship group, 288–289
Knievel, Evel, 263
Knowledge, 11–15
Kroeber, A. L., and Clyde Kluckholm, 66
Ku Klux Klan, 275, 276

Labeling theory, 119–120, 125
Laboratory experiments, 79
Laing, R. D., 285
Laissez-faire policy, 328–329
Langer, Elinor, 75
Language, 68–69, 99, 103–104
Laws, 73–74, 92
Learning your place, 312
Le Bon, Gustave, 251
Legal-rational authority, 342, 360
Legitimate authority, 341, 359
Lenski, Gerhard, 62, 138, 142, 307
Lewis, Oscar, 295
Liebow, Elliot, 52–53
Life chances, 135, 136–138, 156
Life-style approach, 145
Linton, Ralph, 81
Lipset, Seymour Martin, 341
Literacy, 317
Lobbying, 350, 360
Looking-glass self (Cooley), 102, 124, 180
Luther, Martin, 327
Lynd, Robert and Helen, 145

Machismo, 48
MacIver, Robert M., 343
Malthus, Thomas Robert, 215–216
Malthusian prophecy, 214–216
Managerial revolution, 329
Mann, Leon, 68
Mao Tse-tung, 274
Marianismo, 48
Marriage
  forms of, 289, 321
  limitations on, 289–290, 321
Marx, Karl, 9–10, 132–133, 135, 347
Mass hysteria, 257–258
Mass society, 347–349
Master status, 141
Matched-pair technique, 20
Material culture, 70
Matriarchal family, 291, 321
Matrifocal family, 291–292
Mayo, Elton, 113
Mead, George Herbert, 102–105
Mead, Margaret, 108, 111
Meadows, Dennis L., 218
Megalopolis, 229, 244
Melting pot theory, 177–178, 199
Membership groups, 35
Mendel, Gregor J., 167
Merit, selection based on, 234
Merrill, Francis E., 70
Merton, Robert K., 117–119
Methodology, 15–22
  analyzing the vote, 354–355
  causal explanation, 307
  content analysis, 265
  demographic analysis, 21–22, 211
  direct observation, 14
  field experiments, 113
  the interview, 143
  laboratory experiments, 79
  participant observation, 19, 52–53
  sample survey, 18, 24, 183
  See also Scientific method
Metropolitan areas, 228–229, 244
Mexican-Americans, 184–186
Mexicans, 60
Michels, Robert, 240–241
Middle classes, 147, 305–306, 313–314
Migratory movements, 269–270, 271, 280
Milgram, Stanley, 20, 79
Militant minorities, 162, 170
Millenarian movements, 304
Mills, C. Wright, 9, 10, 133, 144, 346
Mind (Mead), 102–103, 125
Miner, Horace, 6
Minority groups, 159–171, 199
  common features of, 161–162
  family condition, 295–296
  goals of, 162–163
  kinds of, 160–161
  problems faced by, 163–164
  See also American Indians; Asian minorities: Black Americans; Discrimination; Jews; Prejudice; Spanish-speaking minorities; Women
Mitford, Jessica, 106
Mobility
  demographic, 215
  geographic, 269–270
  social, 147, 150, 151–155, 156
Mobilization for action, 250
Modal personality, 111, 125
Monogamy, 289, 321
Moore, Wilbert, 131*n*
Moral goals, 310
Mores, 73, 92
Morris, Jan/James, 48
Multiple nuclei theory, 225, 226
Murdock, George Peter, 85, 288
Myth complex, 343

Nation, 339–340, 357, 359
National character, 111, 125
Nationalism, 340, 357, 360
Nationalistic revolutionary movements, 273, 281
Neighborhoods, city, 225–226
Neolocal family, 292
Nisbet, Robert A., 35, 39, 99
Nonconformist, 85
Nonmaterial culture, 70–78
Normality, 112–114
Normative system, 70–72, 91
Norms, 71–72, 91
  changing nature of, 77–78
  deviations from, 114
  religion and, 300
  and social control, 74–77
  socialization as internalization of, 109–111
Novak, Michael, 178
Nuclear family, 290–291, 294, 321

Objective approach, 146
Objectivity, 11, 12, 24
Occupational mobility, 154
Occupational prestige approach, 146
Oligarchy
  bureaucracy and, 240–242, 243
  iron law of, 240, 244
Olsen, Marvin E., 62
Open society, 150–151, 156
Organizational levels, 45
Organizations
  formal, 231–233, 244
  See also Bureaucracy
Out-groups, 34–35
Overpopulation, 217
Overt culture, 85–86

Palmer, Jerry, 118
Parsons, Talcott, 131, 144
Participant observation, 19, 52–53
Patriarchal family, 291, 321
Patrilocal family, 290, 292
Peer group, 100–101
Personality, 95–107, 122–123, 125
  conforming or deviant, 122
  normal vs. abnormal, 112–122
  See also Socialization
Peter Principle, 238
Piece system, 210
Pine Ridge Indian Reservation, 188, 190
Pivotal institutions, 283–284
Pluralism, democratic, 345–346, 360
Pluralistic minorities, 162
Political behavior, 347–349
Political ideology, 343–347
Political parties, 350–352, 360
Political party machines, 338–339
Political power, 340–343
  distribution in U.S., 345–347
Politics, 336–337, 360
Polygamy, 289, 321

Population, 212–219
Post, Emily, 71
Poverty
  culture of, 295–296
  religion and, 305–306
Power, 135, 142–144, 156, 340, 360
  corporate, 329–330
  elites, 339, 346–347
  location and use of, 142–144
  political, 340–343, 345–347
  religion and, 300, 301
Powerlessness, 299–300, 321
Precipitating factors, 250
Preindustrial societies, 63–64
Prejudice, 171–174, 198, 199
Pressure groups. *See* Interest groups
Primary groups, 31–34, 35, 56, 113
Prisoners, 106–107
Profit motive, 327
Programming, social, 80
Propaganda, 262–264, 280
Protestant ethic, 327–328, 359
Public opinion, 259–266, 278, 280
  formation of, 259–260
  function of, 264–266
  manipulation of, 261–262
  measuring, 260–261
Publics, 258–259, 278, 280
Puerto Ricans, 187
Punctuality, 107

Race
  defined, 165–166, 197, 199
  misconceptions about, 164–165
  scholastic success and, 314–317
  status and, 141
  stereotypes of, 172
Racial minorities, 161, 198. *See also* Minority groups
Racism, 166–167, 199
  history of, 167–168
  today, 168–170
Radical lesbians, 272
Rainwater, Lee, 147
Random-assignment techniques, 20
Rebellion, 119
Reference groups, 35–36
Reform, 203
Reform movements, 272–273, 281
Relative deprivation, 269, 280
Religion, 178, 299–306, 319–320, 321
  and capitalism, 327–328
  contemporary trends in, 306–308
  features of, 301–302
  organization of, 302–303
  social class and, 306
  and stratification systems, 305–306
  in U.S., 303–305
Replication, 15
Reputational approach, 145–146
Research, 17, 23, 24
Resocialization, 106–107, 123, 125

Retirement, 47, 335
Retreatism, 119
Revolution, 203
  results of, 274–275
Revolutionary movements, 273–275, 281
Riesman, David, 100, 144
Rising expectations, failure of, 269, 280
Rites of passage, 301, 321
Ritual, 301–302, 322
Ritualism, 119
Role conflict and confusion, 51–52
Role performance, 52–54
Roles, 46, 57
  identifying with, 50
  multiplicity of, 49–51
  recruitment and preparation for, 311, 322
  sex, 294–295
  socialization as learning of, 108–109
  women's, 46–47, 48, 52, 53, 294–295
Rosenhan, D. L., 115
Rules, bureaucratic, 234, 237–239
Ruling class cohesiveness, 129
Ruling elite, 346, 360
Rumors, 255–257, 278, 280
Rural areas, 220
Rural values, traditional, 221–222

Sample survey, 18, 24, 183
Sampling, 261
Sanctions, 76, 92
Sane vs. insane, 115
Sartre, Jean-Paul, 50
Scapegoating, 174
Scarcity, 299–300, 321
Schools
  achievement in, 313–317
  as socialization agents, 100, 312–313
  See also Education
Schuman, Howard and Shirley Hatchett, 183
Scientific method, 11–15, 24
  in sociology, 15–22, 23
Scientific spirit, 12
Secessionist minorities, 162
Secondary group, 32–36, 56
Sector theory, 225, 226
Sects, 303, 322
Segmental roles, 109
Segregation process, 226
Self, acquisition of, 101–105
Self-fulfilling prophecies, 120
Self (Mead), 103–105, 180
Senoi of Malaysia, 42
Sex roles, changes in, 294–295
Sexism, 195, 200
Sexual minority. *See* Women
Sexual norms, 292, 293–294
Sexual stereotypes, inconsistency in, 193
Shibutani, Tamotsu, 256–257
Signals, 67, 91
Significant others, 104
Simmel, Georg, 9
Situational approach, 295–296
Smelser, Neil J., 249, 250
Smith, Adam, 328–329
Social action, 30
Social and cultural change, 201–245
  processes of, 203–205
  theories of, 202–203
Social classes, 129, 134–138, 156
  classifications of, 145–146
  definitions of, 135
  educational success and, 313–317
  religious affiliation and, 306
  sociologists determinations of, 145–151
  U.S., 134–135
Social contagion, 252
  ineffectiveness of, 250
  norms and, 74–77, 92
Social dynamics, 201
Social interaction, 99
  education and, 309–310
  social processes, 39–44, 56
Social mobility, 147, 150, 151–155, 156
  evaluation of, 153–155
  goals, 310
  social movements and, 270–271
  U.S., 152–153
Social movements, 266–277, 278–279, 280
  purpose of, 268–269
  reform, 272–273
  revolutionary, 273–275
  stages of development in, 275–277
  why people join, 269–271
Social organization, 44–54, 57
  in cities, 224, 225–226
  classification according to, 64–65
  levels of, 45
Social power. *See* Authority; Power
Social problems and the economy, 332–335
Social processes, 39–44, 56
Social programming, 80
Social reality level, 45
Social relationship level, 45
Social-scientific model, 10–11, 24
Social statics, 201
Social status, 139–140, 156
Social stratification. *See* Stratification
Social structure, 44–45, 57
Social systems, 44–45, 56–57
Socialism, 330, 359
Socialization, 97, 99–105, 123, 125
  agents of, 100–101
  aims of, 100, 310
  as internalization of norms, 109–111
  political, 352
  as role learning, 108–109
  See also Resocialization
Society, 61–62, 91
  classifications of, 62–65
  and culture, 59–61, 65–69
  as a group, 37–38, 56
  individual in, 94–125
  theoretical models of, 8–11
Sociocultural changes, 205–212, 242

Sociology, 2–4, 24
of economics, 324–325
ethics of, 7
and other social sciences, 4–5
perspective of, 5–8
scientific method in, 15–22
theoretical frameworks of, 8–11
Spanish-speaking minorities, 184–187
Specialization, 233, 332
Standard Metropolitan Statistical Area (SMSA), 229, 244
State and government, 339, 360
Status, 45–49, 57, 135, 138–141, 156
determining, 139–140
group, 140–141
importance of, 138–139
inconsistency, 140–141
multiplicity of, 49–51
social, 139–140
Status quo, religion as subversion of, 301
Stratification 129–134, 157
categories of, 134–144
economic decision making and, 325–326
systems, 146–151, 157
See also Class; Power; Status
Structural conduciveness, 250
Structural discrimination, 176, 199
Structural-functionalism, 10
Structural strain, 250
Subcultures, 86–88, 89, 92, 313
Subjective approach, 146, 147
Suburbs, 226–228, 244
Succession process, 226
Suicide, 211
Sumner, William Graham, 72
Symbolic interaction, 31, 39, 99
Symbolic interactionism, 102–103, 125
Symbols, 67, 91

Taboos, 73, 92, 290, 321
Team spirit, 128
Technology, 207, 244
Telephone workers, 75
Theories, 16–17, 23, 24
Thernstrom, Stephan, 154, 215
Thompson, Daniel, 169
Thompson, Hunter, 348
Tilly, Charles, Louise Tilly, and Richard Tilly, 267
Titmus, Richard M., 331
Tönnies, Ferdinand, 38
Totalitarianism, 345, 360
Tracking, 312
Tradition, 11, 24
Traditional authority, 342, 360
Transmission of culture, 311, 322
Truth
relativity of, 7–8
search for, 11–15
Tumin, Melvin, 181
Turner, Ralph H., 248, 251

Uncle Tom, 169
Unemployment and automation, 333–334
Upper classes, 129
Upwardly mobile, 152
Urban life-styles, 223–224
Urban sprawl, 229, 244
Urban transition, 222–223
Urbanism, 221–222, 245
Urbanization, 219–229, 243, 245
Utopian movements, 271–272, 280

Value goals, 310
Values
of detachment, 21
relativity of, 8
See also Laws; Mores; Norms
Variables, 17–18, 24
Verification, 15
Vertical mobility, 151
Vidich, Arthur J. and Joseph Bensman, 221–222
Voluntary associations, 233, 236, 243, 245
Voluntary groups, 36
Vonnegut, Kurt, 127–128
Voter participation, 352–355

Warner, W. L. and Paul Lunt, 145
WASP values, 177
Weber, Max, 32*n*, 72, 135, 136, 141, 233–235, 327*n*
White, Leslie, 108
Women
job discrimination against, 333
as minority group, 161, 192–197, 198
roles of, 46–47, 48, 52, 294–295
Women's liberation, 195–197, 272, 273
Work
ethic, 327–328, 335–337, 356
retirement from, 335
role of, 334, 356
Wylie, Laurence, 110

Yetman, Norman and C. Hoy Steele, 167

Zangwill, Israel, 178
Zero population growth, 218–219